0 metres 500
0 yards 500

**Jewish Quarter
Josefov**
Pages 82–95

JEWISH QUARTER
JOSEFOV

OLD TOWN
STARÉ MĚSTO

Vltava

NEW TOWN
NOVÉ MĚSTO

**Old Town
Staré Město**
Pages 62–81

**New Town
Nové Město**
Pages 142–157

D0892796

90710 000 323 535

EYEWITNESS TRAVEL

Prague

DK EYEWITNESS TRAVEL

Prague

Main Contributors **Vladimír Soukup**

Project Editor Heather Jones
Art Editor Lisa Kosky
Editors Ferdie McDonald, Carey Combe
Designers Louise Parsons, Nicki Rawson

Contributors
Petr David, Vladimír Dobrovodský,
Nicholas Lowry, Polly Phillimore,
Joy Turner-Kadečková, Craig Turp

Photographers
Jiří Doležal, Jiří Kopřiva, Vladimír Kozlík,
František Přeučil, Milan Posselt,
Stanislav Tereba, Peter Wilson

Illustrators
Gillie Newman, Chris Orr, Otakar Pok, Jaroslav
Staně

This book was produced with the assistance
of Olympia Publishing House, Prague

Printed and bound in China

First published in the UK in 1994 by
Dorling Kindersley Limited
80 Strand, London WC2R 0RL, UK
17 18 19 20 10 9 8 7 6 5 4 3 2 1

Reprinted with revisions
1994, 1995, 1996, 1997, 1998, 1999,
2000, 2001, 2002, 2003, 2004,
2005, 2006, 2008, 2009, 2010, 2011,
2012, 2013, 2014, 2015, 2016, 2017

1994, 2017 © Dorling Kindersley Limited,
London
A Penguin Random House Company

A CIP catalogue record is available from
the British Library.

ISBN 978-0-24127-735-5

Floors are referred to throughout in
accordance with European usage; ie the
"first floor" is the floor above ground level.

MIX
Paper from
responsible sources
FSC™ C018179

Detail of an Art Nouveau frieze on a house
on Kaprova street in the Jewish Quarter

Introducing Prague

Litter Quarter side of Charles Bridge at dusk

The information in this
DK Eyewitness Travel Guide is checked regularly.
Every effort has been made to ensure that this book is as up-to-date as possible
at the time of going to press. Some details, however, such as telephone numbers,
opening hours, prices, gallery hanging arrangements and travel information are
liable to change. The publishers cannot accept responsibility for any consequences
arising from the use of this book, nor for any material on third party websites, and
cannot guarantee that any website address in this book will be a suitable source of
travel information. We value the views and suggestions of our readers very highly.
Please write to: Publisher, DK Eyewitness Travel Guides, Dorling Kindersley,
80 Strand, London, WC2R 0RL, UK, or email: travelguides@dk.com.

◀ **Title page** Prague across the Vltava **Front cover main image** Church of Our Lady before Týn towering over the Old Town Square
Back cover image Panorama of Prague

Contents

Baroque detail of three violins on the façade of a house

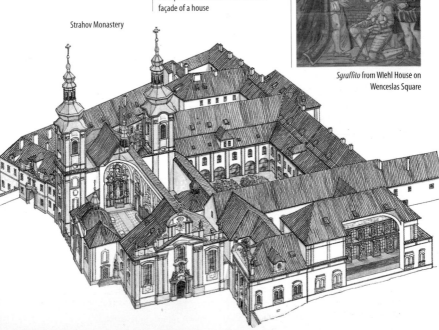

Strahov Monastery

Sgraffito from Wiehl House on Wenceslas Square

HOW TO USE THIS GUIDE

This Eyewitness Travel Guide helps you get the most from your stay in Prague with the minimum of difficulty. The opening section, *Introducing Prague*, locates the city geographically, sets modern Prague in its historical context and describes events through the entire year. It also includes *Prague at a Glance*, which is an overview of the city's main attractions, as well as a feature on the River Vltava. Section two, *Prague Area by Area*, starts on page 60. This is the main sightseeing section, which covers all the important sights, with photographs, maps and drawings. It also includes day trips from Prague and four guided walks around the city. Carefully researched tips for hotels, restaurants, shops and markets, cafés and bars, entertainment and sports are found in *Travellers' Needs*. The last section, the *Survival Guide*, contains useful practical advice on all you need to know, from making a telephone call to using the public transport system.

Finding Your Way Around the Sightseeing Section

Each of the five sightseeing areas in the city is colour-coded for easy reference. Every chapter opens with an introduction to the part of Prague it covers, describing its history and character, followed by a Street-by-Street map illustrating the heart of the area. Finding your way around each chapter is made simple by the numbering system used throughout. The most important sights are covered in detail in two or more full pages.

Colour-coding on each page makes the area easy to find in the book.

Recommended restaurants in the area are listed and plotted on the map.

Numbered circles pinpoint all the listed sights on the area map.

A locator map shows you where you are in relation to surrounding areas.

1 Introduction to the Area
For easy reference, the sights in each area are numbered and plotted on an area map. To help the visitor, this map also shows metro stations, tram stops, river boat boarding points and parking areas. The area's key sights are listed by category: Churches; Museums and Galleries; Historic Streets and Squares; Palaces; and Parks and Gardens.

A suggested route for a walk takes in the most attractive and interesting streets in the area.

Street-by-Street: Prague Castle

2 Street-by-Street Map
This gives a bird's eye view of the most important parts of each sightseeing area. The numbering of the sights ties in with the area map and the fuller descriptions on the pages that follow.

Prague Area Map

The coloured areas shown on this map *(see inside front cover)* are the five main sightseeing areas of Prague – each covered in a full chapter in Prague Area by Area *(pp60–157)*. They are highlighted on other maps throughout the book. In Prague at a Glance *(pp38–51)*, for example, they help locate the top sights. They are also used to plot the routes of the river trip *(pp56–9)* and the four guided walks *(p173)*.

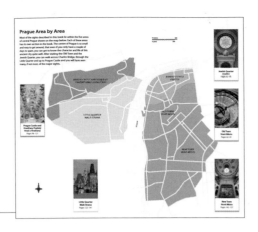

3 Detailed Information on each Sight
All the important sights in Prague are described individually. They are listed in order, following the numbering on the area map. Practical information on opening hours, telephone numbers, admission charges and facilities available is given for each sight. The key to the symbols used can be found on the back flap.

Practical Information lists all the information you need to visit every sight, including a map reference to the Street Finder *(pp250–55)*.

Numbers refer to each sight's position on the area map and its place in the chapter.

The façade of each major sight is shown to help you spot it quickly.

Stars indicate the most interesting architectural details of the building, and the most important works of art or exhibits on view inside.

Numbered circles point out key features of the sight listed in a key.

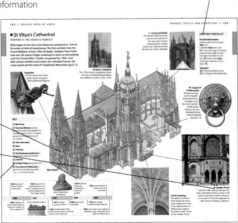

The Visitors' Checklist provides the practical information you will need to plan your visit.

4 Prague's Major Sights
Historic buildings are dissected to reveal their interiors; and museums and galleries have colour-coded floorplans to help you find important exhibits.

INTRODUCING PRAGUE

GREAT DAYS IN PRAGUE

Few cities have as much to offer as Prague, so it can be difficult to decide how best to spend your time. The Old Town is a joy in itself, and you could amble around here admiring its old houses for days. Yet, with some planning, you can see much more of what makes this historic city special. Here are itineraries covering some of the best of the attractions, arranged first by theme and then by length of stay. Price guides on pages 10–11 include travel, food and admission for two adults, while family prices are for two adults and two children.

National Treasures

Two adults
allow at least Kč3,000

- Hradčany Square
- Lunch in the Little Quarter
- Cross the Charles Bridge
- Watch the Old Town Square's Astronomical clock

Morning
Starting at **Hradčany Square**, admire the commanding statue of the first Czechoslovak president, Tomáš Garrigue Masaryk, then walk through První nádvoří to **St Vitus's Cathedral** *(see pp102–105)*, the soul of the Castle. Take a short tour here before moving on to the "Story of Prague Castle" exhibition in **Old Royal Palace** *(see pp106–107)*. For souvenir shopping, go to the artisans' cottages on **Golden Lane** *(see p101)*. Alternatively, head to **Lobkowicz Palace**, and tour the exhibition inside *(see p101)*. Walk

The sumptuous interior of the Spanish synagogue

down U Zlaté studně and Sněmovní to **Little Quarter Square** *(see pp124–5)*, where you can enjoy a late lunch and admire the architectural gems of the Little Quarter.

Afternoon
It is a short walk from here to **Charles Bridge** *(see pp136–9)*, and on to Old Town Square. Time your arrival on the hour to see the **Old Town Square's Astronomical Clock** *(see p76)* in action. The **Old Town Hall Tower** *(see p75)* is well worth a visit for amazing views of Prague Castle and the Little Quarter. Next, choose between seeing the art in the Rococo **Kinský Palace** *(see p72)* or the bare majesty of **Church of St Nicholas** *(see pp72–3)*. After visiting either of these, the narrow streets and shops of the Týn courtyard await exploration. Enjoy a traditional dinner in the elegant surroundings of the **Staroměstská** restaurant *(see p199)*.

Visitors taking a break from sightseeing at the Staroměstská restaurant in Old Town Square

Literary, Art and Religious Landmarks

Two adults
allow at least Kč5,800

- Grand Café Praha – "Kafka's café"
- The Jewish Quarter
- Decorative and Medieval Art collections

Morning
Jewish Prague and Franz Kafka are inseparable, so you may want to start the day with a coffee at **Grand Café Praha** *(see p206)* in Old Town Square. Kafka lived above here and the café was once named after his journalist girlfriend, Milena. Refreshed, head along Pařížská into the **Jewish Quarter** *(see pp82–95)*. Stop at the **Maisel Synagogue** *(see p92)*, then cross the road to the historic **Old Jewish Cemetery** *(see pp88–9)*. A good walk around here, as well as a look inside the **Klausen Synagogue** *(see p87)*, sets you up for lunch. Try **King Solomon** *(see p200)*, one of the best Jewish restaurants in town.

◀ Detail of the painted dome of the Basilica of St Peter and St Paul, Vyšehrad

Afternoon

Admire the Gobelin tapestries at the **Museum of Decorative Arts** *(see p86)*. Stroll along to the **Jewish Town Hall** *(see p87)*, and the **Old-New Synagogue** *(see pp90–91)*. The eastern side of the Jewish Quarter is home to two must-see sights: the glorious **Spanish Synagogue** *(see pp92–3)* and the medieval art in **St Agnes of Bohemia Convent** *(see pp94–5)*. After a day full of culture, it's time for a little quality shopping on Pařížská – a long, straight thoroughfare in the Jewish Quarter. For dinner, head to the **Prague Beer Museum** *(see p200)*, one of the city's many original restaurants.

Family Day

Family of four
allow at least Kč3,500

- **Funicular ride to the Tower**
- **Mirror Maze**
- **Peacocks and a cave**
- **Basilica of St James**

Morning

Take the funicular railway up **Petřín Hill** *(see p141)*, to see Prague's mini-Eiffel Tower – the **Observation Tower** *(see p140)* which has a spiral staircase to the top. The **Mirror Maze** *(see p140)*, a short walk away, will keep youngsters happy, as will the nearby **Štefánik's Observatory** *(see p140)*. Be sure to ask for family tickets. Take the funicular halfway back down the hill for lunch at the **Nebozízek**, *(see p201)* with its outdoor patio and panoramic views.

Afternoon

Take a stroll on **Střelecký Ostrov**, where you can feed the swans. There's more wildlife to be seen at the **Wallenstein Palace and Garden** *(see p126)*, home to peacocks and a bizarre replica of a limestone cave. Walk or take the metro over the river to catch the **Old Town Square's Astronomical Clock** *(see p76)* in action. Then, on to the **Basilica of St James** *(see p67)*.

Wenceslas Square and monument in front of the National Museum

Children will be intrigued by the mummified arm, which has been hanging above the church entrance for several centuries. Finally, stop for a bite to eat at the **Grand Café Orient** *(see p198)*.

History and Heroes

Two adults
allow at least Kč1,100

- **Wenceslas Square – the rise and fall of Communism**
- **Wartime history found in a church**
- **Shopping for antiques**

Morning

Start the day with a walk along **Wenceslas Square** *(see pp144–5)* to see where the Communist regime was toppled. Walk the length of the square and imagine it lined with protestors as it was for weeks in 1989. Pay your respects at the **Monument to the Victims of Communism** *(see p145)*, and to anti-communist martyr Jan Palach, who set himself alight here in 1969 in protest of the Soviet invasion. Just off the Square is the former Gestapo HQ on Politických vězňů (now the Ministry of Industry and Trade), where thousands of Czechs were imprisoned during World War II. Stop for a traditional Czech lunch or delicious local beer at **U Fleků** *(see p155)*.

Afternoon

Walk to the beautiful Baroque **Cathedral of St Cyril and St Methodius** *(see p152)*, where Czech resistance fighters bravely took their own lives in 1942. Bullet holes can still be seen on the wall of the crypt, where a museum chronicles the tragic event. To round off your exploration of Prague's history, end the day antique-browsing. **Military Antiques** in Hybernská *(see p212)*, is a treasure-trove of relics from the Nazi and Soviet occupations, and military bric-a-brac from all periods.

The Mirror Maze, great fun for young and old alike

2 days in Prague

- Tour Prague Castle – a Gothic gem
- Watch the Old Town Square's Astronomical Clock strike the hour
- Visit the poignant sights of the Jewish Quarter

Day 1
Morning Catch scenic tram route 22 up Hradčany hill to **Prague Castle** *(see pp98–9)*. Take a tour of the Gothic **St Vitus's Cathedral** *(see pp102–105)* and the **Old Royal Palace** *(see pp106–107)*.

Afternoon Wander through the stately **Royal Garden** *(see p111)*, then make your way down **Nerudova Street** *(see p130)* to cross **Charles Bridge** *(see pp136–39)*, which is lined with statues of saints. Head to **Old Town Square** *(see pp68–71)* to watch the **Astronomical Clock** *(see p76)* on the **Old Town Hall** *(see pp74–5)* chime the hour. The pretty **Kinský Palace** *(see p72)* features ancient art in the shadow of the spire-topped **Church of Our Lady before Týn** *(see p72)*. End the day by shopping at the market on Havelská Street.

Day 2
Morning Begin by exploring the **Jewish Quarter** *(see pp82–95)*. Visit the **Old Jewish Cemetery** *(see pp88–9)*, with its tilting tomb-stones marked by symbols, the **Pinkas Synagogue** *(see pp86–7)* memorial to Holocaust victims and the 13th-century **Old-New Synagogue** *(see pp90–91)*.

Afternoon Cross the Vltava to the **Little Quarter** *(see pp122–41)*, where shops stand alongside cafés and beer gardens. On **Little Quarter Square** *(see p127)*, the **Church of St Nicholas** *(see pp128–9)* is the height of High Baroque and worthy of a peek inside. Go for a leisurely stroll in **Wallenstein Palace and Garden** *(see p126)* amid bronze statues and wandering peacocks, then see celebrated sculptures and paintings in the **Kampa Museum of Modern Art** *(see p135)*.

Aerial view of Old Town Square, with the Jan Hus Monument in its centre

3 days in Prague

- Cross fortified Charles Bridge, looking at its statues
- Explore the narrow streets and Baroque palaces of the romantic Little Quarter

Day 1
Morning Marvel at Prague's most venerated Gothic survivor, **St Agnes of Bohemia Convent** *(see pp94–5)*, and its medieval art collection. Then walk to **Old Town Square** *(see pp68–71)* to take in the Rococo **Kinský Palace** *(see p72)* and the imposing **Church of Our Lady before Týn** *(see p72)*. Don't miss the **Old Town Hall** *(see pp74–5)* and its crowd-pleasing astronomical clock.

Afternoon Admire the Cubist House of the Black Madonna on **Celetná Street** *(see p67)* en route to the **Powder Gate** *(see p66)*, a

St Vitus's Cathedral, a medieval Gothic masterpiece completed in the 20th century

former city fortification. Afterwards, visit the **Estates Theatre** *(see p67)*, where Mozart conducted operas, the **Church of St Gall** *(see p73)* and Havelská Street market. It's a short walk from here to the magnificent **Charles Bridge** *(see pp136–9)*.

Day 2
Morning Devote your morning to **Prague Castle** *(see pp98–9)*. Survey the city from Hradčanské náměstí before venturing into **St Vitus's Cathedral** *(see pp102–105)* and **St George's Basilica and Convent** *(see pp100–101)*. Take a tour of the **Old Royal Palace** *(see pp106–107)* and the **Royal Garden** *(see p111)*. If there's time, walk along pretty **Golden Lane** *(see p101)*.

Afternoon Head down **Nerudova Street** *(see p130)* to the narrow streets of the **Little Quarter** *(see pp122–41)* and pop into the **Church of St Nicholas** *(see pp128–9)*. The monumental **Wallenstein Palace and Garden** *(see p126)*, peaceful **Kampa Island** *(see p131)* and the **Kafka Museum** *(see p135)* are all nearby.

Day 3
Morning Visit the **Jewish Quarter** *(see pp82–95)*, where the **Old Jewish Cemetery** *(see pp88–9)*, **Old-New Synagogue** *(see pp90–91)* and **Pinkas Synagogue** *(see pp86–7)* honour life in the ghetto.

Afternoon Take a half-hour train ride to Charles IV's summer retreat, **Karlštejn Castle** *(see p169)*, which stands above a wooded valley.

5 days in Prague

- Admire St Agnes of Bohemia Convent
- Take a trip to Charles IV's breathtaking country retreat, Karlštejn Castle
- Listen to a Mozart opera at the Estates Theatre

Day 1

Morning Tour Old Town Square *(see pp68–71)*, taking in the Gothic steeples of the **Church of Our Lady before Týn** *(see p72)*, **Kinský Palace** *(see p72)* and the **Old Town Hall** *(see pp74–5)*, where the **Astronomical Clock** *(see p76)* delights crowds on the hour. Ride the metro to the **Little Quarter** *(see pp122–41)* and ascend the Old Castle Steps to **Prague Castle** *(see pp98–9)*, the historic heart of Bohemia. Explore the **Old Royal Palace** *(see pp106–107)*, visit the Romanesque **St George's Basilica** *(see pp100–101)* and **St Vitus's Cathedral** *(see pp102–105)*. Then, visit the treasure of St Vitus's Cathedral in the nearby Chapel of the Holy Cross.

Afternoon Set opposite the castle complex, the Baroque **Sternberg Palace** *(see pp112–15)* houses the National Gallery's Old Masters. Walk up to the opulent 17th-century shrine of **The Loreto** *(see pp118–19)*, then make your way to **New World** *(see p116)*, a charming street of cottages where royal astronomers and goldsmiths once lived. Take tram 22 to the **Strahov Monastery** *(see pp120–21)*, whose ornate library holds thousands of obscure tomes.

Day 2

Morning Spend your morning exploring the **New Town** *(see pp142–57)*. **Wenceslas Square** *(see pp144–5)* showcases early 20th-century architecture and highlights found here include the Art Nouveau **Hotel Europa** *(see p147)*. The **National Museum** *(see p147)* has had a complete refit, while the **Mucha Museum** *(see p147)* features the early work of Art Nouveau avatar Alphonse Mucha.

Afternoon Head to the Gothic **New Town Hall** *(see p155)*, where Hussites defenestrated their Catholic overlords in 1419. Off **Charles Square** *(see pp150–51)*, a former medieval cattle market, is the **Cathedral of St Cyril and St Methodius** *(see p152)*, where Czech partisans fought with German troops in 1942. The grand **National Theatre** *(see pp156–7)* is a cultural treasure where historic operas by Smetana are staged.

Neo-Classical elegance of the Estates Theatre, where *Don Giovanni* had its debut

Day 3

Morning Immerse yourself in the spirit of medieval Bohemia at **St Agnes of Bohemia Convent** *(see pp94–5)*, which is packed with 13th–16th-century paintings and sculptures. Next, marvel at the **Old-New Synagogue** *(see pp90–91)* and the pseudo-Moorish **Spanish Synagogue** *(see pp92–3)* in the **Jewish Quarter** *(see pp82–95)*. Nearby, the **Old Jewish Cemetery** *(see pp88–9)* and **Pinkas Synagogue** *(see pp86–7)* contain memorials to Prague's Holocaust victims.

Afternoon Explore the **Old Town** *(see pp62–81)*. Start at the **Powder Gate** *(see p66)* and walk down **Celetná Street** *(see p67)*. Turn off for the **Church of St Gall** *(see p73)* and **Bethlehem Chapel** *(see p77)*, where Jan Hus preached. **Charles Street** *(see p80)*, lined with Baroque and Renaissance façades, leads to **Charles Bridge** *(see pp136–9)*.

Day 4

Morning Journey by train to Charles IV's imposing **Karlštejn Castle** *(see p169)*. Don't miss the Chapel of St Catherine, the walls of which are decorated with gems.

Afternoon Back in the city, browse the designer shops on Národní třída, and then enjoy an evening at the **Estates Theatre** *(see p67)* or **Rudolfinum** *(see p86)*.

Day 5

Morning Wander the **Little Quarter** *(see pp122–41)* and the **Wallenstein Palace and Garden** *(see p126)*. On **Little Quarter Square** *(see pp124–5)* is the Baroque **Church of St Nicholas** *(see pp128–9)*. Close by, pretty **Nerudova Street** *(see p130)* is lined with intriguing house signs.

Afternoon Take the funicular railway up **Petřín Hill** *(see p141)* to see the **Observation Tower** *(see p140)*. Enjoy the views, then stroll back to the city via Petřínské Park *(see p141)*.

A tram in the Little Quarter, where buildings have been largely unchanged since the 1700s

Putting Prague on the Map

Prague has a population of just over 1 million and covers 500 sq km (200 sq miles) at its outer limits. It is the capital of the Czech Republic (Czechia) and Bohemia's main metropolis. Prague's geographical position at the centre of Europe makes it a convenient base from which to visit both the Bohemian countryside and many other major cities, such as Nuremberg, Vienna, Bratislava and Budapest.

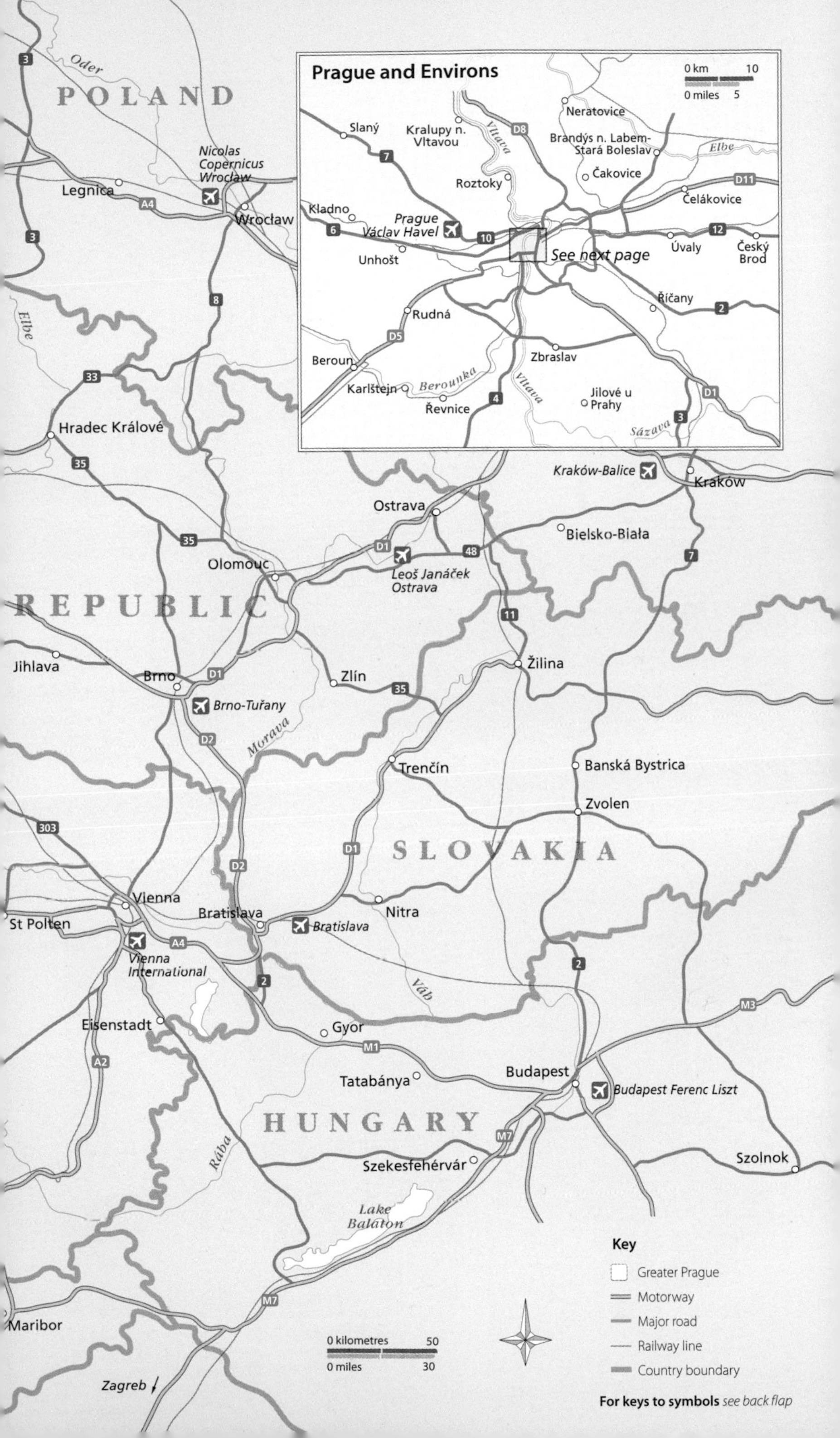
Prague and Environs
0 km 10
0 miles 5
Neratovice
Slaný
Kralupy n. Vltavou
Vltava
D8
Brandýs n. Labem-Stará Boleslav
Elbe
7
Čakovice
Roztoky
D11
Čelákovice
Kladno
Prague Václav Havel
6
10
12
Úvaly
Český Brod
Unhošť
See next page
Říčany
2
Rudná
D5
Beroun
Zbraslav
Karlštejn
Berounka
Řevnice
4
Vltava
Jílové u Prahy
D1
3
Sázava
Oder
POLAND
3
Nicolas Copernicus Wrocław
Legnica
A4
Wrocław
3
8
Elbe
33
Hradec Králové
35
Kraków-Balice
Kraków
Ostrava
Bielsko-Biała
D1
48
35
Olomouc
Leoš Janáček Ostrava
7
REPUBLIC
11
Jihlava
Žilina
Brno
D1
Zlín
35
Brno-Tuřany
D2
Morava
Trenčín
Banská Bystrica
Zvolen
303
D1
SLOVAKIA
D2
Vienna
Bratislava
Nitra
St Polten
Bratislava
A4
Vienna International
2
2
Váh
M3
Eisenstadt
Gyor
M1
A2
Tatabánya
Budapest
Budapest Ferenc Liszt
HUNGARY
M7
Rába
Szolnok
Szekesfehérvár
Lake Balaton
Key
Greater Prague
Motorway
Major road
Railway line
Country boundary
M7
Maribor
0 kilometres 50
0 miles 30
Zagreb
For keys to symbols see back flap

Central Prague

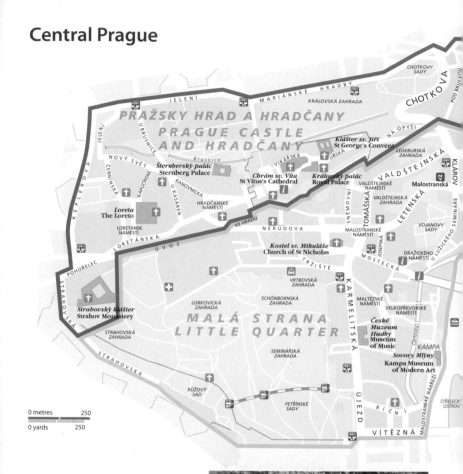

PRAŽSKÝ HRAD A HRADČANY
PRAGUE CASTLE
AND HRADČANY

Šternberský palác
Sternberg Palace

Chrám sv. Víta
St Vitus's Cathedral

Klášter sv. Jiří
St George's Convent

Královský palác
Royal Palace

Malostranská

Loreta
The Loreto

Kostel sv. Mikuláše
Church of St Nicholas

Strahovský klášter
Strahov Monastery

MALÁ STRANA
LITTLE QUARTER

České Muzeum Hudby
Museum of Music

KAMPA

Sovovy Mlýny
Kampa Museum of Modern Art

0 metres   250
0 yards   250

Orb and Cross
An important part of the royal coronation regalia, this orb is now kept at St Vitus's Cathedral *(see pp102–105)*.

For keys to symbols *see back flap*

Church of St Lawrence
Petřín Park offers many sights, as well as outstanding views of Prague *(see p141 and Four Guided Walks, pp176–7)*.

FRANTIŠKU

Klášter sv. Anežky
St Agnes's Convent

REVOLUČNÍ

NA

JOSEFOV
JEWISH QUARTER

U MILOSRDNÝCH

HRADEBNÍ

Staronová synagóga
Old-New Synagogue

HAŠTALSKÁ

Starý židovský hřbitov
Old Jewish Cemetery

DLOUHÁ

MASNÁ

RYBNÁ

KRÁLODVORSKÁ

NÁMĚSTÍ JANA
PALACHA

ŠIROKÁ

Staroměstská

MAISELOVA

ŽATECKÁ

VALENTINSKÁ

PLATNÉŘSKÁ

STAROMĚSTSKÉ
NÁMĚSTÍ

Staroměstská radnice
Old Town Hall

OVOCNÝ
TRH

MARIÁNSKÉ
NÁMĚSTÍ

MALÉ
NÁMĚSTÍ

U RADNICE

Karlův most

KARLOVA

STARÉ MĚSTO
OLD TOWN

NA PŘÍKOPĚ

NEKÁZANKA

PANSKÁ

RŮŽOVÁ

ANENSKÉ
NÁMĚSTÍ

HUSOVA

RYTÍŘSKÁ

U ČÍPU

JINDŘIŠSKÁ

SMETANOVO NÁBŘEŽÍ

BETLÉMSKÉ
NÁMĚSTÍ

SKOŘEPKA

PERLOVÁ

Můstek

POLITICKÝCH

VĚŽNÁ

UHELNÝ
TRH

28. ŘÍJNA

VÁCLAVSKÉ
NÁMĚSTÍ

NA PERŠTÝNĚ

Můstek

OPLETALOVA

most Legií

NÁRODNÍ

Národní třída

SPÁLENÁ

JUNGMANNOVA

i
VÁCLAVSKÉ
NÁMĚSTÍ

WASHINGTONOVA

WILSONOVA

LE GEROVA

Národní divadlo
National Theatre

OSTROVNÍ

Muzeum

V JIRCHÁŘÍCH

VLADISLAVOVA

VODIČKOVA

ŠTĚPÁNSKÁ

KRAKOVSKÁ

ČELAKOVSKÉHO
SADY

MEZIBRÁNSKÁ

OPATOVICKÁ

LAZARSKÁ

KŘEMENCOVA

ČERNÁ

VE SMEČKÁCH

NOVÉ MĚSTO
NEW TOWN

MYSLÍKOVA

ODBORŮ

ŽITNÁ

SOKOLSKÁ

KARLOVO
NÁMĚSTÍ

NA RYBNÍČKU

V TŮNÍCH

HÁLKOVA

Karlovo náměstí

RESSLOVA

KARLOVO
NÁMĚSTÍ

JEČNÁ

LIPOVA

DITTRICHOVA

VÁCLASKÁ

KATEŘINSKÁ

KE KARLOVU

TROJANOVA

NA MORÁNI

VYŠEHRADSKÁ

U NEMOCNICE

PALACKÉHO
NÁMĚSTÍ

Karlovo náměstí

NÁMĚSTÍ POD
EMAUZY

VINIČNÁ

BENÁTSKÁ

BOTANICKÁ
ZAHRADA

NA SLUPI

APOLINÁŘSKÁ

Čechův
most

DVOŘÁKOVO NÁBŘEŽÍ

NÁMĚSTÍ
CURIEOVÝCH

17 LISTOPADU

PAŘÍŽSKÁ

DUŠNÍ

BÍLKOVA

VĚZEŇSKÁ

KOŽNÁ

U OBECNÍHO DVORA

Mánesův most

KŘIŽOVNICKÁ

KOŠÁRKOVO
NÁBŘEŽÍ

KOZÍ

Karlův most

NÁRODNÍ

Jiráskův
most

JIRÁSKOVO
NÁMĚSTÍ

Palackého
most

RAŠÍNOVO NÁBŘEŽÍ

MASARYKOVO NÁBŘEŽÍ

SLOVANSKÝ
OSTROV

NA STRUZE

PŠTROSSOVA

NÁP.

LAVLI

NA ZDERAZE

GORAZDOVA

V i t a v a

Painted House Façade
The Old Town has many
Renaissance and Baroque
houses. Some have colour-
ful mural paintings like this
one in Old Town Square
(see pp68–71).

552   16

Art Nouveau Statue
The New Town has
many examples of Art
Nouveau architecture
(see pp148–9).

THE HISTORY OF PRAGUE

Prague's position at the crossroads of Europe has made it a magnet for foreign traders since prehistoric times. By the early 10th century, Prague had become a thriving town with a large market place, the Old Town Square, and two citadels, Prague Castle and Vyšehrad, from where its first rulers, the Přemyslids, conducted their many family feuds. These were often bloody: in AD 935, Prince Wenceslas was murdered by his brother Boleslav. Wenceslas was later canonized and became the Czechs' best-known patron saint.

During the Middle Ages, Prague prospered, especially during the reign of the Holy Roman Emperor, Charles IV. Under the government of this wise and cultured ruler, Prague grew into a magnificent city, larger than Paris or London. Charles instigated the founding and building of many institutions in Prague, including the first university in Central Europe, Charles University. One of the University's first Czech rectors was Jan Hus, the reforming preacher whose execution for alleged heresy in 1415 led to the Hussite wars. The radical wing of the Hussites, the Taborites, were finally defeated at the Battle of Lipany in 1434. During the 16th century, after a succession of weak kings, the Habsburgs gained control, beginning a rule that would last for almost 400 years. One of the more enlightened of all the Habsburg Emperors was Rudolph II. He brought the spirit of the Renaissance to Prague through his love of the arts and sciences. Soon after his death, in 1618, Prague was the setting for the Protestant revolt which led to the Thirty Years' War. The war's aftermath caused a serious decline in the fortunes of the city that would revive only in the 18th century. Prague's many fine Baroque churches and palaces date from this time.

The 19th century saw a period of national revival and the burgeoning of civic pride. The great public monuments – the National Museum, National Theatre and Rudolfinum – were built. But the Habsburgs still ruled the city, and it was not until 1918 that Prague became the capital of an independent Republic. World War II brought occupation by the German army, followed by four decades of Communism. After the "Velvet Revolution" of 1989, Prague embraced a new era as a modern European capital.

View of Prague Castle and Little Quarter, 1493

◀ *St Wenceslas and St Vitus*, by Bartholomaeus Spränger, c.1600

Rulers of Prague

Three great dynasties have shaped the history of Prague: the Přemyslids, the Luxemburgs and the Habsburgs. According to Slavic legend, the Přemyslids were founded by Princess Libuše *(see p23)*. Her line included St Wenceslas and Přemysl Otakar II, whose death in battle at Marchfeld paved the way for the Luxemburgs. This family produced one of the city's greatest rulers, Charles IV, who was King of Bohemia and Holy Roman Emperor *(see pp26–7)*. In 1526, Prague came under the control of the Austrian House of Habsburg whose rule lasted 400 years, until after World War I, when the newly formed Czechoslovakia gained its independence and was governed by a succession of presidents. Following the dissolution of Czechoslovakia in 1993, the modern day Czech Republic continues to elect presidents.

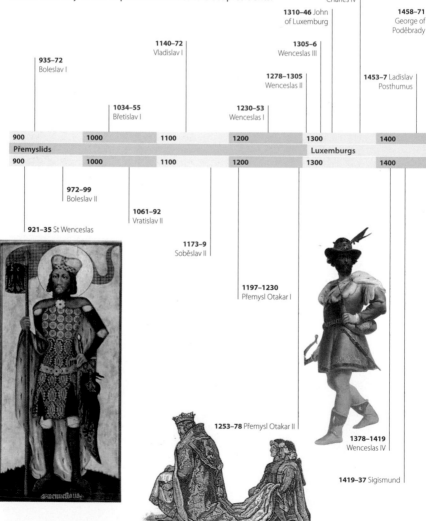

1346–78 Charles IV

1310–46 John of Luxemburg

1458–71 George of Poděbrady

1140–72 Vladislav I

1305–6 Wenceslas III

935–72 Boleslav I

1278–1305 Wenceslas II

1453–7 Ladislav Posthumus

1034–55 Břetislav I

1230–53 Wenceslas I

900	1000	1100	1200	1300	1400

Přemyslids — Luxemburgs

900	1000	1100	1200	1300	1400

972–99 Boleslav II

1061–92 Vratislav II

921–35 St Wenceslas

1173–9 Soběslav II

1197–1230 Přemysl Otakar I

1253–78 Přemysl Otakar II

1378–1419 Wenceslas IV

1419–37 Sigismund

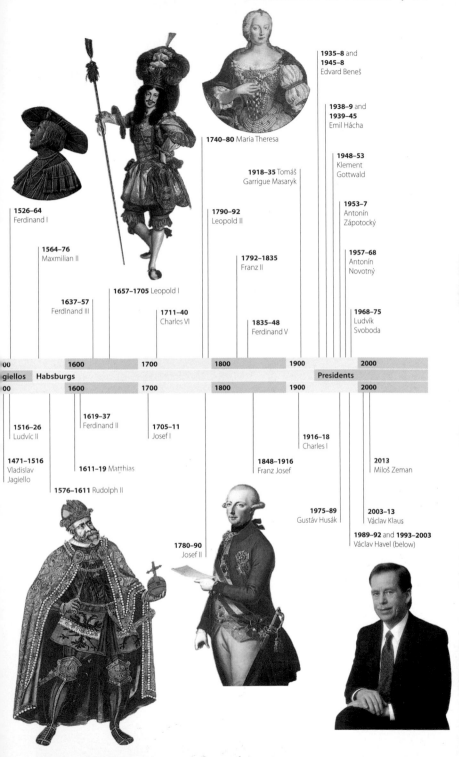

1935–8 and
1945–8
Edvard Beneš

1938–9 and
1939–45
Emil Hácha

1740–80 Maria Theresa

1918–35 Tomáš
Garrigue Masaryk

1948–53
Klement
Gottwald

1526–64
Ferdinand I

1790–92
Leopold II

1953–7
Antonín
Zápotocký

1564–76
Maxmilian II

1792–1835
Franz II

1957–68
Antonín
Novotný

1657–1705 Leopold I

1637–57
Ferdinand III

1711–40
Charles VI

1835–48
Ferdinand V

1968–75
Ludvík
Svoboda

00	1600	1700	1800	1900	2000
giellos	Habsburgs			Presidents	
00	1600	1700	1800	1900	2000

1516–26
Ludvíc II

1619–37
Ferdinand II

1705–11
Josef I

1916–18
Charles I

1471–1516
Vladislav
Jagiello

1611–19 Matthias

1848–1916
Franz Josef

2013
Miloš Zeman

1576–1611 Rudolph II

1975–89
Gustáv Husák

2003–13
Václav Klaus

1780–90
Josef II

1989–92 and 1993–2003
Václav Havel (below)

Prague Under the Přemyslids

Early Celtic tribes, from 500 BC, were the first inhabitants of the area around the Vltava valley. The Germanic Marcomans arrived in 9–6 BC, and gradually the Celts left. The first Slavic tribes came to Bohemia in about 500 AD. Struggles for supremacy led to the emergence of a ruling dynasty, the Přemyslids, around 800 AD. They built two fortified settlements: the first at Prague Castle *(see pp96–111)*, the second at Vyšehrad, a rocky headland on the right bank of the Vltava *(see pp180–81)*. These remained the seats of Czech princes for hundreds of years. One prince crucial to the emerging Czech State was the pious Wenceslas. He enjoyed only a brief reign but left an important legacy in the founding of St Vitus's rotunda *(see pp102–5)*.

Extent of the City
▫ 1000 AD ▫ Today

Boleslav's henchman
raises his sword to strike the fatal blow.

St Cyril and St Methodius
Originally Greeks from Salonica, these two brothers brought Christianity to Great Moravia in about 863. They baptized early Přemyslid, Bořivoj, and his wife Ludmila, grandmother of St Wenceslas.

Second assassin
grapples with the Prince's companion.

Early Coin
Silver coins like this denar were minted in the royal mint of Vyšehrad during Boleslav II's reign from 972–99.

Wild Boar Figurine
Celtic tribes made small talismans of the wild animals that they hunted for food in the forested areas around Prague.

6th century AD Slavs settle alongside Germanic tribes in Bohemia

623–658 Bohemia is part of an empire formed by Frankish merchant, Samo

600 AD

700

500 BC Celts in Bohemia. Joined by Germanic Marcomans in 1st century AD

Bronze head of a Celtic goddess

8th century Tribe of Czechs settle in central Bohemia

Vyšehrad acropolis – first Czech settlement on the right bank of the Vltava

Sword and Helmet

St Wenceslas was buried in the southern apse of the rotunda of St Vitus. His sword and helmet were preserved as relics and today form part of the Cathedral's treasure.

Princess Libuše

The legendary founder of the Přemyslids was Princess Libuše, head of a West Slavic tribe. She took notice of the discord among her clansmen, and succeeded her father to become the first woman ruler. Choosing a humble plough-man (Přemysl-Oráč) as consort and ruler, she began a dynasty that was to last 400 years.

Ploughman Přemysl and Princess Libuše founded a long-lasting dynasty

Wenceslas seeks sanctuary.

A monk closes the door against Wenceslas

Rotunda of St Vitus

Founded by Wenceslas in the early 10th century, the rotunda became a place of pilgrimage after the saint's death in 935. It stood where St Wenceslas Chapel is today.

Roman-arched windows

Assassination of Prince Wenceslas

In 935, the young Wenceslas was murdered on the orders of his brother, Boleslav. This manuscript illustration of 1006 shows the moment when the assassins caught up with the prince as he was about to enter the church for the morning mass.

Curving stone walls

800 Dynasty of Přemyslids founded

Early Christian breast cross

870 Prague Castle founded

921 Wenceslas becomes Prince of Bohemia

993 Bishop Adalbert Vojtěch founds monastery at Břevnov

800	900	1000

863 St Cyril and St Methodius bring Christianity to Great Moravia

935 Wenceslas dies

920 Founding of St George's Basilica at Prague Castle

Bishop Adalbert's bejewelled glove

Early Medieval Prague

Prague Castle steadily grew in importance from the beginning of the 9th century onwards. Prone to frequent fires, its wooden buildings were gradually replaced by stone and the area developed into a sturdy Romanesque fortress with a palace and religious buildings. Clustered around the original outer bailey was an area inhabited by skilled craftsmen and German merchants, encouraged to come and stay in Prague by Vladislav II and, later, Přemysl Otakar II. This came to be known as the "Little Quarter" and achieved town status in 1257. It was joined to the Old Town by a bridge, known as the Judith Bridge.

Extent of the City
☐ 1230   ☐ Today

St George's Convent and Basilica *(see p100)*

Decorative Comb
This ornate, bone, fine-toothed comb was one of the relics of St Adalbert.

The Prince's Palace grew into the Old Royal Palace *(see pp106–107)*.

The White Tower gave access from the west.

St Vitus's Basilica and Chapter House *(see pp102–105)*

Entrance from Old Town

Prague Castle in 1230

Sited on a high ridge, the Romanesque fortress had protective stone walls and easily guarded gates.

Site of Hradčany Square

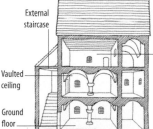

External staircase

Living room

Vaulted ceiling

Ground floor

Romanesque Stone House
These three-storeyed houses were based around a very simple floor plan.

Stone houses were built on what is now Nerudova Street in the Little Quarter *(see p130)*.

St Adalbert with a martyr's palm frond

1040 St Adalbert's remains brought to Prague

1091 Old Town marketplace first mentioned by travellers

1070 Vyšehrad becomes temporary seat of Czech princes

1085 Vratislav I becomes first King of Bohemia

1050

1092–1110 Reign of Bretislav II

1110 Small German settlement in Prague

1091 Great fire at Prague Castle

1091 Great fire at Prague Castle

1110–20 Reign of Bořivoj II

1135 Seat of Czech princes moves from Vyšehrad to Prague Castle

1100

1140 Strahov Monastery founded

115

St Agnes of Bohemia
Sister of Wenceslas I, this devout woman built a convent for the order of the Poor Clares (the female counterparts of the Franciscans) *(see pp94–5)*. She was not canonized until 1989.

Where to See Romanesque Prague

Remains of Prague's history can be seen in the crypt of St Vitus's Cathedral *(see pp102–105)*, and the Old Royal Palace *(see pp106–107)*.

St George's Basilica and Convent
The vaulting in the crypt dates from the 12th century *(see pp100–101)*.

The Black Tower was the exit to Bohemia's second town, Kutná Hora *(see p170)*.

Vratislav II
The Vyšehrad Codex, an illuminated selection from the gospels, was made to mark Vratislav's coronation in 1061.

Little Quarter Square

St Martin's Rotunda
This well-preserved building is in Vyšehrad *(see p46)*.

Přemysl Otakar II
The last great Přemyslid king was killed in battle after carving out a large central European empire.

Little Quarter Coat of Arms
Vladislav II's portrait was incorporated into this 16th-century miniature painting.

Romanesque stone head from Judith Bridge Tower

1182 Romanesque construction of Prague Castle completed

1233 Founding of St Agnes's Convent

1257 Little Quarter receives town status

1258–68 Strahov Monastery rebuilt in Gothic style after fire

1200

1250

1172 Judith Bridge built *(see pp136–9)*

1212 Přemysl Otakar I receives the Sicilian Golden Bull, confirming the sovereignty of Bohemian kings

1278 Přemysl Otakar II dies at Marchfeld

Sicilian Golden Bull

Prague's Golden Age

In the late Middle Ages, Prague attained the height of its glory. The Holy Roman Emperor Charles IV chose Prague as his Imperial residence and set out to make the city the most magnificent in Europe. He founded a university (the Carolinum) and built many fine churches and monasteries in the Gothic style. Of major importance were his town-planning schemes, such as the reconstruction of Prague Castle, the building of a new stone bridge to replace the Judith Bridge, and the foundation of a new quarter, the New Town. A devout Catholic, he owned a large collection of relics which were kept, along with the Crown Jewels, at Karlštejn Castle *(see p169)*.

Extent of the City
1350   Today

Charles IV
wears the Imperial crown, set with sapphires, rubies and pearls.

St Wenceslas Chapel
Proud of his direct descent from the Přemyslids, Charles had this shrine to St Wenceslas built in St Vitus's Cathedral *(see pp102–105)*.

The Emperor
places the piece of the cross in its reliquary.

St Wenceslas Crown
Worn by Charles at his coronation in 1347, the Bohemian crown was based on early Přemyslid insignia.

1280 Old-New Synagogue completed in Gothic style

Town Hall, Old Town Square

1338 John of Luxemburg gives permission to Old Town to build a town hall

1333 Charles IV makes Prague his home

1348 Charles IV founds Charles University

1305   **1320**   **1335**

1306 Přemyslid dynasty ends

Portal of Old-New Synagogue

1310 John of Luxemburg occupies Prague

Votive panel showing Charles, Archbishop Jan Očko and Bohemia's patron saints

1344 Elevation of Prague bishopric to archbishopric

1348 Charles IV founds Prague New Town

St Vitus by Master Theodoric
This is one of a series of paintings of saints by the great Bohemian artist for the Holy Rood Chapel at Karlštejn Castle (c.1365).

A jewelled reliquary cross was made to house the new relic.

University Seal, 1348
The seal depicts the Emperor offering the foundation documents to St Wenceslas.

Building the New Town
This manuscript records Charles IV supervising the building of the New Town during the 14th century.

Charles IV and his Relics

Charles collected holy relics from all over the Empire. In about 1357, he received a part of Christ's cross from the Dauphin. This mural in Karlštejn Castle is thought to be the best likeness of the Emperor.

Where to See Gothic Prague

Prague's rich Gothic legacy includes three of its best-known sights – St Vitus's Cathedral (see pp102–105), Charles Bridge (see pp136–9) and the Old-New Synagogue (see pp90–91). Another very important building from Charles IV's reign is the Carolinum (see p67). The Church of Our Lady before Týn (see p72) has also retained most of its original Gothic features and is worth visiting.

Carolinum This fine oriel window was part of the university (see p67).

Old Town Bridge Tower
The sculptural decoration is by Peter Parler (see p139).

1357 Charles Bridge begun

Sculpture of young Wenceslas IV by Peter Parler in St Vitus's Cathedral

1378 Reign of Wenceslas IV begins

Bethlehem Chapel

1350   **1365**   **1380**   **1395**

1361 Wenceslas IV born, oldest son of Charles

1378 Charles dies

1391 Bethlehem Chapel founded

Hussite Prague

In the early 15th century, Europe shook in fear of an incredible fighting force – the Hussites, followers of the reformist cleric, Jan Hus. Despite simple weapons, they achieved legendary military successes against the Emperor's Catholic crusades, due largely to their religious fervour and to the discipline of their brilliant leader, Jan Žižka, who invented mobile artillery. The Hussites split into two camps, the moderate "Utraquists" *(see p77)* and the radical "Taborites" who were finally defeated at the Battle of Lipany in 1434, paving the way for the moderate Hussite king, George of Poděbrady.

Extent of the City
☐ 1500 ☐ Today

Nobles' Letter of Protest
Several hundred seals of the Bohemian nobility were affixed to a letter protesting about the execution of Jan Hus.

The priest
held a gilded monstrance.

God's Warriors

The early-16th-century Codex of Jena illustrated the Hussite successes. Here, the Hussites, who included artisans and barons, are shown singing their hymn, with their blind leader, Jan Žižka.

Jan Žižka

War Machine

For maximum effect, farm waggons were tied together to form a shield. A chilling array of weapons were unleashed including crossbows, flails and an early form of howitzer.

Jan Hus preaching

1402–13 Jan Hus preaches at Bethlehem Chapel *(see p77)*

1415 Jan Hus burned at the stake at Constance

1419 Defenestration of councillors from New Town Hall

1434 Battle of Lipany

The Taborites made lethal weapons from simple farm tools

1400

1420

1440

1410 Jan Hus excommunicated. Building of Old Town Clock

The chalice, symbol of the Utraquists

1424 Jan Žižka dies

1420 Hussites victorious under Jan Žižka at Vitkov and Vyšehrad

1448 Prague conquered by troops of George of Poděbrady

Satan Dressed as the Pope
Lurid images satirizing the corruption of the church were painted on placards and carried through the streets.

The banner was decorated with the Hussite chalice.

A variety of farm implements were used as makeshift weapons by the peasants.

The peasant army marched behind Jan Žižka.

Hussite Shield
Wooden shields like this one that bears the arms of the city of Prague, were used to fill any gaps in the waggon fortress's tight formation.

Reformer, Jan Hus

Born to poor parents in a small Bohemian town, Jan Hus became one of the most important religious thinkers of his day. His objections to the Catholic Church's corrupt practices, opulent style and wealth were shared by many Czechs – nobles and peasants alike. His reformist preaching in Prague's Bethlehem Chapel earned him a huge following, noticed by the Roman Papacy, and Hus was excommunicated. In 1412, Wenceslas IV, brother of the Emperor Sigismund, asked him to leave Prague. In October 1414, Hus decided to defend his teaching at the Council of Constance. Even though he had the Emperor's safe conduct, he was put in prison. The following year he was declared a heretic and burned at the stake.

Jan Hus at the Stake in 1415
After suffering death at the hands of the Church on 6 July 1415, Jan Hus became a revered martyr of the Czech people.

1458 Coronation of George of Poděbrady *(see p21)*

1485 King Vladislav Jagiello begins to rebuild Royal Palace at Prague Castle

Vladislav Jagiello

1460

1480

1500

1487 First book printed in Prague

1485 Hussite uprising in Prague

1502 Vladislav Hall built

Chalice on the outside of the Church of Our Lady before Týn denotes the Hussite cause

Vladislav Hall

The Renaissance and Rudolph II

With the accession of the Habsburgs, the Renaissance reached Prague. Art and architecture were dominated by the Italians who enjoyed the patronage of the Imperial court, especially that of Rudolph II. The eccentric Rudolph often neglected politics, preferring to indulge his passions for collecting and science. His court was a haven for artists, astrologers, astronomers and alchemists, but his erratic rule led to revolts and an attempt by his brother Matthias to usurp him. In the course of the Thirty Years' War *(see pp32–3)*, many works of art from Rudolph's collection were looted.

Extent of the City
■ 1550   □ Today

Dalibor Tower

Fish pond

Belvedere

Pergola

Rudolph II
A connoisseur of the bizarre, Rudolph was delighted by this vegetable portrait by Giuseppe Arcimboldo (1590).

Orchard

Formal flower beds

Lion House

Mosaic Desk Top
Renaissance table tops with Florentine themes of fountains and gardens were made at Rudolph's court in semi-precious stones.

Rabbi Löw
A revered Jewish sage, he was said to have invented the Golem *(see pp90–91)*.

1526 Habsburg rule begins with Ferdinand I

Ferdinand I

1541 Great fire in Little Quarter, the Castle and Hradčany

1556 Ferdinand I invites Jesuits to Prague

1520

1540

1560

1538–63 Belvedere built

1547 Unsuccessful uprising of towns of Prague against Ferdinand I

Charter for manglers and dyers

Sense of Sight
Jan Brueghel's allegorical painting shows the extent of Rudolph II's huge collection – from globes to paintings, jewels and scientific instruments.

Where to See Renaissance Prague

The Royal Garden *(see p111)* preserves much of the spirit of Renaissance Prague. Paintings and objects from Rudolph's collections can be seen in the Sternberg Palace *(see pp112–15)*, the Picture Gallery of Prague Castle *(see p100)* and the Museum of Decorative Arts *(see p86)*.

At the Two Golden Bears Built in 1590, the house is famous for its symmetrical, carved doorway, one of the most graceful in Prague *(see p73)*.

Tycho Brahe
The Danish astronomer spent his last years living in Prague.

Ball Game Hall

Belvedere The palace is decorated with stone reliefs by Italian architect Paolo della Stella *(see pp110–11)*.

A covered bridge connected the Palace to the garden.

Ball Game Hall Beautiful Renaissance *sgraffito*, heavily restored, covers the façade of this building in the Royal Garden *(see p111)*.

Royal Palace Gardens

No longer a medieval fortress, Prague Castle and its gardens were given over to the pleasure of the King. Here, Rudolph enjoyed ball games, exotic plants and his menagerie.

1583 Prague becomes seat of Imperial court of Rudolph II; great art collection begun	**1609** Publication of Rudolph's Imperial Charter on religious freedom	**1620** Battle of the White Mountain	**1621** Execution in Old Town Square of 27 Protestant leaders
		1612 Rudolph II dies	
1580	**1600**		**1620**

A ten-ducat coin (1603)

1614 Matthias Gate at Prague Castle built

1618 Defenestration of two royal governors from Royal Palace *(see p107)*

Baroque Prague

In 1619, the Czech nobles deposed Habsburg Emperor Ferdinand II as King of Bohemia and elected instead the Protestant ruler Frederick of the Palatinate. The following year, they paid for their defiance at the Battle of the White Mountain, the beginning of the Thirty Years' War. There followed a period of persecution of all non-Catholics, accompanied by the Germanization of the country's institutions. The leaders in the fight against Protestantism were the Jesuits and one of their most powerful weapons was the restoration of Prague's churches in Baroque style. Many new churches also adopted this style.

Extent of the City
☐ 1750 ☐ Today

Mirror Chapel

Church of St Nicholas
This outstanding High Baroque church in the Little Quarter was the work of the great Dientzenhofers *(see pp128–9)*.

Grape Courtyard

Measuring the World
Some monasteries were seats of learning. Strahov *(see pp120–21)* had two libraries built, decorated with Baroque painting. This fresco detail is in the Philosophical Hall.

Holy Saviour Church

Old Town coat of arms – embellished with the Imperial eagle and 12 flags in recognition of the defence of the city against the Swedes

1627 Beginning of Counter-Reformation committee in Prague

1706–14 Decoration of Charles Bridge with statues

1625	1645	1665	1685	1705

1648 Swedes occupy Prague Castle. Treaty of Westphalia and end of Thirty Years' War

1704–53 Building of Church of St Nicholas in the Little Quarter

1631 Saxon occupation of Prague

1634 Wallenstein killed by Irish mercenaries

1676–8 New bastions built to fortify Vyšehrad

A sculpture of **Atlas** (1722) adorns the top of the tower.

Observatory Tower

Battle of the White Mountain In 1620, the Czech army was defeated by Habsburg troops at Bílá Hora (White Mountain), a hill west of Prague *(see p163)*. After the battle, Bohemia became a de facto province of Austria.

St Clement's Church gave its name to the whole complex.

Italian Chapel

Monstrance Baroque monstrances – used to display the communion host – became increasingly elaborate and ornate during this period.

Clementinum

The Jesuits exercised enormous power over education. Between 1653 and 1723, they built this College (see p81). It was the largest complex of buildings after Prague Castle and included three churches, smaller chapels, libraries, lecture halls and an observatory.

Where to See Baroque Prague

The Baroque is everywhere in Prague. Almost all the churches were built or remodelled in Baroque style, the finest being St Nicholas in the Little Quarter *(see pp128–9)*. There are also the grand palaces and smaller houses of the Little Quarter *(see pp122–41)*, the façades in the Old Town *(see pp62–81)*, and statues on churches, street corners and along the parapets of Charles Bridge.

Nerudova Street At the Golden Cup, No. 16, has preserved its typical Baroque house sign *(see p130)*.

Charles Bridge This statue of St Francis Borgia by Ferdinand Brokoff was added in 1710 *(see pp136–9)*.

The National Revival in Prague

The 19th century was one of the most glorious periods in the history of Prague. Austrian rule relaxed, allowing the Czech nation to rediscover its own history and culture. Silent for so long, Czech was re-established as an official language. Civic pride was rekindled with the building of the capital's great showpieces, such as the National Theatre, which utilized the talents of Czech architects and artists. The Jewish Quarter and New Town underwent extensive redevelopment and, with the introduction of public transport, Prague grew beyond its ancient limits.

Extent of the City
🔲 1890   🔲 Today

Smetana's Libuše
Written for the scheduled opening of the National Theatre in 1881, the opera drew on early Czech legend *(see p23)*.

Days of the year

December

Months and zodiac signs revolve around the centre.

Old Town coat of arms

Rudolfinum
A major concert venue beside the Vltava, the building *(see p86)* is richly decorated with symbols of the art of music.

Old Town Square's Astronomical Clock Calendar

In 1866, the revolving dial on Prague's most enduring landmark was replaced by a new one by celebrated artist, Josef Mánes. His studies of Bohemian peasant life are incorporated into pictures symbolizing the months of the year.

1805 Czechs, Austrians and Russians defeated by Napoleon at Battle of Slavkov (Austerlitz)

1818 National Museum founded

Restored clock from the east face of the Town Hall Tower

1848 Uprising of people of Prague against Austrian troops

1800

1820

1840

1815 First public demonstration of a vehicle driven by a steam engine

The battle of Slavkov

1833 Englishman Edward Thomas begins production of steam engines

1838–45 Old Town Hall undergoes reconstruction

1845 First train arrives in Prague

Expo 95 Poster
Vojtěch Hynais designed this poster for the ethnographic exhibition of folk culture in 1895. In the Art Nouveau style, it reflected the new appreciation of regional traditions.

Where to See the National Revival

Many of Prague's remarkable monuments, the National Museum for example, were built around this period. One fine example of Art Nouveau architecture is the Municipal House (see p66), where the Mayor's Room has murals by Mucha. The grand Rudolfinum (see p86) and the National Theatre (see pp156–7) have gloriously-decorated interiors by great artists of the day. The Prague Museum (see p161) has many objects from the late 19th and early 20th centuries as well as the original painting for Mánes' Old Town Square's Astronomical Clock.

Sagittarius

Municipal House
Allegories of civic virtues painted by Alfons Mucha adorn this Art Nouveau interior.

National Museum The Neo-Renaissance façade dominates the skyline (see p147).

Jewish Quarter
From 1897 onwards, the slum housing of the ghetto was replaced with new apartment blocks.

National Theatre The decor has murals by Czech artists, including Aleš (see pp156–7).

National Theatre

Early electric trams

1860

1868 Foundation stone for National Theatre laid

1880

1881 Newly opened National Theatre destroyed by fire, then rebuilt

1883 Re-opening of the National Theatre

1884–91 Building of the National Museum

1883 First public lighting with electric lamps

1891 Jubilee Exhibition

1896 Proper city transport of electric trams starts

1897–1917 Slums of Jewish Ghetto cleared

1900

1912 Municipal House opens

1914 World War I begins

1916 Emperor Franz Josef dies

Prague after Independence

Just 20 years after its foundation in 1918, the Czechoslovak Republic was helplessly caught up in the political manoeuvring that preceded Nazi domination of Europe. Prague emerged from World War II almost unscathed by bombings, no longer part of a Nazi protectorate but of a Socialist republic. Any resistance was brutally suppressed. Ultimately, the intellectuals spoke out, demanding observance of civil rights. Denial of such rights led these dissidents to unite and prepare for the "Velvet Revolution". In the end, it was a playwright, Václav Havel, who was swept into power at Prague Castle to lead the country at the start of a long and often difficult return to independence.

1966 Jiří Menzel's *Closely Observed Trains* wins Oscar for Best Foreign Film, drawing the world's attention to Czech cinema

1967 First Secretary and President, Antonín Novotný, imprisons dissident writers

1968 Moderate Alexander Dubček adopts the programme of liberal reforms known as "Prague Spring". On 21 August, Warsaw Pact occupies Czechoslovakia and over 100 protesters are killed as troops enter Prague

1935 Edvard Beneš succeeds Masaryk as President. Nazi-funded Sudeten German Party, led by Konrad Henlein, makes election gains

1948 Communist Party assumes power under Klement Gottwald; announces 89 per cent support in May elections

1962 Statue of Stalin in Letná Park demolished (replaced, in 1991, by a giant metronome)

1920 Avant-garde left-wing artists form Devětsil movement in Prague's Union Café

Edvard Beneš

1945 The Soviet Red Army enters Prague on 9 May to rapturous welcome, following four days of uprisings. In October, provisional National Assembly set up under Beneš

1958 Premiere of innovative animated film, *The Invention of Destruction* directed by Karel Zeman

1977 Human rights manifesto Charter 77 drawn up after arrest of band, Plastic People

1920	1935	1950	1965

1920	1935	1950	1965

1924 Death of Franz Kafka, author of *The Trial*

1942 Tyrannical Nazi "Protector" for only eight months, Reinhard Heydrich assassinated by Czech resistance

1932 Traditional gymnastic rally or *slet* takes place at Strahov stadium

1952 Most famous of many show trials under Gottwald, Slánský Trial sends 11 senior politicians to gallows as Trotskyites and traitors

1969 Jan Palach burns to death in protest at Soviet occupation

1918 Foundation of Czechoslovak Republic. Tomáš Masaryk first democratically elected President

1938 Munich Agreement hands over parts of Republic to Hitler. Beneš flees country

1955 Largest statue of Stalin in the world unveiled in Letná Park, overlooking city

1979 Playwright Václav Havel founds Committee for the Defence of the Unjustly Persecuted and is sent to prison

Tomáš Masaryk in c.1920, shortly after becoming the country's first President

1960 Czechoslovak Socialist Republic (ČSSR) proclaimed

1939 German troops march into Prague; city declared capital of Nazi Protectorate of Bohemia and Moravia. Emil Hácha is President under the German protectorate

1968 Alexander Dubček elected to post of First Secretary

1989 The "Velvet Revolution"; growing civil discontent prompts demonstrations and strikes. Havel unites opposition groups to form Civic Forum. Temporary Government promises free elections; President Husák resigns and Václav Havel is sworn in by popular demand

The coat of arms of the President of the Czech Republic has the inscription "truth victorious" and the arms for Bohemia (top left, bottom right), Moravia (top right) and Silesia (bottom left)

1990 First democratic elections for 60 years produce 99 per cent turnout, with 60 per cent of vote going to alliance of Civic Forum and People Against Violence

1993 The splitting of Czechoslovakia. Prague becomes capital of new Czech Republic

2002 Prague suffers its worst flooding in 150 years

2015 Prague and Ostrava hold the 79th Ice Hockey World Championships

1999 Czech Republic joins NATO

2004 Czech Republic joins the EU

2016 The UN agrees to officially rename the country Czechia

'80	1995	2010	2025

'80	1995	2010	2025

2013 Miloš Zeman, a former prime minister, wins the Czech Republic's first direct presidential election

2012 Government corruption, spending cuts and tax rises lead to huge anti-government protests in April

1989 Canonization of St Agnes of Bohemia *(see pp94–5)* takes place on 4 November. Vatican commissions painting by dissident Prague-born artist Gustav Makarius Tauc for the occasion. Czech legend that miraculous events will accompany her elevation to sainthood prove correct when the "Velvet Revolution" begins on 17 November

2009 Czech Republic holds presidency of the European Union

2008 Václav Klaus sworn into second five-year term as President

1984 Jaroslav Seifert, signatory of Charter 77, wins Nobel Prize for Literature but cannot collect prize in person

2001 The biggest street protests since the end of Communism force Jiři Hodač to resign as director-general of state television

PRAGUE AT A GLANCE

There are almost 150 places of interest described in the *Area by Area* section of this book. A broad range of sights is covered: from the ancient Royal Palace, which was the site of the Defenestration of 1618 *(see p107)*, to cubist houses built in the Jewish Quarter in the 1920s *(see p93)*; from the peaceful oasis of Petřín Park *(see p141)*, to the bustle of Wenceslas Square *(see pp144–5)*. To help you make the most of your stay, the following 12 pages are a time-saving guide to the best Prague has to offer visitors. Museums and galleries, churches and synagogues, palaces and gardens all have their own sections. Each sight has a cross reference to its own full entry. Below are the attractions that no visitor should miss.

Prague's Top Ten Sights

Old Town Square
See pp68–71

Old Town Hall
See pp74–6

Old Jewish Cemetery
See pp88–9

St Agnes of Bohemia Convent
See pp94–5

Prague Castle
See pp98–9

St Vitus's Cathedral
See pp102–105

Wallenstein Palace and Garden
See p126

Church of St Nicholas
See pp128–9

Charles Bridge
See pp136–9

National Theatre
See pp156–7

◀ A view of the Old Town and Charles Bridge, bustling with people

Prague's Best: Museums and Galleries

With more than 20 museums and almost 100 galleries and exhibition halls, Prague is a city of unexpected and rare delights. Religious masterpieces of the Middle Ages vie with the more recent opulence of Art Nouveau and the giants of modern art. Several galleries have opened since 1989 with many more temporary exhibitions. There are museums devoted to the history of the state, the city of Prague and its people, many of them housed in buildings that are historical landmarks and works of art in themselves. This map gives some of the highlights, with a detailed overview on pages 42–3.

Picture Gallery of Prague Castle
Among the art on display are paintings from the famous collection of Emperor Rudolph II, as well as over 100 works by Titian, Aachen and Rubens.

Sternberg Palace
The collection of European art here is outstanding, represented in works such as *The Feast of the Rosary* by Albrecht Dürer (1506).

Prague Castle and Hradčany

Little Quarter

Vltava

The Loreto
The offerings of devout local aristocrats form the basis of this collection of religious decorative art. In 1721, this jewel-encrusted, tree-shaped monstrance was given to the treasury by Countess Wallenstein.

Smetana Museum
The life and work of this 19th-century Czech composer are remembered beside the river that inspired one of his most famous pieces – the *Vltava*.

Schwarzenberg Palace
The ornate Renaissance palace, formerly the home of the Museum of Military History, is now a gallery exhibiting Baroque art.

Museum of Decorative Arts
Five centuries of arts and crafts are represented here, with particularly impressive collections of Bohemian glass, graphic art and furniture. This carved and painted chest dates from 1612.

St Agnes of Bohemia Convent
This collection includes the 14th-century *Resurrection of Christ* by the Master of the Třeboň Altar.

Jewish Quarter

Maisel Synagogue
One of the most important collections of Judaica in the world is housed in the Maisel Synagogue and other buildings of the State Jewish Museum. The displays include religious artifacts, furnishings and books. This illuminated page is from the manuscript of the Pesach *Haggadah* of 1728.

Old Town

0 metres   500
0 yards   500

New Town

National Museum
The vast skeleton of a whale dominates the other exhibits in one of seven grand halls devoted to zoology. The museum will be closed until 2018 while it undergoes extensive renovation.

Dvořák Museum
This viola, which belonged to the influential 19th-century Czech composer, is among the personal effects and musical scores on display in the charming Villa Amerika.

Exploring the Museums and Galleries

The city's museums give a fascinating insight into the history of the Czechs and of Prague's Jewish population. Also a revelation to visitors unfamiliar with the culture is the art of the Gothic and Baroque periods and of the 19th-century Czech National Revival. The National Gallery's plans to show more collections are underway, with Salmovský Palace the home of temporary exhibitions.

14th-century *Madonna Aracoeli*, St Vitus Treasure, Prague Castle

Czech Painting and Sculpture

The most important and wide-ranging collection in Prague is that of the National Gallery. Its holdings of Czech art are shown at two venues: medieval art is housed at **St Agnes of Bohemia Convent**, and 20th- to 21st-century art is on display at the Trade Fair Palace.

The **Picture Gallery of Prague Castle** is a reminder of Emperor Rudolph II's once-great art collection. Alongside the paintings are documents and other evidence of just how splendid the original collection must have been.

Otto Gutfreund's *Commerce* (1923), Trade Fair Palace

For some of the best Bohemian art, you must visit the Baroque works at the **Schwarzenberg Palace**, just outside the main gate of the Castle. The works here include examples by Baroque masters Karel Škréta and Petr Brandl. On permanent display within the Castle is the St Vitus Treasure, a collection of religious pieces including a Madonna from the School of Master Theodoric.

Centuries of Czech sculpture are housed in the Lapidarium at the **Exhibition Ground**. Among its exhibits is statuary formerly found on the Charles Bridge, and the Marian pillar that used to stand in the Old Town Square.

The collection at the **St Agnes of Bohemia Convent** includes Bohemian and central European Gothic painting and sculpture, including panels painted for Charles IV by Master Theodoric. Works by 19th- and 20th-century Prague artists can be seen at the Prague Gallery. Its branches include the Baroque **Troja Palace**, where the architecture makes a great backdrop. Exhibitions are drawn from the gallery's 3,000 paintings, 1,000 statues and 4,000 prints. The superb museum of 20th- and 21st-century art at the **Trade Fair Palace** represents almost every 20th-century artistic movement. Cubism and Art Nouveau are both represented, as are the 1920s figures of renowned sculptor Otto Gutfreund. The development of

such groundbreaking groups as Osma, Devětsil, Skupina 42 and the 12.15 group is also well documented.

European Painting and Sculpture

On view at **Sternberg Palace** is an exceptional range of master-pieces by Europe's finest artists from antiquity to the 18th century. The most treasured work in the collection is the *Feast of the Rosary* by Albrecht Dürer. Works by 17th-century Dutch masters such as Rubens and Rembrandt also feature.

The museum of 20th- and 21st-century art at the **Trade Fair Palace** has a fine collection of Picassos and Rodin bronzes, as well as works from almost every Impressionist, Post-Impressionist and Fauvist. Three notable self-portraits are those of Paul Gauguin (*Bonjour Monsieur Gauguin*, 1889), Henri Rousseau (1890) and Pablo Picasso (1907). Modern German and Austrian painting is also on show, with works by Gustav Klimt and Egon Schiele. The *Dance of Life*, by Norwegian Edvard Munch, influenced Czech avant-garde art.

The other main venue for European art is the **Picture Gallery of Prague Castle**, which focuses on European painters of the 16th to 18th centuries. As well as Titian's superb *The Toilet of a Young Lady*, there are also works by Rubens and Tintoretto. The exquisite building of **Schwarzenberg Palace** houses a gallery of Baroque art. Whilst the **Kampa Museum of Modern Art** has drawings, paintings and scultures from Central Europe.

Music

Two Czech composers merit their own museums. The **Smetana Museum** is a memorial to the father of Czech music, Bedřich Smetana, whose musical style became closely linked to the national revival. The **Dvořák Museum**, housed in the Villa Amerika, explores the life and work of Antonín Dvořák. Both museums contain personal memorabilia, musical scores and correspondence.

The **Museum of Music** has many rare and historic instruments, and a number of scores by famous composers.

History

The historical collections of the **National Museum** are held at the main Wenceslas Square building. The **Prague Museum** centres on the history of the city, with period rooms, historical prints and a model of Prague in the 19th century, made of paper and wood by the lithographer Antonín Langweil.

Astrolabe from the National Technical Museum

A branch of the museum at Výtoň, on the banks of the Vltava, depicts the way of life of a former settlement. Another at Vyšehrad records the history of this royal seat.

The Museum of Military History, in the Schwarzenberg Palace since 1945 but now at U Památníku 3, displays battle charts, weaponry, uniforms and other military regalia. The Lobkowicz Collection, housed in the 16th century **Lobkowicz Palace** at Prague Castle, includes rare books and manuscripts.

The Jewish Museum is made up of various sites in the Jewish Quarter, including the **Spanish Synagogue, Maisel Synagogue** and the **Old Jewish Cemetery**. Among its collections are holy artifacts from other Jewish communities, brought to Prague by the Nazis as part of a plan for a museum of "an extinct race". Another moving display is of drawings made by children from the Terezín concentration camp.

Decorative Arts

With glassware spanning centuries, from medieval to modern, porcelain and pewterware, furniture and textiles, books and posters, the **Museum of Decorative Arts** in the Jewish Quarter is one of Prague's best, but only a small selection of its holdings is on show. Look out for specialized temporary exhibitions mounted either at the museum itself or at other venues in Prague.

Many other museums have examples of the decorative arts, ranging from grandiose monstrances – including one with 6,222 diamonds – in the treasury of **The Loreto** to simple everyday furnishings in the **Prague Museum**. There is also a fascinating collection of pre-Columbian artifacts from Central America in the **Náprstek Museum**.

Science and Technology

A vast exhibition hall holds the transport section of the **National Technical Museum**. Ranks of vintage cars, motorcycles and steam engines fill the space, and over them hang examples of early flying machines. Other sections in the museum trace the progress of sciences such as electronics. The museum's many other fascinating exhibits include displays on architecture, astronomy and printing and communications.

Finding the Museums and Galleries

Bohemian glass, Museum of Decorative Arts

Prague's Best: Churches and Synagogues

The religious buildings of Prague vividly record the city's changing architectural styles, and many are treasure houses of religious art. But they also reflect Prague's times of religious and political strife, the lives of its people, its setbacks and growth as a city. This map features highlights of their architecture and art, with a more detailed overview on pages 46–7.

St George's Basilica
The heroic saint, sword raised to slay the dragon, is portrayed in this late-Gothic relief, set above the doorway of the magnificent early Renaissance south portal.

St Vitus's Cathedral
The jewel of the cathedral is the Chapel of St Wenceslas. Its walls are decorated with semi-precious stones, gilding and frescoes. Elizabeth of Pomerania, the fourth and last wife of Charles IV, is shown at prayer in the fresco above the Gothic altar.

Prague Castle and Hradčany

Little Quarter

VLTAVA

The Loreto
This shrine to the Virgin Mary has been a place of pilgrimage since 1626. Each hour, its Baroque clock tower chimes a hymn on the carillon of 27 bells.

Church of St Thomas
The skeleton of the martyr St Just rests in a glass coffin below a Crucifixion by Antonín Stevens, one of several superb works of religious art in this church.

Church of St Nicholas
In the heart of the Little Quarter, this is Prague's finest example of High Baroque. The dome over the high altar is so lofty that early worshippers feared it would collapse.

Old-New Synagogue
Prague's oldest synagogue dates from the 13th century. Its Gothic main portal is carved with a vine which bears twelve bunches of grapes symbolizing the tribes of Israel.

Church of Our Lady before Týn
Set back behind a row of arcaded buildings, the many-spired twin towers of the church dominate the eastern end of Old Town Square. The Gothic, Renaissance and Baroque features of the interior create striking contrasts.

Jewish Quarter

Old Town

Basilica of St James
Consecrated in 1374, this basilica was restored to new Baroque glory after a fire in 1689. Typical of its grandeur is this 18th-century monument to chancellor Jan Vratislav of Mitrovice. Fine acoustics and a superb organ make the church a popular venue for concerts.

Slavonic Monastery Emauzy
These cloisters hold a series of precious frescoes from three Gothic masters depicting scenes from the Old and New Testaments.

New Town

| 0 metres | 500 |
| 0 yards | 500 |

Church of St Peter and St Paul
Remodelled many times since the 11th century, the design of this church is now 1890s Neo-Gothic. This striking relief of the Last Judgment marks the main entrance.

Exploring Churches and Synagogues

Religious building began in Prague in the 9th century, reaching its zenith during the reign of Charles IV *(see pp26–7)*. The remains of an 11th-century synagogue have been found, but during the 19th-century clearance of the overcrowded Jewish ghetto, three synagogues were lost. Many churches were damaged during the Hussite rebellions *(see pp28–9)*. The political regime of the 20th century also took its toll, but now, churches and synagogues have been reclaimed and restored, with many open to visitors.

Romanesque

Three reasonably well-preserved Romanesque rotundas, dating from the 11th and 12th centuries, still exist in Prague. The oldest is the **St Martin's Rotunda**; the others are the rotundas of the Holy Rood and of St Longinus. All three are tiny, with naves only 6 m (20 ft) in diameter.

By far the best-preserved and most important Romanesque church in Prague is **St George's Basilica**, founded in 920 by Prince Vratislav I. Extensive

11th-century Romanesque St Martin's Rotunda in Vyšehrad

reconstruction was carried out after a fire in 1142, but its chancel, with some exquisite frescoes on its vaulting, is a Late-Romanesque gem.

The **Strahov Monastery**, founded in 1142 by Prince Vladislav II *(see pp24–5)*, has retained its Romanesque core in spite of fire, wars and extensive renovation.

Gothic

Gothic architecture, with its ribbed vaulting, flying buttresses and pointed arches, reached Bohemia in about 1230 and was soon adopted into religious architecture.

The first religious building in Gothic style was the **St Agnes of Bohemia Convent**, founded in 1233 by Wenceslas I's sister, Agnes. Prague's oldest Jewish house of prayer, the **Old-New Synagogue**, built in 1270, is rather different in style to the churches but is still a superb example of Early Gothic.

The best example of Prague Gothic is **St Vitus's Cathedral**. Its fine tracery and towering

High, Gothic windows at the east end of St Vitus's Cathedral

nave epitomize the style. Other notable Gothic churches are **Our Lady before Týn** and **Our Lady of the Snows**.

Important for its historical significance is the reconstructed Gothic **Bethlehem Chapel** where Jan Hus *(see p29)* preached for 10 years.

The superb Gothic frescoes found in abundance at the **Slavonic Monastery Emauzy** were badly damaged in World War II, but have been restored.

Renaissance

In the 1530s, the influence of Italian artists living in Prague sparked the city's Renaissance movement. The style is more clearly seen in secular than religious building. The Late-Renaissance period, under Rudolph II (1576–1611), offers the best remaining examples.

Domes and Spires

The domes and spires of Prague's churches are the city's main landmarks, as the view from the many vantage points will confirm. You will see a variety of spires, towers and domes: Gothic and Neo-Gothic soar skywards, while Baroque often have rounded cupolas and onion domes. The modern top of the 14th-century Slavonic Monastery, added after the church was struck in a World War II air raid, is a rare example of modernist religious architecture in Prague. Its sweeping, intersecting twin spires are a bold reinterpretation of Gothic themes, and a striking addition to the city's skyline.

Gothic

Church of Our Lady before Týn (1350–1511)

Baroque

Church of St Nicholas in the Little Quarter (1750)

The **High Synagogue** and the **Pinkas Synagogue** retain strong elements of the style: the former in its 1586 exterior, the latter in the reworking of an original Gothic building.

The Church of St Roch in the **Strahov Monastery** is probably the best example of Late-Renaissance "Mannerism".

Renaissance-influenced vaulting, Pinkas Synagogue (1535)

Baroque

The Counter-Reformation (see pp32–3) inspired the building of new churches and the revamping of existing ones for a period of 150 years. Prague's first Baroque church was **Our Lady Victorious**, built in 1611–13.

St Nicholas in the Little Quarter took almost 60 years to build. Its lush interior and frescoed vault make it Prague's most important Baroque building, followed by **The Loreto** (1626–1750), adjoining the **Capuchin Monastery**. The father-and-son team, Christoph and Kilian Ignaz Dientzenhofer designed both buildings, and **St John on the Rock** as well as **St Nicholas** in the Old Town.

A special place in Prague's history was occupied by the Jesuit **Clementinum**. This influential university's church was the **Holy Saviour**. The Baroque style is closely linked with Jesuit teachings: Kilian Ignaz Dientzenhofer was educated here.

Klausen Synagogue (now the Jewish Museum) was built in 1689 with Baroque stuccoed barrel vaults.

Many early buildings were given Baroque facelifts. The Gothic nave of **St Thomas** has Baroque vaulting, and the once-Gothic **St James** went Baroque after a fire in 1689.

19th-century Neo-Gothic portal, Church of St Peter and St Paul

Neo-Gothic

During the height of the 19th-century National Revival (see pp34–5), **St Vitus's Cathedral** was completed, in accordance with the original Gothic plan. Work by Josef Mocker, the movement's leader, aroused controversy, but his **St Peter and St Paul** at Vyšehrad is a well-loved landmark. The triple-naved basilica of **St Ludmila** in Náměstí Míru was also designed by Mocker.

Finding the Churches and Synagogues

Nave ceiling of the Church of St Nicholas in the Little Quarter

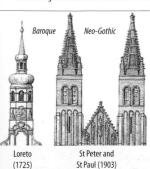

Baroque   Neo-Gothic

Loreto
(1725)

St Peter and
St Paul (1903)

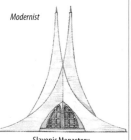

Modernist

Slavonic Monastery
Emauzy (1967)

Prague's Best: Palaces and Gardens

Prague's palaces and gardens are among the most important historical and architectural monuments in the city. Many palaces house museums or galleries *(see pp40–43)*, and some are concert venues. The gardens range from formal, walled oases with fountains and grand statuary, to open spaces beyond the city centre. This map features some of the best palaces and gardens, with a detailed overview on pages 50–51.

Belvedere
The Singing Fountain (1568) stands in front of the exquisite Renaissance summer palace.

Royal Garden
Though redesigned in the 19th century, the Renaissance garden preserves much of its original character. Historic statues still in place include a pair of Baroque lions (1730) guarding the entrance.

Prague Castle and Hradčany

Little Quarter

South Gardens
Starting life as the Castle's defensive bastions, these gardens afford a wonderful view of Prague. First laid out as a park in 1891, their present design was landscaped by Slovene architect Josip Plečnik 40 years later.

Wallenstein Palace
Built in 1624–30 for Duke Albrecht of Wallenstein, this vast Baroque palace was intended to outshine Prague Castle. Over 20 houses and a town gate were demolished to make room for the palace and garden. This Fountain of Venus (1599) stands in front of the arches of the *sala terrena*.

Wallenstein Garden
The garden statues are copies of 17th-century bronzes. The originals were plundered by the Swedes in 1648.

Palace Gardens
In the Baroque period, five palace gardens with spectacular terraces were laid out on the hillside below Prague Castle.

Kinský Palace
The Kinský coat of arms adorns the pink and white stuccoed façade designed by Kilian Ignaz Dientzenhofer. The Rococo palace is part of the National Gallery.

Clam-Gallas Palace
Four giant statues of Hercules (c.1715) by Matthias Bernard Braun show the hero straining to support the weight of the massive Baroque front portals of the palace.

Jewish Quarter

Vltava

Old Town

| 0 metres | 500 |
| 0 yards | 500 |

New Town

Villa Amerika
This charming villa was designed by Kilian Ignaz Dientzenhofer in 1712. It now houses the Dvořák Museum. The garden's sculptural decorations are from the workshop of Antonín Braun.

Kampa Island
A tranquil waterside park was created on the island after the destruction of its original gardens in World War II.

Exploring the Palaces and Gardens

Prague boasts an amazing number of palaces and gardens, spanning centuries. Comparatively few palaces were lost to the ravages of war. Instead, they tended to evolve in style during restoration or enlargement. Palace gardens became fashionable in the 17th century, but could only be laid out where there was space, such as below Prague Castle. More vulnerable to change, most have been relandscaped several times. In the 19th century, and again after 1989, many of the larger parks and private gardens were opened up to the public.

Bronze Singing Fountain in the Royal Garden by the Belvedere

Medieval Palaces

The oldest palace in Prague is the **Old Royal Palace** at Prague Castle. In the basement is the Romanesque ground floor, started in about 1135. It has been rebuilt many times, particularly between the 14th and 16th centuries. The heart of the Palace, Vladislav Hall, dates from the 1490s and is late Gothic in structure. Less well known is the early Baroque **Tuscany Palace**, which has a number of Baroque statues in its attic. Several 17th-century frescoes were unearthed during its reconstruction in the 1990s.

Renaissance Palaces

One of the most beautiful Renaissance buildings in Prague is the 16th-century **Schwarzenberg Palace**. The work of Italian architects, its façade is entirely covered with geometric, two-tone *sgraffito* designs. Italians also worked on the **Belvedere**. Its graceful arcades and columns, all covered with rich reliefs, make this one of the finest Renaissance buildings north of the Alps. The **Martinic Palace**, built in 1563, was the first example of late-Renaissance building in Prague. Soon after came the **Lobkowicz Palace**. Its terracotta relief-decorated windows and plaster *sgraffito* have survived later Baroque modifications. The huge **Archbishop's Palace** was given a later Rococo façade over its Renaissance structure.

Southern façade of Troja Palace and its formal gardens

Baroque Palaces

Many palaces were built in the Baroque style, and examples of all its phases still exist in Prague. A handsome, if ostentatious, early Baroque example is the

Decorative Portals and Gates

The elaborate gates and portals of Prague's palaces are among the most beautiful and impressive architectural features in the city. Gothic and Renaissance portals have often survived, even where the buildings themselves have been destroyed or modified by renovations in a later architectural style. The period of most prolific building was the Baroque, and distinctive portals from this time can be seen framing many a grand entrance around the city. Statues of giants, heroes and mythological figures are often depicted holding up the doorways. These were not merely decorative but acted as an integral element of support.

Gateway to Court of Honour of Prague Castle (1768)

Wallenstein Palace. Similar ostentation is evident in the **Černín Palace**, one of Prague's most monumental buildings. The mid-Baroque had two strands, one opulent and Italianate, the other formal and French or Viennese in influence. **Troja Palace** and **Villa Amerika** are in Italian villa style while the **Sternberg Palace** on Hradčanské náměstí is more Viennese in style. Troja was designed in 1679 by Jean-Baptiste Mathey, who, like the Dientzenhofers *(see p129)*, was a master of the Baroque. The pairs of giants on the portals of the **Clam-Gallas Palace**, and the **Morzin Palace** in Nerudova Street, are a popular Baroque motif. The **Kinský Palace** is a superb Rococo design by Kilian Ignaz Dientzenhofer.

Spring flowers in the Royal Garden of Prague Castle

Gardens

The finest of Prague's palace gardens, such as the **Wallenstein Garden**, are in the Little Quarter. Though the style of Wallenstein Palace is Early Baroque, the garden still displays the geometric formality of the Renaissance, also preserved in the **Royal Garden** behind Prague Castle. The **South Gardens** on the Castle's old ramparts were redesigned in the 1920s.

Many more gardens were laid out in the 17th and 18th centuries, when noble families vied with each other to have fine winter residences in the Little Quarter below the Castle. Many are now the grounds of embassies, but others have been opened to the public. The Ledeburg Garden has been combined with several neighbouring gardens. Laid out on a steep hillside, the **Palace Gardens**, in particular, make ingenious use of pavilions, stairs and terraces from which there are wonderful views of the city. The **Vrtba Garden**, landscaped on the site of former vineyards, is a similar Baroque creation with statues and splendid views. Former palace gardens were also used to create a park on **Kampa Island**.

Ancient trees in Stromovka, formerly a royal deer park

The many old gardens and orchards on Petřín Hill have been transformed into the large public area of **Petřín Park**. Another former orchard is **Vojan Park**, laid out by archbishops in the 13th century. The **Botanical Gardens** is one of the few areas of green open to the public in the New Town.

Generally, the larger parks are situated further out of the city. **Stromovka** was a royal deer park, while **Letná Park** was developed in 1858 on the open space of Letná Plain.

Where to Find the Palaces and Gardens

Troja Palace (c.1703)

Clam-Gallas Palace (c.1714)

PRAGUE THROUGH THE YEAR

Springtime in Prague sees the city burst into colour as its gardens start to bloom. Celebrations begin with the Prague Spring Music Festival. In summer, visitors are entertained by street performers and the city's glorious gardens come into their own. When the weather begins to turn cooler, Prague hosts the Strings of Autumn music festival.

The year often draws to a close with snow on the streets. The ball season starts in December, and in the coldest months, most events are held indoors. At Prague Castle, an all-year-round attraction is the changing of the guard around midday. For details of activities, check the listings magazines *(see p224–5)* or the Prague Information Service *(see p224–5)*.

Concert at Wallenstein Palace during the Prague Spring Music Festival

Spring

As Prague sees its first rays of spring sunshine, the city comes alive. A mass of colours, blooms and cultural events makes this one of the most exciting times of the year to visit. The city's blossoming parks and gardens open their gates again, after the colder months of winter. During April, the temperatures rise and an entertainment programme begins – dominated by the Prague International Spring Music Festival.

Easter

Easter Monday *(dates vary)* is a public holiday. Easter is observed as a religious holiday but it is also associated with a bizarre pagan ritual in which Czech men beat their women with willow sticks in order to keep them fertile during the coming year. The women retaliate by throwing water over their male tormentors. Peace is finally restored when the women present the men with a painted egg. Church services are held during the entire Easter period.

March

Young Bohemia Prague *(March)*. International festival which celebrates young musicians – orchestras and choirs perform and compete.

April

Boat trips *(1 April)*. A number of boats begin trips up and down the Vltava.
Witch-burning *(30 April)*, at the Exhibition Ground *(see p162)*. Concerts accompany this 500-year-old tradition where old

brooms are burnt on bonfires, in a symbolic act to rid nature of evil spirits.

May

Labour Day *(1 May)*. Public holiday celebrated with numerous cultural events.
Mozart's Prague *(early May)*. Celebration of Mozart. International orchestras perform in music halls and churches.
Anniversary of Prague Uprising *(5 May)*. At noon, sirens are sounded for one minute. Flowers are laid at the commemorative plaques of those who died *(see p36)*.
Day of Liberation from Fascism *(8 May)*. Public holiday for VE day. Wreaths are laid on the graves of soldiers at Olšany cemeteries.
Prague International Book Fair *(third week in May)*, Industrial Palace *(see p162)*. The best of Czech and international authors.
Prague Food Festival *(last weekend in May)*. Great food, top chefs and a fun atmosphere at this festival of Czech gastronomy.
Prague International Marathon *(dates vary)*.

The Prague Spring International Music Festival

This international festival presents a busy programme of concerts, ballet and opera from 12 May to 3 June. Music lovers can hear a huge selection of music played by some of the best musicians in the world. The main venue is the Rudolfinum *(see p86)* but others include churches and palaces – some of which are only open to the public on these occasions. The festival begins on the anniversary of Bedřich Smetana's death *(see p81)*. A service is held at his grave in Vyšehrad *(see p180)*, and in the evening there is a concert at the Municipal House *(see p66)* where musicians perform his most famous work, *Má Vlast* (My Country). Municipal House is also where the festival ends.

Bedřich Smetana

Average Daily Hours of Sunshine

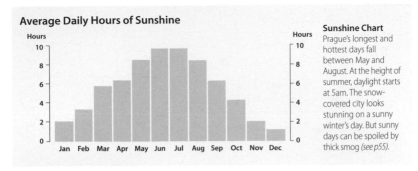

Hours

10
8
6
4
2
0

Jan Feb Mar Apr May Jun Jul Aug Sep Oct Nov Dec

Hours

10
8
6
4
2
0

Sunshine Chart
Prague's longest and hottest days fall between May and August. At the height of summer, daylight starts at 5am. The snow-covered city looks stunning on a sunny winter's day. But sunny days can be spoiled by thick smog (see p55).

Czechs and tourists enjoying the beauty of Vyšehrad Park on a sunny afternoon

Summer

Summer arrives with high temperatures, frequent, sometimes heavy, showers and thousands of visitors. This is a beautiful, if busy, time to visit. Every weekend, Czechs set out for the country to go hiking in the surrounding hills or stay in country cottages. Those remaining in Prague visit the reservoirs and lakes, just outside the city to try and escape the heat. There is a wealth of entertainment on offer as culture moves into the open air taking over the squares, streets and gardens. Street performers, buskers and classical orchestras all help to keep visitors entertained. Many cafés have tables outside allowing you to quench your thirst while watching the fun.

June

Mayoral Boat Race (first weekend in June), Primátorky. Rowing races are held on the river Vltava, just below Vyšehrad. **Summer Concerts** (throughout the summer). Prague's gardens (see pp48–51) are the attractive and popular setting for a large number of free classical and brass-band concerts. One of the city's most famous, and spectacular, outdoor classical concerts is held by Křižík Fountain at the Exhibition Ground (see p162). Full orchestras play to the stunning backdrop of coloured lights and water, synchronized to the music by computer.
Prague Museum Night (second Saturday in June). From 7pm until midnight, buses take visitors from Staroměstská metro station to various museums and galleries, with free entry.
Anniversary of the Murder of Reinhard Heydrich's Assassins (18 June). A mass is held in remembrance at

the Cathedral of St Cyril and St Methodius (see p152) for those who died there. **Battle Re-enactments** (throughout summer), held in Prague's palaces and gardens. **Dance Prague** (end of May to last week of June). An international festival of contemporary dance at the Ponec Theatre (see p218).

July

Remembrance of the Slavonic Missionaries (5 July). Public holiday in honour of St Cyril and St Methodius (see p152).
Anniversary of Jan Hus's Death (6 July). A public holiday when flowers are laid at the the memorial of 15th-centruy religious reformer and martyr Jan Hus (see pp28–9).

August

Czech Open (third week of August). International youth sports festival.

Changing of the Guard at Prague Castle

Average Monthly Rainfall

Rainfall Chart
Prague has plenty of rain throughout the year. The wettest months are October and November, but there are frequent light showers in the summer months as well. Winter snowfalls can be quite heavy, but they are rarely severe.

Autumn

When the gardens below Prague Castle take on the shades of red and gold, and visitors start to leave, the city gets ready for the cold winter months. This is also the traditional mushroom-gathering season when you encounter people with baskets full of freshly picked mushrooms. Market places are flooded with fruit and vegetables. The tree-lined slopes above the Vltava take on the beautiful colours of autumn. September and October still have a fair number of warm and sunny days, although November often sees the first snowfalls. Football fans fill the stadiums and the popular steeplechase course at Pardubice reverberates to the cheers of fans.

Cellist performing at Dvořákova Praha in the Rudolfinum

September
Prague Grand Prix *(first or second Saturday in September)*. Running competition in the centre of Prague.
Dvořákova Praha *(dates vary)*, International music festival in the Rudolfinum *(see p86)*.
Kite competitions *(third Sunday in September)*, on Letná Plain in front of Sparta Stadium. Despite being very popular with children, these competitions are open to anyone with a kite – young or old.
St Wenceslas *(28 September)*. A sacred music festival is held for the feast of the patron saint.
Běchovice-Praha *(last Sunday in September)*. This 10-km (6-mile)- road race has been run since 1897. The race starts from Běchovice, a suburb of Prague, and ends in Žižkov.
Strings of Autumn *(September–October)*. This music festival blending tradition and innovation takes place in various venues around Prague.

October
Golden Prague *(time varies)*, Nová Scéna of National Theatre. International TV festival of prize-winning programmes.
The Great Pardubice Steeplechase *(second Sunday in October)*, held at Pardubice, east of Prague. This horse race has been run since 1874 and is considered to be one of the most difficult in Europe.
The Day of the Republic *(28 October)*. Despite the splitting up of Czechoslovakia into two separate republics, the founding of the country in 1918 is still a public holiday.

November
Velká Kunratická *(second Sunday in November)*. Popular, but gruelling, cross-country race in Kunratice forest. Anyone can enter.
Celebration of the Velvet Revolution *(17 November)*. Peaceful demonstrations take place around Wenceslas Square *(see pp144–5)*.

A view of St Vitus's Cathedral through autumn trees

Average Monthly Temperature

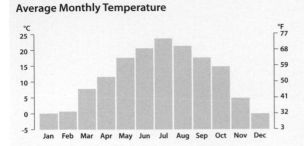

Temperature Chart
The chart shows the average minimum and maximum temperatures for each month in Prague. The summer usually remains comfortably warm, while the winter months can get bitterly cold and temperatures often drop below freezing.

Winter

If you are lucky enough to catch Prague the morning after a snowfall with the sun shining, the effect is magical. The view over the Little Quarter rooftops with their pristine white covering is a memorable sight. Unfortunately, Prague is rarely at its best during the winter months. The weather is changeable. Foggy days with temperatures just above freezing can quickly go down to -5° C (23° F). Pollution and Prague's geographical position in the Vltava basin, lead to smog being trapped just above the city.

As if to try and make up for the winter weather's shortcomings, the theatre season reaches its climax and there are a number of premieres. Balls and dances are held in these cold months. Just before Christmas Eve, large barrels containing live carp – which is the traditional Czech Christmas delicacy – appear on the streets. Christmas trees adorn the city, and carol singers

Snow-capped rooftops in the Little Quarter

can be heard on street corners. Christmas mass is held in most churches and New Year's Eve is celebrated, in time-honoured style, throughout the entire city.

December

Christmas markets (*throughout December*), Můstek and Anděl metro stations, Náměstí Míru, Palackého náměstí, Old Town Square. Stalls sell Christmas decorations, gifts, hot wine, punch and the traditional Czech carp (*see p195*).
Christmas Eve, Christmas Day and Boxing Day (*24, 25 and 26 December*). Public holidays. Mass is held in churches throughout the city.
Swimming competitions in the Vltava (*26 December*). Hundreds of hardened and determined swimmers gather at the Vltava to swim in temperatures of around 3° C (37° F).
New Year celebrations (*31 December*). Crowds of people congregate around Wenceslas and Old Town Square.

January

New Year's Day (*1 January*). Public holiday.

February

Dances and Balls (*early February*).
Bohemian Carnevale Praha (*second and third weeks of February*). Museums, schools and shops host performances of traditional Czech festivities.

Public Holidays

New Year's Day (1 Jan)
Easter Monday
Labour Day (1 May)
Day of Liberation from Fascism (8 May)
Remembrance of the Slavonic Missionaries (5 Jul)
Anniversary of Jan Hus's death (6 Jul)
St Wenceslas (28 Sep)
Foundation of Czechoslovakia (28 Oct)
Fall of Communism (17 Nov)
Christmas Eve, Christmas Day, Boxing Day (24–26 Dec)

Barrels of the traditional Christmas delicacy, carp, on sale in Prague

A RIVER VIEW OF PRAGUE

The Vltava river has played a vital part in the city's history *(see pp22–3)* and has provided inspiration for artists, poets and musicians throughout the centuries.

Up until the 19th century, parts of the city were exposed to the danger of heavy flooding. To try and alleviate the problem, the river's embankments have been strengthened and raised many times, in order to try to prevent the water penetrating too far (the foundations of today's embankments are made of stone or concrete). During the Middle Ages, year after year of disastrous flooding led to the decision to bury the areas affected under 2 m (6 ft) of earth to try to minimize the damage. Although this strategy was only partially effective, it meant that the ground floors of many Romanesque and Gothic buildings were preserved and can still be seen today, such as in the Church of St Francis *(see pp80–81)*.

In 2002 however, a state of emergency was declared as flooding devastated large parts of the city. Despite its destructive side, the Vltava has provided a vital method of transport for the city, as well as a source of income. As technology improved, the river became increasingly important; water mills, weirs and water towers were built. In 1912, a large hydroelectric power plant was built on Štvanice Island, supplying almost a third of Prague's electricity. To make the river navigable, eight dams, a large canal and weirs were constructed along the Slapy-Prague-Mělník stretch, where the Vltava flows into the river Elbe. For the visitor, an excursion on one of the many boats and paddle steamers that travel up and down the river is worthwhile. There are trips to Troja *(see pp166–7)* and as far as Slapy Lake. Catching a boat from one of the piers on the river is a pleasant way to see the city from a different perspective.

A view of the steamboat landing stage (přístaviště parníků) on Rašínovo nábřeží

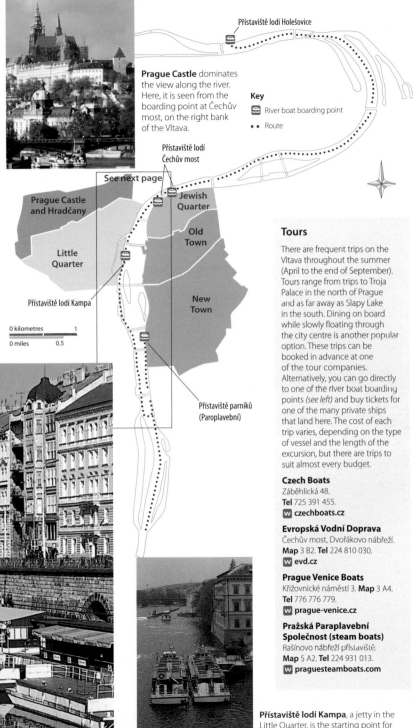

Přístaviště lodí Holešovice

Prague Castle dominates the view along the river. Here, it is seen from the boarding point at Čechův most, on the right bank of the Vltava.

Key

River boat boarding point

Route

Přístaviště lodí Čechův most

See next page

Prague Castle and Hradčany

Jewish Quarter

Old Town

Little Quarter

Přístaviště lodí Kampa

New Town

0 kilometres 1
0 miles 0.5

Přístaviště parníků (Paroplavební)

Tours

There are frequent trips on the Vltava throughout the summer (April to the end of September). Tours range from trips to Troja Palace in the north of Prague and as far away as Slapy Lake in the south. Dining on board while slowly floating through the city centre is another popular option. These trips can be booked in advance at one of the tour companies. Alternatively, you can go directly to one of the river boat boarding points *(see left)* and buy tickets for one of the many private ships that land here. The cost of each trip varies, depending on the type of vessel and the length of the excursion, but there are trips to suit almost every budget.

Czech Boats
Záběhlická 48.
Tel 725 391 455.
W czechboats.cz

Evropská Vodní Doprava
Čechův most, Dvořákovo nábřeží.
Map 3 B2. **Tel** 224 810 030.
W evd.cz

Prague Venice Boats
Křižovnické náměstí 3. **Map** 3 A4.
Tel 776 776 779.
W prague-venice.cz

Pražská Paraplavební Společnost (steam boats)
Rašínovo nábřeží přístaviště.
Map 5 A2. **Tel** 224 931 013.
W praguesteamboats.com

Přístaviště lodí Kampa, a jetty in the Little Quarter, is the starting point for some of the organized boat trips along the Vltava.

Prague River Trip

Taking a trip on the Vltava gives you a unique view of many of the city's historic monuments. Although the left bank was the site of the first Slavonic settlement in the 9th century, it was the right bank, heavily populated by merchants and traders, that developed into a thriving and bustling commercial centre, and the tradition continues today. The left bank was never developed as intensively and much of it is still an oasis of parks and gardens. The river's beauty is enhanced by the numbers of swans which have made it their home.

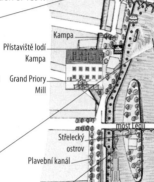

Hanavský Pavilion
This flamboyant cast-iron staircase is part of a pavilion built for the Jubilee Exhibition of 1891.

Little Quarter Bridge Towers
The smaller tower was built in 1158 to guard the entrance to the original Judith Bridge, while the larger one was built on the site of an old Romanesque tower in 1464 (see p136).

Karlův

Kampa

Přístaviště lodí
Kampa

Grand Priory
Mill

most Legií

Střelecký
ostrov

Plavební kanál

Vltava Weir
The thickly wooded slopes of Petřín Hill tower above one of several weirs on the Vltava. During the 19th century, this weir, along with others on this stretch, were built to make the river navigable to ships.

The Vltava Statue
on the northern tip of Children's Island is where, every year, wreaths are placed in memory of the drowned.

Jiráskův most

Palackého most

Little Quarter Water Tower
Built in 1560, the tower supplied river water to 57 fountains throughout the Little Quarter.

Apartment buildings of Art Nouveau design

| 0 metres | | 500 |
| 0 yards | | 500 |

Key
- • Boat trip

Železniční most

To Troja

Čechův most

Přístaviště lodí

Přístaviště lodí

súv most

Charles Bridge

Rudolfinum
This allegorical statue of music by Antonín Wagner is one of two which decorate the imposing entrance to the Neo-Renaissance concert hall *(see p86)*.

The Clementinum, a former Jesuit college, is one of the largest buildings in the city *(see p81)*.

The Old Town Bridge Tower was built as part of the city's 14th-century fortifications *(see p139)*.

Smetana Museum

Weir

Weir

National Theatre
This symbol of the Czech revival, with its spectacularly decorated roof, has dominated the skyline of the right bank since the 1880s *(see pp156–7)*.

The Šitka Water Tower, with its late-18th-century Baroque roof, was originally built in 1495 and pumped water to the New Town.

Slovanský ostrov

The Dancing House
This charming, quirky office building has become a symbol of post-Velvet Revolution modern architecture.

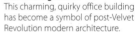

Přístaviště parníků

The Memorial to František Palacký commemorates the life of this eminent 19th-century Czech historian and was built in 1905.

The Na Slovanech Monastery was built in 1347 by Charles IV. Its two modern steeples are easily recognizable from the river.

Výtoň Excise House
The coat of arms on this 16th-century New Town house – built to collect duty on timber transported along the river – dates from 1671.

Church of St Peter and St Paul
The Neo-Gothic steeples on this much-rebuilt church were designed by František Mikeš and erected in 1903. They are the dominant feature of Vyšehrad rock *(see pp180–81)*.

An aerial view of the Old Town Square ▶

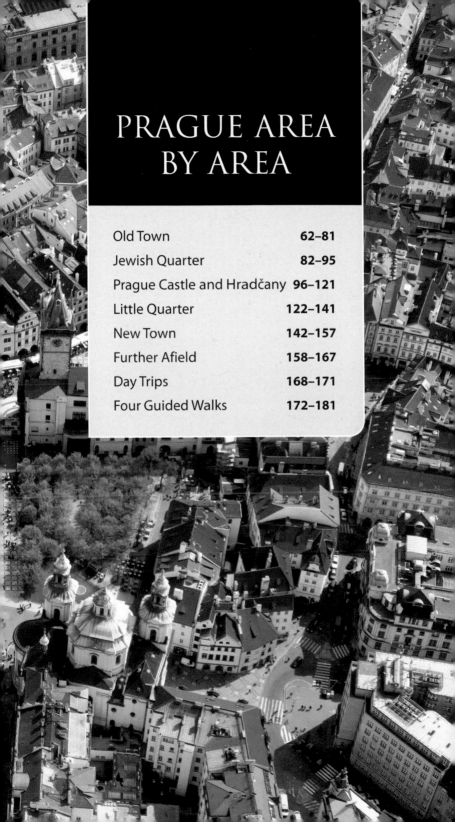

PRAGUE AREA BY AREA

OLD TOWN
STARÉ MĚSTO

The heart of the city is the Old Town and its central square. In the 11th century, the settlements around the Castle spread to the right bank of the Vltava. A market-place in what is now Old Town Square (Staroměstské náměstí) was mentioned for the first time in 1091. Houses and churches sprang up around the square, determining the random network of streets, many of which survive. The area gained the privileges of a town in the 13th century, and, in 1338, a Town Hall. This and other great buildings, such as Clam-Gallas Palace and the Municipal House, reflect the importance of the Old Town.

Sights at a Glance

Churches
- ❹ Basilica of St James
- ❽ Church of Our Lady before Týn
- ⓫ Church of St Nicholas
- ⓮ Church of St Gall
- ⓯ Church of St Martin in the Wall
- ⓱ Church of St Giles
- ⓲ Bethlehem Chapel
- ㉒ Church of St Francis

Museums and Galleries
- ⓰ Náprstek Museum
- ㉔ Smetana Museum

Historic Streets and Squares
- ❸ Celetná Street
- ❼ Old Town Square pp68–71
- ⓴ Mariánské Square
- ㉑ Charles Street
- ㉕ Knights of the Cross Square

Historic Monuments and Buildings
- ❶ Powder Gate
- ❷ Municipal House
- ❻ Carolinum
- ❿ Jan Hus Monument

- ⓬ Old Town Hall pp74–6
- ⓭ House at the Two Golden Bears
- ㉓ Clementinum

Theatres
- ❺ Estates Theatre

Palaces
- ❾ Kinský Palace
- ⓳ Clam-Gallas Palace

☐ **Restaurants** see pp198–9

1 Las Adelitas
2 Ambiente Brasileiro
3 Atmoška
4 Bellevue
5 Country Life
6 Divinis
7 Francouzská Restaurace
8 Golden Tikka
9 Grand Café Orient
10 Kabul
11 Klub Architektů
12 Kogo
13 Lehká hlava

14 Maitrea
15 Mlýnec
16 Pepe Lopez
17 Platina
18 Raw Deli
19 Red Pif
20 Restaurace U Tří Zlatých Lvů
21 Staroměstská
22 Století
23 Le Terroir
24 U Provaznice
25 U Tří růží
26 V Zátiší
27 VinodiVino
28 Zdenek's Oyster Bar

See Street Finder maps 3, 4

0 metres   250
0 yards   250

◀ A close up of the famous Old Town Square's Astronomical Clock

For keys to symbols see back flap

Street-by-Street: Old Town (East)

Free of traffic (except for a few horse-drawn carriages) and ringed with historic buildings, Prague's Old Town Square (Staroměstské náměstí) ranks among the finest public spaces in any city. Streets like Celetná and Ovocný trh are also pedestrianized. In summer, café tables spill out onto the cobbles, and though the area draws tourists by the thousands, the unique atmosphere has not yet been destroyed.

❽ Church of Our Lady before Týn
The church's Gothic steeples are the Old Town's most distinctive landmark.

❾ Kinský Palace
This stunning Rococo palace now serves as an art gallery.

⓫ Church of St Nicholas
This Baroque church's imposing façade dominates a corner of the square.

STAROMĚSTSKÉ NÁMĚSTÍ

MALÉ NÁMĚSTÍ

❼ ★ Old Town Square
This late-19th-century watercolour by Václav Jansa shows how little the square has changed in over a century.

❿ Jan Hus Monument
Religious reformer Hus is a symbol of integrity, and the monument brings together the highest and lowest points in Czech history.

ŽELEZNÁ

The Štorch house has painted decoration based on designs by Mikuláš Aleš showing St Wenceslas on horseback.

⓭ House at the Two Golden Bears
The carved Renaissance portal is the finest of its kind in Prague.

U Rotta is a former ironmonger's shop, decorated with colourful paintings by the 19th-century artist Mikuláš Aleš.

⓬ ★ Old Town Hall
The famous astronomical clock draws a crowd of visitors every hour.

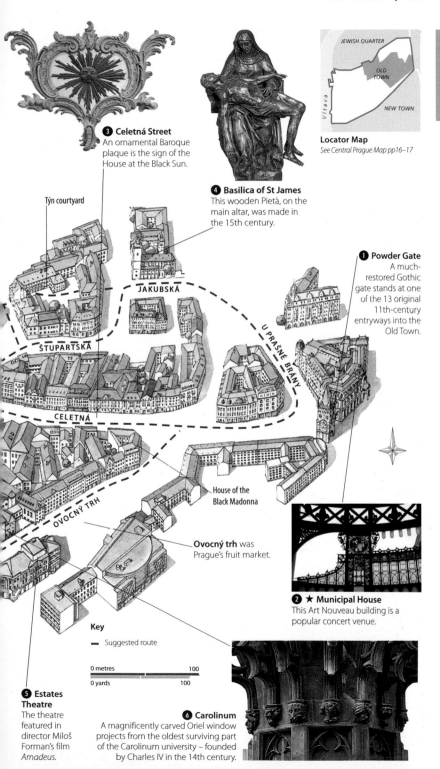

3 Celetná Street
An ornamental Baroque plaque is the sign of the House at the Black Sun.

4 Basilica of St James
This wooden Pietà, on the main altar, was made in the 15th century.

Locator Map
See Central Prague Map pp16–17

Týn courtyard

JAKUBSKÁ

U PRAŠNÉ BRÁNY

1 Powder Gate
A much-restored Gothic gate stands at one of the 13 original 11th-century entryways into the Old Town.

ŠTUPARTSKÁ

CELETNÁ

OVOCNÝ TRH

House of the Black Madonna

Ovocný trh was Prague's fruit market.

2 ★ Municipal House
This Art Nouveau building is a popular concert venue.

Key

— Suggested route

0 metres	100
0 yards	100

5 Estates Theatre
The theatre featured in director Miloš Forman's film *Amadeus*.

6 Carolinum
A magnificently carved Oriel window projects from the oldest surviving part of the Carolinum university – founded by Charles IV in the 14th century.

❶ Powder Gate

Prašná Brána

Náměstí Republiky. **Map** 4 D3. **Tel** 725 847 875. Ⓜ Náměstí Republiky. 🚊 5, 8, 24, 26. **Open** 10am–6pm daily (to 8pm Mar & Oct; to 10pm Apr–Sep). 📷 🅆 **muzeumprahy.cz**

There has been a gate here since the 11th century, when it formed one of the 13 entrances to the Old Town. In 1475, King Vladislav II laid the foundation stone of the New Tower, as it was to be known. A coronation gift from the city council, the gate was modelled on Peter Parler's Old Town bridge tower built a century earlier. The gate had little defensive value; its rich sculptural decoration was intended to add prestige to the adjacent palace of the Royal Court. Building was halted eight years later when the king had to flee because of riots. On his return in 1485, he opted for the safety of the Castle. Kings never again occupied the Royal Court.

The gate acquired its present name when it was used to store gunpowder in the 17th century. The sculptural decoration, badly damaged during the Prussian occupation in 1757, was replaced in 1876.

The Powder Gate viewed from outside the Old Town

Karel Špillar's mosaic *Homage to Prague* on Municipal House's façade

❷ Municipal House

Obecní Dům

Náměstí Republiky 5. **Map** 4 D3. **Tel** 222 002 101. Ⓜ Náměstí Republiky. 🚊 5, 8, 24, 26. Gallery: **Open** for guided visits only, 10am–8pm daily. 📷 obligatory. ♿ 📷 🅆 **obecnidum.cz**

Prague's most prominent Art Nouveau building stands on the site of the former Royal Court palace, the King's residence between 1383 and 1485. Abandoned for centuries, what remained was used as a seminary and later as a military college. It was demolished in the early 1900s to be replaced by the present cultural centre (1905–11) with its exhibition halls and auditorium, designed by Antonín Balšánek assisted by Osvald Polívka.

The exterior is embellished with stucco and allegorical statuary. Above the main entrance, there is a huge semicircular mosaic entitled *Homage to Prague* by Karel Špillar. Inside, topped by an impressive glass dome, is Prague's principal concert venue and the core of the entire building, the Smetana Hall, sometimes also used as a ballroom. The interior of the building is decorated with works by leading Czech artists of the first decade of the century, including Alfons Mucha *(see p149)*.

There are numerous smaller halls, conference rooms and offices that are normally closed but for which you can arrange a guided tour, or you can simply relax in one of the cafés or restaurants.

On 28 October 1918, Prague's Municipal House was the scene of the momentous proclamation of the new independent state of Czechoslovakia.

Decorative detail by Alfons Mucha

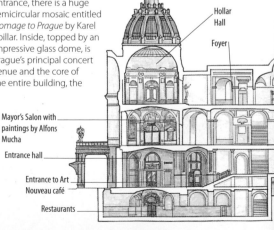

Hollar Hall

Foyer

Mayor's Salon with paintings by Alfons Mucha

Entrance hall

Entrance to Art Nouveau café

Restaurants

❸ Celetná Street
Celetná Ulice

Map 3 C3. 🚇 Náměstí Republiky.

One of the oldest streets in
Prague, Celetná follows an old
trading route from eastern
Bohemia. Its name comes from
the plaited bread rolls that were
first baked here in the Middle
Ages. It gained prestige in the
14th century as a section of the
Royal Route *(see pp174–5)* used
for coronation processions.
Foundations of Romanesque and
Gothic buildings can be seen in
some of the cellars, but most of
the houses with their picturesque
signs are Baroque remodellings.

At No. 34, the House of the
Black Madonna is a fine
example of Cubist architecture.
The building was designed by
Josef Gočár in 1911 and is
home to the historic Grand
Café Orient *(see p206)*, the
only surviving Cubist café
in the world. There is a Cubist
gallery on the ground floor.

❹ Basilica of St James
Bazilika Sv. Jakuba

Malá Štupartská 6. **Map** 3 C3.
🚇 Můstek, Náměstí Republiky.
Tel 224 828 816. **Open** 9:30am–
noon & 2–4pm Tue–Sat (to 3:30pm
Fri), 2–4pm Sun. 🕐 6:45am Mon–
Fri, 5pm Thu–Fri, 8am Sat, 8:30am
& 10:30am Sun.

This basilica was originally the
Gothic presbytery of a Minorite
monastery. The order (a branch
of the Franciscans) was invited

Baroque organ loft in the Basilica of St James

to Prague by King Wenceslas I
in 1232. The church was rebuilt in
the Baroque style after a fire
in 1689, allegedly started by
agents of Louis XIV. Over 20 side
altars were added, decorated
with works by painters such
as Jan Jiří Heinsch, Petr Brandl
and Václav Vavřinec Reiner.
The tomb of Count Vratislav of
Mitrovice (1714–16), designed
by Johann Bernhard Fischer von
Erlach and executed by sculptor
Ferdinand Brokoff, is the most
beautiful Baroque tomb in
Bohemia. The count is said to
have been accidentally buried
alive – his corpse was later
found sitting up in the tomb.
Hanging on the right of the
entrance is a mummified
forearm. It has been there for
several centuries, ever since a
thief tried to steal the jewels
from the Madonna on the
high altar. The Virgin grabbed
his arm and held on so tightly
it had to be cut off.

Because of its long nave, the
church has excellent acoustics,

and many concerts and recitals
are given here. There is also a
magnificent organ built in 1702.

❺ Estates Theatre
Stavovské Divadlo

Ovocný trh 1. **Map** 3 C4. **Tel** 224 901
448 (tickets), 224 901 506 (groups),
221 714 161 (weekends, for
individuals). 🚇 Můstek. **Open** for
guided tours and performances only.
📷 🎫 ♿ 🌐 **narodni-divadlo.cz**

Built by Count Nostitz in 1783,
this opera theatre is one of
Prague's finest examples of Neo-
Classical elegance. It is a mecca
for Mozart fans *(see p218)*. On 29
October 1787, Mozart's opera,
Don Giovanni had its debut here
with Mozart conducting. In 1834,
the musical *Fidlovačka* premiered
here; one of the songs, "Where
is my Home?", became the
Czech national anthem.

❻ Carolinum
Karolinum

Ovocný trh 3. **Map** 3 C4. **Tel** 224 491
850. 🚇 Můstek. **Closed** to the public.
Open for special exhibitions.

At the core of the university
founded by Charles IV in 1348
is the Carolinum. The chapel,
arcade and walls still survive,
together with a fine oriel
window, but in 1945, the courtyard was reconstructed in
Gothic style. In the 15th and 16th
centuries, the university played
a leading role in the movement
to reform the church. After the
Battle of the White Mountain
(see pp32–3), the university was
taken over by the Jesuits.

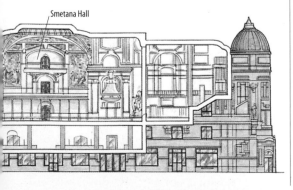
Smetana Hall

❼ Old Town Square: East and North Sides

Staroměstské Náměstí

Some of Prague's colourful history is preserved around the Old Town Square in the form of its buildings. On the north side of the Square, the Pauline Monastery is the only surviving piece of original architecture. The east side boasts two superb examples of the architecture of their times: the House at the Stone Bell, restored to its former appearance as a Gothic town palace, and the Rococo Kinský Palace. An array of pastel-coloured buildings completes the Square.

★ House at the Stone Bell
At the corner of the building, the bell is the sign of this medieval town palace.

Kinský Palace
C G Bossi created the elaborate stucco decoration on the façade of this Rococo palace *(see p72)*.

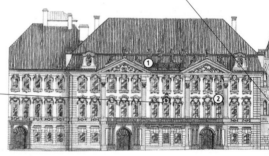

East Side

North Side

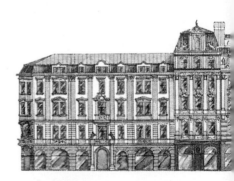

KEY

① **Statues by Ignaz Platzer from 1760–65**

② **Rococo stucco work**

③ **Entrance to Týn Church**

④ **A solid gold effigy of the Virgin Mary**

⑤ **Romanesque arcaded house with 18th-century façade**

⑥ **Restaurant U Sv. Salvatora façade** dates from 1696.

★ Church of St Nicholas
Besides its original purpose as a parish church and, later, a Benedictine monastery church, this has served as a garrison church and a concert hall *(see p72)*.

East and north side

Jan Hus Monument

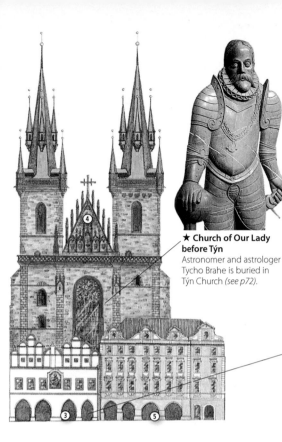

★ Church of Our Lady before Týn
Astronomer and astrologer Tycho Brahe is buried in Týn Church *(see p72)*.

Týn School
Gothic rib vaulting is a primary feature of this building, which was a school from the 14th to the mid-19th century.

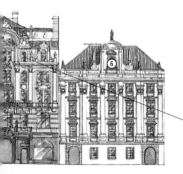

Ministerstvo pro místní rozvoj
Architect Osvald Polívka designed this Art Nouveau building in 1898, with figures of firefighters on the upper façade. It houses the Ministry of Local Development.

Staroměstské náměstí, 1793
The engraving by Filip and František Heger shows the Old Town Square teeming with people and carriages. The Old Town Hall is on the left.

⑦ Old Town Square: South Side

Staroměstské Náměstí

A colourful array of houses of Romanesque or Gothic origin, with fascinating house signs, graces the south side of the Old Town Square. The block between Celetná Street and Železná Street is especially attractive. The Square has always been a busy focal point, and today offers visitors a tourist information centre, as well as a number of restaurants, cafés, shops and galleries.

Franz Kafka (1883–1924)

The author of two of the most influential novels of the 20th century, *The Trial* and *The Castle*, Kafka spent most of his short life in the Old Town. From 1893 to 1901, he studied in the Kinský Palace *(see p72)*, where his father later had a shop. He worked as an insurance clerk, but frequented Berta Fanta's literary salon at the Stone Ram, Old Town Square, along with others who wrote in German. Hardly any of his work was published in his lifetime.

U Lazara (At Lazarus's)
Romanesque barrel vaulting testifies to the house's early origins, though it was rebuilt during the Renaissance. The ground floor houses the Staroměstská restaurace.

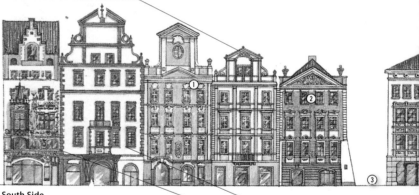

South Side

★ Štorch House
The late-19th-century painting of St Wenceslas on horseback by Mikuláš Aleš appears on this ornate Neo-Renaissance building, also known as At the Stone Madonna.

KEY

① **At the Stone Table**
② **At the Golden Unicorn**
③ **Železná Street**
④ **At the Storks**
⑤ **The arcade** houses the Grand Café Praha.
⑥ **At the Blue Star**
⑦ **U Orloje restaurant**
⑧ **Melantrichova Passage**

★ At the Stone Ram
The early 16th-century house sign shows a young maiden with a ram. The house has been referred to as At the Unicorn due to the similarity between the one-horned ram and a unicorn.

Melantrichova Passage
This narrow passageway leads to the Old Town Square, with the Old Town Hall and its astronomical clock.

South side

Jan Hus Monument

At the Red Fox
A golden Madonna and Child look down from the Baroque façade of an originally Romanesque building.

At the Ox
Named after its 15th-century owner, the burgher Ochs, this house features an early 18th-century stone statue of St Anthony of Padua.

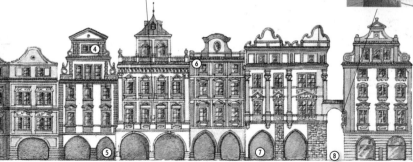

1338 Old Town becomes municipality

Leopold II's Royal Procession through the Old Town Square in 1791

1735 Church of St Nicholas completed

1948 Klement Gottwald proclaims Communist state from balcony of Kinský Palace

1150	1300	1450	1600	1750	1900	2050

1200 Square is meeting point of trade routes and important market

1365 Building of present Týn Church

1621 Execution of 27 anti-Habsburg leaders in square *(see p75)*

1689 Fire destroys large part of Old Town

1784 Unification of Prague towns

1915 Unveiling of Jan Hus Monument

Hus Monument (detail)

Statue of the Madonna on Our Lady before Týn

❽ Church of Our Lady before Týn

Kostel Matky Boží Před Týnem

Staroměstské náměstí 14. **Map** 3 C3. **Tel** 222 318 186. Ⓜ Staroměstská, Můstek. **Open** 10am–1pm & 3–5pm Tue–Sat, 10am–noon Sun. ⏰ 6pm Tue–Thu, 3pm Fri, 8am Sat, 9:30am & 9pm Sun. 🖼 Ⓦ tyn.cz

Dominating the Old Town Square are the magnificent multiple steeples of this historic church. The present Gothic building was started in 1365 and soon became associated with the reform movement in Bohemia. From the early 15th century until 1620, Týn was the main Hussite church in Prague. The Hussite king, George of Poděbrady, took Utraquist communion *(see Church of St Martin in the Wall p77)* here and had a gold chalice – the Utraquist symbol – mounted on the façade. After 1621, the chalice was melted down to become part of the statue of the Madonna that replaced it.

On the northern side of the church is a beautiful entrance portal (1390) decorated with scenes of Christ's passion. The dark interior has some notable features, including Gothic sculptures of *Calvary*, a pewter font (1414) and a 15th-century Gothic pulpit. Behind the church is the Týn Courtyard, with its numerous architectural styles.

❾ Kinský Palace

Palác Kinských

Staroměstské náměstí 12. **Map** 3 C3. **Tel** 224 810 758. Ⓜ Staroměstská. **Open** 10am–6pm Tue–Sun. 🖼 ✏ ♿ Ⓦ ngprague.cz

This lovely Rococo palace, designed by Kilian Ignaz Dientzenhofer, has a pretty pink and white stucco façade crowned with statues of the four elements by Ignaz Franz Platzer. It was bought from the Golz family in 1768 by Štěpán Kinský, an Imperial diplomat. In 1948, Communist leader, Klement Gottwald, used the balcony to address a huge crowd of party members – a key event in the crisis that led up to his *coup d'état*. The National Gallery now uses the Kinský Palace for its "Arts of Asia and Africa" exhibition.

Kinský arms on Kinský Palace

❿ Jan Hus Monument

Pomník Jana Husa

Staroměstské náměstí. **Map** 3 B3. Ⓜ Staroměstská.

At one end of the Old Town Square stands the massive monument to the religious reformer and Czech hero, Jan Hus *(see pp28–9)*. Hus was burnt at the stake after being pronounced a heretic by the Council of Constance in 1415. The monument by Ladislav Šaloun was unveiled in 1915 on the 500th anniversary of his death. It shows two groups of people, one of victorious Hussite warriors, the other of Protestants forced into exile 200 years later, and a young mother symbolizing national rebirth. The dominant figure of Hus emphasizes the moral authority of the man who gave up life rather than his beliefs.

⓫ Church of St Nicholas

Kostel Sv. Mikuláše

Staroměstské náměstí. **Map** 3 B3. **Tel** 602 958 927. Ⓜ Staroměstská. **Open** 10am–4pm daily (from noon Sun). ⏰ 10am Sun, noon Wed. Ⓦ svmikulas.cz

There has been a church here since the 12th century. It was the Old Town's parish church and meeting place until Týn Church was completed in the 14th century. After the Battle of the White Mountain in 1620 *(see pp32–3)*, the church became part of a Benedictine monastery. The present church by Kilian Ignaz Dientzenhofer, was completed in 1735. Its dramatic white façade is studded with statues by Antonín Braun. When in 1781 Emperor Joseph II

Defiant Hussites on the Jan Hus Monument in Old Town Square

Church of St Nicholas in the Old Town

closed all monasteries not engaged in socially useful activities, the church was stripped bare. In World War I, the church was used by the troops of Prague's garrison. The colonel in charge took the opportunity to restore the church with the help of artists who might otherwise have been sent to the front. The dome has frescoes of the lives of St Nicholas and St Benedict by Kosmas Damian Asam. In the nave is a huge crown-shaped chandelier. At the end of the war, the church of St Nicholas was given to the Czechoslovak Hussite Church. The church is now a popular concert venue.

⓬ Old Town Hall

Staroměstská Radnice

See pp74–6.

⓭ House at the Two Golden Bears

Dům U Dvou Zlatých Medvědů

Kožná 1. **Map** 3 B4. Ⓜ Můstek.
Closed to the public.

If you leave the Old Town Square by the narrow Melantrichova Street, make a point of turning into the first alleyway on the

left to see the portal of the house called "At the Two Golden Bears". The Renaissance building was constructed from two earlier houses in 1567. The portal was added in 1590, when wealthy merchant Lorenc Štork secured the services of court architect Bonifaz Wohlmut, who had designed the spire on the tower of St Vitus's Cathedral *(see pp102– 105)*. His ornate portal with reliefs of two bears is one of the most beautiful in Prague. Arcades dating from the 16th century have been preserved in the inner courtyard. In 1885, Egon Erwin Kisch, known as the "Furious Reporter", was born here. A German-speaking Jewish writer and journalist, he was feared for the force of his left-wing rhetoric.

⓮ Church of St Gall

Kostel Sv. Havla

Havelská. **Map** 3 C4. Ⓜ Můstek.
Tel 222 318 186. **Open** 11:30am–1pm daily. ⬆ 12:15pm Mon–Fri, 8am Sun. ✉ ♿ Ⓦ **tyn.cz**

Dating from around 1280, this church was constructed to serve an autonomous German community in the area known as Gall's Town (Havelské Město). In the 14th century, this was merged with the Old Town. In the 18th century, the church was given a Baroque facelift by Giovanni Santini-Aichel, who created a bold façade decorated with statues of saints by Ferdinand Brokoff. Rich interior furnishings include paintings by the leading Baroque artist Karel Škréta, who is buried here. Prague's best-known market has been held in Havelská Street since the Middle Ages, these days it sells such items as flowers, vegetables, toys and clothes.

A statue on the façade of St Gall's

Carved Renaissance portal of the House at the Two Golden Bears

⑫ Old Town Hall

Staroměstská Radnice

One of the most striking buildings in Prague is the Old Town Hall, established in 1338 after King John of Luxembourg agreed to set up a town council. Over the centuries a number of old houses were knocked together as the Old Town Hall expanded, and it now consists of a row of colourful Gothic and Renaissance buildings, most of which have been carefully restored after heavy damage inflicted by the Nazis in the 1945 Prague Uprising. The tower is 69.5 m (228 ft) high and offers a spectacular view of the city.

Gothic Door
This late Gothic main entrance to the Town Hall and Tower was carved by Matthias Rejsek. The entrance hall is filled with wall mosaics after designs by the Czech painter Mikuláš Aleš.

Old Town Coat of Arms
Above the inscription, "Prague, Head of the Kingdom", is the coat of arms of the Old Town, which was adopted in 1784 for the whole city.

KEY

① Temporary art exhibitions

② Tourist information and entrance to Tower

③ Former house of Volflin of Kamen

④ Entrance hall decorated with mosaics

⑤ Viewing gallery

⑥ Steps to gallery

⑦ Calendar *(see pp34–5)*.

Old Council Hall
This 19th-century engraving features the well-preserved 15th-century ceiling.

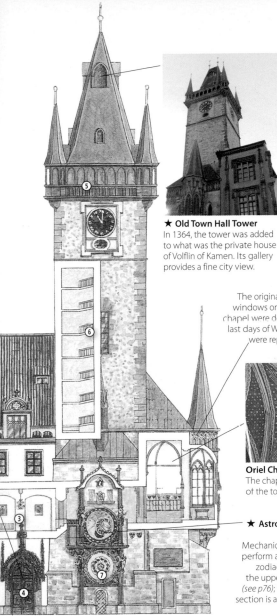

VISITORS' CHECKLIST

Practical Information
Staroměstské náměstí 1.
Map 3 C3. **Tel** 236 002 629.
W **staromestskaradnicepraha.cz**
Tower: **Open** 11am–10pm Mon,
9am–10pm Tue–Sun. &
Halls: **Open** 11am–6pm Mon,
9am–6pm Tue–Sun.

Transport
Staroměstská (line A), Můstek
(A & B). 17, 18.

★ Old Town Hall Tower
In 1364, the tower was added to what was the private house of Volflin of Kamen. Its gallery provides a fine city view.

Oriel Chapel
The original stained-glass windows on the five-sided chapel were destroyed in the last days of World War II, but were replaced in 1987.

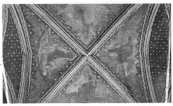

Oriel Chapel Ceiling
The chapel, which was built on the first floor of the tower in 1381, has an ornate ceiling.

★ Astronomical Clock
Mechanical figures perform above the zodiac signs in the upper section (see p76); the lower section is a calendar.

Executions in the Old Town Square
A bronze tablet below the Old Town Hall chapel records the names of the 27 Protestant leaders executed here by order of the Catholic Emperor Ferdinand on 21 June 1621. This was the humiliating aftermath of the Battle of the White Mountain (see pp32–3). This defeat led to the emigration of Protestants unwilling to give up their faith, a Counter-Reformation drive and Germanization.

Town Hall Clock

Orloj

The Town Hall acquired its first clock at the beginning of the 15th century. According to legend, in 1490, when it was rebuilt by a master clockmaker called Hanuš (real name Jan Z Růže), the councillors were so anxious to prevent him from recreating his masterpiece elsewhere, that they blinded the poor man. Though the clock has been repaired many times since, the mechanism was perfected by Jan Táborský between 1552 and 1572.

The Apostles

Vanity and Greed

Arabic numerals 1–24

Astronomical Clock with the sun in Aries

Blue, representing the daylight hours

Calendar by Josef Mánes *(see pp34–5)*

Death

The Turk, a symbol of lust

Vojtěch Sucharda's Apostles, sculpted after the last set was burnt in 1945

Apostles

The centrepiece of the show that draws a crowd of spectators every time the clock strikes the hour is the procession of the 12 Apostles. First the figure of Death, the skeleton on the right of the clock, gives a pull on the rope that he holds in his right hand. In his left hand is an hourglass, which he raises and inverts. Two windows then open and the clockwork Apostles (or to be precise 11 of the Apostles plus St Paul) move slowly round, led by St Peter.

At the end of this part of the display, a cock crows and the clock chimes the hour. The other moving figures are a Turk, who shakes his head from side to side, Vanity, who looks at himself in a mirror and Greed, adapted from the original medieval stereotype of a Jewish moneylender.

Astronomical Clock

The clockmaker's view of the universe had the Earth fixed firmly at the centre. The purpose of the clock was not to tell you the exact time but to imitate the supposed orbits of the sun and moon about the Earth. The hand with the sun, which points to the hour, in fact records three different kinds of time. The outer ring of medieval Arabic numerals measures Old Bohemian time, in which a day of 24 hours was reckoned from the setting of the sun. The ring of Roman numerals indicates time as we know it. The blue part of the dial represents the visible part of the sky. This is

divided into 12 parts. In so-called Babylonian time, the period of daylight was divided into 12 hours, which would vary in length from summer to winter.

The clock also shows the movement of the sun and moon through the 12 signs of the zodiac, which were of great importance in 16th-century Prague.

The figures of Death and the Turk

⓯ Church of St Martin in the Wall
Kostel Sv. Martina Ve Zdi

Martinská 8. **Map** 3 B5. **Tel** 734 767 335. Ⓜ Národní třída, Můstek. 🚊 6, 9, 17, 18, 22. **Open** 3–5pm Mon–Sat. ⛪ Sun: 10:30am (German), 7:30pm (Czech). Ⓦ **martinvezdi.eu**

This 12th-century church became part of the city wall during the fortification of the Old Town in the 13th century, hence its name. It was the first church where blessed wine, usually reserved for the clergy, was offered to the congregation as well as bread. This was a basic tenet of belief of the moderate Hussites *(see pp28–9)*, the Utraquists, who took their name from the Latin *sub utraque specie*, "in both kinds". In 1787, the church was converted into workshops, but rebuilt in its original form in the early years of this century.

⓰ Náprstek Museum
Náprstkovo Muzeum

Betlémské náměstí 1. **Map** 3 B4. **Tel** 224 49 / 511. Ⓜ Národní třída, Staroměstská. 🚊 6, 9, 17, 18, 22. **Open** 10am–6pm Tue–Sun. ♿ 🅿 Ⓦ **nm.cz**

Vojta Náprstek, art patron and philanthropist, created this museum as a tribute to modern industry following a decade of exile in America after the 1848 revolution *(see pp34–5)*. On his return in 1862, inspired by London's Victorian museums, he began his collection. He created the Czech Industrial Museum by joining five older buildings together, and in the process virtually destroyed the family brewery and home – an 18th-century house called At the Haláneks (U Halánků). He later turned to ethnography and the collection now consists of artifacts from Asian, African and Native American cultures, including weapons and ritual objects from the Aztecs, Toltecs and Mayas. The museum is part of the National Museum. Regular temporary exhibitions on a range of subjects are also staged here.

Ceiling fresco by Václav Vavřinec Reiner in Church of St Giles

⓱ Church of St Giles
Kostel Sv. Jiljí

Husova 8. **Map** 3 B4. **Tel** 224 218 440. Ⓜ Národní třída. 🚊 6, 9, 18, 22. **Open** timings vary. ⛪ 6:30pm daily (also 9:30am & noon Sun in Polish).

Despite the Gothic portal on the southern side, this church is essentially Baroque. Founded in 1371 on the site of a Romanesque church, it became a Hussite parish church in 1420. Following the Protestant defeat in 1620 *(see pp32–3)*, Ferdinand II presented the church to the Dominicans, who built a huge friary on its southern side. It has now been returned to the Dominicans, religious orders having been abolished under the Communists.

The vaults of the church are decorated with frescoes by the painter Václav Vavřinec Reiner, who is buried in the nave before the altar of St Vincent. The main fresco, a glorification of the Dominicans, shows St Dominic and his friars helping the pope defend the Catholic Church from non-believers.

⓲ Bethlehem Chapel
Betlémská Kaple

Betlémské náměstí 4. **Map** 3 B4. **Tel** 224 248 595. Ⓜ Národní třída, Staroměstská. 🚊 6, 9, 17, 18, 22. **Open** 10am–6pm daily. ♿ 🅿 Ⓦ **bethlehemchapel.eu**

The present "chapel" is a reconstruction of a hall built by the followers of the radical preacher Jan Milíč z Kroměříže in 1391–4. The hall was used for preaching in Czech. Between 1402 and 1413 Jan Hus *(see pp28–9)* preached in the Chapel. Influenced by the teachings of the English religious reformer John Wycliffe, Hus condemned the corrupt practices of the Church, arguing that the Scriptures should be the sole source of doctrine. After the Battle of the White Mountain in 1620 *(see pp32–3)*, when Protestant worship was outlawed, the building was handed over to the Jesuits, who rebuilt it with six naves. In 1786, it was almost demolished. After World War II, the Chapel was reconstructed following the design shown in old illustrations.

Illustration of Jan Hus preaching in the Bethlehem Chapel

Street-by-Street: Old Town (West)

The narrow streets near Charles Bridge follow Prague's medieval street plan. For centuries, Charles Street (Karlova) was the main route across the Old Town. The picturesque, twisting street is lined with shops and houses displaying Renaissance and Baroque façades. In the 17th century, the Jesuits bought up a vast area of land to the north of the street to house the complex of the Clementinum university.

② Church of St Francis
This Baroque church is noteworthy for its huge cupola and its underground corridors, which are all that remains of the original Church of St Francis.

㉓ ★ Clementinum
This plaque records the founding in 1783 of a state-supervised seminary in place of the old Jesuit university.

The Old Town Bridge Tower dates from 1380. The Gothic sculptural decoration on the eastern façade was from Peter Parler's workshop. The kingfisher was the favourite personal symbol of Wenceslas IV (son of Charles IV) in whose reign the tower was completed (see p139).

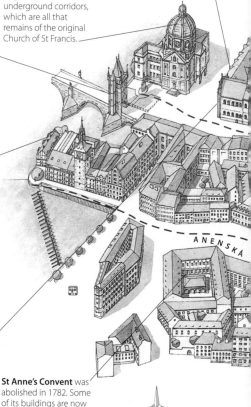

㉔ ★ Smetana Museum
A museum devoted to the life and work of composer Bedřich Smetana is housed in this Neo-Renaissance building set on the riverfront, which was once an old waterworks.

ANENSKÁ

St Anne's Convent was abolished in 1782. Some of its buildings are now used by the National Theatre (see pp156–7).

0 metres		100
0 yards		100

㉕ Knights of the Cross Square
From the façade of the Church of the Holy Saviour, blackened statues overlook the small square.

Key

— Suggested route

20 Mariánské Square
The square used to be flooded so often, it was called "the puddle". The Art Nouveau sculptures on the balcony of the New Town Hall, built here in 1911, are by Stanislav Sucharda.

Locator Map
See Central Prague Map pp16–17

Observatory tower

MARIÁNSKÉ NÁMĚSTÍ

19 Clam-Gallas Palace
One of Prague's grandest Baroque palaces and full of wonderful statuary, the restored Clam-Gallas is open for concerts.

KARLOVA

LILIOVÁ

HUSOVA

To Old Town Square

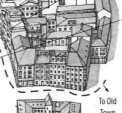

21 Charles Street
Among the many decorated houses along the ancient street, be sure to look out for this Art Nouveau statue of the legendary Princess Libuše (see p23) surrounded by roses at No. 22/24.

ŘETĚZOVÁ

17 Church of St Giles
Much of the Baroque sculpture, like this angel on the altar (1738), is by František Weiss.

18 Bethlehem Chapel
In this spacious chapel, rebuilt in the 1950s, Hus and other reformers preached to huge congregations.

⑲ Clam-Gallas Palace

Clam-Gallasův Palác

Husova 20. **Map** 3 B4.
⬛ Staroměstská. **Open** for concerts and temporary exhibitions only; usually 10am–6pm Tue–Sun.

The interior of this magnificent Baroque palace suffered during its use as a store for the city archives, but it has been restored to its former glory. The palace, designed by Viennese court architect Johann Bernhard Fischer von Erlach, was built in 1713–30 for the Supreme Marshal of Bohemia, Jan Gallas de Campo. Its grand portals, each flanked by two pairs of Hercules sculpted by Matthias Braun, give a taste of what lies within. The main staircase is also decorated with Braun statues, set off by a ceiling fresco, *The Triumph of Apollo* by Carlo Carlone. Clam-Gallas Palace also has a theatre, where Beethoven performed.

⑳ Mariánské Square

Mariánské Náměstí

Map 3 B3. ⬛ Staroměstská, Můstek.

Two statues dominate the square from the corners of the forbidding Town Hall, built in 1912. One illustrates the story of the long-lived Rabbi Löw *(see p90)* finally being caught by the Angel of Death. The other is the Iron Man, a local ghost condemned to roam the Old Town after murdering his mistress. A niche in the garden wall of the Clam-Gallas Palace houses a statue of the River Vltava, depicted as a nymph pouring water from a jug. There is a story that an old soldier once made the nymph sole beneficiary of his will.

The square is a popular meeting point and often attracts visitors in the winter months with a Christmas market.

A 19th-century sign on the House at the Golden Snake

㉑ Charles Street

Karlova Ulice

Map 3 A4. ⬛ Staroměstská.

Dating back to the 12th century, this narrow, winding street was part of the Royal Route *(see pp174–5)*, along which coronation processions passed on the way to Prague Castle. Many original Gothic and Renaissance houses remain, most converted into shops to attract tourists.

A café at the House at the Golden Snake (No. 18) was established in 1714 by an Armenian, Deodatus Damajan, who handed out slanderous pamphlets from here. It is now a restaurant. Look out for At the Golden Well (No. 3), which has a magnificent Baroque façade and stucco reliefs of saints including St Roch and St Sebastian, who are believed to offer protection against plagues.

㉒ Church of St Francis

Kostel Sv. Františka

Křižovnické náměstí 3. **Map** 3 A4. **Tel** 221 108 255. ⬛ Staroměstská. 🚋 17, 18. 🚌 207. **Open** 10am–7pm daily. ✝ 7am Mon–Fri, 9am Sun.

The Baroque Church of St Francis was constructed between 1679 and 1685 by architects Gaudenzio Casanova and Domenico Canevalle, and was built on the remains of the original church of St Francis of Assisi of 1270. The church has a striking 40m-(130ft-)high cupola. Statues of Bohemian patrons stand in alcoves in the façade. The interior is richly appointed with frescoes and important artwork.

Matthias Braun's statues on a portal of the Clam-Gallas Palace (c.1714)

Former Jesuit Church of the Holy Saviour in the Clementinum

Underground corridors contain tombstones and fragments of the former church.

㉓ Clementinum

Klementinum

Křížovnická 190, Karlova 1, Mariánské náměstí 5. **Map** 3 A4. **Tel** 733 129 252 (tours). Ⓜ Staroměstská. 🚊 17, 18. Library: **Open** 9am–10pm Mon–Sat (to 7pm Sat). Church of the Holy Saviour: **Open** for services and events. 🔲 7pm Tue, 2pm & 8pm Sun. 🔲 🔲 🔲 🔲 every half hour from 10am–7pm daily (Nov & Dec: to 6pm, Jan & Feb: to 4:30pm). Ⓦ **klementinum.com**

In 1556, Emperor Ferdinand I invited the Jesuits to Prague to help bring the Czechs back into the Catholic fold. They established their headquarters in the former Dominican monastery of St Clement, hence the name Clementinum. This soon became an effective rival to the Carolinum *(see p67)*, the Utraquist university. Prague's first Jesuit church, the Church of the Holy Saviour (Kostel sv. Salvátora) was built here in 1601. Its façade, with seven large statues of saints by Jan Bendl (1659), is dramatically lit up at night. Expelled in 1618, the Jesuits were back two years later more determined than ever to stamp out heresy. In 1622, the two universities were merged, resulting in the Jesuits gaining a virtual monopoly on higher education in Prague. They searched for books in

Czech and then burnt them by the thousand. Between 1653 and 1723, the Clementinum expanded eastwards. Over 30 houses and three churches were pulled down to make way for the new complex. When in 1773 the pope dissolved their order, the Jesuits had to leave Prague and education was secularized. The Clementinum became the Prague University library, today the National Library. Look out for classical concerts performed in the beautiful Mirror Chapel (Zrcadlová kaple). You can also take a tour of the library and Mirror Chapel.

㉔ Smetana Museum

Muzeum Bedřicha Smetany

Novotného lávka 1. **Map** 3 A4. **Tel** 222 220 082. Ⓜ Staroměstská. 🚊 17, 18. **Open** 10am–5pm Wed–Mon. 🔲 for a fee. Ⓦ **nm.cz**

A former Neo-Renaissance waterworks beside the Vltava has been turned into a memorial to Bedřich Smetana (1824–1884), the father of Czech music. The museum contains documents, letters, scores and instruments detailing the composer's life and work. Smetana was a fervent patriot, and his music helped inspire the Czech national revival. Deaf towards the end of his life, he never heard his cycle of symphonic poems, *Má Vlast* (My Country), being performed.

Statue of Charles IV (1848) in Knights of the Cross Square

㉕ Knights of the Cross Square

Křižovnické Náměstí

Map 3 A4. Ⓜ Staroměstská. 🚊 17, 18 🚌 207. Church of St Francis: **Open** 10am–7pm for services and concerts. 🔲 7am Mon–Fri, 9am Sun. 🔲 🔲

This small square in front of the Old Town Bridge Tower offers fine views across the Vltava. On the north side is the Church of St Francis (Kostel sv. Františka, *see p80*), once part of the monastery of the crusading Knights of the Cross with the Red Star. In summer, concerts of popular Classical and Baroque music take place in this beautiful Baroque church most evenings at 8pm. To the east is the Church of the Holy Saviour, part of the huge Clementinum complex. In the square stands a large bronze Neo-Gothic statue of Charles IV.

Sgraffito façade of the Smetana Museum

JEWISH QUARTER
JOSEFOV

In the Middle Ages, there were two distinct Jewish communities in Prague's Old Town: Jews from the west had settled around the Old-New Synagogue, Jews from the Byzantine Empire around the Old Shul (on the site of today's Spanish Synagogue). The two settlements gradually merged and were confined in an enclosed ghetto. For centuries, Prague's Jews suffered from oppressive laws – in the 16th century, they had to wear a yellow circle as a mark of shame. Rudolph II's more enlightened reign saw the Jewish Mayor Mordechai Maisel *(see p92)* appointed chief financial advisor. Discrimination was further relaxed by Joseph II, and the Jewish Quarter was named Josefov after him. In 1850, the area became officially incorporated into Prague. The city authorities decided to raze the ghetto slum in the 1890s because the lack of sanitation made it a health hazard. However, the Town Hall, the Old Jewish Cemetery and a number of synagogues were saved.

Sights at a Glance

Synagogues and Churches
4 Pinkas Synagogue
5 Klausen Synagogue
6 *Old-New Synagogue pp90–91*
7 High Synagogue
9 Maisel Synagogue
10 Church of the Holy Ghost
11 Spanish Synagogue
13 Church of St Simon and St Jude
14 Church of St Castullus

Concert Hall
1 Rudolfinum

Museums and Galleries
2 Museum of Decorative Arts
15 *St Agnes of Bohemia Convent pp94–5*

Historic Buildings
8 Jewish Town Hall
12 Cubist Houses

Cemeteries
3 *Old Jewish Cemetery pp88–9*

◻ **Restaurants**
See pp199–200
1 Aldente Trattoria Vineria
2 Apetit

3 Bake Shop
4 La Belle Epoque
5 La Casa Argentina
6 La Degustation
7 Dinitz
8 La Finestra in Cucina
9 Fish and Chips
10 Grosseto Marina
11 King Solomon
12 Krčma
13 Lokál
14 Mistral Café
15 My Raw Café
16 Prague Beer Museum
17 V Kolkovně
18 La Veranda

See Street Finder map 3

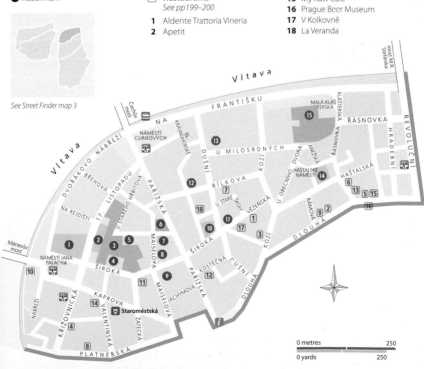

Street-by-Street: Jewish Quarter

Though the old ghetto has disappeared, much of the area's fascinating history is preserved in the synagogues around the Old Jewish Cemetery, while the newer streets are lined with many delightful Art Nouveau buildings. The old lanes to the east of the former ghetto lead to the quiet haven of St Agnes's Convent, beautifully restored as a branch of the National Gallery.

⑥ ★ Old-New Synagogue
The Gothic hall with its distinctive crenellated gable has been a house of prayer for over 700 years.

③ ★ Old Jewish Cemetery
Thousands of gravestones are crammed into the ancient cemetery.

⑫ Cubist Houses
One of the new architectural styles used in the rebuilding of the old Jewish Quarter was based on the ideas of Cubism.

⑦ High Synagogue
The interior has splendid Renaissance vaulting.

⑤ Klausen Synagogue
The exhibits of the Jewish Museum include this alms box, dating from about 800.

② ★ Museum of Decorative Arts
Stained glass panels on the staircase depict the crafts represented in the museum's wide-ranging collection.

④ Pinkas Synagogue
The walls are now a moving memorial to the Czech Jews killed in the Holocaust.

⑧ Jewish Town Hall
The 16th-century building still serves the Czech Jewish community.

⑨ Maisel Synagogue
The original synagogue was built for Mayor Mordechai Maisel in 1591.

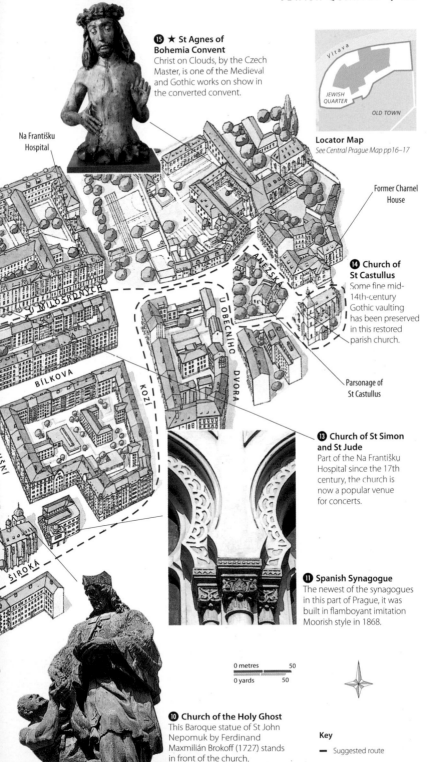

⓯ ★ St Agnes of Bohemia Convent
Christ on Clouds, by the Czech Master, is one of the Medieval and Gothic works on show in the converted convent.

Na Františku Hospital

Locator Map
See Central Prague Map pp16–17

Former Charnel House

⓮ Church of St Castullus
Some fine mid-14th-century Gothic vaulting has been preserved in this restored parish church.

Parsonage of St Castullus

⓭ Church of St Simon and St Jude
Part of the Na Františku Hospital since the 17th century, the church is now a popular venue for concerts.

⓫ Spanish Synagogue
The newest of the synagogues in this part of Prague, it was built in flamboyant imitation Moorish style in 1868.

0 metres 50
0 yards 50

⓾ Church of the Holy Ghost
This Baroque statue of St John Nepomuk by Ferdinand Maxmilián Brokoff (1727) stands in front of the church.

Key
— Suggested route

For keys to symbols *see back flap*

Stage of the Dvořák Hall in the Rudolfinum

❶ Rudolfinum

Alšovo nábřeží 12. **Map** 3 A3.
🚇 Staroměstská. 🚊 17, 18. 🚌 207.
Philharmonic: **Tel** 227 059 227. Galerie
Rudolfinum: **Tel** 227 059 205.
Open 10am–6pm Tue–Sun (to 8pm Thu).
🖂 ♿ 🖥 🌐 **ceskafilharmonie.cz**

As well as being home to the
Czech Philharmonic Orchestra,
the Rudolfinum is one of the
most impressive landmarks on
the Old Town bank of the Vltava.
Many of the major concerts of
the Prague Spring International
Music Festival (see p52) are held
here. There are several concert
halls here, and the sumptuous
Dvořák Hall is one of the finest
creations of 19th-century
Czech architecture.

The Rudolfinum was built
between 1876 and 1884 to a
design by Josef Zítek and Josef
Schulz and named in honour
of Crown Prince Rudolph of
Habsburg. Like the National
Theatre (see pp156–7), it is an
outstanding example of Czech
Neo-Renaissance style. The
curving balustrade is decorated
with statues of distinguished
Czech, Austrian and German
composers and artists.

Also known as the House
of Artists (Dům umělců), the

building houses the Galerie
Rudolfinum, a collection of
modern art. Between 1918
and 1939, and for a brief
period after World War II, the
Rudolfinum was the seat of
the Czechoslovak parliament.

❷ Museum of Decorative Arts
Uměleckoprůmyslové Muzeum

17. listopadu 2. **Map** 3 B3. **Tel** 251
093 111. 🚇 Staroměstská. 🚊 17, 18.
🚌 207. **Open** 10am–6pm Tue–Sun
(to 7pm Tue). 🚼 🖂 ♿ 🖥
🌐 **upm.cz**

For some years after its foundation in 1885, the museum's
collections were housed in the
Rudolfinum. The present building,
designed by Josef Schulz in

French Neo-Renaissance style,
was completed in 1901. The
museum's glass collection is one
of the largest in the world, but
only a fraction of it is ever on
display. Pride of place goes to
the Bohemian glass, of which
there are many fine Baroque
and 19th- and 20th-century
pieces. Medieval and Venetian
Renaissance glass are also
well represented.

Among the permanent
exhibitions of other crafts are
Meissen porcelain, the Gobelin
tapestries and displays covering
fashion, textiles, photography
and printing. The fine furniture
collection has exquisitely carved
escritoires and bureaux from the
Renaissance. On the mezzanine
floor are halls for temporary
exhibitions and an extensive
art library housing more than
100,000 publications.

❸ Old Jewish Cemetery
Starý Židovský Hřbitov

See pp88–9.

❹ Pinkas Synagogue
Pinkasova Synagoga

Široká 3. **Map** 3 B3. **Tel** 222 749 211.
🚇 Staroměstská. 🚊 17, 18. 🚌 207.
Open 9am–6pm Sun–Fri (Nov–
Mar: to 4:30pm). 🚼 🖂 ♿
🌐 **jewishmuseum.cz**

The synagogue was founded
in 1479 by Rabbi Pinkas and
enlarged in 1535 by his great-
nephew Aaron Meshulam
Horowitz. It has been rebuilt
many times over the centuries.
Excavations have turned up
fascinating relics of life in the
medieval ghetto, including a

Names of Holocaust victims on a wall of the Pinkas Synagogue

mikva or ritual bath. The core of the present building is a hall with Gothic vaulting. The gallery for women was added in the early 17th century.

The synagogue now serves as a memorial to all the Jewish Czechoslovak citizens who were imprisoned in Terezín concentration camp and later deported to various Nazi extermination camps. The names of the 77,297 who did not return are inscribed on the synagogue walls. The building houses a moving exhibition of children's drawings from the Terezín concentration camp.

➎ Klausen Synagogue

Klausová Synagoga

U starého hřbitova. **Map** 3 B3. **Tel** 222 317 191. Ⓜ Staroměstská. 🚋 17, 18. 🚌 207. **Open** 9am–6pm Sun–Fri (Nov–Mar: to 4:30pm). 🎧 ♿ Ⓦ **jewishmuseum.cz**

18th-century silver-gilt Torah shield in the High Synagogue

Before the fire of 1689, this site was occupied by a number of small Jewish schools and prayer houses known as *klausen*. The name was preserved in the Klausen Synagogue, built on the ruins and completed in 1694. The High Baroque structure has a fine barrel-vaulted interior with rich stucco decorations. It now houses Hebrew prints and manuscripts and an exhibition of Jewish traditions and customs, tracing the history of the Jews in Central Europe back to the early Middle Ages. Many exhibits relate to famous figures in the city's Jewish community including the 16th-century Rabbi Löw (*see p90*), who, according to legend, created an artificial man out of clay and bought it to life.

19th-century Torah pointer in Klausen Synagogue

Adjoining the synagogue is a building that looks like a tiny medieval castle. It was built in 1906 as the ceremonial hall of the Jewish Burial Society.

In 1944, an exhibition was put on here detailing the history of the Prague ghetto.

➏ Old-New Synagogue

Staronová Synagoga

See pp90–91.

➐ High Synagogue

Vysoká Synagoga

Červená 2. **Map** 3 B3. **Tel** 224 800 849. Ⓜ Staroměstská. 🚋 17, 18. 🚌 207. **Open** for services only: 8:30am & 2pm Mon–Fri, 1:30pm Sat. Ⓦ **kehilaprag.cz**

Like the Jewish Town Hall, the building of the High Synagogue was financed by Mordechai Maisel, mayor of the Jewish Town, in the 1570s. Originally, the two buildings formed a single complex and to facilitate communication with the Town Hall, the main hall of the synagogue was on the first floor.

It was not until the 19th century that the two buildings were separated and the synagogue was given a staircase and street entrance. You can still see the original Renaissance vaulting and stucco decoration.

➑ Jewish Town Hall

Židovská Radnice

Maiselova 18. **Map** 3 B3. **Tel** 224 800 849. Ⓜ Staroměstská. 🚋 17, 18. 🚌 207. **Closed** to the public.

The core of this attractive blue and white building is the original Jewish Town Hall, built in 1570–77 by architect Panacius Roder at the expense of the immensely rich mayor, Mordechai Maisel. In 1763, it acquired a new appearance in the flowery style of the Late Baroque. The last alterations date from 1908, when the southern wing was enlarged.

The building is one of the few monuments that survived far-reaching sanitation of this medieval part of Prague at the beginning of the 20th century. On the roof stands a small wooden clock tower with a distinctive green steeple. The right to build the tower was originally granted to the Jewish community after their part in the defence of Charles Bridge against the Swedes in 1648 (*see pp32–5*). On one of the gables there is another clock. This one has Hebrew figures and, because Hebrew reads from right to left, hands that turn in an anti-clockwise direction. The Town Hall is now the seat of the Council of Jewish Religious Communities in the Czech Republic.

Façade and clock tower of the Jewish Town Hall

❸ Old Jewish Cemetery

Starý Židovský Hřbitov

This remarkable site was, for over 300 years, the only burial ground permitted to Jews. Founded in 1478, it was slightly enlarged over the years but still basically corresponds to its medieval size. Because of the lack of space, people had to be buried on top of each other, up to 12 layers deep. Today, you can see over 12,000 gravestones crammed into the tiny space, but several times that number are thought to have been buried here. The last burial was of Moses Beck in 1787.

View across the cemetery towards the western wall of the Klausen Synagogue

David Gans' Tombstone
The tomb of the writer and astronomer (1541–1613) is decorated with the symbols of his name – a star of David and a goose (*Gans* in German).

KEY

① **The oldest tomb** is that of the writer Rabbi Avigdor Kara (1439).

② **The Pinkas Synagogue** is the second-oldest in Prague *(see pp86–7)*.

③ **Jewish printers**, Mordechai Zemach (d 1592), and his son Bezalel (d 1589), are buried under this square gravestone.

④ **Rabbi David Oppenheim** (1664–1736) was the chief rabbi of Prague. He owned the largest collection of old Hebrew manuscripts and prints in the city.

⑤ **Mordechai Maisel** (1528–1601) was Mayor of Prague's Jewish Town and a philanthropist.

⑥ **The Museum of Decorative Arts** *(see p86)*.

⑦ **The Neo-Romanesque Ceremonial Hall**

⑧ **Klausen Synagogue** *(see p87)*.

⑨ **The Nephele Mound** was where infants who died under a year old were buried.

⑩ **The gravestone of Moses Beck**

★ **14th-Century Tombstones**
Embedded in the wall are fragments of Gothic tombstones brought here from an older Jewish cemetery which was discovered in 1866 in Vladislavova Street in the New Town.

Prague Burial Society
Founded in 1564, the group carried out ritual burials and performed charitable work in the community. Members of the society wash their hands after leaving the cemetery.

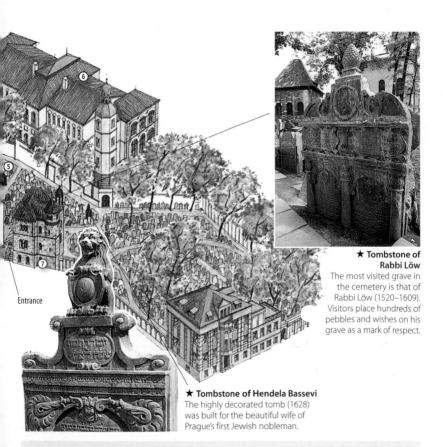

★ **Tombstone of Rabbi Löw**
The most visited grave in the cemetery is that of Rabbi Löw (1520–1609). Visitors place hundreds of pebbles and wishes on his grave as a mark of respect.

Entrance

★ **Tombstone of Hendela Bassevi**
The highly decorated tomb (1628) was built for the beautiful wife of Prague's first Jewish nobleman.

Understanding the Gravestones

From the late 16th century onwards, tombstones in the Jewish cemetery were decorated with symbols denoting the background, family name or profession of the deceased person.

Blessing hands:
Cohen family

A pair of
scissors: tailor

A stag: Hirsch or
Zvi family

Grapes: blessing
or abundance

⊙ Old-New Synagogue

Staronová Synagoga

Built around 1270, this is the oldest synagogue in Europe and one of the earliest Gothic buildings in Prague. The synagogue has survived fires, the slum clearances of the 19th century and many Jewish pogroms. Residents of the Jewish Quarter have often had to seek refuge within its walls and today it is still the religious centre for Prague's Jews. It was originally called the New Synagogue until another synagogue was built nearby – this was later destroyed.

★ **Jewish Standard**
The historic banner of Prague's Jews is decorated with a Star of David and within it the hat that had to be worn by Jews in the 14th century.

Rabbi Löw and the Golem

The scholar and philosophical writer Rabbi Löw, director of the Talmudic school (which studied the Torah) in the late 16th century, was also thought to possess magical powers. He was supposed to have created a figure, the Golem, from clay and then brought it to life by placing a magic stone tablet in its mouth.

The Golem went berserk and the Rabbi had to remove the tablet. He hid the creature among the Old-New Synagogue's rafters.

Rabbi Löw and the Golem

KEY

① **Candlestick holder**

② **14th-century stepped brick gable**

③ **These windows** formed part of the 18th-century extensions built to allow women a view of the service.

④ **The tympanum** above the Ark is decorated with 13th-century leaf carvings.

⑤ **The cantor's platform** and its lectern is surrounded by a wrought-iron Gothic grille.

★ **Five-rib Vaulting**
Two massive octagonal pillars inside the hall support the five-rib vaults.

Right-hand Nave
The glow from the bronze chandeliers provides light for worshippers using the seats lining the walls.

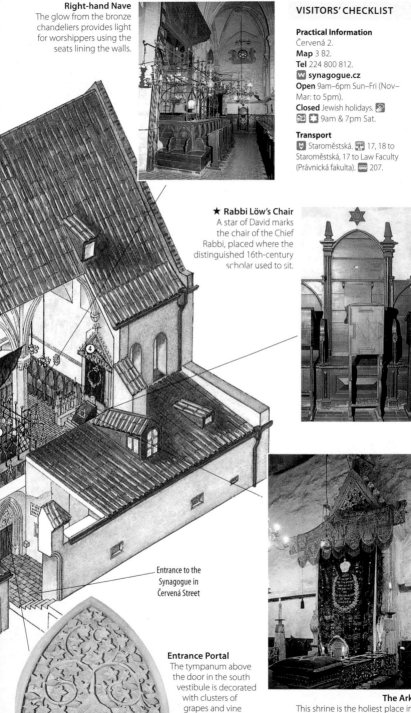

VISITORS' CHECKLIST

Practical Information
Červená 2.
Map 3 B2.
Tel 224 800 812.
W **synagogue.cz**
Open 9am–6pm Sun–Fri (Nov–Mar: to 5pm).
Closed Jewish holidays.
9am & 7pm Sat.

Transport
Staroměstská. 17, 18 to Staroměstská, 17 to Law Faculty (Právnická fakulta). 207.

★ Rabbi Löw's Chair
A star of David marks the chair of the Chief Rabbi, placed where the distinguished 16th-century scholar used to sit.

Entrance to the Synagogue in Červená Street

Entrance Portal
The tympanum above the door in the south vestibule is decorated with clusters of grapes and vine leaves growing on twisted branches.

The Ark
This shrine is the holiest place in the synagogue and holds the sacred scrolls of the Torah.

18th-century silver Torah crown in the Maisel Synagogue

⑨ Maisel Synagogue
Maiselova Synagoga

Maiselova 10. **Map** 3 B3. **Tel** 222 749 211. Ⓜ Staroměstská. 🚊 17, 18. 🚌 207. **Open** Apr–Oct: 9am–6pm Sun–Fri; Nov–Mar: 9am–4:30pm Sun–Fri. 🖼 🚫 ♿ Ⓦ **jewishmuseum.cz**

When it was first built, at the end of the 16th century, this was a private house of prayer for the use of mayor Mordechai Maisel and his family. Maisel had made a fortune lending money to Emperor Rudolph II to finance wars against the Turks, and his synagogue was the most richly decorated in the city. The original building was a victim of the fire that devastated the Jewish Town in 1689 and a new synagogue was built in its place. Its present crenellated, Gothic appearance dates from the start of the 20th century. Since the 1960s, the Maisel Synagogue has housed a fascinating collection of Jewish silver and other metalwork dating from Renaissance times to the 20th century. It includes many Torah crowns, shields and finials. Crowns and finials were used to decorate the rollers on which the text of the Torah (the five books of Moses) was kept. The shields were hung over the mantle that was draped over the Torah and the

pointers were used to follow the text so that it was not touched by readers' hands. There are also objects such as wedding plates, lamps and candlesticks. By a tragic irony, nearly all these Jewish treasures were brought to Prague by the Nazis from synagogues throughout Bohemia and Moravia with the intention of founding a museum of a vanished people.

⑩ Church of the Holy Ghost
Kostel Sv. Ducha

Elišky Krásnohorské. **Map** 3 B3. Ⓜ Staroměstská. 🚊 17, 18. 🚌 207. **Open** only for services. ✝ 9:30am Sun. 🚫 ♿

This church stands on the narrow strip of Christian soil that once separated the two Jewish communities of the Middle Ages – the Jews of the eastern and western rites. Built in the mid-14th century, the single-naved Gothic church was originally part of a convent of Benedictine nuns. The convent was destroyed in 1420 during the Hussite Wars *(see pp28–9)* and not rebuilt.

The church was badly damaged in the Old Town fire of 1689. The exterior preserves the original Gothic buttresses and high windows, but the vault of the nave was rebuilt in Baroque style after the fire. The furnishings

too are mainly Baroque. The high altar dates from 1760, and there is an altar painting of *St Joseph* by Jan Jiří Heintsch (c.1647–1712). In front of the church stands a stone statue of St John Nepomuk *(see p85)* distributing alms (1727) by the Baroque sculptor Ferdinand Maxmilián Brokoff. Inside the church, there are a few earlier statues, including a 14th-century *Pietà* (the heads of the figures are later, dating from 1628), a Late Gothic statue of St Ann and early 16th-century busts of St Wenceslas and St Adalbert.

The soaring Gothic architecture of the Church of the Holy Ghost

⑪ Spanish Synagogue
Španělská Synagoga

Vězeňská 1, Dušní 12. **Map** 3 B2. **Tel** 222 749 211. Ⓜ Staroměstská. 🚊 17, 18. 🚌 207. **Open** Apr–Oct: 9am–6pm Sun–Fri; Nov–Mar: 9am–4:30pm Sun–Fri. 🖼 ♿ Ⓦ **jewishmuseum.cz**

Prague's first synagogue, known as the Old School (Stará škola), once stood on this site. In the 11th century, the Old School was the centre of the community of Jews of the eastern rite, who lived strictly apart from Jews of the western rite, who were concentrated round the Old-New Synagogue.

The present building dates from the second half of the

Motif of the Ten Commandments on the Spanish Synagogue's façade

19th century. The exterior and interior are both pseudo-Moorish in appearance. The rich stucco decorations on the walls and vaults are reminiscent of the Alhambra in Spain, hence the name. Once closed to the public, the Spanish Synagogue now houses a permanent exhibition dedicated to the history of the Jews from emancipation to the present.

⓬ Cubist Houses
Kubistické Domy

Elišky Krásnohorské, 10–14. **Map** 3 B2. 🚇 Staroměstská. 🚋 17, 18. 🚌 207. **Closed** to the public.

The rebuilding of the old Jewish Quarter at the turn of the 20th century gave Prague's architects scope to experiment with many new styles. Most of the blocks in this area are covered with flowing Art Nouveau decoration, but on the corner of Bílkova and Elišky Krásnohorské, there is a plain façade with a few simple repeated geometrical shapes. This is an example of Cubist architecture, a fashion that did not really catch on in the rest of Europe, but was very popular with the avant-garde in Bohemia and Austria before and after World War I. This block was built for a cooperative of teachers in 1919–21.

At No. 7 Elišky Krásnohorské, you can see the influence of Cubism in the curiously geometric figures supporting the windows. Another interesting Cubist building is the House of the Black Madonna in Celetná *(see p67)*.

⓭ Church of St Simon and St Jude
Kostel Sv. Šimona A Judy

Dušní/U milosrdných. **Map** 3 B2. **Tel** 222 321 352. 🚇 Staroměstská. 🚋 17, 18. 🚌 207. **Open** for concerts. 👟 🅦 **fok.cz**

Members of the Bohemia Brethren built this church with high Late Gothic windows in 1615–20. Founded in the mid-15th century, the Brethren agreed with the Utraquists

Cubist-style figures framing a window in Elišky Krásnohorské Street

(see p77) in directing the congregation to receive both bread and wine at Holy Communion. In other respects, they were more conservative than other Protestant sects, continuing to practise celibacy and Catholic sacraments such as confession. After the Battle of the White Mountain *(see pp32–3)*, the Brethren were expelled from the Empire.

The church was then given to a Catholic order, the Brothers of Mercy, becoming part of a monastery and hospital. Tradition has it that the monastery's wooden steps were built from the scaffold on which 27 Czechs were executed in 1621 *(see p75)*. In the 18th century, the city's first anatomy

Detail of the Baroque façade of the Church of St Simon and St Jude

lecture hall was established here and the complex continues to serve as a hospital – the Na Františku. The church is now used as a venue for concerts.

⓮ Church of St Castullus
Kostel Sv. Haštala

Haštalské náměstí. **Map** 3 C2. 🚋 5, 8, 24, 26. 🚌 207. **Open** times vary. ✝ 11am 1st & last Sun of month. 🚫 ♿

This peaceful little corner of Prague takes its name – Haštal – from the parish church of St Castullus. One of the finest Gothic buildings in Prague, the church was erected on the site of an older Romanesque structure in the second quarter of the 14th century. Much of the church had to be rebuilt after the fire of 1689, but the double nave on the north side survived. It has slender pillars supporting a delicate ribbed vault.

The interior furnishings are mainly Baroque, though there are remains of wall paintings of about 1375 in the sacristy and a metal font decorated with figures dating from about 1550. Standing in the Gothic nave is an impressive sculptural group depicting *Calvary* (1716) from the workshop of Ferdinand Maxmilián Brokoff.

⓯ St Agnes of Bohemia Convent

Klášter Sv. Anežky České

In 1234, a convent of the Poor Clares was founded here by Agnes, sister of King Wenceslas I. She was not canonized until 1989. The convent, one of the very first Gothic buildings in Bohemia, was abolished in 1782 and used to house the poor and as storage space, later falling into disrepair. Following painstaking restoration in the 1960s, it has recovered much of its original appearance and is now used by the National Gallery to display a large collection of medieval painting and sculpture from Bohemia and Central Europe, dating from 13th–16th centuries.

First floor

Gallery Guide

The permanent exhibition is housed on the first floor of the old convent in a long gallery and smaller rooms around the cloister. The works are arranged chronologically.

Ground floor

★ **Votive panel of Archbishop Jan Očko of Vlašim**
This detailed panel, painted around 1370 by an anonymous artist, shows Charles IV kneeling before the Virgin in Heaven.

★ **The Annunciation of Our Lady**
Painted around 1350 by the renowned Master of the Vyšší Brod Altar, this panel is one of the oldest and finest works in the museum.

Steps to first-floor gallery

★ **Strakonice Madonna**
This 700-year-old statue evokes the Classical French sculpture found in such places as Reims Cathedral.

Terrace café

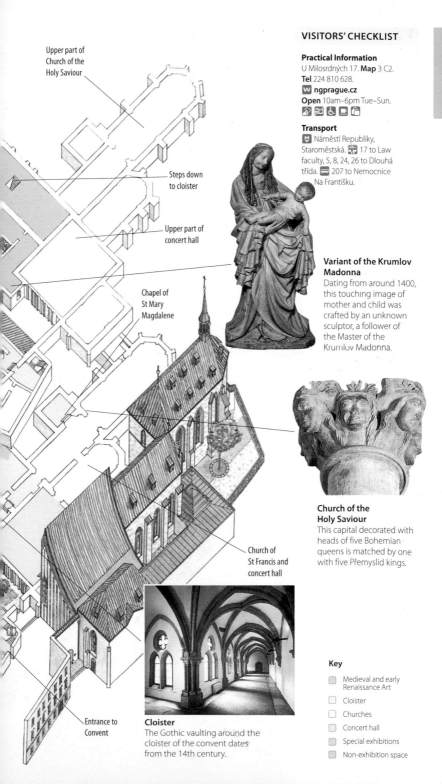

Upper part of
Church of the
Holy Saviour

Steps down
to cloister

Upper part of
concert hall

Chapel of
St Mary
Magdalene

Church of
St Francis and
concert hall

Entrance to
Convent

**Variant of the Krumlov
Madonna**
Dating from around 1400,
this touching image of
mother and child was
crafted by an unknown
sculptor, a follower of
the Master of the
Krumlov Madonna.

**Church of the
Holy Saviour**
This capital decorated with
heads of five Bohemian
queens is matched by one
with five Přemyslid kings.

Cloister
The Gothic vaulting around the
cloister of the convent dates
from the 14th century.

Key

▢ Medieval and early
Renaissance Art

▢ Cloister

▢ Churches

▢ Concert hall

▢ Special exhibitions

▢ Non-exhibition space

PRAGUE CASTLE AND HRADČANY

PRAŽSKÝ HRAD A HRADČANY

The history of Prague begins with the Castle, founded in the 9th century by Prince Bořivoj. Its commanding position high above the river Vltava soon made it the centre of the lands ruled by the Přemyslids. The buildings enclosed by the Castle walls included a palace, three churches and a monastery. In about 1320, a town called Hradčany was founded in part of the Castle's outer bailey. The Castle has been rebuilt many times, most notably in the reigns of Charles IV and Vladislav Jagiello. After a fire in 1541, the badly damaged buildings were rebuilt in Renaissance style and the Castle enjoyed its cultural heyday under Rudolph II. Since 1918, it has been the seat of the president of the Republic. The Changing of the Guard takes place every hour. At noon, the ceremony includes a fanfare.

Sights at a Glance

Churches and Monasteries
- 2 St Vitus's Cathedral pp102–105
- 5 St George's Basilica and Convent
- 18 Capuchin Monastery
- 19 The Loreto pp118 19
- 22 Strahov Monastery pp120–21

Palaces
- 4 Old Royal Palace pp106–107
- 10 Belvedere
- 13 Archbishop's Palace
- 15 Martinic Palace
- 20 Černín Palace and Garden

Historic Buildings
- 3 Powder Tower
- 8 Dalibor Tower

Museums and Galleries
- 1 Picture Gallery of Prague Castle
- 7 Lobkowicz Palace
- 12 Riding School
- 14 Sternberg Palace pp112–15
- 16 Schwarzenberg Palace

Historic Streets
- 6 Golden Lane
- 17 New World
- 21 Pohořelec

Parks and Gardens
- 9 South Gardens
- 11 Royal Garden

Restaurants
see p201
1. Host
2. Kavárna Nový Svět
3. Malý Buddha
4. Peklo
5. Villa Richter

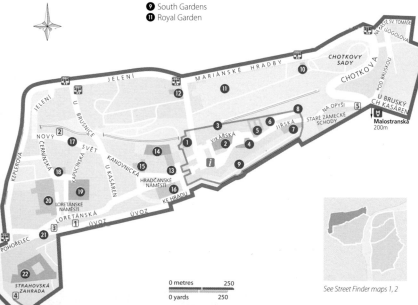

See Street Finder maps 1, 2

◀ Ceiling fresco, *The Heavenly Banquet*, found in the Strahov Monastery   **For keys to symbols** *see back flap*

Street-by-Street: Prague Castle

Despite periodic fires and invasions, Prague Castle has retained churches, chapels, halls and towers from every period of its history, from the Gothic splendour of St Vitus's Cathedral to the Renaissance additions of Rudolph II, the last Habsburg to use the Castle as his principal residence. The courtyards date from 1753–75 when the whole area was rebuilt in Late Baroque and Neo-Classical styles. The Castle became the seat of the Czechoslovak president in 1918, and the current president of the Czech Republic has his office here.

Hradčanské námĕsti and the Archbishop's Palace

❶ Picture Gallery of Prague Castle
Renaissance and Baroque paintings hang in the restored stables of the castle.

❸ Powder Tower
Used in the past for storing gun-powder and as a bell foundry, the tower is now a museum.

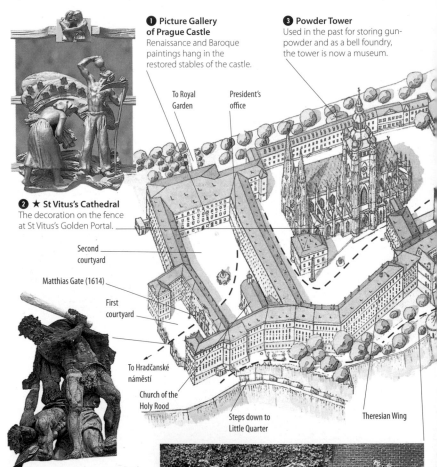

❷ ★ St Vitus's Cathedral
The decoration on the fence at St Vitus's Golden Portal.

To Royal Garden

President's office

Second courtyard

Matthias Gate (1614)

First courtyard

To Hradčanské námĕstí

Church of the Holy Rood

Steps down to Little Quarter

Theresian Wing

The Castle gates are crowned by copies of 18th-century statues of Fighting Giants by Ignaz Platzer.

❾ South Gardens
18th-century statues decorate the gardens laid out in the old ramparts.

6 ★ Golden Lane
The picturesque artisans' cottages along the inside of the castle wall were built in the late 16th century for the Castle's guards and gunners.

Locator Map
See Central Prague Map pp16–17

White Tower

St. George's Convent

8 Dalibor Tower
This grim tower is named for a prisoner who played his violin in return for food.

Toy Museum

Old Castle steps to Malostranská Metro

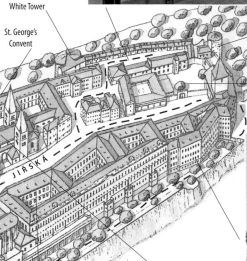

JIŘSKÁ

Key

— Suggested route

0 metres 60
0 yards 60

Rosenberg Palace

7 Lobkowicz Palace
Exquisite works of art from the Lobkowicz family's private collection are housed here.

4 ★ Old Royal Palace
The uniform exterior of the palace conceals many fine Gothic and Renaissance halls. Coats of arms cover the walls and ceiling of the Room of the New Land Rolls.

5 St George's Basilica
The vaulted chapel of the royal Bohemian martyr St Ludmilla is decorated with 16th-century paintings.

❶ Picture Gallery of Prague Castle
Obrazárna Pražského Hradu

Prague Castle, the second courtyard.
Map 2 D2. **Tel** 224 373 531.
🚇 Malostranská, Hradčanská.
🚊 22. **Open** 9am–5pm daily (Nov–Mar: to 4pm). 📷 ♿ 🌐 **hrad.cz**

The gallery was created in 1965 to hold works of art collected since the reign of Rudolph II *(see pp30–31)*. Though most of the collection was looted by the Swedes in 1648, many interesting paintings remain. Works from the 16th–18th centuries form the bulk of the collection, but there are also sculptures, among them a copy of a bust of Rudolph by Adriaen de Vries. Highlights include Titian's *The Toilet of a Young Lady*, Rubens' *The Assembly of the Olympic Gods* and Guido Reni's *The Centaur Nessus Abducting Deianeira*. Master Theodoric, Paolo Veronese, Tintoretto and, the Czech Baroque artists, Jan Kupecký and Petr Brandl are among other artists represented. The Picture Gallery houses many of Rudolph's best paintings.

You can also see the remains of the Castle's first church, the 9th-century Church of our Lady, thought to have been built by Prince Bořivoj, the first Přemyslid prince to be baptized a Christian *(see pp22–3)*. The site was discovered during reconstruction.

❷ St Vitus's Cathedral
Chrám Sv. Víta

See pp102–105.

❸ Powder Tower
Prašná Věž

Prague Castle, Vikářská. **Map** 2 D2.
Tel 224 372 434. 🚇 Malostranská, Hradčanská. 🚊 22. **Open** Apr–Oct: 9am–5pm daily; Nov–Mar: 9am–4pm daily. 📷 ♿ ♿ ♿

A tower was built here in about 1496 by the King Vladislav II's architect Benedikt Ried as a cannon bastion overlooking the Stag Moat. The original was destroyed in the fire of 1541, but it was rebuilt as the home and workshop of gunsmith and bell founder Tomáš Jaroš. In 1549, he made Prague's largest bell, the 18-tonne Sigismund, for the bell tower of St Vitus's Cathedral.

During Rudolph II's reign (1576–1612), the tower became a laboratory for alchemists. It was here that adventurers such as Edward Kelley performed

View of the Powder Tower from across the Stag Moat

experiments that convinced the emperor they could turn lead into gold.

In 1649, when the Swedish army was occupying the Castle, gunpowder exploded in the tower, causing serious damage. Nevertheless, it was used as a gunpowder store until 1754, when it was converted into flats for the sacristans of St Vitus's Cathedral. Today, the tower houses a permanent exhibition of Czech military history.

❹ Old Royal Palace
Starý Královský Palác

See pp106–107.

❺ St George's Basilica and Convent
Bazilika Sv. Jiří

Jiřské náměstí. **Map** 2 E2. **Tel** 224 371 111. 🚇 Malostranská, Hradčanská. 🚊 22. **Open** Apr–Oct: 9am–5pm daily; Nov–Mar: 9am–4pm daily. 📷 ♿ ♿ 🌐 **hrad.cz**

Founded by Prince Vratislav (915–21), the basilica pre-dates St Vitus's Cathedral and is the best-preserved Romanesque

Titian's *The Toilet of a Young Lady* in the Picture Gallery of Prague Castle

church in Prague. It was enlarged in 973 when the adjoining St George's Convent was established here, and rebuilt following a fire in 1142. The massive twin towers and austere interior have been scrupulously restored to give a good idea of the church's original appearance. However, the rusty red façade was a 17th-century Baroque addition.

Buried in the church is St Ludmila, widow of the 9th-century ruler Prince Bořivoj *(see pp22–3)*. She became Bohemia's first female Christian martyr when she was strangled as she knelt at prayer. Other members of the Přemyslid dynasty buried here include Vratislav. His austere tomb stands on the right-hand side of the nave at the foot of the curving steps that lead up to the choir. The impressive Baroque grille opposite encloses the tomb of Boleslav II (972–99). The adjacent former Benedictine nunnery is the oldest convent building in Bohemia. It was founded in 973 by Princess Mlada, sister of Boleslav II. Throughout the Middle Ages, the convent, together with the basilica, formed the heart of the castle complex.

Façade of St George's Basilica, with the towers in the background

❻ Golden Lane
Zlatá Ulička

Map 2 E2. Ⓜ Malostranská, Hradčanská. 🚋 22. 🚻

Named after the goldsmiths who lived here in the 17th century, this short, narrow street is one of the most picturesque in Prague. One side of the lane is lined with tiny, brightly painted houses which were built right into the arches of the Castle walls. They were constructed in the late 1500s for Rudolph II's 24 Castle guards. A century later, the goldsmiths moved in and modified the buildings. But by the 19th century, the area had degenerated into a slum and was populated by Prague's poor and the criminal community. In the 1950s, all the remaining tenants were moved out and the area restored to something like its original state. The house at number 20 is the oldest and the least altered in appearance. Most of the houses were converted into shops selling books, Bohemian glass and other souvenirs for tourists, who flock to the narrow lane.

Golden Lane has been home to some well-known writers, including the Nobel prize-winning poet Jaroslav Seifert, and Franz Kafka *(see p70)* who stayed at No. 22 with his sister for a few months in 1916–17. Because of its name, legends have spread about the street being filled with alchemists huddled over their bubbling alembics trying to produce gold for Rudolph II. In fact, the alchemists had laboratories in Vikářská, the lane between St Vitus's Cathedral and the Powder Tower.

❼ Lobkowicz Palace
Lobkovický Palác

Jiřská 3. **Map** 2 E2. **Tel** 233 312 925 (to book a guided tour). Ⓜ Malostranská. 🚋 5, 12, 18, 20, 22. **Open** 10am–6pm daily. 🚻 📷 ♿ 🖥 🖳 **lobkowicz.cz** Toy Museum: **Tel** 224 372 294. **Open** 9:30am–5:30pm daily.

Dating from 1570, this is one of the palaces that sprang up after the fire of 1541, when Hradčany was largely destroyed. Some original *sgraffito* on the façade has been preserved, but most of the present palace is Carlo Lurago's 17th-century reconstruction for the Lobkowicz family, who had inherited it in 1627. The most splendid room is the 17th-century banqueting hall with mythological frescoes by Fabian Harovník.

The palace once formed part of Prague's National Museum, but has since been returned to the Lobkowicz family. It now houses the valuable Princely Collections, an exhibition of paintings, decorative arts, original music scores annotated by Beethoven and Haydn, and musical instruments.

Opposite the palace, at No. 6, is a delightful toy museum claiming to be the world's second largest, with toys from ancient Greece to the present. The collection includes toys made from wood and tin, dolls and teddy bears.

One of the tiny houses in Golden Lane

❷ St Vitus's Cathedral

Katedrála Sv. Víta, Václava a Vojtěcha

Work began on the city's most distinctive landmark in 1344 on the orders of John of Luxembourg. The first architect was the French Matthew of Arras. After his death, Swabian Peter Parler took over. His masons' lodge continued to work on the building until the Hussite Wars. Finally completed by 19th- and 20th-century architects and artists, the cathedral houses the crown jewels and the tomb of "Good King" Wenceslas *(pp22–3)*.

St Vitus's Cathedral
This 19th-century engraving shows how the cathedral looked before the additions made in 1872–1929.

Gargoyles
On the ornate west front, gutter spouts are given their traditional disguise.

KEY

① **West front**

② **The Rose Window**, located above the portals, was designed by František Kysela in 1925–7. It depicts scenes from the biblical story of the creation.

③ **Twin west spires**

④ **Nave**

⑤ **Triforium**

⑥ **The Renaissance bell tower** is capped with a Baroque "helmet".

⑦ **Chancel**

⑧ **To Royal Palace** *(see pp106–107)*.

⑨ **The tomb of St Wenceslas** is connected to an altar, decorated with semi-precious stones.

Main entrance

Bust of Peter Parler on triforium

926 Rotunda of St Vitus built by St Wenceslas	**1344** King John of Luxembourg founds Gothic cathedral. French architect Matthew of Arras begins work		**1619** Calvinists take over cathedral as house of prayer	**1872** Joseph Mocker begins work on the west nave	

1000	**1200**	**1400**	**1600**	**1800**

| **1060** Building of triple-naved basilica begins on orders of Prince Spytihněv | *Tomb of Přemysl Otakar II* | **1421** Hussites occupy St Vitus's | **1589** Royal tomb completed | **1770** New steeple added to tower after fire |
| | | **1356** Masterbuilder Peter Parler summoned to continue work on the cathedral | | **1929** Consecration of completed cathedral, nearly 1,000 years after death of St Wenceslas |

★ Flying Buttresses
The slender buttresses that surround the exterior of the nave and chancel, supporting the vaulted interior, are richly decorated like the rest of the cathedral.

★ Chapel of St Wenceslas
The bronze ring on the chapel's north portal was thought to be the one to which St Wenceslas clung as he was murdered by his brother Boleslav *(see pp22–3).*

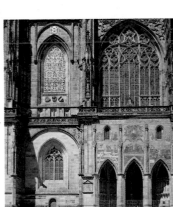

★ Golden Portal
Until the 19th century, this was the main cathedral entrance, and it is still used on special occasions. Above it is a mosaic of *The Last Judgment* by 14th-century Venetian craftsmen.

Gothic Vaulting
The skills of architect Peter Parler are never more clearly seen than in the delicate fans of ribbing that support the three Gothic arches of the Golden Portal.

A Guided Tour of St Vitus's Cathedral

A walk around St Vitus's takes you back through a thousand years of history. Go in through the west portal to see some of the best elements of the modern, Neo-Gothic style and continue past a succession of side chapels to catch glimpses of religious artifacts, saintly relics and works of art from Renaissance paintings to modern statuary. Allow plenty of time to visit the richly decorated, jewel-encrusted St Wenceslas Chapel before you leave.

② **Chancel**
The chancel was built by Peter Parler from 1372. It is remarkable for the soaring height of its vault, counter-pointed by the intricacy of the webbed Gothic tracery.

① **Alfons Mucha Window**
The cathedral contains many superb examples of 20th-century Czech stained glass, notably *St Cyril and St Methodius*.

Cathedral organ (1757)

New sacristy

Main entrance (West Portal)

Thun Chapel

Chapel of St Ludmilla

The Four Eras of St Vitus's

Excavations have revealed sections of the northern apse of St Wenceslas's original rotunda, and architectural and sculptural remains of the later basilica, beneath the existing cathedral. The western, Neo-Gothic end is a faithful completion of the 14th-century plan.

Key

☐ Rotunda, 10th century
▨ Basilica, 11th century
☐ Gothic cathedral, 14th century
☐ 19th- and 20th-century additions to cathedral

Leopold II is shown in a contemporary engraving being crowned King of Bohemia at the cathedral in September 1791. Mozart composed an opera, *La Clemenza di Tito*, in honour of the occasion.

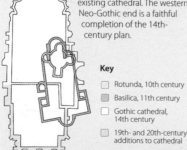

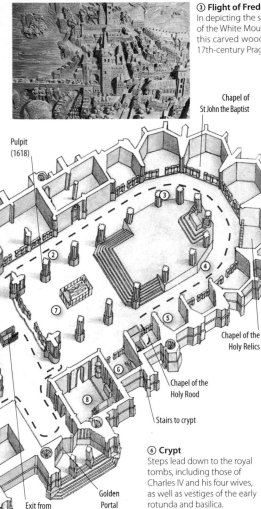

③ **Flight of Frederick of the Palatinate**
In depicting the sad aftermath of the Battle of the White Mountain in 1620 *(see p33)*, this carved wooden panel shows 17th-century Prague in fascinating detail.

Chapel of
St John the Baptist

Pulpit
(1618)

④ **Tomb of St John Nepomuk**
Crafted from solid silver in 1736, this elaborate tomb honours the saint who became the focus of a Counter-Reformation cult *(see p137)*.

Chapel of the
Holy Relics

⑤ **Royal Oratory**
The vault of the 15th-century Late-Gothic oratory is carved with branches instead of ribs.

Chapel of the
Holy Rood

Stairs to crypt

⑥ **Crypt**
Steps lead down to the royal tombs, including those of Charles IV and his four wives, as well as vestiges of the early rotunda and basilica.

Key

— Tour route

Golden
Portal

Exit from
crypt

⑧ **St Wenceslas Chapel**
Gothic frescoes with scenes from the Bible and the life of the saint cover the walls, interspersed with a patchwork of polished gemstones and fine gilding. Every object is a work of art – this golden steeple held the wafers and wine for Holy Communion.

⑦ **Royal Mausoleum**
Ferdinand I died in 1564. His beloved wife and son, Maximilian II, are buried alongside him in the mausoleum.

❹ Old Royal Palace

Starý Královský Palác

From the time Prague Castle was first fortified in stone in the 11th century *(see pp24–5)*, the palace was the seat of Bohemian princes. The building consists of three different architectural layers. A Romanesque palace built by Soběslav I around 1135 forms the cellars of the present building. Přemysl Otakar II and Charles IV then added their own palaces above this, while the top floor, built for Vladislav Jagiello, contains the massive Gothic Vladislav Hall. During the period of Habsburg rule, the palace housed government offices, courts and the old Bohemian Diet (parliament). In 1924, it was extensively restored.

Riders' Staircase
These wide and gently sloping steps, with their Gothic rib vault, were used by knights on horse-back to get to Vladislav Hall for indoor jousting competitions.

The Diet, the medieval parliament, was also the throne room. Destroyed by fire in 1541, it was rebuilt by Bonifaz Wohlmut in 1563.

An overhead passage from the palace leads to the Royal Oratory in St Vitus's Cathedral *(see p105)*.

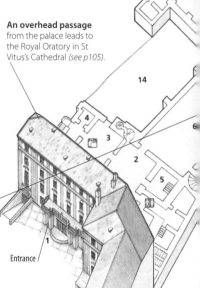

14
4
3
2
6
5
1
Entrance

Vladislav Hall
This hall's magnificent rib vaulting was designed by Benedikt Ried in the 1490s. The Royal Court was very like a public market in the 17th century, but it is used today for the swearing-in of Czech presidents.

Přemysl Otakar II, 1230–78

1253 Palace reconstructed by Přemysl Otakar II

1618 Defenestration from Bohemian Chancellery

1041 Castle besieged and palace burnt

1541 Fire destroys large part of Castle

1766–8 Building of Theresian Wing

900	1100	1300	1500	1700	1900

Late 9th century Founding of Prague Castle by Prince Bořivoj

1340 Charles IV rebuilds palace

1370s Peter Parler rebuilds All Saints' Chapel

Decorated door of office in Old Royal Palace

1135 Rebuilding undertaken by Soběslav I

1502 Completion of Vladislav Hall by Benedikt Ried after nine years

1924 Palace undergoes exten-sive restoration

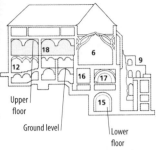

Upper floor
12
18
6
9
16
17
15
Ground level
Lower floor

All Saints' Chapel was built by Peter Parler for Charles IV. After the 1541 fire, its vault had to be rebuilt and it was redecorated in the Baroque style.

11

10

9

The Theresian Way was built to house the office registers.

Plan and Cross Section of Old Royal Palace

The cross section of the palace shows the three distinct levels of the building, all constructed at different times. The plan shows how Vladislav Hall dominates the entire palace structure.

Key to Old Royal Palace

- ☐ Romanesque and Early Gothic
- ☐ Late Gothic
- ☐ Rebuilt after 1541 fire
- ☐ Baroque and later

1	Eagle Fountain	**10**	All Saint's Chapel
2	Vestibule	**11**	Diet Hall
3	Green Chamber	**12**	Rider's staircase
4	King's Bedchamber	**13**	Court of Appeal
5	Romanesque tower	**14**	Palace courtyard
6	Vladislav Hall	**15**	Hall of the Romanesque palace
7	Bohemian Chancellery	**16**	Old Land Rolls
8	Imperial Council Room steps	**17**	Palace of Charles IV
9	Terrace	**18**	New Land Rolls

VISITORS' CHECKLIST

Practical Information
Prague Castle, third courtyard.
Map 2 D2.
Tel 224 373 102.
Open Apr–Oct: 9am–5pm daily;
Nov–Mar: 9am–4pm daily; last adm: 1hr before closing.

Transport
🚇 Hradčanská, up K Brusce, then through the Royal Garden; Malostranská, left up Klárov, then up Old Castle Steps. 🚋 22 to Prague Castle (Pražský hrad).

Bohemian Chancellery
This 17th-century Dutch-style stove decorates the former royal offices of the Habsburgs. The chancellery is the site of the 1618 defenestration.

Defenestration of 1618

Painting by Václav Brožík, 1889

On 23 May 1618, more than 100 Protestant nobles, led by Count Thurn, marched into the palace to protest against the succession to the throne of the intolerant Habsburg Archduke Ferdinand. The two Catholic Governors appointed by Ferdinand, Jaroslav Martinic and Vilém Slavata, were confronted and, after a row, the Protestants threw both the Governors and their secretary, Philipp Fabricius, out of the eastern window. Falling some 15 m (50 ft), they survived by landing in a dung heap. This event signalled the beginning of the Thirty Years' War. The Catholics attributed the survival of the Governors to the intervention of angels.

The New Land Rolls
These rooms are decorated with the crests of clerks who worked here from 1561 to 1774.

Old prison in the 15th-century Dalibor Tower, part of the city fortifications

❽ Dalibor Tower

Daliborka

Prague Castle, Zlatá ulička. **Map** 2 E2. Ⓜ Malostranská. 🚊 12, 18, 20, 22. **Open** 9am–5pm daily (Nov–Mar: to 4pm). 📷 ♿ W hrad.cz

This 15th-century tower with a conical roof was part of the fortifications built by King Vladislav Jagiello *(see p29)*. His coat of arms can be seen on the outer wall. The tower also served as a prison and is named after its first inmate, Dalibor of Kozojedy, a young knight sentenced to death for harbouring some outlawed serfs. While awaiting execution, he was kept in an underground dungeon, into which he had to be lowered through a hole in the floor.

According to legend, while in prison he learnt to play the violin. People sympathetic to his plight came to listen to his playing and provided him with food and drink, which they lowered on a rope from a window – prisoners were often left to starve to death. The story was used by Bedřich Smetana in his opera *Dalibor*. The tower ceased to serve as a prison in 1781. Visitors can see part of the old prison.

❾ South Gardens

Jižní Zahrady

Prague Castle (access from Old Castle Steps, New Castle Steps or Old Royal Palace). **Map** 2 D3. Ⓜ Malostranská. 🚊 12, 18, 20, 22. **Open** Apr–Oct: 10am–6pm daily (May & Sep: to 7pm; Jun & Jul: to 9pm; Aug: to 8pm). W hrad.cz

The gardens occupy the long narrow band of land below the Castle overlooking the Little Quarter. Several small gardens have been linked to form what is now known as the South Gardens. The oldest, the Paradise Garden (Rajská zahrada), laid out in 1562, contains a circular pavilion built for Emperor Matthias in 1617. Its carved wooden ceiling shows the coloured emblems of the 39 countries of the Habsburg Empire. The Garden on the Ramparts (Zahrada Na valech) dates from the 19th century. It occupies a former vegetable patch and is famous as the site of the defenestration of 1618 *(see p107)*, when two Imperial governors were thrown from a first-floor window. Two obelisks were subsequently erected by Ferdinand II to mark the spots where they landed. Modifications were carried out in the 1920s by Josip Plečnik, who built the Bull Staircase leading to the Paradise Garden and the observation terrace. Below the terrace, in the former Hartig Garden, is a Baroque music pavilion designed by Giovanni Battista Alliprandi. Beside it stand four statues of Classical gods by Antonín Braun.

Alliprandi's music pavilion in the South Gardens

❿ Belvedere

Belvedér

Prague Castle, Royal Garden. **Map** 2 E1. Ⓜ Malostranská, Hradčanská. 🚊 22 to Královský Letohrádek. **Open** 10am–6pm Tue–Sun during exhibitions only. 📷 ♿

Built by Ferdinand I for his beloved wife Anne, the Belvedere is one of the finest Italian Renaissance buildings north of the Alps. Also known

The Belvedere, Queen Anne's summer palace in the Royal Garden beside Prague Castle

◀ Prague Castle and the spires of St Vitus's Cathedral

Antonín Braun's statue of *The Allegory of Night* in front of the Ball Game Hall

as Queen Anne's Summerhouse (Letohrádek Královny Anny), it is an arcaded building with slender Ionic columns topped by a roof shaped like an inverted ship's hull clad in blue-green copper. The main architect was Paolo della Stella, who was also responsible for the ornate reliefs inside the arcade. Work began in 1538 but was interrupted by the great Castle fire of 1541 and not completed until 1564.

In the middle of the small geometrical garden in front of the palace stands the Singing Fountain. Dating from 1568, it owes its name to the musical sound the water makes as it hits the bronze bowl, though you have to listen closely to appreciate the effect. The fountain was cast by Tomáš Jaroš, the famous bell founder, who lived and worked in the Powder Tower *(see p100)*.

Many of the Belvedere's works of art were plundered by the Swedish army in 1648. The statues stolen included Adriaen de Vries's 16th-century bronze of *Mercury and Psyche*, now in the Louvre in Paris. Today, the Belvedere is used as an art gallery.

⓫ Royal Garden
Královská Zahrada

Prague Castle, U Prašného mostu. **Map** 2 D2. 🚇 Malostranská, Hradčanská. 🚋 22. **Open** May–Oct: 10am–6pm daily (May & Sep: to 7pm; Jun & Jul: to 9pm; Aug: to 8pm). 🅿 ♿ 🌐 **hrad.cz**

The garden was created in 1535 for Ferdinand I. Its appearance has been altered over time, but some examples of 16th-century garden architecture have survived, notably the Belvedere and the Ball Game Hall (Míčovna), built by Bonifaz Wohlmut in 1569. The building is covered in beautiful, though much restored, Renaissance *sgraffito*, a form of decoration created by cutting a design

through the wet top layer of plaster on to a contrasting undercoat. The garden is beautiful in spring when thousands of tulips bloom. This is where tulips were first acclimatized to Europe.

⓬ Riding School
Jízdárna

Prague Castle. **Map** 2 D2. **Tel** 224 373 232. 🚇 Malostranská, Hradčanská. 🚋 22. **Open** 10am–6pm during exhibitions.

The 17th-century Riding School forms one side of U Prašného mostu, a road which runs to the northern side of Prague Castle via Deer Moat. In the 1920s, it was converted into an exhibition hall, which now holds important exhibitions of painting and sculpture. A garden provides excellent views of St. Vitus's Cathedral and the northern fortifications of the castle.

⓭ Archbishop's Palace
Arcibiskupský Palác

Hradčanské náměstí 16. **Map** 2 D3. 🚇 Malostranská, Hradčanská. 🚋 22. **Closed** to the public.

Ferdinand I bought this sumptuous palace in 1562 for the first Catholic Archbishop since the Hussite Wars *(see pp28–9)*. An imposing building, it has four wings and four courtyards. It replaced the old Archbishop's Palace in the Little Quarter, which had been destroyed during the wars, and has remained the Archbishop's seat in Prague ever since. In the period after the Battle of the White Mountain *(see pp32–3)*, it was a powerful symbol of Catholic domination of the city and the Czech lands. Its spectacular cream-coloured Rococo façade was designed by Johann Joseph Wirch in the 1760s for Archbishop Antonín Příchovský, whose coat of arms sits proudly above the portal.

Příchovský coat of arms

⓮ Sternberg Palace
Šternberský Palác

Franz Josef Sternberg founded the Society of Patriotic Friends of the Arts in Bohemia in 1796. Fellow noblemen would lend their finest pictures and sculpture to the society, which had its headquarters in the early 18th-century Sternberg Palace. Since 1949, the fine Baroque building has been used to house the National Gallery's collection of European art, with its superb range of Old Masters.

The Lamentation of Christ
Frozen, sculptural figures make this one of the finest paintings by Lorenzo Monaco (1408).

Cardinal Cesi's Garden in Rome
Henrick van Cleve's painting (1548) provides a valuable image of a Renaissance collections of antiquities. The garden was later destroyed.

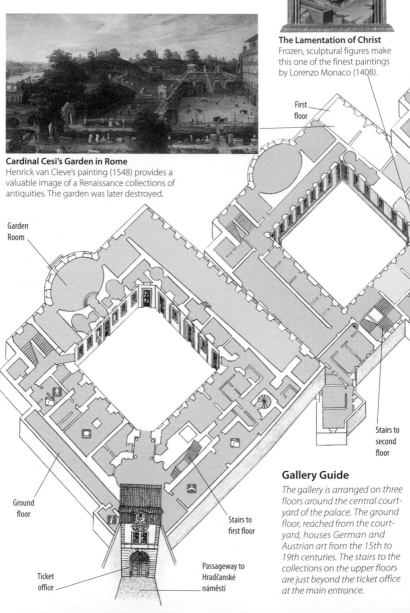

Garden Room

First floor

Stairs to second floor

Ground floor

Stairs to first floor

Ticket office

Passageway to Hradčanské náměstí

Gallery Guide

The gallery is arranged on three floors around the central court-yard of the palace. The ground floor, reached from the court-yard, houses German and Austrian art from the 15th to 19th centuries. The stairs to the collections on the upper floors are just beyond the ticket office at the main entrance.

★ Scholar in his Study
In this painting from 1634, Rembrandt used keenly observed detail to convey wisdom in the face of the old scholar.

Chinese Cabinet

Second floor

Stairs down to other floors and exit

Paradise (1618)
Roelandt Savery studied models of exotic animals, brought to Prague by Persian nobles, at the court of Emperor Rudolf II. He was then able to paint real animals.

★ Head of Christ
Painted by El Greco in the 1590s, this portrait emphasizes the humanity of Christ. At the same time, the curious square halo framing the head gives the painting the qualities of an ancient icon.

★ The Martyrdom of St Thomas
This magnificent work is by Peter Paul Rubens, the foremost Flemish painter of the 17th century.

Key
- German and Austrian Art 1400–1800
- Flemish and Dutch Art 1400–1600
- Italian Art 1400–1500
- Flemish and Dutch Art 1600–1800
- French Art 1400–1800
- Icons, Classical and Ancient Art
- Venice 1700–1800 and Goya
- Spanish Art 1400–1800
- Naples and Venice 1600–1700
- Italian Art 1500–1600
- Non-exhibition space

Exploring the Sternberg Collections

The National Gallery's collection of European art at the Sternberg Palace ranks among the country's best collections. The museum is divided into three separate viewing areas. Its extensive holdings of German and Austrian art of the 15th to 19th centuries are exhibited just off the courtyard on the ground floor. A small collection of art from antiquity and religious icons, as well as a larger display of early Italian and Dutch art, occupy the first floor. Most of the real treasures are on the second floor, where the museum displays works of Italian, Spanish, French and Dutch masters from the 16th to 18th centuries.

Icons, Classical and Ancient Art

Two small rooms on the first floor are occupied by an odd assortment of paintings that do not quite fit in with the rest of the collection. These include a *Portrait of a Young Woman* dating from the 2nd century AD, which was discovered during excavations at Fayoum in Egypt in the 19th century.

The second room, on the left as you enter the main viewing area, holds icons of the Orthodox church – some are Byzantine, some Italo-Greek and some Russian. A fine example on show here is a later 16th-century work, *Christ's Entry into Jerusalem* from Russia. The collection of icons on display offers examples from a variety of the most important Mediterranean and Eastern European centres.

Christ's Entry into Jerusalem, a 16th-century Russian icon

German and Austrian Art (1400–1800)

This collection is massive and it could take half a day to see everything. One of the most celebrated paintings in the Sternberg's collection is Albrecht Dürer's *The Feast of the Rosary*, painted during the artist's stay in Venice in 1506. The work has a particular

significance for Prague since it was bought by Emperor Rudolph II. The two figures in front of the Virgin and Child are Maximilian I (Rudolph's great-great-grandfather) and Pope Julius II.

The collection also includes works by several other important German painters of the Renaissance, including Hans Holbein the Elder and the Younger and Lucas Cranach the Elder. Cranach is represented by a striking *Adam and Eve*, whose nudes show the spirit of the Renaissance, tempered by Lutheran Reform.

Italian Art (1400–1700)

When you enter the gallery of early Italian art on the first floor, you are greeted by a splendid array of richly gilded early diptychs and triptychs from the churches of Tuscany and northern Italy. Most came originally from the d'Este collection at Konopiště Castle (*see p169*). Of particularly high quality are the two triangular panels of saints by the 14th-century Sienese painter Pietro Lorenzetti and a moving *Lamentation of Christ* by Lorenzo Monaco.

A fascinating element of the collection is the display of Renaissance bronze statuettes. Fashionable amongst Italian nobility of the 15th century, these little bronzes were at first cast from famous or newly discovered works of antiquity. Later, sculptors began to use the medium more freely – Padua, for example, specialized in the depiction of small animals – and producers also adapted items for use as decorative household goods such as oil lamps, ink pots and door knockers. This small collection has representative works from all the major Italian producers except Mantua and, while many variations can be found in other museums throughout the world, there are some pieces here that are both unique and outstanding examples of the craft. On the second floor, among the

The Feast of the Rosary by Dürer (1506)

Don Miguel de Lardizábal (1815) by Francisco Goya

16th-century Italian works on display, are some delightful surprises. These include *St Jerome* by the Venetian painter, Tintoretto, and *The Annunciation to the Shepherds* and *Portrait of an Elderly Man* by another Venetian, Jacopo Bassano. There is also an expressive portrait by the Florentine mannerist, Bronzino, of *Eleanor of Toledo*, the wife of Cosimo de' Medici.

Flemish and Dutch Art (1400–1800)

The collections of Flemish and Dutch art on the first and second floors are rich and varied, ranging from rural scenes by Pieter Brueghel the Elder to portraits by Rubens and Rembrandt. Highlights of the former include an altarpiece showing the *Adoration of the Magi* by Geertgen tot Sint Jans. Other early works of great interest include *St Luke Drawing the Virgin* by Jan Gossaert (c.1515), one of the first works of art from the Netherlands to show the clear influence of the Italian Renaissance. The collection from the 17th century on the second floor includes several major works, notably by Peter Paul Rubens who, in 1639, sent two paintings to the Augustinians of the Church of St Thomas (*see p127*) in the Little Quarter. The originals were lent to the gallery in 1896 and replaced by copies. The violence and drama of *The Martyrdom of St Thomas* is in complete

contrast to the spiritual calm of *St Augustine*. Two other fine portraits are those of Rembrandt's *Scholar in His Study* and Frans Hals' *Portrait of Jasper Schade*.

Also on display is a wide assortment of paintings by other, less-prominent, artists who nonetheless represent the enormous range and quality of this period.

Spanish and French Art (1400–1800)

French art on the second floor is represented chiefly by the 17th-century painters Simon Vouet (*The Suicide of Lucretia*), Sébastien Bourdon and Charles Le Brun. Spanish painting is even less well represented, but two of the collection's finest works are a haunting *Head of Christ* by El Greco, which is the only work by this important artist on display in the Czech Republic, and a noble half-length portrait of the politician *Don Miguel de Lardizábal* by Goya.

The Chinese Cabinet

After several years of difficult restoration work, this curiosity on the second floor is once again open to the public. The richly decorated little chamber was part of the original furnishings of the Sternberg Palace, and was designed as an intimate withdrawing room away from the bustle of the grand state rooms. In its plethora of decorative styles, Baroque mingles with Far Eastern motifs and techniques, which were fashionable at the turn of the 18th century. The vaulted ceiling features the Star of the Sternbergs among its geometric decorations. Black lacquered walls are embellished with cobalt blue and white medallions in golden frames, while gilded shelves once held rare Oriental porcelain.

Eleanor of Toledo (1540s) by the painter Agnolo Bronzino

⓯ Martinic Palace

Martinický Palác

Hradčanské náměstí 8. **Map** 1 C2.
Tel 777 798 040. 🚇 Malostranská,
Hradčanská. 🚋 22. 🎫 only (call
ahead to arrange). ♿
🌐 **martinickypalac.cz**

In the course of the palace's
restoration in the early 1970s,
workmen uncovered the original
16th-century façade decorated
with ornate cream and brown
sgraffito (see p111). The exterior
depicts Old Testament scenes,
including the story of Joseph
and Potiphar's wife. More *sgraffito*
in the internal courtyard shows
the story of Samson and the
Labours of Hercules.

Martinic Palace was enlarged
by Jaroslav Bořita of Martinic,
who was one of the imperial
governors thrown from a
window of the Royal Palace
in 1618 *(see p107)*.

According to an old legend,
between 11pm and midnight,
the ghost of a fiery black dog
appears at the palace and acc-
ompanies walkers as far as the
Loreto *(see pp118–19)*. You can
tour the palace or visit a small
museum of musical machines,
such as gramophones.

⓰ Schwarzenberg Palace

Schwarzenberský Palác

Hradčanské náměstí 2. **Map** 2 D3.
Tel 233 081 713. 🚇 Malostranská,
Hradčanská. 🚋 22. **Open** 10am–6pm
Tue–Sun. ♿ 📷 ♿ 🌐 **ngprague.cz**

From a distance, the façade of
this grand Renaissance palace
appears to be clad in projecting
pyramid-shaped stonework. On
closer inspection, this turns out
to be an illusion created by
sgraffito patterns
incised on a flat
wall. Built originally

for the Lobkowicz
family by the Italian
architect Agostino Galli
in 1545–76, the gabled
palace is Florentine
rather than Bohemian
in style. It passed
through several
hands before the
Schwarzenbergs, a
leading family in the
Habsburg Empire,
bought it in 1719.
Much of the interior
decoration has survived,
including four painted
ceilings on the second
floor dating from 1580.
This palace once housed
the Museum of Military
History, now located at
U Památníku 3. Following
renovation, the palace became
home to the National Gallery's
collection of Baroque art.

In the square outside is the
statue of Tomáš G Masaryk,
Czechoslovakia's first president.

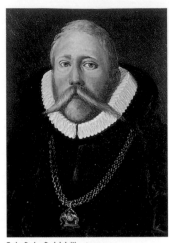

Tycho Brahe, Rudolph II's astronomer

⓱ New World

Nový Svět

Map 1 B2. 🚋 22, 25 to Brusnice.

Now a charming street of
small cottages, Nový Svět
(New World) used to be the
name of this area of Hradčany.
Developed in the mid-14th
century to provide houses for
the castle workers, the area was
twice destroyed by fire, the last
time being in 1541. Most of the
cottages date from the 17th
century. They have been spruced
up, but are otherwise unspoilt
and very different in character
from the rest of Hradčany.

In defiance of their poverty,
the inhabitants of these cottages
chose golden house signs to
identify their modest houses –
you will see depictions of a
Golden Pear, a Grape, a Foot,
a Bush and an Acorn. Plaques
identify No. 1 as the former
home of Rudolph II's brilliant
court astronomer, Tycho Brahe,
and No. 25 as the 1857 birthplace of the great Czech
violinist František Ondříček.

⓲ Capuchin Monastery

Kapucínský Klášter

Loretánské náměstí 6. **Map** 1 B3.
🚋 22, 25. **Closed** to the public
except the church. ✝ 6pm Mon–Sat,
8:30am Sun.

Bohemia's first Capuchin monastery was founded here in
1600. It is connected to the
neighbouring Loreto *(see
pp118–19)* by an overhead
roofed passage. Attached to
the monastery is the Church
of Our Lady Queen of Angels,
a single-naved building with
plain furnishings, typical of
the ascetic Capuchin order.

The church is famous for
its miraculous statue of the
Madonna and Child. Emperor
Rudolph II liked the statue so
much he asked the Capuchins
to give it to him to place in
his private chapel. The monks
agreed, but then the statue

The Carmelite monastery next to the Schwarzenberg Palace

The ornate altar, Church of Our Lady Queen of Angels in the Capuchin Monastery

somehow found its way back to the church. Three times Rudolph had the Madonna brought back, but each time she returned to her original position. The Emperor eventually gave up, left her where she was and presented her with a gold crown and a robe.

Each year, at Christmas, crowds of visitors come to see the church's Baroque nativity scene of life-sized figures dressed in period costumes.

⓳ The Loreto

Loreta

See pp118–19.

⓴ Černín Palace and Garden

Černínský Palác a Zahrada

Loretánské náměstí 5. **Map** 1 B3. 🚋 22, 25. Palace: **Closed** to the public. Garden: **Open** May–Oct: 10am–5pm daily. ♿ Ⓦ **mzv.cz**

Constructed in 1668 for Count Černín of Chudenice, the Imperial Ambassador to Venice, Prague's Černín Palace is arguably the Italian architect Francesco Caratti's masterpiece. It is 150 m (500 ft) long with a row of 30 massive Corinthian half-columns running the length of its upper storeys. The palace towers over the attractive, small, grassy square that lies between it and the Loreto.

The huge building suffered as a result of its prominent position on one of Prague's highest hills. It was looted by the French in 1742 and badly damaged in the Prussian bombardment of the city in 1757. In 1851, the impoverished Černín family sold the palace to the state and it became a barracks. After the creation of Czechoslovakia in 1918, the palace was restored to its original design and became the Ministry of Foreign Affairs.

Capital on Černín Palace

In 1948, Jan Masaryk, the son of Czechoslovakia's first president, was found dead in his pyjamas below his bathroom window at the age of 61. It is widely believed he was murdered by the new communist regime.

㉑ Pohořelec

Map 1 B3. 🚋 22, 25.

First settled in 1375, this is one of the oldest parts of Prague. The name is of more recent origin: Pohořelec means "place destroyed by fire", a fate the area has suffered three times in the course of its history – the last time being in 1741. It is now a large open square on a hill high over the city and part of the main access route to Prague Castle. In the centre stands a large monument to St John Nepomuk (1752) *(see p137)*, thought to be by Johann Anton Quitainer. The houses around the square are mainly Baroque and Rococo. In front of the Jan Kepler grammar school stands a monument to Kepler and his predecessor as astronomer at the court of Rudolph II, Tycho Brahe, who died in a house on the school site in 1601.

Černín Palace, with its Corinthian half-columns

⑲ The Loreto
Loreta

Ever since its construction in 1626, the Loreto has been an important place of pilgrimage. It was commissioned by Kateřina of Lobkowicz, a Czech aristocrat who was very keen to promote the legend of the Santa Casa of Loreto *(see opposite)*. The heart of the complex is a copy of the house believed to be the Virgin Mary's. The Santa Casa was enclosed by cloisters in 1661, and a Baroque façade 60 years later by Christoph and Kilian Ignaz Dientzenhofer. The grandiose design and miraculous stories about the Loreto were part of Ferdinand II's campaign to recatholicize the Czechs *(see pp32–3)*.

Bell Tower
Enclosed in this large Baroque tower is a set of 30 bells cast 1683–91 in Amsterdam by Claudy Fremy.

★ **Loreto Treasury**
This gold-plated, diamond-encrusted monstrance, for displaying the host, is one of the valuable liturgical items in the Loreto treasury, most of which originated in the 16th to 18th centuries.

Entrance from Loretánské náměstí

KEY

① **Chapel of St Ann**
② **Chapel of St Francis Seraphim**
③ **Fountain decorated with a sculpture of the Resurrection**
④ **Chapel of St Joseph**
⑤ **Chapel of the Holy Rood**
⑥ **Chapel of St Anthony of Padua**
⑦ **Chapel of Our Lady of Sorrows**
⑧ **This fountain sculpture** is a copy of *The Ascension of the Virgin Mary*, taken from Jan Brüderle's 1739 sandstone statue, now in the Lapidarium *(see p162)*.

Baroque Entrance
The balustrade above the Loreto's front entrance is decorated with statues of St Joseph and St John the Baptist by Ondřej Quitainer.

★ Santa Casa
Stucco figures of many of the Old Testament prophets and reliefs from the life of the Virgin Mary by Italian artists decorate the chapel.

VISITORS' CHECKLIST

Practical Information
Loretánské náměstí 7, Hradčany.
Map 1 C3.
Tel 220 516 740.
W loreta.cz
Open Apr–Oct: 9am–5pm daily; Nov–Mar: 9:30am–4pm daily.
7:30am Sat, 6pm Sun.

Transport
22, 25 to Pohořelec.

★ Church of the Nativity
Gruesome relics, including fully clothed skeletons with death masks made of wax, line the walls of this 18th-century church. The frescoes are by Václav Vavřinec Reiner.

Legend of the Santa Casa

The original house, said to be where the Archangel Gabriel told Mary about the future birth of Jesus, is in the small Italian town of Loreto. It was believed that angels transported the house from Nazareth to Loreto in 1278 following threats by infidels. After the Protestants' defeat in 1620 *(see pp32–3)*, Catholics promoted the legend, and 50 replicas of the Loreto were built in Bohemia and Moravia. This, the grandest, became the most important in Bohemia, and received many visitors.

The stuccoed Santa Casa

17th-Century Cloister
Built originally as a shelter for the many pilgrims who visited the shrine, the cloister is covered with frescoes.

㉒ Strahov Monastery

Strahovský Klášter

When it was founded in 1140 by an austere religious order, the Premonstratensians, Strahov rivalled the seat of the Czech sovereign in size. Destroyed by fire in 1258, it was rebuilt in the Gothic style, with later Baroque additions. Its famous library, in the theological and philosophical halls, is over 800 years old and despite being ransacked by many invading armies, is one of the finest in Bohemia. Strahov also escaped Joseph II's 1783 dissolution of the monasteries by changing its library into a research institute. It is now a working monastery and museum.

Statue of St John
A Late-Gothic, painted statue of St John the Evangelist situated in the Theological Hall, has the saint's prayer book held in a small pouch.

Entrance to main courtyard of the monastery

★ **Church of Our Lady**
The interior of this Baroque church is highly decorated. Above the arcades of the side naves, there are 12 paintings with scenes from the life of St Norbert, founder of the Premonstratensian order, by Jiří Neunhertz.

KEY

① **Baroque organ on which Mozart played**

② **The Museum** of National Literature is devoted to works by Czech writers.

③ **Refectory**

④ **Baroque tower**

⑤ **The façade** of the Philosophical Hall is decorated with vases and a gilded medallion of Joseph II by Ignaz Platzer.

Entrance to Church of Our Lady

Church Façade
The elaborate statues, by Johann Anton Quitainer, were added to the western façade of the church when it was remodelled by the architect Anselmo Lurago in the 1750s.

View from Petřín Hill
A gate at the eastern end of the first courtyard leads to Petřín Hill, part of which was once the monastery's orchards.

VISITORS' CHECKLIST

Practical Information
Královská Kanonie Premonstrátů na Strahově. Strahovské nádvoří 1.
Map 1 B4.
Tel 233 107 730.
W strahovskyklaster.cz
Open 9am–noon & 1–5pm daily.
Philosophical Hall, Theological Hall, Church of Our Lady, Picture Gallery: **Open** 9:30–11:30am & noon–5pm daily. **Closed** Easter Sun, 24 & 25 Dec.

Transport
22, 25.

★ Theological Hall
One of the 17th-century astronomical globes by William Blaeu that line the hall. The stucco and wall paintings relate to librarianship.

ntrance to braries

★ Philosophical Hall
The ceiling fresco depicts the *Struggle of Mankind to Know Real History* by Franz Maulbertsch. It was built in 1782 to hold the Baroque bookcases and their valuable books from a dissolved monastery near Louka, in Moravia.

Strahov Gospel Book
A facsimile of this superb and precious 9th-century volume is now on display in the Theological Hall.

LITTLE QUARTER
MALÁ STRANA

The Little Quarter is the part of Prague least affected by recent history. Hardly any new building has taken place here since the late 18th century and the quarter is rich in splendid Baroque palaces and old houses with attractive signs. Founded in 1257, it is built on the slopes below the Castle hill with magnificent views across the river to the Old Town.

The centre of the Little Quarter has always been Little Quarter Square (Malostranské náměstí), dominated by the Church of St Nicholas. The Grand Prior's millwheel at Kampa Island still turns, pilgrims still kneel before the Holy Infant of Prague in the Church of Our Lady Victorious, and music rings out from churches and palaces as it did when Mozart stayed here.

Sights at a Glance

Churches
- ❷ Church of St Thomas
- ❹ *Church of St Nicholas pp128–9*
- ❾ Church of Our Lady Victorious
- ⓭ Church of Our Lady beneath the Chain
- ㉓ Church of St Lawrence

Parks and Gardens
- ❽ Vrtba Garden
- ⓲ Vojan Park
- ⓳ Palace Gardens
- ㉑ Observation Tower
- ㉒ Mirror Maze
- ㉔ Štefánik's Observatory
- ㉖ Petřín Park
- ㉗ Funicular Railway

Museums
- ❺ Museum Montanelli
- ⓱ Kafka Museum
- ⓳ Kampa Museum of Modern Art
- ㉘ Museum of Music

Historic Monuments
- ㉕ Hunger Wall

Historic Restaurants and Beer Halls
- ⓯ At the Three Ostriches

Historic Streets and Squares
- ❸ Little Quarter Square
- ❻ Nerudova Street
- ❼ Italian Street
- ❿ Maltese Square
- ⓬ Grand Priory Square
- ⓰ Bridge Street

Bridges and Islands
- ⓫ Kampa Island
- ⓮ *Charles Bridge pp136–9*

Palaces
- ❶ Wallenstein Palace and Garden
- ㉙ Michna Palace

☐ Restaurants
see pp201–202
- 1 Bar Bar
- 2 Bohemia Bagel
- 3 Café Lounge
- 4 Café de Paris
- 5 Café Savoy
- 6 Coda
- 7 Kočár z Vídně
- 8 Konírna
- 9 Luka Lu
- 10 Malostranská beseda
- 11 Nebozízek
- 12 Restaurace Tbilisi
- 13 Spices
- 14 Terasa U Zlaté Studně
- 15 U Knoflíčků
- 16 U Kocoura
- 17 U Malého Glena
- 18 U Malířů

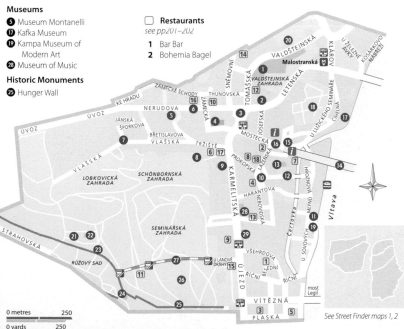

0 metres 250
0 yards 250

See Street Finder maps 1, 2

◀ An early-morning view across Charles Bridge

For keys to symbols *see back flap*

Street-by-Street: Around Little Quarter Square

The Little Quarter, most of whose grand Baroque palaces now house embassies, has preserved much of its traditional character. The steep, narrow streets and steps have an air of romantic mystery, and you will find fascinating buildings adorned with statues and house signs at every turn. Some of the old buildings now house smart restaurants.

❺ Museum Montanelli
This contemporary museum hosts international exhibitions of modern art.

Thun-Hohenstein Palace (1721–6) has a doorway crowned with two sculpted eagles by Matthias Braun. The palace is now the seat of the Italian embassy.

At the Three Little Fiddles, now a restaurant, acquired its house sign when it was the home of a family of violin makers around 1700.

❻ ★ Nerudova Street
This historic street leading up to Prague Castle is named after the 19th-century writer Jan Neruda.

Morzin Palace has a striking Baroque façade with a pair of sculpted moors.

Schonborn Palace

❼ Italian Street
From the 16th to the 18th century, houses in the street, like the House at the Golden Scales, were occupied by Italian craftsmen.

❽ Vrtba Garden
Laid out in about 1720 by František Maximilián Kaňka, these fine Baroque terraces provide good views over the rooftops of the Little Quarter.

Key

— Suggested route

| 0 metres | 100 |
| 0 yards | 100 |

For keys to symbols *see back flap*

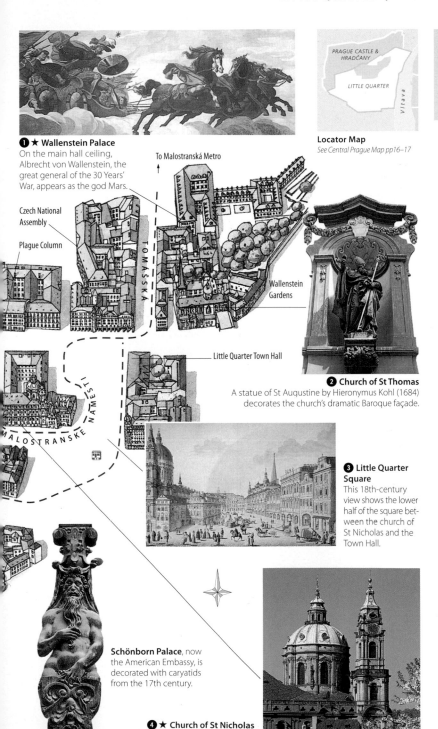

❶ ★ **Wallenstein Palace**
On the main hall ceiling, Albrecht von Wallenstein, the great general of the 30 Years' War, appears as the god Mars.

Locator Map
See Central Prague Map pp16–17

To Malostranská Metro

Czech National Assembly

Plague Column

Wallenstein Gardens

Little Quarter Town Hall

❷ **Church of St Thomas**
A statue of St Augustine by Hieronymus Kohl (1684) decorates the church's dramatic Baroque façade.

❸ **Little Quarter Square**
This 18th-century view shows the lower half of the square between the church of St Nicholas and the Town Hall.

Schönborn Palace, now the American Embassy, is decorated with caryatids from the 17th century.

❹ ★ **Church of St Nicholas**
The cupola and bell tower of this Baroque church are the best-known landmarks of the Little Quarter.

❶ Wallenstein Palace and Garden

Valdštejnský Palác a Zahrada

Valdštejnské náměstí 4. **Map** 2 E3.
🚇 Malostranská. **Tel** 257 075 707.
🚊 12, 18, 20, 22. Palace: **Open** 10am–
5pm Sat & Sun. 🎧 call in advance to
arrange. 📷 ♿ from Valdštejnská.
Garden: **Open** Apr–Oct: 10am–6pm
daily (Jun–Sep: 10am–7pm). Riding
school: **Open** for exhibitions 9am–
7pm Tue–Sun. ♿ from Valdštejnské
náměstí. 🌐 **senat.cz**

The main hall of Wallenstein Palace

The first large secular building of the Baroque era in Prague, the palace stands as a monument to the fatal ambition of military commander Albrecht von Wallenstein (1581–1634). His string of victories over the Protestants in the 30 Years' War *(see pp32–3)* made him vital to Emperor Ferdinand II. Already showered with titles, Wallenstein started to covet the crown of Bohemia. When he dared to negotiate independently with the enemy, he was killed on the emperor's orders by mercenaries in the town of Cheb in 1634.

Wallenstein's intention was to overshadow even Prague Castle with his palace, built between 1624 and 1630. To obtain a suitable site, he had to purchase 23 houses, three gardens and the municipal brick kiln. The magnificent main hall rises to a height of two storeys with a ceiling fresco of Wallenstein himself portrayed as Mars, the god of war, riding in a triumphal chariot. The architect, Andrea Spezza, and nearly all the artists employed in the decoration of the palace were Italians.

Today, the palace is used as the home of the Czech Senate (the upper house of parliament) and is open to the public. The gardens are laid out as they were when Wallenstein dined in the huge *sala terrena* (garden pavilion) that looks out over a fountain and rows of bronze statues. These are copies of works by Adriaen de Vries that were stolen by the Swedes in 1648 *(see pp32–3)*. There is also a pavilion with fine frescoes showing scenes from the legend of the Argonauts and the Golden Fleece. Wallenstein was a holder of the Order of the Golden Fleece, the highest order of chivalry of the Holy Roman Empire. At the far end of the garden is a large ornamental pond with a central statue. Behind this stands the old Riding School, now used to house special exhibitions by the National Gallery. Both gardens and riding school have undergone substantial restoration.

Copy of a bronze statue of Eros
by Adriaen de Vries

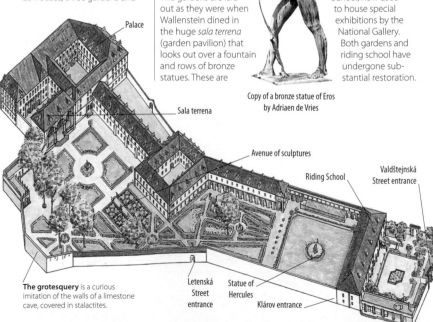

Palace

Sala terrena

Avenue of sculptures

Riding School

Valdštejnská
Street entrance

The grotesquery is a curious imitation of the walls of a limestone cave, covered in stalactites.

Letenská
Street
entrance

Statue of
Hercules

Klárov entrance

❷ Church of St Thomas
Kostel Sv. Tomáše

Josefská 8. **Map** 2 E3. **Tel** 257 530 556.
🚇 Malostranská. 🚊 12, 20, 22.
Open 11:30am–1pm & 4–6pm Mon–
Sat. ✝ 12:15pm Mon–Sat (and 6pm
Sat in English); 9:30am (Czech), 11am
(English), 12:30pm (Spanish), 6pm
(Czech) in summer and 5pm (Czech)
in winter Sun. ▨ 🔉 (call in advance).

Founded by Wenceslas II in 1285
as the monastery church of
the Augustinians, the original
Gothic church was completed
in 1379. In the Hussite period
(see pp28–9), this was one of the
few churches to remain Catholic.
As a result, it suffered serious fire
damage. During the reign of
Rudolph II *(see pp30–31)*, St
Thomas's developed strong
links with the Imperial court.
Several members of Rudolph's
entourage were buried here,
such as court architect Ottavio
Aostalli and the sculptor
Adriaen de Vries.

In 1723, the church was struck
by lightning and Kilian Ignaz
Dientzenhofer was called in
to rebuild it. The shape of the
original church was preserved
in the Baroque reconstruction
but, apart from the spire, the
church today betrays little of
its Gothic origins. The interior
of the dome and the curving
ceiling frescoes in the nave
were painted by Václav Vavřinec
Reiner. Above the altar are
copies of paintings by Rubens
The Martyrdom of St Thomas
and a picture of St Augustine.

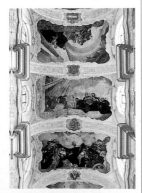

Baroque ceiling in the nave of the
Church of St Thomas

Arcade in front of buildings on the north side of Little Quarter Square

The originals are found in the
Sternberg Palace *(see pp112–15)*.
The English-speaking Catholic
community of Prague meets in
this church.

❸ Little Quarter Square
Malostranské Náměstí

Map 2 E3. 🚇 Malostranská.
🚊 12, 20, 22.

The square has been the centre
of life in the Little Quarter since
its foundation in 1257. It started
life as a large marketplace in the
outer bailey of Prague Castle.
But soon, buildings sprang up
in the middle of the square
dividing it in half and a gallows
and pillory were erected in its
lower part.

Most of the houses around
the square have a medieval
core, but all were rebuilt in
the Renaissance and Baroque
periods. The centre of the
square is dominated by the
splendid Baroque church of
St Nicholas. The large building
beside it was a Jesuit college.
Along the upper side of the
square, facing the church, runs
the vast Neo-Classical façade of
Lichtenstein Palace. In front
of it stands a column raised
in honour of the Holy Trinity
to mark the end of a plague
epidemic in 1713.

Other important buildings
include the Little Quarter
Town Hall with its splendid
Renaissance façade and the
Sternberg Palace, built on the

site of the outbreak of the fire of
1541, which destroyed most
of the Little Quarter. Beside it
stands the Smiřický Palace.
Its turrets and hexagonal
towers make it an unmistakable
landmark on the northern side
of the lower square. The Baroque
Kaiserstein Palace is situated at
the eastern side. On the façade
is a bust of the great Czech
soprano Emmy Destinn (Ema
Destinnová), who lived there
between 1908 and 1914. She
often sang with the famous
Italian tenor Enrico Caruso.

❹ Church of St Nicholas
Kostel Sv. Mikuláše

See pp128–9.

❺ Museum Montanelli
Muzeum Montanelli

Nerudova 13. **Map** 2 D3. **Tel** 257 531
220. 🚇 Malostranská. 🚊 12, 20, 22.
Open 2–6pm Tue–Sun (from 1pm Sat
& Sun). ▨ 📷 🔉 🏠 📷
Ⓦ **muzeummontanelli.com**

The Museum Montanelli
(MuMo) is one of a handful
of small private museums
in the Czech Republic. MuMo's
aim is to present imaginative,
modern art in a historical
setting, while maintaining the
DrAK Foundation's permanent
collection. There is an impressive
selection of educational programmes for children, including
weekend workshops.

❹ Church of St Nicholas

Kostel Sv. Mikuláše

The Church of St Nicholas divides and dominates the two sections of Little Quarter Square. Building began in 1703, and the last touches were put to the glorious frescoed nave in 1761. It is the acknowledged masterpiece of father-and-son architects Christoph and Kilian Ignaz Dientzenhofer, Prague's greatest exponents of the High Baroque style, although neither lived to see the completion of the magnificent church. The statues, frescoes and paintings inside the building are by leading artists of the day, and include a fine *Crucifixion* of 1646 by Karel Škréta. Extensive renovation in the 1950s reversed the damage caused by 200 years of leaky cladding and condensation.

Altar Paintings
The side chapels hold many works of art. This painting of St Michael is by Francesco Solimena.

★ Pulpit
Dating from 1765, the ornate pulpit is by Richard and Peter Prachner. It is lavishly adorned with golden cherubs.

KEY

① **Chapel of St Ann**

② **The curving façade** has a number of statues, one of which is St Paul, by John Frederick Kohl. The façade was completed in 1710 by Christoph Dientzenhofer, who was influenced by Italian architects Borromini and Guarini.

③ **The dome** was completed by Kilian Ignaz Dientzenhofer in 1751, shortly before his death.

④ **The belfry**, added in 1751–6, was the last part to be built. It houses a museum of musical instruments.

⑤ **Chapel of St Francis Xavier**

⑥ **Chapel of St Catherine**

Entrance from west side of Little Quarter Square

Baroque Organ
A fresco of St Cecilia, patron saint of music, watches over the superb organ. Built in 1746, the instrument was played by Mozart in 1787.

VISITORS' CHECKLIST

Practical Information
Malostranské náměstí. **Map** 2 E3.
Tel 257 534 215. **Open** 9am–5pm
daily (Nov–Mar: to 4pm). 🎫 🛈
8:30pm Sun. 🚹 Belfry: **Tel** 725
847 927. **Open** 10am–6pm daily
(Apr–Sep: to 10pm; Mar & Oct: to
8pm). 🎫 **w** stnicholas.cz

Transport
Ⓜ Malostranská. 🚊 12, 20, 22.

★ Dome Fresco
František Palko's fresco, *The Celebration
of the Holy Trinity* (1753–4), fills the 70-m
(230-ft)-high dome.

Entrance to Belfry

★ Statues of the Church Fathers
The great teachers by Ignaz Platzer stand
at the four corners of the transept. St Cyril
dispatches a pagan with his crozier.

High Altar
A copper statue of St Nicholas by
Ignaz Platzer surmounts the high
altar. Below it, the painting of
St Joseph is by Johann Lukas Kracker,
who also painted the nave fresco.

The Dientzenhofer Family

Christoph Dientzenhofer (1655–1722)
came from a family of Bavarian
master builders. His son Kilian Ignaz
(1689–1751) was born in Prague and
educated at the Jesuit Clementinum
(*see p81*). They were responsible for the
greatest treasures of Jesuit-influenced
Prague Baroque architecture. The
Church of St Nicholas, their last work,
was completed by Kilian's son-in-law,
Anselmo Lurago.

Kilian Ignaz Dientzenhofer

❻ Nerudova Street
Nerudova Ulice

Map 2 D3. 🚇 Malostranská. 🚋 12, 20, 22. 🚌 292.

A picturesque narrow street leading up to Prague Castle, Nerudova is named after the poet and journalist Jan Neruda, who wrote many short stories set in this part of Prague. He lived in the house called At the Two Suns (No. 47) between 1845 and 1857.

Up until the introduction of house numbers in 1770, Prague's houses were distinguished by signs. Nerudova's houses have a splendid selection of heraldic beasts and emblems. As you make your way up Nerudova's steep slope, look out in particular for the Red Eagle (No. 6), the Three Fiddles (No. 12), the Golden Horseshoe (No. 34), the Green Lobster (No. 43) and the White Swan (No. 49) as well as the Old Pharmacy museum (No. 32).

There are also a number of grand Baroque buildings in the street, including the Thun-Hohenstein Palace (No. 20, now the Italian embassy) and the Morzin Palace (No. 5, the Romanian embassy). The latter has a façade with two massive statues of moors (a pun on the name Morzin) supporting a semicircular balcony on the first floor. Another impressive façade is that of the Church of Our Lady of Unceasing Succour, the church of the Theatines, an order founded during the Counter-Reformation.

❼ Italian Street
Vlašská Ulice

Map 1 C4. 🚇 Malostranská. 🚋 12, 20, 22. 🚌 292.

Italian immigrants started to settle here in the 16th century. Many were artists or craftsmen employed to rebuild and redecorate the Castle. If you approach the street from Petřín, on the left you will see the former Italian Hospital, a Baroque building with an arcaded courtyard. Today, it maintains its traditional

Italian Street, heart of the former colony of Italian craftsmen

allegiance as the cultural section of the Italian embassy.

The grandest building in the street is the former Lobkowicz Palace, now the German embassy. One of the finest Baroque palaces in Prague, it has a large oval hall on the ground floor leading out onto a magnificent garden. Look out too for the pretty stucco sign on the house called At the Three Red Roses, dating from the early 18th century.

❽ Vrtba Garden
Vrtbovská Zahrada

Karmelitská 25. **Map** 2 D4. **Tel** 272 088 350. 🚇 Malostranská. 🚋 12, 20, 22. **Open** Apr–Oct: 10am–6pm daily. 🚻 **w** vrtbovska.cz

Behind Vrtba Palace lies a beautiful Baroque garden with balustraded terraces. From the highest part of the garden,

there are magnificent views of Prague Castle and the Little Quarter. The Vrtba Garden was designed by František Maximilián Kaňka in about 1720. The statues of Classical gods and stone vases are the work of Matthias Braun and the paintings in the *sala terrena* (garden pavilion) in the lower part of the garden are by Václav Vavřinec Reiner.

❾ Church of Our Lady Victorious
Kostel Panny Marie Vítězné

Karmelitská 9. **Map** 2 E4. **Tel** 257 533 646. 🚋 12, 20, 22. Church: **Open** 8:30am–7pm Mon–Sat, 8:30am–8pm Sun. Museum of the Prague Infant Jesus: **Open** 9:30am–5:30pm Mon–Sat, 1–6pm Sun. 🔔 9am & 6pm (Czech) Mon–Fri, 5pm (English) Thu, 9am & 6pm (Czech), 5pm (Spanish) Sat, 10am & 7pm (Czech), noon (English), 5pm (French), 6pm (Italian) Sun. 🏛 **w** pragjesu.info

The first Baroque building in Prague was the Church of the Holy Trinity, built for the German Lutherans by Giovanni Maria Filippi. It was finished in 1613 but after the Battle of the White Mountain *(see p33)*, the Catholic authorities gave the church to the Carmelites, who rebuilt it and renamed it in honour of the victory. The fabric has survived including the portal. Enshrined on a marble altar in the right aisle is a glass case containing the Holy Infant Jesus of Prague (better known by its Italian name – *il Bambino di Praga*).

The Infant Jesus on the altar of the Church of Our Lady Victorious

This wax effigy has a record of miracle cures and is one of the most revered images in the Catholic world. It was brought from Spain and presented to the Carmelites in 1628 by Polyxena of Lobkowicz. The Museum of the Prague Infant Jesus, adjacent to the church, traces its history. Among the items on display are the various robes that adorn the statue. The colours of the robes change with the liturgical calendar: white at Christmas and Easter, purple for Lent, red for Holy Week and green the rest of the year.

⑩ Maltese Square

Maltézské Náměstí

Map 2 E4. 🚊 12, 20, 22.

The pretty square takes its name from the Priory of the Knights of Malta, which used to occupy this part of the Little Quarter. At the northern end stands a group of sculptures featuring St John the Baptist by Ferdinand Brokoff – part of a fountain erected in 1715 to mark the end of a plague epidemic.

Most of the buildings were originally Renaissance houses belonging to prosperous townspeople, but in the 17th and 18th centuries, the Little Quarter was taken over by the Catholic nobility and many were converted to flamboyant Baroque palaces. The largest, Nostitz Palace, stands on the southern side. It was built in the mid-17th century, then in about 1720, a balustrade was added with Classical vases and statues of emperors. The palace now houses the Ministry of Culture and in summer, concerts are held here. The Japanese embassy is housed in the Turba Palace (1767), an attractive pink Rococo building designed by Joseph Jäger.

Ferdinand Brokoff's statue of John the Baptist in Maltese Square

Čertovka (the Devil's Stream) with Kampa Island on the right

⑪ Kampa Island

Kampa

Map 2 F4. 🚊 6, 9, 12, 20, 22.

Kampa, an island formed by a branch of the Vltava known as the Devil's Stream (Čertovka), is a delightfully peaceful corner of the Little Quarter. The stream got its name in the 19th century, allegedly after the diabolical temper of a lady who owned a house nearby in Maltese Square. For centuries, the stream was used as a millrace and from Kampa, you can see the remains of three old mills. Beyond the Grand Prior's Mill, the stream disappears under a small bridge below the piers of Charles Bridge. From here, it flows between rows of houses. Predictably, the area has become known as "the Venice of Prague", but instead of gondolas, you will see canoes.

For most of the Middle Ages, there were only gardens on Kampa, though the island was also used for washing clothes and bleaching linen. In the 17th century, the island became well-known for its pottery markets. There are some enchanting houses from this period

around Na Kampě Square. Most of the land from here to the southern tip of the island is a park, created from several old palace gardens.

The island all but vanished beneath the Vltava during the floods of 2002, which caused widespread devastation to homes, businesses and historic buildings, many of which needed to be restored.

⑫ Grand Priory Square

Velkopřevorské Náměstí

Map 2 F4. Ⓜ Malostranská. 🚊 12, 20, 22.

On the northern side of this small leafy square stands the former seat of the Grand Prior of the Knights of Malta. In its present form, the palace dates from the 1720s. The doorways, windows and decorative vases were made at the workshop of Matthias Braun. On the opposite side of the square is the Buquoy Palace, now the French embassy, a delightful Baroque building roughly contemporary with the Grand Prior's Palace.

The only incongruous feature is a painting of John Lennon with "give peace a chance" graffitied alongside. The "Lennon Peace Wall" has graced the Grand Prior's garden since Lennon's death.

Street-by-Street: Little Quarter Riverside

On either side of Bridge Street lies a delightful half-hidden world of gently decaying squares, picturesque palaces, churches and gardens. When you have run the gauntlet of the trinket-sellers on Charles Bridge, escape to Kampa Island to enjoy a stroll in its informal park, the views across the Vltava weir to the Old Town and the flocks of swans gliding along the river.

The Church of St Joseph dates from the late 17th century. The painting of *The Holy Family* (1702) on the gilded high altar is by the leading Baroque artist Petr Brandl.

The House at the Golden Unicorn in Lázeňská Street has a plaque commemorating the fact that Beethoven stayed here in 1796.

16 Bridge Street
A major thoroughfare for 750 years, the narrow street leads to Little Quarter Square.

To Little Quarter Square

12 Grand Priory Square
The Grand Prior's Palace is the former seat of the Knights of Malta and dates from the 1720s. Its street wall features colourful murals and graffiti.

13 Church of Our Lady beneath the Chain
Two massive towers survive from when this was a fortified priory.

28 Museum of Music
This museum houses a vast collection of beautifully hand-crafted musical instruments.

9 Church of Our Lady Victorious
This Baroque church houses the famous effigy, the Holy Infant of Prague.

MOSTECKÁ

LÁZEŇSKÁ

KARMELITSKÁ

NEBOVIDSKÁ

10 Maltese Square
Grand palaces surround the oddly shaped square. This coat of arms decorates the 17th-century Nostitz Palace, a popular venue for concerts.

0 metres		100
0 yards		100

Key

— Suggested route

For keys to symbols *see back flap*

18 Vojan Park
Quiet shady paths have been laid out under the apple trees of this former monastery garden.

Locator Map
See Central Prague Map pp16–17

15 At the Three Ostriches
A restaurant and hotel have kept the sign of a seller of ostrich plumes.

U LUŽICKÉHO SEMINÁŘE

14 ★ Charles Bridge
The approach to this magnificent 14th-century bridge, with its Baroque statues, passes under an arch below a Gothic tower.

Čertovka (the Devil's Stream)

Lichtenstein Palace

NA KAMPĚ

The Grand Priory Mill
has had its wheel meticulously restored, though it now turns very slowly in the sluggish water of the Čertovka, the former millrace.

11 ★ Kampa Island
This 19th-century painting by Soběslav Pinkas shows boys playing on Kampa. The island's park is still a popular place for children.

⓭ Church of Our Lady beneath the Chain
Kostel Panny Marie Pod Řetězem

Lázeňská/Velkopřevorské náměstí 4.
Map 2 E4. **Tel** 257 530 876.
🚇 Malostranská. 🚃 12, 20, 22.
Open for concerts and services.
✝ 5:30pm Wed, 10am Sun. ♿

This church, the oldest in the Little Quarter, was founded in the 12th century. King Vladislav II presented it to the Knights of St John, the order which later became known as the Knights of Malta. It stood in the centre of the Knights' heavily fortified monastery that guarded the approach to the old Judith Bridge. The church's name refers to the chain used in the Middle Ages to close the monastery gatehouse.

A Gothic presbytery was added in the 13th century, but a century later, the original Romanesque church was demolished. Although a new portico was built with a pair of massive square towers, work was then abandoned, and the old nave became a courtyard between the towers and the church. This was given a Baroque facelift in 1640 by Carlo Lurago. The painting by Karel Škréta on the high altar shows the Virgin Mary and John the Baptist coming to the aid of the Knights of Malta in the naval victory over the Turks at Lepanto in 1571.

⓮ Charles Bridge
Karlův Most

See pp136–9.

Fresco that gave At the Three Ostriches its name

View along Bridge Street through the tower on Charles Bridge

⓯ At the Three Ostriches
U Tří Pštrosů

Dražického náměstí 12.
Map 2 F3. **Tel** 777 876 667.
🚇 Malostranská. 🚃 12, 20, 22.

Many of Prague's colourful house signs indicated the trade carried on in the premises. In 1597, Jan Fux, an ostrich-feather merchant, bought this house by Charles Bridge. At the time, ostrich plumes were very fashionable as decoration for hats among courtiers and officers at Prague Castle. Fux even supplied feathers to foreign armies. So successful was his business that in 1606 he had the house rebuilt and decorated with a large fresco of ostriches. The building is now an expensive hotel and restaurant.

⓰ Bridge Street
Mostecká Ulice

Map 2 E3. 🚇 Malostranská.
🚃 12, 20, 22.

Since the Middle Ages, this street has linked Charles Bridge with the Little Quarter Square. Crossing the bridge from the Old Town you can see the doorway of the old customs house built in 1591 in front of the Judith Tower. On the first floor of the tower, there is a 12th-century relief of a king and a kneeling man.

Throughout the 13th and 14th centuries, the area to the north of the street was the Court of the Bishop of Prague. This was destroyed during the Hussite Wars *(see pp28–9)*, but one of its Gothic towers is preserved in the courtyard of the house called At the Three Golden Bells. It can be seen from the higher of the two bridge towers. The street is lined with a mixture of Renaissance and Baroque houses. As you walk up to Little Quarter Square, look out for the house called At the Black Eagle on the left. It has rich sculptural decoration and a splendid Baroque wrought-iron grille. Kaunic Palace, also on the left, was built in the 1770s. Its Rococo façade has striking stucco decoration and sculptures by Ignaz Platzer.

⓱ Kafka Museum
Kafkovo Muzeum

Cihelná 2b. **Map** 2 F3. 🚇 Malostranská.
Tel 257 535 373. 🚊 12, 18, 20, 22.
Open 10am–6pm daily. 🎟 📷
Ⓦ **kafkamuseum.cz**

This museum houses the long-term exhibition "The City of Franz Kafka and Prague". The author Franz Kafka was born in Prague in 1883. He wrote visionary works that are considered some of the most important of the 20th century, including *The Trial*, *The Metamorphosis* and *The Castle*.

The exhibition has two sections. Existential Space imagines Prague as a mystical space and explores how the city shaped Kafka's life, while Imaginary Topography examines how Kafka turned Prague into a fantastical place in his works, transcending reality.

⓲ Vojan Park
Vojanovy Sady

U lužického semináře 17. **Map** 2 F3.
Tel 257 531 839. 🚇 Malostranská.
🚊 5, 12, 18, 20, 22. **Open** 8am–5pm daily (to 7pm in summer, to 4pm Dec & Jan).

A tranquil spot hidden behind high white walls, the park dates back to the 17th century, when it was the garden of the Convent of Barefooted Carmelites. Two chapels erected by the Order have survived among the park's lawns and fruit trees. One is the Chapel of Elijah, who, because of his Old Testament associations with Mount Carmel, is regarded as the founder of the Order. His chapel takes the form of a stalagmite and stalactite cave. The other chapel, dedicated to St Theresa, was built in the 18th century as an expression of gratitude for the convent's preservation during the Prussian siege of Prague in 1757.

⓳ Kampa Museum of Modern Art
Muzeum Kampa

U Sovových mlýnů 2. **Map** 2 F4.
Tel 257 286 147. 🚊 6, 9, 12, 20, 22.
Open 10am–6pm daily. 🎟 📷 🎟
Ⓦ **museumkampa.cz**

Housed in the historic Sova mill, the Kampa Museum of Modern Art has an impressive collection of Central European art. The museum was founded by the Czech-American couple Jan and Meda Mládek to house their private collection of drawings, paintings and sculptures. Among the artists on display are abstract painter Frantisek Kupka and Czech cubist sculptor Otto Gutfreund.

The 18th-century statue of Hercules located in the Palace Gardens

⓴ Palace Gardens
Palácové Zahrady

Valdštejnská 14 **Map** 2 F3.
🚇 Malostranská. 🚊 5, 12, 18, 20, 22.
Open Apr & Oct: 10am–6pm; May–Sep: 10am–7pm daily. 🎟
Ⓦ **palacove-zahrady.cz**

The steep southern slope below Prague Castle was covered with vineyards and gardens during the Middle Ages. But in the 16th century, nobles laid out formal terraced gardens based on Italian Renaissance models. Most of these gardens were rebuilt during the 18th century and decorated with Baroque statuary and fountains. Five of the gardens – including those belonging to the former Ledebour (Ledeburg), Černín and Pálffy Palaces – have been linked together.

From their terraces, the gardens boast magnificent views of Prague. The Ledeburg Garden, designed in the early 18th century, has a fine *sala terrena* (garden pavilion) by Giovanni Battista Alliprandi. The Pálffy Garden was laid out in the mid-18th century with terraces and loggias. The most beautiful of the five, and architecturally the richest, is the Kolowrat-Černín Garden, created in 1784 by Ignaz Palliardi. The highest terrace has a *sala terrena* with statues and Classical urns. Below this is an assortment of staircases and archways, and the remains of Classical statuary.

The foot of the Palace Gardens

⑭ Charles Bridge (Little Quarter Side)

Karlův Most

Prague's most familiar monument, Charles Bridge, was founded by Charles IV in 1357, and connects the Old Town with the Little Quarter. It is now pedestrianized but at one time could take four carriages abreast. Many of the statues on the bridge are copies; the originals are kept in the Lapidarium of the National Museum *(see p162)* and at Vyšehrad *(see p181)*. The Gothic Old Town Bridge Tower *(see p139)* is one of the finest buildings of its kind.

★ View from Little Quarter Bridge Tower
The tall pinnacled wedge tower, gives a superb view of the city of 100 spires. The shorter tower is the remains of Judith Bridge.

St Adalbert, 1709
Adalbert, Bishop of Prague, founded the Church of St Lawrence *(see p140)* on Petřín Hill in 991. He is known to the Czechs as Vojtěch.

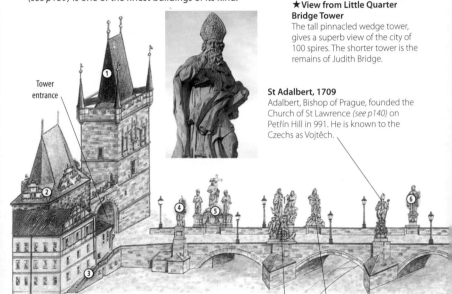

Tower entrance

KEY

① **Little Quarter Bridge Tower**

② **Judith Bridge Tower**, 1158

③ **Steps to Saská Street**

④ **St Wenceslas**, 1859

⑤ **Christ between St Cosmas and St Damian**, 1709

⑥ **St Philip Benizi**, 1714

⑦ **St Cajetan**, 1709

⑧ **Steps to Kampa Island**

⑨ **St Nicholas Tolentino**, 1708

⑩ **St Augustine**, 1708

⑪ **St Jude Thaddaeus**, 1708

⑫ **St Francis of Assisi**, with two angels, 1855

⑬ **St Anthony of Padua**, 1707

⑭ **St Ludmilla with Little Václav**, 1720

St John de Matha, St Felix de Valois and the Blessed Ivan, 1714
These saints, sculpted by Ferdinand Brokoff, founded the Trinitarian Order of mendicants to collect money to buy the freedom of Christians enslaved by the infidels (represented at the foot of the sculpture).

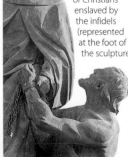

St Vitus, 1714
This engraving of the statue shows the 3rd-century martyr with the lions which were supposed to maul him, but licked him instead. St Vitus is the patron saint of dancers and often invoked against convulsive disorders.

★ **St Luitgard, 1710**
This statue, regarded as the most artistically remarkable on the bridge, was sculpted by Matthias Braun when he was only 26. It is based on the blind Cistercian nun's celebrated vision when Christ appeared and she kissed his wounds.

★ **St John Nepomuk, 1683**
Reliefs on the bridge depict the martyrdom of St John Nepomuk. Here, the saint is polished bright from people touching it for good luck.

St Vincent Ferrer and St Procopius, 1712
This detail shows a rabbi saddened by St Vincent's success in converting many Jews to Christianity. St Procopius is one of Bohemia's patron saints.

St John Nepomuk

The cult of St John Nepomuk, canonized in 1729, was promoted by the Jesuits to rival the revered Jan Hus (see p29). Jan Nepomucký, vicar-general of the Archdiocese of Prague, was arrested in 1393 by Wenceslas IV along with the archbishop and others who had displeased him. The king had St John thrown off Charles Bridge, where he drowned. Statues modelled on the one placed here in 1683 are seen throughout central Europe, especially on bridges. Catholics would later argue that St John was killed for failing to reveal the confessions of the queen.

⓮ Charles Bridge (Old Town Side)

Karlův Most

Until 1741, Charles Bridge was the only crossing over the Vltava. It is 520 m (1,706 ft) long and is built of sandstone blocks, rumoured to be strengthened by mixing mortar with eggs. The bridge was commissioned by Charles IV in 1357 to replace the Judith Bridge and built by Peter Parler. The bridge's original decoration was a simple cross. The first statue – of St John Nepomuk – was added in 1683, inspired by Bernini's sculptures on Rome's Ponte Sant'Angelo.

St Francis Xavier, 1711
The Jesuit missionary is supported by one Moorish, one Tartar and two Oriental converts, plus a pagan prince awaiting baptism.

★ **17th-Century Crucifixion**
For 200 years, the wooden crucifix stood alone on the bridge. The gilded Christ dates from 1629 and the Hebrew words "Holy, Holy, Holy Lord", were paid for by a Jew as punishment for blasphemy.

KEY

① **St Norbert, St Wenceslas and St Sigismund**, 1853

② **St Francis Borgia**, 1710

③ **St John the Baptist**, 1855

④ **St Christopher**, 1857

⑤ **St Cyril and St Methodius**, 1938

⑥ **St Ann**, 1707

⑦ **St Joseph with Jesus**, 1854

⑧ **Pietà**, 1859

⑨ **St Barbara, St Margaret and St Elizabeth**, 1707

⑩ **St Ivo**, 1711

⑪ **Old Town Bridge Tower**

Thirty Years' War
In the last hours of this war, the Old Town was saved from the Swedish army. The truce was signed in the middle of the bridge in 1648.

1357 Charles IV commissions new bridge		**1621** Heads of ten Protestant nobles exhibited on the Old Town Bridge Tower	**1648** Swedes damage part of the bridge and Old Town Bridge Tower	*1890 flood damage*
1342 Judith Bridge destroyed by floods				**2002** Bridge survives huge flood unscathed
1100	**1300**	**1500**	**1700**	**1900**
	1158 Europe's second medieval stone bridge, Judith Bridge, is built	**1393** St John Nepomuk thrown off Bridge on the orders of Wenceslas IV	**1890** Three arches destroyed by flood	**1938** Karel Dvořák's sculpture of St Cyril and St Methodius
		Sculptor Matthias Braun (1684–1738)	**1713** Bridge decorated with 21 statues by Braun, Brokoff and others	

The Madonna, St Dominic and St Thomas, 1708
The Dominicans (known in a Latin pun as *Domini canes*, the dogs of God), are shown with the Madonna and their emblem, a dog.

VISITORS' CHECKLIST

Practical Information
Map 3 A4. **Tel** 224 220 569.
Old Town Bridge Tower: **Open** 10am–6pm daily (Apr–Sep: to 10pm; Mar & Oct: to 8pm).

Transport
17, 18 to Karlovy lázně.

Madonna and St Bernard, 1709
Cherubs and symbols of the Passion, including the dice, the cock and the centurion's gauntlet, form part of the statue.

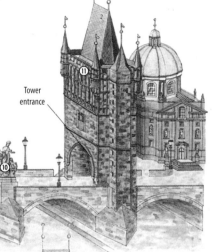

Tower entrance

★ Old Town Bridge Tower

This magnificent Gothic tower, designed by Peter Parler, was built at the end of the 14th century. An integral part of the Old Town's fortifications, it was badly damaged in 1648 and the west side still bears the scars.

Bridge Tower sculptures by Peter Parler include St Vitus, the bridge's patron saint, Charles IV *(left)* and Wenceslas IV.

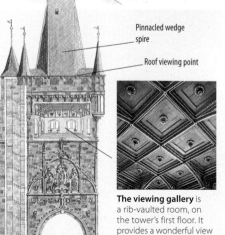

Pinnacled wedge spire

Roof viewing point

The viewing gallery is a rib-vaulted room, on the tower's first floor. It provides a wonderful view of Prague Castle and the Little Quarter.

㉑ Observation Tower

Petřínská Rozhledna

Petřín. **Map** 1 C4. **Tel** 257 320 112.
🚊 6, 9, 12, 20, 22, then take funicular railway. 🚌 143, 176, 191. **Open** 10am–10pm daily (Mar & Oct: to 8pm; Nov–Feb: to 6pm). 🎫 ♿ 🖥
W petrinska-rozhledna.cz

The most conspicuous landmark in Petřín Park is an imitation of the Eiffel Tower, built for the Jubilee Exhibition of 1891. The octagonally shaped tower is only 60 m (200 ft), a quarter the height of the Eiffel Tower, but its top is higher above sea level. A spiral staircase of 299 steps leads up to the viewing platform. A lift is also available. On a clear day, you can see as far as Bohemia's highest peak, Sněžka in the Krkonoše (Giant) Mountains, 150 km (100 miles) to the northeast.

㉒ Mirror Maze

Zrcadlové Bludiště

Petřín. **Map** 1 C4. **Tel** 725 831 634.
🚊 6, 9, 12, 20, 22, then take funicular railway. 🚌 143, 176, 191. **Open** 10am–10pm daily (Mar, Oct: to 8pm; Nov–Feb: to 6pm). 🎫 ✉ ♿
W petrinska-rozhledna.cz

With its distorting mirrors, the maze is a relic of the Exhibition of 1891, like the Observation Tower. It is in a wooden pavilion in the shape of the old Špička Gate, part of the Gothic fortifications of Vyšehrad *(see pp180–81)*. This amusement house moved to Petřín at the end of the exhibition.

The 100-year-old Observation Tower overlooking the city

When you have navigated your way through the maze, your reward is to view the vivid diorama of *The Defence of Prague against the Swedes*, which took place on Charles Bridge *(see p138)* in 1648, badly damaging the Old Town Bridge Tower.

㉓ Church of St Lawrence

Kostel Sv. Vavřince

Petřín. **Map** 1 C5. **Tel** 224 497 707. 🚊 6, 9, 12, 20, 22, then funicular railway. 🚌 143, 176, 191. **Open** for concerts (mainly Prague Spring, *see p52*). ♿

According to legend, the church was founded in the 10th century by the pious Prince Boleslav II and St Adalbert on the site of a pagan shrine. The ceiling of the sacristy is decorated with a painting illustrating this legend. The painting dates from the

18th century, when the Romanesque church was swallowed up by a large new Baroque structure, featuring a cupola flanked by two onion-domed towers. The small Calvary Chapel, dating from 1735, is situated to the left of the church.

㉔ Štefánik's Observatory

Štefánikova Hvězdárna

Petřín 205. **Map** 2 D5. **Tel** 257 320 540.
🚊 6, 9, 12, 20, 22, then funicular railway. 🚌 143, 176, 191. **Open** Tue–Sun; opening hours vary monthly, so phone ahead or check the website. 🎫 ✉ ♿
W observatory.cz

Since 1930, Prague's amateur astronomers have been able to enjoy the facilities of this observatory on Petřín Hill. You can use its telescopes to view the craters of the moon or unfamiliar distant galaxies. There is an exhibition of old astronomical instruments, and various special events for kids are held on Saturdays and Sundays.

㉕ Hunger Wall

Hladová Zeď

Újezd, Petřín, Strahovská.
Map 2 D5. 🚊 6, 9, 12, 20, 22, then funicular railway. 🚌 143, 176, 191.

The great fortifications built around the southern edge of the Little Quarter on the orders of Charles IV in 1360–62 have been known for centuries as the Hunger Wall. Nearly 1,200 m (1,300 yards) of the wall survive, complete with crenellated battlements and a platform for marksmen on its inner side. It runs from Újezd across Petřín Park to Strahov. The story behind the name is that Charles commissioned its construction with the aim of providing employment to the poor during a period of famine. It is true that a great famine did break out in Bohemia in the 1360s, and the two events, the people's hunger and the building of the wall, became permanently associated.

Diorama of *The Defence of Prague against the Swedes* in the Mirror Maze

Nebozízek, the station halfway up Petřín's funicular railway

㉖ Petřín Park

Petřínské Sady

Map 2 D5. 🚊 6, 9, 12, 20, 22, then take funicular railway. *See Four Guided Walks pp176–7.*

To the west of the Little Quarter, Petřín Hill rises above the city to a height of 318 m (960 ft). The name derives either from the Slavonic god Perun, to whom sacrifices were made on the hill, or from the Latin name Mons Petrinus, meaning "rocky hill". A forest used to stretch from here as far as the White Mountain (*see p33*). In the 12th century, the southern side of the hill was planted with vineyards, but by the 18th century, most of these had been transformed into gardens and orchards.

Today, a path winds up the slopes of Petřín, offering fine views of Prague. In the park is the *Monument to the Victims of Communism* (2002) by the sculptor Olbram Zoubek and a monument to Romantic poet Karel Hynek Mácha.

㉗ Funicular Railway

Lanová Dráha

Újezd. **Map** 2 D5. 🚊 6, 9, 12, 20, 22. In operation 9am–11:30pm daily (winter: to 11:20pm). 🅿️ (also valid for public transport). 🚹 🆆 **dpp.cz**

Built to carry visitors to the 1891 Jubilee Exhibition up to the Observation Tower at the top of Petřín Hill, the funicular was

Karel Hynek Mácha statue in Petřín Park

originally powered by water. In this form, it remained in operation until 1914, then between the wars was converted to electricity. In 1965, it had to be shut down because part of the hillside collapsed – coal had been mined here during the 19th century. Shoring up the slope and rebuilding the railway took 20 years, but since its reopening in 1985, it has proved a reliable way of getting up Petřín Hill. At the halfway station, Nebozízek, there is a restaurant (*see p201*) with fine views of the Castle and the city.

㉘ Museum of Music

České Muzeum Hudby

Karmelitská 2, Praha 1, Malá Strana. **Map** 2 E4. **Tel** 257 257 777. Ⓜ Malostranská. 🚊 12, 20, 22. **Open** 10am–6pm Wed–Mon. 🅿️ 🚹 🆆 **nm.cz**

Housed in the former 17th-century Baroque Church of St Magdalene, the Museum of Music seeks to present musical instruments not only as fine specimens of craftsmanship and artistry, but also as mediators between man and music.

The museum is run by the National Museum (*see p147*). Exhibits include a look at the diversity of popular 20th-century music as preserved in television, film, photographs and sound recordings. Also examined is the production of handcrafted instruments, the history of

musical notation and the social occasions linked to certain instruments. Earphones offer high-quality sound reproduction of original recordings made on the instruments displayed. The museum's collections can be accessed via the study room, and there is a listening studio for the library of recordings.

㉙ Michna Palace (Tyrš House)

Michnův Palác (Tyršův Dům)

Újezd 40. **Map** 2 E4. **Tel** 257 007 111. 🚊 12, 20, 22.

In about 1580, Ottavio Aostalli built a summer palace for the Kinský family on the site of an old Dominican convent. In 1623, the building was bought by Pavel Michna of Vacínov, a supply officer in the Imperial Army, who had grown rich after the Battle of the White Mountain. He commissioned a Baroque building that he hoped would rival the palace of his late commander, Wallenstein (*see p126*).

In 1767, the palace was sold to the army and over the years it became a crumbling ruin. After 1918, it was bought by Sokol (a physical culture association) and converted into a gym and sports centre with a training ground in the old palace garden and, dating from 1925, the oldest swimming pool in Prague. The restored palace was renamed Tyrš House in honour of Sokol's founder.

Restored Baroque façade of the Michna Palace (Tyrš House)

NEW TOWN
NOVÉ MĚSTO

The New Town, founded in 1348 by Charles IV, was carefully planned and laid out around three large central marketplaces: the Hay Market (Senovážné Square), the Cattle Market (Charles Square) and the Horse Market (Wenceslas Square). Twice as large as the Old Town, the area was mainly inhabited by tradesmen and craftsmen such as blacksmiths, wheelwrights and brewers. During the late 19th century, much of the New Town was demolished and completely redeveloped, giving it the appearance it has today.

Sights at a Glance

Churches and Monasteries
2 Church of Our Lady of the Snows
9 Church of St Ignatius
12 Cathedral of St Cyril and
   St Methodius
14 Church of St John on the Rock
15 Slavonic Monastery Emauzy
17 Church of St Catherine
20 Church of St Stephen
23 Church of St Ursula

Historic Buildings
5 Hotel Europa
10 Jesuit College
13 Faust House
21 New Town Hall

Theatres and Opera Houses
7 State Opera
24 National Theatre pp156–7

Historic Squares
1 Wenceslas Square
11 Charles Square

Museums and Galleries
4 Museum of Communism
6 National Museum

8 Mucha Museum
19 Dvořák Museum

Historic Restaurants and Beer Halls
18 Chalice Restaurant
22 U Fleků

Parks and Gardens
3 Franciscan Garden
16 Botanical Gardens

☐ **Restaurants** see pp202–204

1 Alcron
2 Bresto
3 Café Louvre
4 Cafe Slavia
5 Čestr
6 Cicala Trattoria
7 Como
8 Dynamo
9 El Emir
10 Fama
11 Ginger & Fred
12 Home Kitchen
13 Klub Cestovatelů
14 Lemon Leaf
15 Miss Saigon
16 Miyabi
17 Nota Bene
18 Novoměstský Pivovar
19 Renommé
20 Solidní Jistota
21 Suterén
22 Svatováclavská Cukrárna
23 U Emy Destinnové
24 U Pinkasů
25 Ultramarin
26 Universal
27 Žofín Garden
28 Zvonice

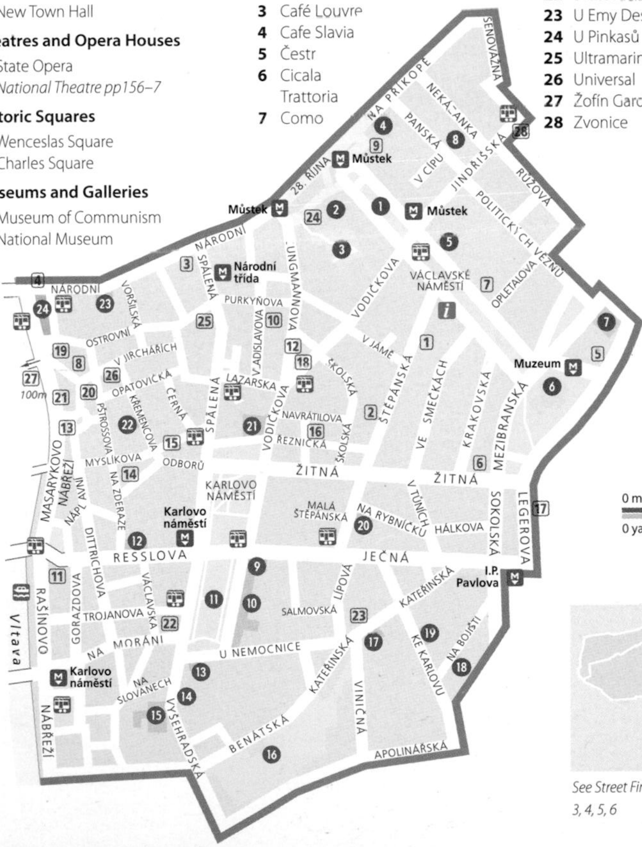

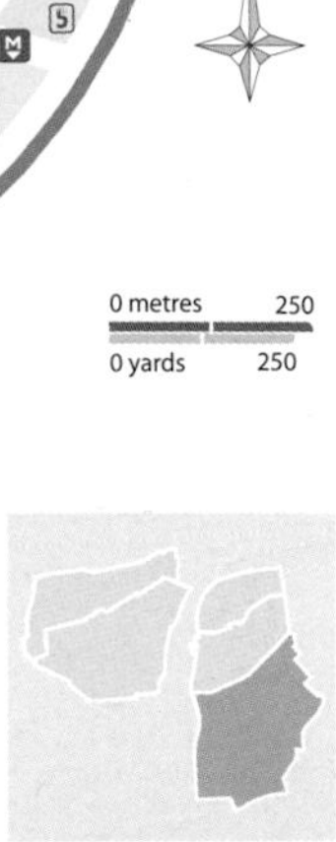

0 metres   250
0 yards   250

See Street Finder maps
3, 4, 5, 6

◄ The ornate interior of the National Theatre

For keys to symbols see back flap

Street-by-Street: Wenceslas Square

Hotels and restaurants occupy many of the buildings around Wenceslas Square, though it remains an important commercial centre – the square began life as a medieval horse market. As you walk along, look up at the buildings, most of which date from the turn of last century, when the square was redeveloped. There are fine examples of the decorative styles used by Czech architects of the period. Many blocks have covered arcades leading to shops, clubs, theatres and cinemas.

Koruna Palace (1914) is an ornate block of shops and offices. Its corner turret is topped with a crown (koruna).

To Powder Gate

NA PŘÍKOPĚ

Můstek Ⓜ

U Pinkasů (see p203) became one of Prague's most popular beer halls when it started serving Pilsner Urquell (see pp196–7) in 1843.

Ⓜ Můstek

❷ Church of Our Lady of the Snows
The towering Gothic building is only part of a vast church planned during the 14th century.

Můstek Ⓜ

Můstek Ⓜ

VODIČKOVA

Jungmann Square is named after Josef Jungmann (1773–1847), an influential scholar of language and lexicographer, and there is a statue of him in the middle. The Adria Palace (1925) used to be the Laterna Magika Theatre (see p218), which was where Václav Havel's Civic Forum worked in the early days of the 1989 Velvet Revolution.

❸ Franciscan Garden
An old monastery garden has been laid out as a small park with this fountain, rosebeds, trellises and a children's playground.

Lucerna Palace

Wiehl House, named after its architect Antonín Wiehl, was completed in 1896. The five-storey building is in striking Neo-Renaissance style, with a loggia and colourful sgraffito. Mikuláš Aleš designed some of the Art Nouveau figures.

❶ ★ Wenceslas Square
The dominant features of the square are the bronze, equestrian statue of St Wenceslas (1912) and the National Museum behind it. St Wenceslas, a former prince who was murdered by his brother Boleslav, is the patron saint of Bohemia.

Locator Map
See Central Prague Map pp16–17

The Assicurazioni Generali Building was where Franz Kafka *(see p70)* worked as an insurance clerk for 10 months in 1906–7.

❺ ★ Hotel Europa
Both the façade and the interior of the hotel (1906) preserve most of their original Art Nouveau features.

The Monument to the Victims of Communism is close to the spot where Jan Palach immolated himself in 1969 in protest at the Warsaw Pact invasion. An unofficial shrine has been maintained here since 1989.

❻ ★ National Museum
The grand building with its monumental staircase was completed in 1890 as a symbol of national prestige.

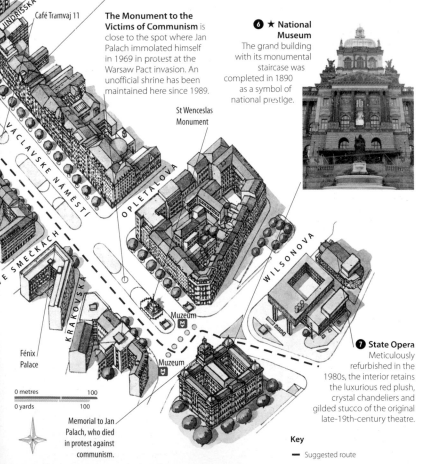

Café Tramvaj 11

JINDŘIŠSKÁ

VÁCLAVSKÉ NÁMĚSTÍ

St Wenceslas Monument

OPLETALOVA

WILSONOVA

V SMEČKÁCH

KRAKOVSKÁ

Muzeum Ⓜ

Muzeum Ⓜ

Fénix Palace

0 metres   100
0 yards   100

Memorial to Jan Palach, who died in protest against communism.

❼ State Opera
Meticulously refurbished in the 1980s, the interior retains the luxurious red plush, crystal chandeliers and gilded stucco of the original late-19th-century theatre.

Key

— Suggested route

For keys to symbols *see back flap*

Wenceslas Monument in Wenceslas Square

❶ Wenceslas Square
Václavské Náměstí

Map 3 C5. Ⓜ Můstek, Muzeum.
🚃 3, 9, 14, 24.

The square has witnessed many key events in Czech history. It was here that the student Jan Palach burnt himself to death in 1969, and in November 1989, a protest rally in the square against police brutality led to the Velvet Revolution and the overthrow of Communism.

Wenceslas "Square" is something of a misnomer, for it is some 750 m (825 yd) long and only 60 m (65 yd) wide. Originally a horse market, today it is lined with hotels, restaurants, clubs and shops, reflecting the seamier side of global consumerism. The huge equestrian statue of St Wenceslas that looks the length of the square from in front of the National Museum was erected in 1912. Cast in bronze, it is the work of Josef Myslbek, the leading Czech sculptor of the late 19th century. At the foot of the pedestal, there are several other statues of Czech patron saints. A memorial near the statue commemorates the victims of the former Communist regime.

❷ Church of Our Lady of the Snows
Kostel Panny Marie Sněžné

Jungmannovo náměstí 18. **Map** 3 C5. **Tel** 222 246 243. Ⓜ Můstek. **Open** 9am–6pm daily. 🕐 7am, 8am & 6pm Mon–Fri, 8am & 6pm Sat, 9am, 10:15am, 11:30am & 6pm Sun. ♿ Ⓦ **pms.ofm.cz**

Charles IV founded this church to mark his coronation in 1347. The name refers to a 4th-century miracle in Rome, when the Virgin Mary appeared to the pope in a dream telling him to build a church to her on the spot where snow fell in August. Charles's church was never completed, and the building we see today was just the presbytery of the projected church. Over 33 m (110 ft) high, it was finished in 1397, and was originally part of a Carmelite monastery. On the northern side, there is a gateway with a 14th-century pediment that marked the entrance to the church graveyard.

A steeple was added in the early 1400s, but further building was halted by the Hussite Wars *(see pp28–9)*. The Hussite firebrand Jan Želivský preached at the church and was buried here after his execution in 1422. The church suffered damage in the wars, and in 1434, the steeple was destroyed. For a long time, the church was left to decay. In 1603, Franciscans restored the building. The intricate net vaulting of the ceiling dates from this period, the original roof having collapsed. Most of the interior decoration, apart from the 1450s

pewter font, is Baroque. The monumental three-tiered altar is crowded with statues of saints, and is crowned with a crucifix.

❸ Franciscan Garden
Františkánská Zahrada

Map 3 C5. Ⓜ Můstek. **Open** Apr–Sep: 7am–10pm (Oct: to 8pm; Nov–Mar: 8am–7pm). ♿

Originally the garden of a Franciscan monastery, the area was opened to the public in 1950 as a tranquil oasis close to Wenceslas Square. By the entrance is a Gothic portal leading down to a cellar restaurant – U Františkánů (At the Franciscans). In the 1980s, several of the beds were replanted with herbs, cultivated by the Franciscans in the 17th century.

❹ Museum of Communism
Muzeum Komunismu

Na Příkopě 10. **Map** 3 C4. **Tel** 224 212 966. Ⓜ Můstek. **Open** 9am–9pm daily. Ⓦ **muzeumkomunismu.cz**

This museum explores how Communism affected various areas of Prague society, such as politics, sports and everyday life, during the totalitarian regime of 1948 to 1989.

On display are original artifacts, gathered from the museum's archive, along with other rare items acquired from public and private collections. These include photos, propaganda material and film footage. There is also a recreation of an interrogation room, complete with a spotlight and a typewriter.

A view of the Church of Our Lady of the Snows from the Franciscan gardens

Façade of the State Opera, formerly the New German Theatre

❺ Hotel Europa
Hotel Evropa

Václavské náměstí 25. **Map** 4 D5.
🅼 Můstek. 🚊 3, 9, 14, 24.

Currently in the midst of a major renovation project, the Hotel Europa is a wonderfully preserved reminder of the golden age of hotels. It was built in highly decorated Art Nouveau style between 1903 and 1906. Not only has its splendid façade crowned with gilded nymphs survived, but many of the interiors on the ground floor have remained virtually intact, including all the original bars, large mirrors, panelling and light fittings.

❻ National Museum
Národní Muzeum

Václavské náměstí 68. **Map** 6 E1.
Tel 224 497 111. 🅼 Muzeum.
🚊 11, 13. **Closed** until 2018; visit building at Vinohradská 1 from 10am–6pm Tue–Sun until then. 🆆 **nm.cz**

The vast Neo-Renaissance building at the upper end of Wenceslas Square houses the National Museum. Designed by Josef Schulz as a triumphal affirmation of the Czech national revival, it was completed in 1890. The entrance is reached by a ramp decorated with allegorical statues. Seated by the door are History and Natural History.
   The collections are mainly devoted to mineralogy, archaeology, anthropology, numismatics and natural history.

A Pantheon also contains busts and statues of Czech scholars, writers and artists. The building is undergoing extensive restoration, which is expected to be complete in 2018. Until then, temporary exhibitions are housed in the so-called New Building nearby.

❼ State Opera
Státní Opera

Wilsonova 4/Legerova 75. **Map** 4 E5.
Tel 224 901 866/448. 🅼 Muzeum.
🚊 3, 9, 14, 24. **Open** for performances only. *See Entertainment p218 & p220.*
🆆 **narodni-divadlo.cz**

The first theatre built here, the New Town Theatre, was pulled down in 1885 to make way for the present building. This was originally known as the New German Theatre, built to rival the Czechs' National Theatre *(see pp156–7)*. A Neo-Classical frieze decorates the pediment above the columned loggia at the front of the theatre. The figures include Dionysus and Thalia, the muse of comedy. The interior is stuccoed, and original paintings in the auditorium and on the curtain have been preserved. In 1945, the theatre became the city's main opera house.

❽ Mucha Museum
Muchovo Muzeum

Panská 7. **Map** 4 D4. **Tel** 224 216 415.
🅼 Můstek, Náměstí Republiky.
🚊 3, 9, 14, 24, 26. **Open** 10am–6pm daily. 📷 🖥 📷 🆆 **mucha.cz**

The 18th-century Kaunicky Palace is home to the first museum dedicated to this Czech master of Art Nouveau. A selection of more than 100 exhibits include paintings and drawings, sculptures, photographs and personal memorabilia. The central courtyard becomes a terrace for the café in the summer, and there is a museum shop offering exclusive gifts with Mucha motifs.

Prints and other souvenirs for sale at the Mucha Museum shop

Art Nouveau in Prague

The decorative style known as Art Nouveau originated in Paris in the 1890s. It quickly became international as most of the major European cities quickly responded to its graceful, flowing forms. In Prague it was called "Secese", and at its height in the first decade of the 20th century, dying out during World War I, when it seemed frivolous and even decadent. There is a wealth of Art Nouveau in Prague, both in the fine and decorative arts and in architecture. In the New Town and the Jewish Quarter *(see pp82–95)*, entire streets were demolished at the turn of the century and built in the new style.

Praha House
This house was built in 1903 for the Prague Insurance Company. Its name is in gilt Art Nouveau letters at the top.

Architecture

Art Nouveau made its first appearance in Prague at the Jubilee exhibition of 1891. Architecturally, the new style was a deliberate attempt to break with the 19th-century tradition of monumental buildings. In Art Nouveau, the important aspect was ornament, either painted or sculpted, often in the form of a female figure, applied to a fairly plain surface. This technique was ideally suited to wrought iron and glass, popular at the turn of the century. These materials were light but strong. The effect of this, together with Art Nouveau decoration, created buildings of lasting beauty.

Hotel Central
Built by Alois Dryák and Bedřich Bendelmayer in 1900, the façade of this hotel has plasterwork shaped like tree branches.

Hlahol Choir Building
The architect Josef Fanta embellished this building, dating from 1905, with mosaics and sculptures by Karl Mottl and Josef Pekárek.

Hotel Meran
Finished in 1904, this grand Art Nouveau building is notable for its fine detailing inside and out.

Ornate pilasters

Decorative statues

Brass and wrought-iron balustrade

Hlavní nádraží
Prague's main railway station was completed in 1901. With its huge interior glazed dome and elegant sculptural decoration, it shows many Art Nouveau features.

Decorative and Fine Arts

Many painters, sculptors and graphic artists were influenced by Art Nouveau. One of the most successful exponents of the style was the artist Alfons Mucha (1860–1939). He is celebrated chiefly for his posters. Yet he designed stained glass (*see p104*), furniture, jewellery, even postage stamps. It is perhaps here, in the decorative and applied arts, that Art Nouveau had its fullest expression in Prague. Artists adorned every type of object – doorknobs, curtain ornaments, vases and cutlery – with tentacle- and plant-like forms in imitation of the natural world from which they drew their inspiration.

Záboj and Slavoj
These mythical figures (invented by a forger of old legends) were carved by Josef Myslbek for Palacký Bridge in 1895. They are now in Vyšehrad.

Postage Stamp
A bold stamp design by Alfons Mucha marked the founding of the Czechoslovak Republic in 1918.

Glass Vase
This iridescent green vase made of Bohemian glass has relief decoration of intertwined threads. It is in the Museum of Decorative Arts.

Poster for Sokol Movement
Mucha's colour lithograph for the sixth national meeting of the Sokol gymnastic movement (1912) is in Tyrš's Museum (Physical Culture and Sports).

Curtain Ornament and Candlestick
The silver and silk ornament adorns the Mayor's room of the Municipal House. The candlestick by Emanuel Novák with fine leaf design is in the Museum of Decorative Arts.

Where to See Art Nouveau in Prague

Detail of doorway, Široká 9, Jewish Quarter

Architecture
Apartment Building,
    Na příkopě 7
Hanavský Pavilion *p161*
Hlahol Choir Building,
    Masarykovo nábřeží 10
Hlavní nádraží, Wilsonova
Hotel Central,
    Hybernská 10
Hotel Europa *p147*
Industrial Palace *p162* and Four
    Guided Walks *pp178–9*
Ministerstvo pro místní
    rozvoj *p69*
Municipal House *p66*
Palacký Bridge (Palackého most)
Praha House, Národní třída 7
Wiehl House *p144*

Painting
Trade Fair Palace *pp164–5*

Sculpture
Jan Hus Monument *p72*
Vyšehrad Garden and Cemetery
    p160 and Four Guided
    Walks *pp180–81*

Decorative Arts
Mucha Museum *p147*
Museum of Decorative Arts *p86*
Prague Museum *p161*

Street-by-Street: Charles Square

The southern part of the New Town resounds to the rattle of trams, as many routes converge in this part of Prague. Fortunately, the park in Charles Square (Karlovo náměstí) offers a peaceful and welcome retreat. Some of the buildings around the Square belong to the University and the statues in the centre represent writers and scientists, reflecting the academic environment. There are several Baroque buildings and towards the river stands the historic 14th-century Slavonic Monastery.

The Czech Technical University was founded on the square in 1867 in a grand Neo-Renaissance building.

Charles Square Centre

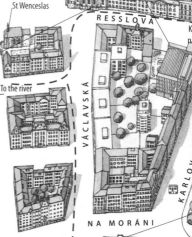

Church of St Wenceslas

RESSLOVA

VÁCLAVSKÁ

KARLOV

NA MORÁNI

To the river

⑫ ★ Cathedral of St Cyril and St Methodius
A plaque and a bullet-scarred wall are reminders of a siege in 1942, when German troops attacked Czech and Slovak paratroopers hiding here after assassinating Nazi Reinhard Heydrich.

⑪ ★ Charles Square
The centre of the square is a pleasant 19th-century park with lawns, formal flowerbeds, fountains and statues.

To metro Karlovo náměstí

Church of St Cosmas and St Damian

VYŠEHRADSKÁ

PODSLOVANY

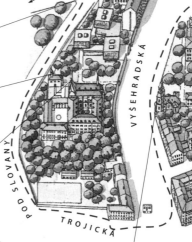

⑮ Slavonic Monastery Emauzy
In 1965, a pair of modern concrete spires by František Černý were added to the church of the 14th-century monastery.

TROJICKÁ

⑭ Church of St John on the Rock
This view of the organ and ceiling shows the dynamic Baroque design of Kilian Ignaz Dientzenhofer.

9 Church of St Ignatius
The sun rays and gilded cherubs on the side altars are typical of the gaudy decoration in this Baroque church built for the Jesuits.

Eliška Krásnohorská was a 19th-century poet who wrote the libretti for Smetana's operas. A statue of her was put up here in 1931.

JEČNÁ

A statue of Jan Purkyně (1787–1869), an eminent physiologist and pioneer of cell theory, was erected in 1961. It is the most recent of the many memorials in the square.

10 Jesuit College
Founded in the mid-17th century, this imposing building has been a hospital since the suppression of the Jesuits in 1773 (see pp32–3).

U NEMOCNICE

18th-century Institute of Gentlewomen (now a hospital)

13 Faust House
In the 18th century, this house was owned by Count Ferdinand Mladota of Solopysky. The chemical experiments he performed reinforced the associations that gave the building its name.

BENÁTSKÁ

16 Botanical Gardens
Though part of the Charles University, the gardens are open to the public and are known for their profusion of rare plants. They make a pleasant place to relax.

0 metres	100
0 yards	100

Key
— Suggested route

For keys to symbols see back flap

Sculptures on the façade of the Jesuit College by Tomasso Soldati

❾ Church of St Ignatius
Kostel Sv. Ignáce

Ječná 2. **Map** 5 C2. **Tel** 221 990 200. Ⓜ Karlovo náměstí. 🚋 3, 4, 6, 10, 16, 18, 22, 24. **Open** 6am–noon & 3:30–6:30pm daily. ✝ 6:15am, 7:30am & 5:30pm Mon–Sat (6:30am Sat); 7am, 9am, 11am (in Latin) & 5:30pm Sun. 🌐 **kostelignac.cz**

With its wealth of gilding and flamboyant stucco decoration, St Ignatius is typical of the Baroque churches built by the Jesuits to impress people with the glamour of their faith. The architects – Carlo Lurago, who started work on the church in 1665, and Paul Ignaz Bayer, who added the tower in 1687 – were also responsible for the adjoining Jesuit College.

The painting on the high altar of *The Glory of St Ignatius* (St Ignatius Loyola, founder of the Jesuit order) is by Jan Jiří Heinsch.

The Jesuits continued to embellish the interior right up until the suppression of their order in 1773, adding stuccowork and statues of Jesuit and Czech saints.

❿ Jesuit College
Jezuitská Kolej

Karlovo náměstí 36. **Map** 5 B2. Ⓜ Karlovo náměstí. 🚋 3, 4, 6, 10, 14, 16, 18, 21, 22, 24. **Closed** to the public.

Half the eastern side of Charles Square is occupied by the former college of the Jesuit order in the New Town. As in other parts of Prague, the Jesuits were able to demolish huge swathes of the city to put up another bastion of their formidable education system. The college was built between 1656 and 1702 by Carlo Lurago and Paul Ignaz Bayer. The two sculptured portals are the work of Johann Georg Wirch who extended the building in 1770. After the suppression of the Jesuit order in 1773, the college was converted into a military hospital. It is now part of Charles University.

⓫ Charles Square
Karlovo Náměstí

Map 5 B2. Ⓜ Karlovo náměstí. 🚋 3, 4, 6, 10, 16, 18, 22, 24.

Since the mid-19th century, the square has been a park. Though surrounded by busy roads, it is a pleasant but somewhat shabby place to sit and read or watch people walking their dogs.

The square began life as a vast cattle market, when Charles IV founded the New Town in 1348. Other goods sold in the square included firewood, coal and pickled herring from barrels. In the centre of the market, Charles had a wooden tower built, where the coronation jewels were put on display once a year. In 1382, the tower was replaced by a chapel, from which, in 1437, concessions made to the Hussites by the pope at the Council of Basle were read out to the populace.

⓬ Cathedral of St Cyril and St Methodius
Katedrála Sv. Cyrila a Metoděje

Resslova 9. **Map** 5 B2. **Tel** 224 920 686. Ⓜ Karlovo náměstí. 🚋 3, 4, 6, 10, 16, 18, 22, 24. Museum: **Open** 9am–5pm Tue–Sun (Nov–Mar: Tue–Sat). Church: **Open** 8–9:30am Sat, 9am–noon Sun. ✝ 8am Tue, 8am & 5pm Sat, 9:30am Sun. 🅿 ✉ ♿ 🌐 **pamatnik-heydrichiady.cz**

This Baroque church, with a pilastered façade and a small central tower, was built in the 1730s. It was dedicated to St Charles Borromeo and served as the church of a community of retired priests, but both were closed in 1783. In the 1930s, the church was restored and given to the Czechoslovak Orthodox Church, and rededicated to St Cyril and St Methodius, the 9th-century "Apostles to the Slavs" (*see pp22–3*). In May 1942, parachutists who assassinated Reinhard Heydrich, the Nazi governor of Czechoslovakia, hid in the crypt along with members of the Czech Resistance. Surrounded by German troops, they took their own lives rather than surrender. Bullet holes made by German machine guns during the siege can still be seen below the memorial plaque on the outer wall of the crypt, which now houses a museum of these times.

Main altar in the Cathedral of St Cyril and St Methodius

⓭ Faust House
Faustův Dům

Karlovo náměstí 40, 41. **Map** 5 B3.
🅼 Karlovo náměstí. 🚊 3, 4, 10, 16, 18, 22, 24. **Closed** to the public.

Prague thrives on legends of alchemy and pacts with the devil, and this Baroque mansion has attracted many. There has been a house here since the 14th century when it belonged to Prince Václav of Opava, an alchemist and natural historian. In the 16th century, it was owned by the alchemist Edward Kelley. The chemical experiments of Count Ferdinand Mladota of Solopysky, who owned the house in the mid-18th century, gave rise to its association with the legend of Faust.

The Baroque façade of Faust House, the site of many legends

⓮ Church of St John on the Rock
Kostel Sv. Jana Na Skalce

Vyšehradská 49. **Map** 5 B3. **Tel** 732 601 378. 🚊 3, 4, 10, 16, 18, 22, 24. **Open** for services only. 🕇 11am Sun (in German). ✉

One of Prague's smaller Baroque churches, St John on the Rock is one of Kilian Ignaz Dientzen-hofer's most daring designs. Its twin square towers are set at a sharp angle to the church's narrow façade and the interior is based on an octagonal floorplan. The church was completed in 1738, but the double staircase leading up to the west front was not added until the 1770s. On the high altar, there is a wooden version of Jan Brokof's statue of St John Nepomuk *(see p137)*, which stands on the Charles Bridge.

⓯ Slavonic Monastery Emauzy
Klášter Na Slovanech-Emauzy

Vyšehradská 49. **Map** 5 B3. **Tel** 224 917 662. 🚊 3, 4, 7, 10, 16, 17. Monastery church: **Open** 11am–5:30pm Mon–Fri (also Sat in summer; Nov–Mar: to 2pm). 🕇 10am daily. 🅿 ✉ ♿ 🆆 emauzy.cz

Both the monastery and its church were almost destroyed in an American air raid in 1945. During their reconstruction, the church was given a pair of modern reinforced concrete spires.

The monastery was founded in 1347 for the Croatian Benedictines, whose services were held in the Old Slavonic language, hence its name "Na Slovanech". In the course of Prague's tumultuous religious history, it has since changed hands many times. In 1446, a Hussite order was formed here, then in 1635, the monastery was acquired by Spanish Benedictines. In the 18th century the complex was given a thorough Baroque treatment, but in 1880, it was taken over by some German Benedictines, who rebuilt almost everything in Neo-Gothic style. The monastery has managed to preserve some historically important 14th-century wall paintings in the cloister, though many were damaged in World War II.

Remains of 14th-century wall paintings in the Slavonic Monastery

⓰ Botanical Gardens
Botanická Zahrada

Na slupi 16. **Map** 5 B3. **Tel** 221 951 879. 🚊 18, 24. Glasshouses: **Open** 10am–5pm daily (Feb & Mar: to 4pm; Nov–Jan: to 3:30pm). Gardens: **Open** Feb–Oct: 10am–7:30pm daily (Feb, Mar, Sep & Oct: to 6pm). 🅿 ✉ ♿ 🆆 bz-uk.cz

Charles IV founded Prague's first botanical garden in the 14th century. This is a much later institution. The university garden was founded in the Smíchov district in 1775 but moved here in 1897. The huge greenhouses date from 1938.

Special botanical exhibitions and shows of exotic birds and tropical fish are often held here. One star attraction of the gardens is the giant water lily, *Victoria cruziana*, whose huge leaves can support a small child. During the summer, it produces dozens of flowers that only survive for a day.

Entrance to the university's Botanical Gardens

The octagonal, Gothic-style steeple of the Church of St Catherine

⑰ Church of St Catherine
Kostel Sv. Kateřiny

Kateřinská 30. **Map** 5 C3. 🚊 4, 10, 16, 22. **Open** only for services. 🕇 10am Sun.

St Catherine's stands in the garden of a former convent, founded in 1354 by Charles IV to commemorate his victory at the 1332 Battle of San Felice in Italy. In 1420, during the Hussite revolution *(see pp28–9)*, the convent was demolished, but in the 16th century, it was rebuilt by Kilian Ignáz Dientzenhofer as an Augustinian monastery. The monastery closed in 1787. Since 1822, it has been used as a hospital. In 1737 a new Baroque church was built, but the slender steeple of the old Gothic church was retained. Its octagonal shape has gained it the nickname of "the Prague minaret".

⑱ Chalice Restaurant
Restaurace U Kalicha

Na bojišti 12–14. **Map** 6 D3. **Tel** 224 912 557. 🚇 IP Pavlova. 🚊 4, 6, 10, 16, 22. **Open** 11am–11pm daily (book ahead). ♿ 🆆 ukalicha.cz

This Pilsner Urquell beer hall owes its fame to the novel *The Good Soldier Švejk* by Jaroslav Hašek. It was Švejk's favourite drinking place and the establishment trades on the popularity of the best-known

character in 20th-century Czech literature. The staff dress in period costume from World War I, the era of this novel. If you receive something you didn't order, return it immediately to avoid having to pay for it.

⑲ Dvořák Museum
Muzeum Antonína Dvořáka

Ke Karlovu 20. **Map** 6 D2. **Tel** 22 49 18 013. 🚇 IP Pavlova. 🚊 4, 10, 22. 🚌 291. **Open** 10am–1:30pm & 2–5pm Tue–Sun and for concerts. 🎧 🆒 📷 🆆 nm.cz

One of the most enchanting secular buildings of the Prague Baroque now houses the Antonín Dvořák Museum. On display are Dvořák scores and editions of his works, plus photos and memorabilia of the 19th-century Czech composer, including his piano, viola and desk.

The building is by the great Baroque architect Kilian Ignaz Dientzenhofer *(see p129)*. Just two storeys high with an elegant tiered mansard roof, the house was completed in 1720 for the Michnas of Vacínov and was originally known as the Michna Summer Palace. It later became known as Villa Amerika, after a nearby inn called Amerika. Between the two pavilions flanking the house is a fine iron gateway, a replica of

the Baroque original. In the 19th century, the villa and garden fell into decay. The garden statues and vases, from the workshop of Matthias Braun, date from about 1735. They are original but heavily restored, as is the interior of the palace. The ceiling and walls of the large room on the first floor are decorated with 18th-century frescoes by Jan Ferdinand Schor.

⑳ Church of St Stephen
Kostel Sv. Štěpána

Štěpánská. **Map** 5 C2. **Tel** 221 990 200. 🚊 4, 10, 16, 22. **Open** only for services. 🕇 11am Sun. 🆒

Founded by Charles IV in 1351 as the parish church of the upper New Town, St Stephen's was finished in 1401 with the completion of the multi-spired steeple. In the late 1600s, the Branberg Chapel was built on to the north side of the church. It contains the tomb of the prolific Baroque sculptor Matthias Braun.

Most of the subsequent Baroque additions were removed when the church was scrupulously re-Gothicized in the 1870s by Josef Mocker. There are several fine Baroque paintings, however, including *The Baptism of Christ* by Karel

Baroque façade of Villa Amerika, home of the Dvořák Museum

Gothic pulpit in the Church of St Stephen

Škréta at the end of the left hand aisle and a picture of St John Nepomuk *(see p137)* by Jan Jiří Heinsch to the left of the 15th-century pulpit. The church's greatest treasure is undoubtedly a beautiful Gothic panel painting of the Madonna, known as *Our Lady of St Stephen's*, which dates from 1472.

The impressive exterior of the New Town Hall, flanked by a Gothic tower

㉑ New Town Hall
Novoměstská Radnice

Karlovo náměstí 23. **Map** 5 B1.
🚇 Karlovo náměstí. 🚋 3, 4, 6, 10, 16, 18, 22, 24. **Tel** 224 948 229. Tower:
Open Apr–Nov: 10am–6pm Tue–Sun.

In 1960, a statue of Hussite preacher Jan Želivský was unveiled in front of the New Town Hall. It commemorates the first and bloodiest of many defenestrations. On 30 July 1419, Želivský led a crowd of demonstrators to the Town Hall to demand the release of some prisoners. When they were refused, they stormed the building and threw the Catholic councillors out of the windows. Those who survived the fall were finished off with pikes.

The Town Hall already existed in the 1300s; the Gothic tower was added in the mid-15th century and contains an 18th-century chapel. In the 16th century, it acquired an arcaded courtyard. After the joining-up of the four towns of Prague in 1784, the Town Hall ceased to be the seat of the municipal administration and became a courthouse and a prison. It is now used for cultural and social events.

㉒ U Fleků

Křemencova 11. **Map** 5 B1. **Tel** 224 934 019. 🚇 Národní třída, Karlovo náměstí. 🚋 3, 4, 6, 9, 10, 16 18, 22, 24. Museum: **Open** 10am–4pm Mon–Sat. 🍴 📷 ♿ 🏠 🌐 **ufleku.cz**

Records indicate that beer was brewed here as early as 1459. This archetypal Prague beer hall has been fortunate in its owners, who have kept up the tradition of brewing as an art rather than just a means of making money. In 1762, the brewery was purchased by Jakub Flekovský, who named it U Fleků (At the Fleks). The present brewery, the smallest in Prague, makes a special strong, dark beer. There is also a small museum of Czech brewing history and a restaurant, which is popular with tourists. Note, any welcome drinks will be added to your bill.

Ornate clock outside U Fleků, a traditional beer hall

㉓ Church of St Ursula
Kostel Sv. Voršily

Národní 8. **Map** 3 A5. **Tel** 224 930 511.
🚇 Národní třída. 🚋 6, 9, 18, 22.
🕙 5pm daily. For tours, call 22 49 30 511. Concerts: 📧

The delightful Baroque church of St Ursula was built as part of an Ursuline convent founded in 1672. The original sculptures still decorate the façade and in front of the church stands a group of statues featuring St John Nepomuk (1747) by Ignaz Platzer the Elder. The light airy interior has a frescoed, stuccoed ceiling and on the various altars, there are lively Baroque paintings. The main altar has one of St Ursula.

The adjoining convent has been returned to the Ursuline order and is now a Catholic school. In the building on the right-hand side of the church is the entrance to the Institute of Endocrinology.

㉔ National Theatre

Národní Divadlo

This gold-crested theatre has always been an important symbol of the Czech cultural revival. Work started in 1868, funded largely by voluntary contributions. The original Neo-Renaissance design was by the Czech architect Josef Zítek. After its destruction by fire, Josef Schulz was given the job of rebuilding the theatre, and all the best Czech artists of the period contributed towards its spectacular decoration. During the late 1970s and early 1980s, the theatre was restored and the New Stage was built by architect Karel Prager. Further renovations have been made since.

The theatre from Marksmen's (Střelecký) Island

★ **Auditorium**
The elaborately painted ceiling is adorned with allegorical figures representing the arts by František Ženíšek.

KEY

① **The five arcades** of the loggia are decorated with lunette paintings by Josef Tulka, entitled Five Songs.

② **The New Stage auditorium**

③ **Laterna Magika**

④ **A bronze three-horse chariot**, designed by Bohuslav Schnirch, carries the Goddess of Victory.

⑤ **The startling** sky-blue roof covered with stars is said to symbolize the summit all artists should aim for.

★ **Lobby Ceiling**
This ceiling fresco is the final part of a triptych painted by František Ženíšek in 1878 depicting the *Golden Age of Czech Art*.

★ **Stage Curtain**
This sumptuous gold and red stage curtain, showing the origin of the theatre, is the work of designer Vojtěch Hynais.

VISITORS' CHECKLIST

Practical Information
Národní třída 2, Nové Město.
Map 3 A5. **Tel** 224 901 448.
Box office: **Open** 8am–6pm daily.
Auditorium: **Open** only during performances. ♿
🌐 **narodni-divadlo.cz**

Transport
Ⓜ Národní třída, line B. 🚊 6, 9, 17, 18, 22 to Národní divadlo.

Façade Decoration
This standing figure on the attic of the western façade is one of many figures representing the Arts sculpted by Antonín Wagner in 1883.

National Theatre Fire

On 12 August 1881, just days before the official opening, the National Theatre was completely gutted by fire. It was thought to have been started by metalworkers on the roof. But just six weeks later, enough money had been collected to rebuild the theatre. It was finally opened two years late in 1883 with a performance of Czech composer Bedřich Smetana's opera *Libuše (see p34)*.

The President's Box
The former royal box, lined in red velvet, is decorated with famous historical figures from Czech history by Václav Brožík.

FURTHER AFIELD

Visitors to Prague, finding the old centre packed with sights, tend to ignore the suburbs. It is true that once you start exploring away from the centre, the language can become more of a problem. However, it is well worth the effort, first to escape the crowds of tourists milling around the Castle and the Old Town Square, and second to realize that Prague is a living city as well as a picturesque time capsule. Most of the museums and other sights in the first part of this section are easily reached by Metro, tram or even on foot. If you are prepared to venture a little further, do not miss the grand palace at Troja or the monastery at Březnov – which was the first in Bohemia, founded in 993, and later rebuilt in Baroque style. The Day Trips *(pp168–71)* include visits to castles close to Prague and the historic spa towns of Marienbad and Karlsbad, which attracted the first tourists to Bohemia during the 19th century.

Sights at a Glance

Museums and Galleries
- ⑤ Prague Museum
- ⑦ National Technical Museum
- ⑧ *Trade Fair Palace pp164–5*
- ⑬ Villa Müller

Monasteries
- ⑭ Březnov Monastery

Cemeteries
- ② Olšany Cemeteries

Historic Districts
- ① Vyšehrad
- ③ Žižkov
- ④ Náměstí Míru

Historic Sites
- ⑮ White Mountain and Star Hunting Lodge

Historic Buildings
- ⑩ *Troja Palace pp166–7*

Parks and Gardens
- ⑥ Letná Park

- ⑨ Exhibition Ground and Stromovka Park
- ⑪ Prague Zoo
- ⑫ Prague Botanical Gardens

Key

▨	Central Prague
▢	Greater Prague
▬	Major road
═	Minor road
⹀	Tunnel

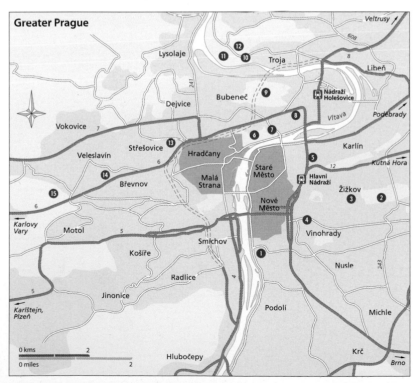

Greater Prague

◀ A view of the splendid Imperial Hall in Troja Palace

For keys to symbols *see back flap*

Vyšehrad Cemetery, where some of Prague's most famous figures are buried

❶ Vyšehrad

Map 5 B5. 🅜 Vyšehrad. 🚋 3, 6, 7, 17, 18, 24. Vyšehrad Cemetery: **Open** 8am–6pm daily (May–Sep: to 7pm, Nov–Feb: to 5pm).Basilica of St Peter and St Paul: **Open** 10am–6pm daily (Sep–Mar: to 4pm). 🚏 Rotunda of St Martin: **Open** by appt (Tel: 22 49 11 353). 🆆 **praha-vysehrad.cz**

A rocky outcrop above the Vltava, Vyšehrad means "castle on the heights" *(see pp180–81)*. It was fortified in the 10th century and, at times, used as the seat of the Přemyslid princes *(see pp22–3)*. The area has great historical and mythological significance, and in the 1870s, it became the site of a national cemetery. Many luminaries of Czech culture are buried here, including the composers Antonín Dvořák *(see p154)* and Bedřich Smetana *(see p81)*, who paid tribute to the second seat of the Přemyslid dynasty in his opera *Libuše (see p34)*. Each year, a service is held at Smetana's grave to mark the beginning of the Prague Spring International Music Festival *(see p52)*.

Within the walls of Vyšehrad are many fascinating sights, such as the huge twin-spired Basilica of St Peter and St Paul, the 11th-century Rotunda of St Martin, the mysterious Devil's Column and the castle walls themselves *(see pp180–81)*. From these walls, there are superb views over the Vltava river and across Prague.

The streets around the fortress feature some fine Cubist houses, on Rašínovo nábřeží, Libušina and the corner of Přemyslova and Neklanova.

❷ Olšany Cemeteries

Olšanské Hřbitovy

Vinohradská 153, Jana Želivského. **Tel** 26 73 10 652. 🅜 Želivského. 🚋 5, 10, 11, 13, 16. **Open** Mar, Apr & Oct: 8am–6pm daily; May–Sep: 8am–7pm daily; Nov–Feb: 8am–5pm daily.

At the northwest corner of the main cemetery stands the small Church of St Roch (1682), protector against the plague – the first cemetery was founded here in 1679 specifically for the burial of plague victims. In the course of the 19th century, the old cemetery was enlarged and new ones developed, including a Russian cemetery,

Grave in the Olšany Cemeteries

distinguished by its old-fashioned Orthodox church (1924–5), and a Jewish cemetery, where Franz Kafka *(see p70)* is buried. Tombs include those of painter Josef Mánes (1820–71) who worked during the Czech Revival movement *(see pp34–5)*, and Josef Jungmann (1773–1847), compiler of a five-volume Czech–German dictionary.

Equestrian statue in Žižkov of Jan Žižka, leader of the Hussites at the battle of Vítkov

❸ Žižkov

🅜 Florenc. National Memorial Vítkov, U památníku 1900. **Tel** 222 781 676. 🚌 133, 175. **Open** 10am–6pm Wed–Sun. 🚏 🖥 🆆 **nm.cz** Žižkov Television Tower: **Open** 8am–midnight daily. 🚏 🅿 ⬧ 🖥 📷 🆆 **towerpark.cz**

This quarter of Prague was the scene of a historic victory for the Hussites *(see pp28–9)* over Crusaders sent by the Emperor Sigismund to destroy them. On 14 July 1420 on Vítkov hill, a tiny force of Hussites defeated an army of several thousand well-armed men. The determined, hymn-singing Hussites were led by the one-eyed Jan Žižka.

In 1877, the area around Vítkov was renamed Žižkov in honour of Žižka's victory, and in 1950, a bronze equestrian statue of Žižka by Bohumil Kafka was erected on the hill. About 9 m (30 ft) high, this is the largest equestrian statue in the world. It stands in front of the National Memorial, built in 1928–38 in honour of the Czechoslovak legionaries, and rebuilt and extended after World War II. The building now houses a branch of the National Museum *(see p147)*, a permanent exhibition on Czechoslovak history.

Relief by Josef Myslbek on the portal of St Ludmilla in Náměstí Míru

Žižkov's main landmark is the nearby television transmitter, at 216 m (709 ft) the city's tallest building. Ten giant sculptures of babies by Czech artist David Černý crawl on its outside.

❹ Náměstí Míru

Map 6 F2. 🚇 Náměstí Míru. 🚊 4, 10, 16, 22. 🚌 135. Church of St Ludmila:
Open Apr–Sep: 9am–4pm Mon–Sat, noon–4pm Sun. 🚪 4:30pm daily, 9am, 11am & 4:30pm Sun.
🌐 **ludmilavinohrady.cz**

This attractive square, with a well-kept central garden, is the focal point of the mostly residential Vinohrady quarter. At the top of its sloping lawns stands the attractive, brick Neo-Gothic Church of St Ludmila (1888–93), designed by Josef Mocker, architect of the west end of St Vitus's Cathedral *(see pp102–105)*. Its twin octagonal spires are 60 m (200 ft) high. On the tympanum of the main portal is a relief of Christ with St Wenceslas and St Ludmila by the great 19th-century sculptor Josef Myslbek. Leading artists also contributed designs for the stained-glass windows.

The outside of the square is lined with attractive buildings, including the Vinohrady Theatre *(see p219)*, a spirited Art Nouveau building completed in 1907. The façade is crowned by two huge winged figures sculpted by Milan Havlíček, symbolizing Drama and Opera.

❺ Prague Museum

Muzeum Hlavního Města Prahy

Na Poříčí 52. **Map** 4 F3. **Tel** 22 48 16 773. 🚇 Florenc. 🚊 3, 8. **Open** 9am–6pm Tue–Sun. 🚗
🌐 **muzeumprahy.cz**

The collection records the history of Prague from primeval times. A new museum was built to house the exhibits in the 1890s. Its Neo-Renaissance façade is rich with stucco and sculptures, and the interior walls are painted with historic views of the city. Some of the impressive items on display include examples of Prague china and furniture, relics of the medieval guilds and paintings of Prague through the ages. The most remarkable exhibit is the paper and wood model of Prague by Antonín Langweil. Completed in 1834, it covers 20 sq m (25 sq yards). The scale of the extraordinarily accurate model is 1:500.

❻ Letná Park

Letenské Sady

Map 3 A1. 🚇 Malostranská, Hradčanská. 🚊 1, 5, 8, 12, 17, 18, 20, 22, 25, 26.

Across the river from the Jewish Quarter, a large plateau overlooks the city. It was here that armies gathered before attacking Prague Castle. Since the mid-19th century, it has been a wooded park.

On the terrace at the top of the granite steps that lead up from the embankment stands a curious monument – a giant metronome built in 1991. It was installed after the Velvet Revolution on the pedestal formerly occupied by the gigantic stone statue of Stalin leading the people, which was blown up in 1962. A far more durable monument is the Hanavský Pavilion, a Neo-Baroque cast iron structure, built for the 1891 Exhibition. It was later dismantled and erected on its present site in the park, where it houses a popular restaurant and café. The park has a popular beer garden in summer at its eastern end.

A handsome wooden pavilion in Letná Park

7 National Technical Museum
Národní Technické Muzeum

Kostelní 42. **Tel** 220 399 111. 🚊 1, 8, 12, 17, 24, 25, 26. **Open** 9am–5:30pm Mon–Fri, 10am–6pm Sat & Sun. 🖼 📷 🚻 ♿ **W** ntm.cz

Though it tries to keep abreast of all scientific developments, the museum's strength is its collection of machines from the Industrial Revolution to the present day, one of the largest in Europe. The section on the History of Transportation is filled with locomotives, railway carriages, bicycles, motorcars and motorcycles, with aeroplanes and a hot-air balloon suspended overhead.

The photography and cinematography section is well worth a visit, as is the collection of astronomical instruments. The section on measuring time is also popular, especially on the hour, when everything starts to chime at once. In the basement, there is a huge reconstruction of a coal mine, with tools tracing the development of mining from the 15th to the 19th century. The museum also features exhibitions on the history of printing, architecture and civil engineering.

8 Trade Fair Palace
Veletržní palác

See pp164–5.

9 Exhibition Ground and Stromovka Park
Výstaviště a Stromovka

🚊 12, 17, 24. Exhibition Ground: **Open** 10am–11pm daily. 🚻 📷 Stromovka Park: **Open** 24hrs daily. Lapidarium: **Tel** 724 412 257. **Open** 10am–4pm Wed, noon–6pm Thu–Sun. ♿ **W** nm.cz

Laid out for the Jubilee of 1891, with the Art Nouveau Industrial Palace as its centrepiece, the Exhibition Ground has a lively funfair and is great for a family day out. All kinds of exhibitions, sporting events and concerts

The Elephant Valley pavilion at Prague Zoo

are staged in summer. The large park to the west was the former royal hunting enclosure and deer park, first established in the late 16th century. The name Stromovka means "place of trees". Opened to the public in 1804, the park is still an ideal place for a walk. The Lapidarium holds an exhibition of 11th- to 19th-century sculpture, including some originals from Charles Bridge *(see pp136–9)*. On display are decorated windows, spouts, fountains, groups of statues and memorials.

10 Troja Palace
Trojský Zámek

See pp166–7.

11 Prague Zoo
Zoologická Zahrada

U trojského zámku 3/120. **Tel** 29 61 12 230. Ⓜ Holešovice, then 🚌 112. **Open** Jun–Aug: 9am–9pm daily; Apr, May, Sep, Oct: 9am–6pm daily; Nov–Feb: 9am–4pm daily; Mar: 9am–5pm daily. 🚻 ♿ 📷 **W** zoopraha.cz

Attractively situated on a rocky slope overlooking the right bank of the Vltava, the zoo was founded in 1924. The second most popular attraction in the

country, after Prague Castle, it now covers an area of 58 hectares (143 acres), and there is a chair lift to take visitors to the upper part.

The zoo houses almost 5,000 animals, representing close to 700 species, 50 of them extremely rare in the wild. It is best known for its breeding programme of Przewalski's horses, the only species of wild horse in the world. In addition, there are 12 pavilions, including Elephant Valley, Hippo House, Lemur Island, Bird Outlands and a Children's Zoo.

12 Prague Botanical Gardens
Botanická Zahrada Troja

Nádvorní 134. **Tel** 234 148 111. Ⓜ Holešovice, then 🚌 112. **Open** 9am–8pm daily (Apr: to 6pm; Nov–Feb: to 4pm; Mar & Oct: to 5pm). **Closed** Tropical greenhouse: Mon. 🚻 ♿ **W** botanicka.cz

The Troja Botanical Gardens are a short walk from the zoo. Visitors can enjoy a large tropical greenhouse, Japanese gardens, open-air exhibitions, and an impressive park. There is also a National Heritage vineyard and chapel on-site.

⑬ Villa Müller
Müllerova Vila

Nad Hradním vodojemem 14.
🚇 Hradčanská, then 🚋 1, 18 to Ořechovka. 🅿️ ⏰ Tue, Thu, Sat & Sun: 9am, 11am, 1pm, 3pm & 5pm; reservations needed (Tel: 224 312 012). 🌐 **muzeumprahy.cz**

A severe, white concrete façade, asymmetric windows and a flat roof characterize the Villa Müller. It was designed by Modernist architect Adolf Loos and built in 1928–30 by construction entrepreneur František Müller for himself and his wife Milada, who were leading lights of Czech society at that time. Loos used his innovative spatial theory known as "Raumplan" in the design of both the outside and the inside of the building, so that all the spaces look and feel interconnected. The roof terrace at the top of the house provides a "framed" view of Prague cathedral in the distance.

In contrast to the building's functional exterior, the interiors combine traditional furnishings with vibrant use of marble, wood and silk. The villa fell into disrepair during the 1950s, and in 1995, ownership passed to the city of Prague. A programme of restoration took place between 1997 and 2000, when it was opened to the public as a National Cultural Monument.

⑭ Břevnov Monastery
Břevnovský Klášter

Markétská 28. **Tel** 220 406 111. 🚋 22, 25. ⏰ only. On request Mon–Fri (call 220 406 270); 10am, 2pm Sat & Sun; also 4pm Apr–Oct. 🅿️ 📷 🌐 **brevnov.cz**

From the surrounding suburban housing, you would never guess that Břevnov is one of the oldest parts of Prague. A flourishing community grew up here around the Benedictine abbey founded in 993 by Prince Boleslav II *(see p22)* and Bishop Adalbert (Vojtěch) – the first monastery in Bohemia. An ancient well called Vojtěška marks the spot where prince and bishop are said to have met and decided to found the monastery.

The gateway, courtyard and most of the present monastery buildings are by the great Baroque architects Christoph and Kilian Ignaz Dientzenhofer *(see p129)*. The monastery Church of St Margaret was completed in 1715, and is based on a floorplan of overlapping ovals, as ingenious as any of Bernini's churches in Rome. In 1964, the crypt of the original 10th-century church was discovered below the choir and is open to the public. Of the other buildings, the most interesting is the Theresian Hall, with a painted ceiling dating from 1727.

The 16th-century Star Hunting Lodge in its peaceful surroundings

⑮ White Mountain and Star Hunting Lodge
Bílá Hora a Hvězda

Obora Hvězda. 🚇 Petřiny. 🚋 1, 18, 22, 25. Obora Hvězda (game park): **Open** 24hrs daily. Summer House Hvězda: **Tel** 220 612 230. **Open** May–Sep: 10am–6pm Tue–Sun. 🅿️ 📷

The Battle of the White Mountain *(see p33)*, fought on 8 November 1620, had a very different impact for the two main communities of Prague. For the Protestants, it was a disaster that led to 300 years of Habsburg domination; for the Catholic supporters of the Habsburgs, it was a triumph, so they built a memorial chapel on the hill. In the early 1700s, this chapel was converted into the grander Church of Our Lady Victorious and decorated by leading Baroque artists, including Václav Vavřinec Reiner.

In the 16th century, the woodland around the battle site had been a royal game park. The hunting lodge, completed in 1556, survives today. This fascinating building is shaped as a six-pointed star – *hvězda* means star. On site is a small exhibition about the building and its history. Also on show are exhibits relating to the Battle of the White Mountain and temporary exhibitions about Czech culture.

Modernist Villa Müller, seen from the garden

❽ Trade Fair Palace

Veletržní Palác

The National Gallery in Prague opened its museum of
20th- and 21st-century art in 1995, housed in a reconstruction
of a former Trade Fair building of 1929. Since 2000, it has also
housed a 19th-century collection. Its vast, skylit spaces make
an ideal backdrop for the paintings, which range from French
19th-century art and superb examples of Impressionism and
Post-Impressionism, to works by Munch, Klimt, Picasso and
Miró, as well as a splendid collection of Czech modern
art. The collection is subject to rearrangement
so the location of artworks may change.

Grand Meal (1951–5)
Mikuláš Medek's works range
from post-war Surrealism
to 1960s Abstraction.

Fourth Floor

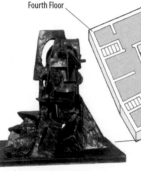

Cubist Bust (1913–14)
Otto Gutfreund was one of the first
artists to apply the principles of Cubism
to sculpture, and this work marks his
move towards abstract art.

Third
Floor

Cleopatra (1942–57)
This painting by Jan Zrzavý, a major
representative of Czech modern art,
took the artist 45 years to complete
and is his best-known piece.

St Sebastian (1912)
This self-portrait by Bohumil
Kubišta takes its inspiration
from the martyrdom of St
Sebastian, who was persecuted
by being bound to a tree and
shot with arrows.

Pomona (1910)
Aristide Maillol was a pupil of
Rodin. This work is part of an
exceptional collection of bronzes.

Key

☐ Czech Art 1900–1930
☐ 19th- and 20th-century French Art
☐ Czech Art 1930–present day
☐ 20th-century Foreign Art
☐ Temporary exhibition space
☐ Non-exhibition space

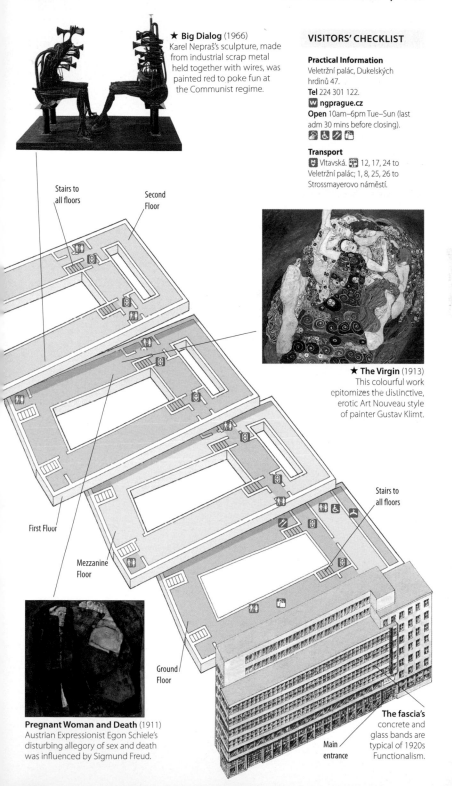

★ **Big Dialog** (1966)
Karel Nepraš's sculpture, made from industrial scrap metal held together with wires, was painted red to poke fun at the Communist regime.

VISITORS' CHECKLIST

Practical Information
Veletržní palác, Dukelských hrdinů 47.
Tel 224 301 122.
W **ngprague.cz**
Open 10am–6pm Tue–Sun (last adm 30 mins before closing).

Transport
Vltavská. 12, 17, 24 to Veletržní palác; 1, 8, 25, 26 to Strossmayerovo náměstí.

Stairs to all floors

Second Floor

★ **The Virgin** (1913)
This colourful work epitomizes the distinctive, erotic Art Nouveau style of painter Gustav Klimt.

First Floor

Stairs to all floors

Mezzanine Floor

Ground Floor

Pregnant Woman and Death (1911)
Austrian Expressionist Egon Schiele's disturbing allegory of sex and death was influenced by Sigmund Freud.

Main entrance

The fascia's concrete and glass bands are typical of 1920s Functionalism.

⑩ Troja Palace

Trojský Zámek

One of the most striking summer palaces in Prague, Troja was built in the late 17th century by Jean-Baptiste Mathey for Count Sternberg, a member of a leading Bohemian aristocratic family. Situated at the foot of the Vltava Heights, the exterior of the palace was modelled on a Classical Italian villa, while its garden was laid out in formal French style. The magnificent interior took over 20 years to complete and is full of extravagant frescoes expressing the Sternberg family's loyalty to the Habsburg dynasty. Troja houses a good collection of 19th-century art.

Terracotta urn on the garden balustrade of Troja Palace

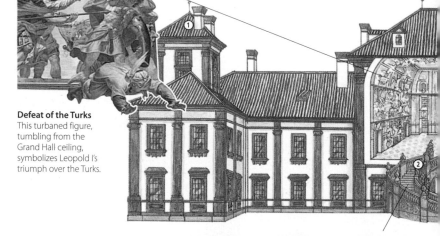

Defeat of the Turks
This turbaned figure, tumbling from the Grand Hall ceiling, symbolizes Leopold I's triumph over the Turks.

★ Garden Staircase
The two sons of Mother Earth which adorn the sweeping oval staircase (1685–1703) are part of a group of sculptures by Johann Georg Heermann and his nephew Paul, depicting the struggle of the Olympian Gods with the Titans.

KEY

① Belvedere turret

② Statue of Olympian God

③ Statues of sons of Mother Earth

④ **Chinese Rooms** feature 18th-century murals of Chinese scenes. This room makes a perfect backdrop for a ceramics display.

⑤ Stucco decoration

VISITORS' CHECKLIST

Practical Information
U trojského zámku 1, Prague 7.
Tel 283 851 614.
W **ghmp.cz**
Open Apr–Oct: 10am–6pm Tue–
Thu, Sat & Sun, 1–6pm Fri.

Transport
see p57. Holešovice,
then 112.

★ **Grand Hall Fresco**
The frescoes in the Grand Hall
(1691–7), by Abraham Godyn,
depict the story of the first
Habsburg Emperor, Rudolph I, and
the victories of Leopold I over the
archenemy of Christianity, the
Sublime Porte (Ottoman Empire).

**Personification
of Justice**
Abraham Godyn's
image of Justice gazes
from the lower east wall
of the Grand Hall.

★ **Landscaped Gardens**

Sloping vineyards were levelled,
hillsides excavated and terraces
built to fulfil the elaborate and
grandiose plans of French
architect, Jean-Baptiste Mathey,
for the first Baroque French-style
formal gardens in Bohemia.
The palace and its geometric
network of paths, terracing,
fountains, statuary and beautiful
terracotta vases, is best viewed
from the south of the garden
between the two orangeries.
The gardens have been carefully
restored according to Mathey's
original plans.

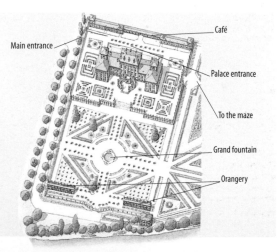

Café

Main entrance

Palace entrance

To the maze

Grand fountain

Orangery

Day Trips from Prague

The sights that attract most visitors away from the city are Bohemia's picturesque medieval castles. Karlštejn, for example, stands in splendid isolation above wooded valleys that have changed little since the Emperor Charles IV hunted there in the 14th century. We have chosen four castles, very varied in character. There are regular organized tours *(see p225)* to the major sights around Prague, to the historic mining town of Kutná Hora and, if you have more time to spare, to the famous spa towns of Karlsbad and Marienbad in western Bohemia.

Sights at a Glance

Castles
❶ Veltrusy
❷ Karlštejn
❸ Konopiště
❹ Křivoklát

Historic Towns
❺ Kutná Hora
❻ Karlsbad
❼ Marienbad

Key

≈ Motorway
▬ Major road
≈ Minor road

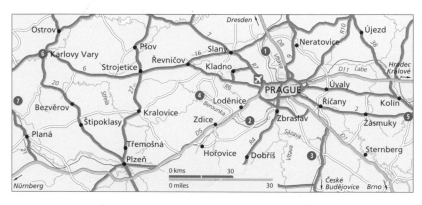

❶ Veltrusy Château

Veltruský Zámek

20 km (12 miles) N of Prague. **Tel** 315 781 146. 🚉 from Masarykovo to Kralupy nad Vltavou, then bus. **Open** Apr: 8:30am–5pm Sat & Sun (last tour 4pm); May–Oct: 8:30am–5pm Tue–Sun (Jun–Aug: to 7pm; last tour 4pm). 🅿 🛈 🛒 ♿ 🖥 **zamek-veltrusy.cz** Park: **Open** dawn to nightfall daily. Nelahozeves Castle: **Tel** 315 709 111. 🚉 from Masarykovo to Nelahozeves – zámek. **Open** Apr–Oct: 9am–5pm Tue–Sun. 🅿 🛈 🛒 🖼
🖥 **zamek-nelahozeves.cz**

Veltrusy is a small town beside the Vltava, famous for the 18th-century château built by the aristocratic Chotek family. The building is in the shape of a cross, with a central dome and a staircase adorned with statues representing the months of the year and the seasons.

The estate was laid out as an English-style landscaped deer park, covering an area of 300 hectares (750 acres). Near the entrance, there is still an enclosure with a herd of deer. The Vltava flows along one side and

dotted around the grounds are summer houses.

The Doric and Maria Theresa pavilions, the orangery and the grotto date from the late 18th century. The park is planted with some 100 different kinds of tree.

Across the river, and accessible from Veltrusy by bus or train, is **Nelahozeves Castle**. This Renaissance castle houses an exhibition entitled "Private Spaces: A Noble Family At

Home", depicting the life of the Lobkowicz family over five centuries. Some 12 rooms have been fitted out with period furnishings. On display in the library are the family archives. The family's art treasures are housed in Lobkowicz Palace *(see p101)*. The birthplace of Czech composer Antonín Dvořák is nearby.

Every year, Nelahozeves hosts a popular classical music festival, Dvořákova Nelahozeves.

Karlštejn Castle, built by Emperor Charles IV in the 14th century

❷ Karlštejn Castle

25 km (16 miles) SW of Prague. **Tel** 311 681 617. 🚊 from Smíchov or Hlavní nádraží to Karlštejn (1.5 km/1 mile from castle. The uphill walk takes around 40 minutes). **Open** late Jul–early Jan: days and times vary; call to check. Chapel of the Holy Rood: May–Oct: Tue–Sun (Jul & Aug: daily). 🎟️ 📷 compulsory (book in advance). 📧
🌐 **hradkarlstejn.cz**

The castle was founded by Charles IV as a country retreat, a treasury for the crown jewels and a symbol of his divine right to rule the Holy Roman Empire. It stands on a crag above the River Berounka. The castle is largely a 19th-century reconstruction by Josef Mocker. The original building work (1348–67) was supervised by French master mason Matthew of Arras, and then by Peter Parler. You can still see the audience hall and the bedchamber of Charles IV in the Imperial Palace. On the third floor, the Emperor's quarters are below those of the Empress.

The central tower houses the Church of Our Lady, decorated with faded 14th-century wall paintings. A narrow passage leads to the tiny Chapel of St Catherine, the walls of which are adorned with semi-precious stones set into the plaster.

❸ Konopiště Castle

40 km (25 miles) SE of Prague. **Tel** 317 721 366. 🚊 from Hlavní nádraží to Benešov, then local bus. **Open** Apr–Nov: 10am–noon & 1–4pm Tue–Sun (Jun–Aug: to 5pm; Oct & Nov: to 3pm). 🎟️ 📷 📧 ✏️ 🏠
🌐 **zamek-konopiste.cz**

Though it dates back to the 13th century, this moated castle is essentially a late 19th-century creation. In between, Konopiště had been rebuilt by Baroque architect František Kaňka and in front of the bridge across the moat is a gate (1725) by Kaňka and sculptor Matthias Braun.

In 1887, Konopiště was bought by Archduke Franz Ferdinand, who later became heir to the Austrian throne. It was his assassination in 1914 in

View of the castle at Křivoklát, dominated by the Great Tower

Sarajevo that triggered off World War I. To escape the Habsburg court's disapproval of his wife, he spent much of his time at Konopiště and amassed arms, armour and Meissen porcelain, all on display in the fine furnished interiors. However, the abiding memory of the castle is of the hundreds of stags' heads lining the walls.

The many hunting trophies lining the walls at Konopiště Castle

❹ Křivoklát Castle

45 km (28 miles) W of Prague. **Tel** 313 558 440. 🚊 from Hlavní nádraží via Beroun or from Masarykovo nádraží via Rakovník (1 km/0.6 miles) from castle). **Open** Jul & Aug: 9am–6pm daily; Apr & Oct: 10am–4pm Tue–Sun; May, Jun & Sep 9am–5pm Tue–Sun; Nov: 11am–3pm Sat & Sun.
🎟️ 📷 📧 🏠 🌐 **krivoklat.cz**

This castle, like Karlštejn, owes its appearance to the restoration work of Josef

Mocker. It was originally a hunting lodge belonging to the early Přemyslid princes and the seat of the royal master of hounds. In the 13th century, King Wenceslas I built a stone castle here, which remained in the hands of Bohemia's kings and the Habsburg emperors until the 17th century.

Charles IV spent some of his childhood here and returned from France in 1334 with his first wife Blanche de Valois. Their daughter Margaret was born in the castle. To amuse his queen and young princess, Charles ordered the local villagers to trap nightingales and set them free in a wooded area just below the castle. Today, you can still walk along the "Nightingale Path".

The royal palace is on the eastern side of the triangular castle. This corner is dominated by the Great Tower, 42 m (130 ft) high. You can still see some 13th-century stonework, but most of the palace dates from the reign of Vladislav Jagiello. On the first floor there is a vaulted Gothic hall, reminiscent of the Vladislav Hall in the Old Royal Palace at Prague Castle (see pp106–107). It has an oriel window and a beautiful loggia, and the chapel has a finely carved Gothic altar. Below the chapel, the Augusta Prison is named for Bishop Jan Augusta of the Bohemian Brethren, imprisoned here in the mid-16th century. The dungeon now houses a grim assortment of torture instruments.

❺ Kutná Hora

70 km (45 miles) E of Prague. **Tel** 327 512 378 (tourist information). 🚆 from Hlavní nádraží, to Kutná Hora, then bus 1 to Kutná Hora-Město. 🚌 from Florenc. **W kutnahora.cz** Italian Court: **Open** Mar & Oct: 10am–5pm; Apr–Sep: 9am–6pm; Nov–Feb: 10am–4pm daily. 🎭 🎫 Hrádek: **Open** Apr & Oct: 9am–5pm Tue–Sun; May, Jun & Sep: 9am–6pm Tue–Sun; Jul & Aug: 10am–6pm Tue–Sun; Nov: 10am–4pm Tue–Sun. 🎭 🎫 Stone House: **Open** as Hrádek. 🎭 🎫 Cathedral of St Barbara: **Open** Apr–Oct: 9am–6pm daily; Mar, Nov & Dec: 10am–5pm daily; Jan & Feb: 10am–4pm daily. 🎭 🎫

The town originated as a small mining community in the second half of the 13th century. When rich deposits of silver were found, the king took over the licensing of the mines and Kutná Hora became the second most important town in Bohemia.

In the 14th century, five to six tonnes of pure silver were extracted here each year, making the king the richest ruler in Central Europe. The Prague *groschen*, a silver coin that circulated all over Europe, was minted here in the Italian Court (Vlašský; dvůr), so-called because Florentine experts were employed to set up the mint. Strongly fortified, it was also the ruler's seat in the town. In the late 14th century, a

superb palace with reception halls and the Chapel of St Wenceslas and St Ladislav, below which lay the royal treasury, were constructed.

When the silver started to run out in the 16th century, the town began to lose its importance; the mint finally closed in 1727. The Italian Court later became the town hall. On the ground floor, you can still see a row of forges. Since 1947, a mining museum has been housed in another building, the Hrádek, which was originally a fort. A visit includes a tour of a medieval mine. There is museum in the Stone House (Kamenný dům), a restored Gothic building of the late 15th century.

To the southwest of the town stands the Cathedral of St Barbara, begun in 1380 by the workshop of Peter Parler, also the architect of St Vitus's Cathedral *(see pp102–105)*. The presbytery (1499) has a fine net vault and windows with intricate tracery. The slightly later nave vault is by royal architect Benedikt Ried. The murals show mining scenes. The cathedral, with its three massive and tent-shaped spires rising above a forest of

The Italian Court, Kutná Hora's first mint

flying buttresses, is a wonderful example of Bohemian Gothic.

In Sedlec, a suburb of Kutná Hora, is the Ossuary of All Saints church, where thousands of human bones have been fashioned into furnishings and decorative objects.

❻ Karlsbad

Karlovy Vary

140 km (85 miles) W of Prague. **Tel** 355 321 171. 🚆 from Hlavní nádraží. 🚌 from Florenc. 🛈 Lázeňská 14 (355 321 176). **W karlovyvary.cz**

Legend has it that Charles IV *(see pp26–7)* discovered one of the sources of mineral water that would make the town's fortune when one of his stag-hounds fell into a hot spring. In 1522, a medical description of the springs was published, and by the end of the 16th century, over 200 spa buildings had been built there. Today, there are 12 hot mineral springs – *vary* means hot springs. The best-known is the Vřídlo, which rises to a height of 12 m (40 ft). At 72°C, it is also the hottest. The water is good for digestive disorders, but you do not have to drink it; you can take the minerals in the form of salts.

The town is also known for its production of decorated Karlovy Vary china and brightly-coloured Moser glass, and for

The Bohemian Gothic Cathedral of St Barbara in Kutná Hora

summer concerts and other cultural events, including an international film festival in early June. As one of Europe's leading film events, it attracts a host of international stars.

Outstanding among the local historic monuments is the Baroque parish church of Mary Magdalene by Kilian Ignaz Dientzenhofer (1732–6). More modern churches built for foreign visitors include a Russian church (1896) and an Anglican one (1877). The 19th-century Mill Colonnade (Mlýnská kolonáda) is by Josef Zítek, architect of the National Theatre *(see pp156–7)* in Prague.

❼ Marienbad

Mariánské Lázně

170 km (105 miles) W of Prague.
🚉 from Hlavní nádraží. 🚌 from Florenc. ℹ️ Hlavní 47 (354 622 474).
🌐 **marianskelazne.cz**

This delightful spa town lost in the forests of West Bohemia once drew royalty and celebrities to its elegant parks and spa houses. The area's health-giving waters – *lázně* means bath (or spa) – have been known since the 16th century, but the spa was not founded until the beginning of the 19th century. The waters are used to treat all kinds of disorders; mud baths are also popular.

Most of the spa buildings date from the latter half of the 19th century. The great cast-iron colonnade with frescoes by Josef

Bronze statue of a chamois at Jelení skok (Stag's Leap), Karlsbad

Vylet'al is still an impressive sight. In front of it is a "singing fountain", its jets of water now controlled by computer. Churches were provided for visitors of all denominations, including an Evangelical church (1857), an Anglican church (1879) and the Russian Orthodox church of St Vladimír (1902). Visitors can learn the history of the spa in the house called At the Golden Grape (U zlatého hroznu), where

the German poet Johann Wolfgang von Goethe stayed in 1823. Musical visitors during the 19th century included the composers Weber, Wagner and Bruckner, while writers such as Ibsen, Gogol, Mark Twain and Rudyard Kipling also found its treatments beneficial. King Edward VII also came here and in 1905 he agreed to open the golf course (Bohemia's first), despite hating the game.

The cast-iron colonnade at Marienbad, completed in 1889

FOUR GUIDED WALKS

Prague offers some good opportunities for walking. In the centre of the city, many streets are pedestrianized and the most important sights are confined to quite a small area *(see pp16–17)*. Here are four guided walks of varied character. The first passes through a main artery of the city, from the Powder Gate on the outskirts of the Old Town to St Vitus's Cathedral in Prague Castle, crossing Charles Bridge at its mid-point. This is the Royal Coronation Route, followed for centuries by Bohemian kings. Away from the busy centre, the second and third of the walks take in the peace and tranquillity of two of Prague's loveliest parks – Petřín and the Royal Enclosure. Petřín Park is rewarding for its spectacular views of the city. The Royal Enclosure is outside the centre in the old royal hunting park. The final walk is in Vyšehrad – an ancient fortress, steeped in history and atmosphere. The views from Vyšehrad of the Vltava and Prague Castle are unparalleled.

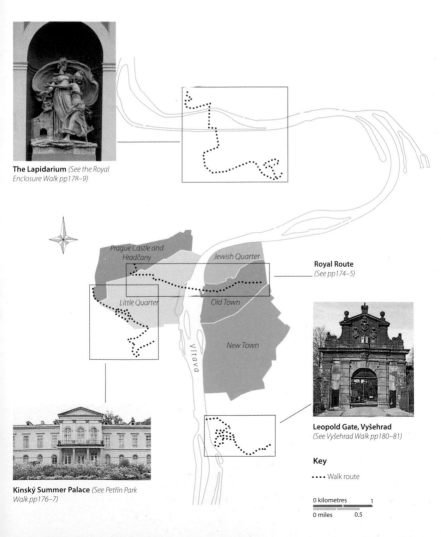

The Lapidarium *(See the Royal Enclosure Walk pp178–9)*

Prague Castle and Hradčany

Jewish Quarter

Royal Route
(See pp174–5)

Little Quarter

Old Town

New Town

Vltava

Leopold Gate, Vyšehrad
(See Vyšehrad Walk pp180–81)

Key

•••• Walk route

0 kilometres 1

0 miles 0.5

Kinský Summer Palace *(See Petřín Park Walk pp176–7)*

◀ View of Old Town Square, bustling with tourists

A Two-Hour Walk along the Royal Route

The Royal Route originally linked two important royal seats: the Royal Court – on the site of the Municipal House and where the walk starts – and Prague Castle, where the walk finishes. The name of this walk derives from the coronation processions of the Bohemian kings and queens who passed along it. Today, these narrow streets offer a wealth of historical and architecturally interesting sights, shops and cafés, making the walk one of Prague's most popular. For more details on the Old Town, the Little Quarter and Hradčany turn to *pages 62–81, 122–41* and *96–121* respectively.

Figural *sgraffito* covers the façade of the Renaissance House At the Minute

History of the Royal Route

The first major coronation procession to travel along this route was for George of Poděbrady *(see p28)* in 1458. The next large procession took place in 1743, when Maria Theresa was crowned with great pomp – three Turkish pavilions were erected just outside the Powder Gate. September 1791 saw the coronation of Leopold II. This procession was led by cavalry, followed by mounted drummers, trumpeters and soldiers and Bohemian lords. Some 80 carriages came next, carrying princes and bishops. The most splendid were each drawn by six pairs of horses, flanked by servants with red coats and white leather trousers, and carried the ladies-in-waiting. The last great coronation procession along the Royal Route – for Ferdinand V – was in 1836 with over 3,391 horses and four camels.

From the Powder Gate to Old Town Square

At Náměstí Republiky, turn towards the Municipal House *(see p66)* and walk under the Gothic Powder Gate ① *(see p66)*. Here, at the city gates, the monarch and a large retinue of church dignitaries, aristocrats and foreign ambassadors were warmly welcomed by leading city represen-tatives. The gate leads into one of Prague's oldest streets, Celetná *(see p67)*. It was here the Jewish community and the crafts guilds, carrying their insignia, greeted their king. The street is lined with Baroque and Rococo houses. At house No. 36 was the Mint ②. It moved here after the

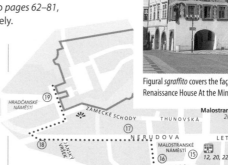

③ House of the Black Madonna

mint at Kutná Hora *(see p170)* was occupied by Catholic troops in the Hussite Wars *(see pp28–9)*. It minted coins from 1420 to 1784. The House of the Black Madonna ③ is a product of Cubist architecture. Revellers would watch processions from the taverns At the Spider ④ and At the Vulture ⑤.

At the end of Celetná Street is the Old Town Square ⑥ *(see pp68–71)*. Here, the processions halted beside Church of Our Lady before Týn ⑦ *(see p72)* for pledges of loyalty from the

⑪ The distinct Baroque façade of the House At the Golden Well in Karlova Street

university. Keep to the left of the square, past No. 17, At the Unicorn ⑧, then No. 20, Smetana House, where the composer began a music school in 1848. Proceed to the Old Town Hall ⑨ (*see pp74–6*). Here, the municipal guard and a band waited for the royal procession and city dignitaries cheered from the temporary balcony around the hall.

Along Karlova Street and across Charles Bridge

Walk past the sgraffitoed façade of the House at the Minute and into Malé náměstí ⑩, where merchants waited with members of the various religious orders. Bear left off the square, then turn right into gallery-filled Karlova Street.

was considered to be a good omen. But only a few months later, he died. Walk under the Old Town Bridge Tower ⑫ and over Charles Bridge ⑬ and then under the Little Quarter Towers ⑭ (*see pp136–9*).

The Little Quarter

The walk now follows Mostecká Street. On entering the Little Quarter, the mayor handed the city keys to the king and the artillery fired a salute. At the end of this street is Little Quarter Square ⑮ (*see p127*) and the Baroque Church of St Nicholas ⑯ (*see pp128–9*). The procession passed the church to the sound of its bells.

Leave this picturesque square by Nerudova Street ⑰

The route ends at the Castle's Matthias Gate ⑲. The procession ended with the coronation held at St Vitus's Cathedral.

A decorative house sign in Celetná Street

Beyond Husova Street is an attractive Baroque house, At the Golden Well ⑪. Further on is the 16th-century Clementinum (*see p81*), where the clergy stood. You then pass into Knights of the Cross Square (*see p81*). When Leopold II's procession passed through here, the clouds lifted, which

(*see p130*). Poet and writer Jan Neruda, who immortalized hundreds of Little Quarter characters in books like *Mala Strana Tales*, grew up and worked at No. 47, The Two Suns ⑱. Cross the street, turn sharp right and walk up the Castle ramp, which leads you to Hradčanské Square.

Key

••• Walk route

— City wall

```
0 metres        300
0 yards         300
```

Tips for Walkers

Starting point: Náměstí Republiky.
Length: 2.4 km (1.5 miles).
Getting there: Line B goes to Náměstí Republiky metro station. At Hradčany, you can get tram 22 back into town.
Stopping off points: Rest beneath the sunshades of the outdoor cafés on Old Town Square or Karlova Street in the summer. There are plenty of cafés and restaurants on Malostranské náměstí, as well as along Nerudova Street.

Coronation procession passing through the Knights of the Cross Square

For keys to symbols *see back flap*

A Two-Hour Walk through Petřín Park

Part of the charm of this walk around this large and peaceful hillside park are the many spectacular views over the different areas of Prague. The Little Quarter, Hradčany and the Old Town all take on a totally different aspect when viewed from above. The tree-covered gardens are dotted with châteaux, pavilions and statues and criss-crossed by winding paths leading you to secret and unexpected corners. For more on the sights of Petřín Hill see pages 140–41.

⑤ One of the gateways in the Hunger Wall

③ Interior of the Church of St Michael

Kinský Square to Hunger Wall

The walk starts at náměstí Kinských in Smíchov. Enter Kinský Garden through a large enclosed gateway. This English-style garden was founded in 1827 and named after the wealthy Kinský family, supporters of Czech culture in the 19th century.

Take the wide cobbled and asphalt path on your left to the Kinský Summer Palace ①. This 1830s pseudo-classical building was designed by Jindřich Koch and its façade features Ionic columns terminating in a triangular tympanum. Inside the building is a large hall of columns with a triple-branched staircase beautifully decorated with statues. The Ethnographical Museum, housed here, holds a permanent exhibition of folk art.

Next to the museum is a 1913 statue of the actress Hana Kvapilová.

About 50 m (150 ft) above the palace is the lower lake ②, where a small waterfall trickles into a man-made pond. Keep going up the hill until you reach the Church of St Michael ③, on your left. This 18th-century wooden folk church was moved here from a village in the Ukraine.

Follow the path up the hill for about 20 m (60 ft), then go to the top of the steps to a wide asphalt path known as the Observation Path for its beautiful views of the city. Turn right and further on your left is the small upper lake ④ with a 1950s bronze statue of a seal at its

Sunbathers on Petřín Hill

centre. Keep following the Observation Path; ahead of you stands a Neo-Gothic gate. This allows you to pass through the city's old Baroque fortifications.

Hunger Wall to Observation Tower

Continue along the path to the Hunger Wall ⑤ *(see p140)*. This was a major part of the Little Quarter's fortifications; the wall still runs from Újezd Street across Petřín Hill and up to

Strahov Monastery. Passing through the gate in the wall brings you to Petřín Park. Take the wide path to the left below the wall and walk up the hill beside the wall until you cross the bridge which spans the funicular railway *(see p141)*. Below on your right you can see the Nebozízek restaurant *(see p201)* famed for its views. On either side of the path are small sandstone rockeries. Most are entrances to reservoirs, built in the 18th and 19th centuries, to bring water to Strahov Monastery; others are left over from the unsuccessful attempts at mining the area. Walk up to the summit of the hill. On your right is the Mirror Maze ⑥ *(see p140)*. Facing the maze is the 12th-century Church of St Lawrence ⑦ *(see p140)*, renovated in 1740 in the Baroque style.

Key

••• Walk route

— Hunger wall

0 metres   300

0 yards   300

Observation Tower to Strahov Monastery

A little further on stands the Observation Tower ⑧ *(see p140)*. This steel replica of the Eiffel Tower in Paris is 60 m (200 ft) high. Opposite the tower is the main gate of the Hunger Wall. Pass through, turn left and follow the path to the Rose Garden ⑨.

The garden was planted by the city of Prague in 1932, and features a number of attractive sculptures. When you look down to the far end of the garden you can see Štefánik's Observatory *(see p140)*. This was rebuilt from a municipal building in 1928 by the Czech Astronomical Society and was then modernized in the 1970s. It now houses a huge telescope and is open in the evenings to the public.

Returning to the Observation Tower, follow the wall on the left, passing some chapels of the Stations of the Cross dating from 1834. Then pass through a gap in the Hunger Wall, turn right, and walk past a charming Baroque house. About 50 m (150 ft) beyond this, you pass through another gap in the Hunger Wall on your right. Turn left into a large orchard above Strahov Monastery ⑩ *(see pp120–21)* for spectacular views of the city. Leave by the same hole in the wall that you came in by, turn right, and walk downhill along the wall, through the orchard and past tennis courts to the Strahov

⑦ Sgraffitoed façade of the Calvary Chapel next to the Church of St Lawrence

Monastery courtyard. You can catch tram 22 from here, or linger in the peaceful monastery grounds. If you feel energetic, you can walk back down the hill.

Tips for Walkers

Starting point: náměstí Kinských in Smíchov.

Length: 2.7 km (1.7 miles). The walk includes steep hills.

Getting there: The nearest metro station to the starting point is Anděl. Trams 6, 9, 12 and 20 go to náměstí Kinských (Kinský Square).

Stopping off points: There is a restaurant, Nebozízek, half way up Petřín Hill and in the summer a few snack bars are open at the summit of the Hill near the Observation Tower.

Hradčany and the Little Quarter from the summit of Petřín Hill

A Two-Hour Walk in the Royal Enclosure

The royal enclosure, more popularly called Stromovka, is one of the largest parks in Prague. It was created around 1266 during the reign of Přemysl Otakar II, who fenced the area in and built a small hunting château in the grounds. In 1804, it was opened to the public and became Prague's most popular recreational area. The large park of Troja Palace and the zoological garden are on the opposite river bank.

⑥ A bust on the Academy of Fine Arts

The Exhibition Ground (Výstaviště)

From U Výstaviště ①, pass through the gate to the old Exhibition Ground. This was created for the 1891 Jubilee Exhibition. Since the late 19th century, it has been used for exhibitions and entertainment.

The large Lapidarium of the National Museum ② is on your right. This Neo-Renaissance exhibition pavilion was rebuilt in 1907 in the Art Nouveau style, and decorated with reliefs of figures from Czech history. Many architectural monuments and sculptures from the 11th to the 19th centuries are also housed here.

Facing you is the Industrial Palace ③, a vast Neo-Renaissance building constructed of iron which was partially destroyed by fire in 2008. Walk to the right of the building and you will come to Křižík's Fountain ④. This was restored in 1991 in honour of the Czechoslovakia Exhibition. It was designed by the great inventor František Křižík (1847–1941), who established Prague's first public electric lighting system. During summer, the fountain is illuminated at night by computer-controlled lights which synchronize with the music (see p53). Behind the fountain, there is a permanent fairground. On the left

② The Art Nouveau Lapidarium

ZOOLOGICKÁ ZAHRADA

U TROJSKÉHO ZÁMKU

POD HAVRÁNKOU

POVLTAVSKÁ

POVLTAVSKÁ

CÍSAŘSKÝ OSTROV

Vltava

jezdecké závodiště

ZA ELEKTRÁRNOU

průplav

STROMOVKA

⑩ The summer palace created from a medieval Hunting Château

0 metres		500
0 yards		500

Key

••• Walk route

=== Railway line

of the Industrial Palace is a circular building which houses Marold's Panorama ⑤. This was painted by Luděk Marold in 1898 and depicts the Battle of Lipany, which ended the Hussite Wars. As you walk back to the Exhibition Ground entrance, you pass the Academy of Fine Arts ⑥, decorated with 18 busts of artists. On leaving the Exhibition Ground, turn sharp right. Following the outer edge of the Ground, you will pass the Planetarium ⑦ on your left, which has interactive exhibitions; walk straight ahead, take the road down the slope, then turn left into a wide avenue of chestnut trees.

The Royal Enclosure

Continue for some way along the avenue until you reach a simple building among trees, on your left. Behind this is the Rudolph Water Tunnel ⑧, a grand monument of the age of Rudolph II (see pp30–31). Hewn into rock, the aqueduct is over 1,000 m (3,000 ft) long. Now sadly

⑭ The grand façade of Troja Palace (see pp166–7)

defaced by graffiti, it was built in 1584 to carry water from the Vltava to Rudolph's newly constructed lakes in the Royal Park.

Continue along the path until you reach the derelict Royal Hall ⑨. Built in the late 17th century, it was converted into a restaurant, then rebuilt in 1855 in Neo-Gothic style. Beyond the Royal Hall, at the bend in the main path, take a steep left fork up through woods to the former Hunting Château ⑩. This medieval building was built for the Bohemian kings who used this park as a hunting reserve. The Château was then later enlarged, and in 1805 was changed again by Jiří Fischer into a Neo-Gothic summer palace. Until 1918, this was a residence of the Governor of Bohemia. Today, it is used to house the extensive library of newspapers and magazines of the National Museum. Retrace your steps to the main path, walk

ahead and take the first small path on the right which will lead you into a pleasant late-16th-century formal garden ⑪. Return to the main path and turn right. At the fork, take the path which bends to the right along the railway embankment then turn left under the railway line to a canal ⑫.

Walk over the bridge, turn left along the canal, then right across the island. Cross the Vltava ⑬ and turn left into Povltavská Street where a wall marks the boundary of Troja Park. Carry along to the south entrance of the gardens of Troja Palace ⑭ (see pp166–7), and then wander through them up to the palace itself.

Tips for Walkers

Starting point: U Výstaviště in Holešovice.

Length: 5 km (3 miles). The walk goes up a very steep incline to the former Hunting Château.

Getting there: Trams 12, 17 and 24 run to the starting point. The nearest metro stations are Vltavská or Nádraží Holešovice on line C, ten minutes walk away. At the end of the walk, you can get on bus No. 112 at Troja to Nádraží Holešovice metro station.

Stopping off points: There are a number of restaurants and kiosks in the Exhibition Ground. All the gardens are tranquil spots in which to rest. If you feel like a boat trip down the Vltava, there are often trips starting from the bridge over the canal to Palacký Bridge (see p57).

⑦ Prague Planetarium, the largest in the Czech Republic

For keys to symbols see back flap

A One-Hour Walk in Vyšehrad

According to ancient legend, Vyšehrad was the first seat of Czech royalty. It was from this spot that Princess Libuše is said to have prophesied the future glory of the city of Prague (*see pp22–3*). However, archaeological research indicates that the first castle on Vyšehrad was not built until the 10th century. The fortress suffered a turbulent history and was rebuilt many times. Today, it is above all a peaceful place with parks and unrivalled views of the Vltava valley and Prague. The fascinating cemetery is the last resting place of many famous Czech writers, actors, artists and musicians.

⑤ Decorative sculpture on the Baroque Leopold Gate

⑩ The ruin of Libuše's Baths on the cliff face of Vyšehrad Rock

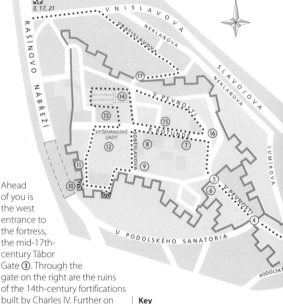

Key

• • • Walk route

— Castle wall

0 metres 200
0 yards 200

V Pevnosti

From Vyšehrad metro ①, take the exit for the Congress Centre Prague ②, walk up the steps and continue straight ahead with views of Prague Castle to your right. Go down the incline and straight ahead into the quiet street Na Bučance. Cross the road, turn right at the end, and you find yourself on V Pevnosti, facing the brick walls of the original Vyšehrad Citadel.

Ahead of you is the west entrance to the fortress, the mid-17th-century Tábor Gate ③. Through the gate on the right are the ruins of the 14th-century fortifications built by Charles IV. Further on are the ruins of the original Gothic gate, Špička ④. Past that is the sculpture-adorned Leopold Gate ⑤, one of the most impressive parts of these 17th-century fortifications. It adjoins the brick walls ⑥ that were widened during the French occupation of 1742.

K rotundě to Soběslavova Street

Turn right out of the gate and just after St Martin's Rotunda, turn left into K rotundě.

18th-century engraving by I G Ringle, showing Vyšehrad and the Vltava

A few metres on your left, almost concealed behind high walls, is the New Deanery ⑦. Situated at the corner of K rotundě and Soběslavova streets is the Canon's House ⑧. Turn left down Soběslavova to see the excavations of the foundations of the Basilica of St Lawrence ⑨. This was built by Vratislav II, the first Bohemian king, in the late 11th century, but was destroyed by the Hussites (*see pp28–9*) in

1420. About 20 m (65 ft) past the basilica, turn right on to the fortified walls for a stunning view of Prague.

Vyšehrad Rock

The wooded outcrop of rock on which Vyšehrad was built drops in the west to form a steep rock wall to the river – a vital defensive position. On the summit of the rock are the Gothic ruins of the so-called Libuše's Baths ⑩. This was a defence bastion of the medieval castle. To the left of the bastion is a grassy patch where the remains of a 14th-century Gothic palace ⑪ have been found.

⑭ The elaborate memorial to the composer Antonín Dvořák in Vyšehrad Cemetery

Vyšehrad Park

The western part of Vyšehrad has been transformed into a park. Standing on the lawn south of the Church of St Peter and St Paul are four groups of statues ⑫ by the 19th-century sculptor Josef Myslbek. The works represent figures from early Czech history – including the legendary Přemysl and Libuše *(see pp22–3)*. The statues were originally on Palacký Bridge, but were damaged during the US bombardment of February 1945. After being restored, they were taken to Vyšehrad Park. The park was the site of a Romanesque palace, which was connected to the neighbouring church by a bridge. Another palace was built here in the reign of Charles IV *(see pp26–7)*.

The Church of St Peter and St Paul

This twin-spired church ⑬ dominates Vyšehrad. It was founded in the latter half of the 11th century by Vratislav II and was enlarged in 1129. In the mid-13th century, it burned down and was replaced by an Early

⑫ Statue of Přemysl and Princess Libuše by Josef Myslbek in Vyšehrad Park

Gothic church. Since then, it has been redecorated and restored many times in a variety of styles. In 1885, it was finally rebuilt in Neo-Gothic style, the twin steeples being added in 1902. Note the early 12th-century stone coffin, thought to be of St Longinus, and a mid-14th-century Gothic panel painting *Our Lady of the Rains* on the altar in the third chapel on the right.

Vyšehrad Cemetery and the Pantheon

The cemetery ⑭ was founded in 1869 as the burial place for some of the country's most famous figures, such as Bedřich Smetana *(see p81)*. Access is through a gate at the front. On the east side of the cemetery is the Slavín (Pantheon) – built in 1890 for the most honoured citizens of the Czech nation, including the sculptor Josef Myslbek.

Leave the cemetery by the same gate and return down K rotundě. On your left is the Devil's Column ⑮, said to be left by the devil after losing a wager with a priest. At the end is St Martin's Rotunda *(see p46)* ⑯, a small Romanesque church built in the late 11th century and restored in 1878. Turn left, walk down hill to Cihelná (Brick) Gate ⑰, built in 1741 and home to a small museum that houses six of the original statues from Charles Bridge. Go down Vratislavova Street to Výtoň tram stop on the Vltava Embankment.

Tips for Walkers

Starting point: Vyšehrad metro station, line C.
Length: 1.5 km (1 mile).
Getting there: The walk starts at Vyšehrad metro station and ends at Výtoň tram stop. Trams 3, 17 and 21 go back to the city centre.
Stopping-off points: Relax in the park next to the church of St Peter and St Paul. There is a café in front of the Basilica of St Lawrence and more outdoor cafés in the summer.

For keys to symbols *see back flap*

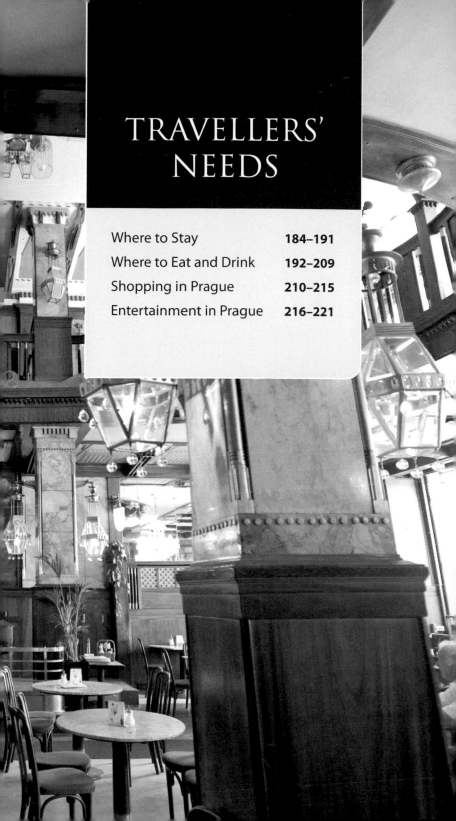

TRAVELLERS'
NEEDS

WHERE TO STAY

Since the "Velvet Revolution" of 1989, Prague has become one of the most visited cities in Europe. Thanks to investment in new hotels, helped by huge injections of foreign capital, Prague has developed enough accommodation to meet every tourist need. Many old hotels have been rebuilt, while others have been fully refurbished. It may be hard to find inexpensive accommodation in the city, however, there are a good number of hotels offering surprisingly reasonable rates as competition grows intense. Several are centrally located and even feature designer touches, as well as good service. Cheaper hotels tend to be old-fashioned places in the centre of the city, or smaller, pension-type hotels located in the suburbs. Staying in a flat or a room in a private home can also save you money. This type of accommodation is usually booked through an agency *(see p186)*. Hostels and campsites offer other budget options *(see p186)*.

The tastefully decorated lobby of Lindner Hotel Prague Castle *(see p190)*

Where to Look

As Prague is such a small city, it is best to stay near the centre, close to all the main sights, restaurants and shops. Many hotels are found around Wenceslas Square. Here, you are at the hub of everything, and the prices of some of the hotels reflect this. Other popular areas include the nearby Náměstí Republiky, and the area around Old Town Square, a few minutes' walk from Charles Bridge. Hotels here include large, international establishments, hostels, and some small, much more exclusive hotels.

To the south, in the New Town, there are several cheaper hotels only a few metro stops from Old Town Square. But the area is less picturesque, and some of the streets suffer from heavy volumes of traffic. For a view of the river Vltava, stay in the Jewish Quarter, although most hotels here are expensive. There are also a few botels (floating hotels) moored along the embankments away from the city centre. These can be a good option for budget travellers and make for an unusual stay.

Over Charles Bridge, in the Little Quarter, you will find a handful of interesting hotels in delightful surroundings, but there are far fewer by Prague Castle in Hradčany. Further north of this area, there are some large and particularly unappealing hotels.

Two areas close to the centre worth considering are Vinohrady and Anděl. Quality facilities, plus a variety of restaurants makes these neighbourhoods interesting options. The city's suburbs too, have a number of rather nondescript places. These may have good facilities, but they can be as expensive as their equivalents in the centre, with the added inconvenience of travelling time and cost – bear in mind that the metro stops at midnight, and taxis can become costly. Parking can be difficult; if you have a car, make sure the hotel you book has parking places available. It's usually better to find a hotel slightly out of the centre if you plan to drive, as these are more likely to have available parking.

How to Book

To reserve a room, you can telephone, email or book online (the best deals are often found online). It is advisable

Well-appointed room with city views in Riverside Praha *(see p191)*

to get confirmation of your booking in writing or via email and bring it with you when you check in as it can save you some time on arrival. Most hotel receptionists speak English, so you can always ring them for advice; otherwise, ask your tour operator for help. A number of UK operators specialize in Prague *(see p187)*.

The most popular seasons are Christmas, New Year and Easter, as well as summer, when rooms are often hard to find and more expensive.

Facilities

Following the large investment in many of Prague's hotels, most rooms now have en suite WC and shower or bath, Internet, telephone and TV, which may also offer movie and satellite channels. Many hotels offer a reasonably priced laundry service, and the larger hotels usually have 24-hour room service and mini bars. Guests are expected to vacate rooms by midday, but most hotels are happy to keep luggage safe if you are leaving later.

Czech staff generally speak good English so you should encounter few communication problems *(see p224)*.

Discount Rates

The price structure for hotels in Prague is fairly flexible. Check the hotel's website for good rates. Popular websites such as **agoda.com**, **booking.com**, **expedia.com** and **hotels.com** may also offer good deals.

Hidden Extras

All hotels include tax (currently at 21 per cent) and service charges in their tariff, but do check these details when you book. Telephone charges can be a shock when you receive your bill, so be aware of the mark-up rate. A few surviving telephone boxes in the city take phone cards and some take credit cards, but it may be more practical to use roaming facilities on your mobile phone

Entrance to Hotel Paříž, housed in a protected monument *(see p191)*

since EU roaming rates are now very low *(see p232)*. Some expensive hotels charge an extra fee for breakfast, others include a continental breakfast, but hot dishes cost extra. Buffet-style continental breakfasts are popular, and usually offer fresh fruit, cereals, yogurt, cold meat and cheese, juice and jugs of coffee and tea.

The elegant bar area at the Augustine Hotel *(see p190)*

Tipping is not common and is not expected by hotel staff. As in most countries, single travellers receive no favours. There are few single rooms, particularly in newer hotels, and a supplement is charged for single occupancy of a double room; you'll pay about 70–80 per cent of the standard rate.

Disabled Travellers

Most of the newer hotels in Prague have wheelchair access *(see p226)*. For information on accommodation suitable for the disabled, contact **Accessible Prague** or the Embassy of the Czech Republic in your country.

Travelling with Children

Children are accommodated by most hotels, either in family rooms or with extra beds. Reliable baby-sitting services are sometimes available in high-end establishments or small inns. Highchairs are readily available. It is worth asking if there are discounts, or if children can stay free in their parents' rooms.

Pension in a quiet street of a historic neighbourhood

Private Rooms and Self-Catering Apartments

Over the past few years, the number of private rooms to rent in Prague has grown enormously. Although cheap and popular, they may be some distance from the city centre. Private rooms in homes start at about Kč1,000 per person per night, usually with breakfast. There are also self-contained apartments – a fairly central one-bedroom apartment costs about Kč2,000 per night. Most agencies that offer private rooms also rent out apartments *(see Directory opposite)*.

To book a room or apartment, tell the agency exactly what you want, for how many, when and in which area. The agency will then suggest places. Find out the exact location and the nearest metro before accepting; if you are in Prague, see it yourself. Make sure you receive written or emailed confirmation of a booking to take with you. On arrival in Prague, pay the agency in cash; they give you a voucher to take to the room or apartment (sometimes you can pay the owner directly). If the agency requires advance payment by banker's draft, go direct to the accommodation with your receipt. Agencies may ask for a deposit on bookings from abroad, or charge a registration fee payable in Prague.

Hostels

There are many hostels in Prague offering cheap beds year-round. Useful websites include www. hostels.com, www.hostel bookers.com, www.bed.cz, and www.hostelworld.com.

A few hostels operate curfews, so it's worth checking this before you book. It is rarely necessary to bring your own sleeping bag as most hostels tend to provide bed sheets and blankets for free. Sometimes it can be better value to choose a hostel further away from the city centre, as even with the addition of transport costs, these can be cheaper than some of the more central establishments, which can cost just as much as a cheap hotel.

If you are visiting between June and mid-September, it's worth investigating the thousand or so very basic student rooms available to the public in the summer holidays at Charles University's dormitories (Tel: 22 49 30 010). These are an excellent option for the budget traveller. Locations do vary; some are in the city centre, while others are on the outskirts so check the address carefully before booking. However, all have good public transport links. Some other Czech colleges also offer a similar service.

Camping

Most campsites in or near Prague are closed from November to the start of April. They are very cheap with basic facilities, but are well served by transport. The largest site is at **Camp Dana Troja**, 3 km (1.5 miles) north of the city centre. **Aritma Džbán**, 4 km (2.5 miles) west, is open all year for tents, and **Intercamp Hostel Kotva** is 6 km (4 miles) south of the city on the banks of the Vltava.

Pensions

In the Czech Republic, pensions, or guesthouses, are a cosy, inexpensive type of accommodation. They offer guests reasonably priced standard rooms with en suite bathrooms, and most include breakfast in the price. Look out for their signs along the roads approaching Prague – the word *pension* is usually in green. Pensions tend to be located outside the city centre and are therefore most convenient for visitors who are arriving by car.

Luxury and Boutique Hotels

Prague has many luxury hotels, including well-known international chains such as Four Seasons, Hilton, Intercontinental and Radisson Blu. These establishments are renowned for the quality of their services and amenities.

Boutique hotels offer a similar level of quality, plus individual designs and colour schemes.

The entrance to Domus Henrici in Hradčany *(see p188)*

Most upmarket hotels have a concierge who can help guests with theatre tickets and dinner reservations. You can also turn to your hotel concierge for help when making travel arrangements and sightseeing plans, and if you need to make use of local services or deal with an emergency. It is polite to tip a concierge who has helped during your stay.

Recommended Hotels

The accommodation options listed over the next few pages are divided up into five categories: **Luxury**, **Boutique/Design**, **Hotels with Character**, **Budget** and **Apartments**. The list, which should satisfy all tastes and budgets, has been compiled by taking location, amenities and service into account. The descriptions

highlight the unique aspects of the property to help narrow down your decision of where to stay. Any establishment highlighted as a "DK Choice" offers an extra special experience – either in terms of superlative service, beautiful interiors and rooms, top-notch amenities, an excellent on-site restaurant, superb views, or a combination of these.

DIRECTORY

Disabled Travellers

Accessible Prague
Moravanů 51, Praha 6.
Tel 608 531 753.
w accessible
prague.com

Embassy of the Czech Republic
26–30 Kensington Palace Gardens, London W8 4QY.
Tel 020 7243 1115.
w mzv.cz/london

UK and Czech Agencies

Cresta Holidays
Thomas Cook Business Park, Conningsby, Peterborough PE3 8SB.
Tel 0844 800 7020.
w crestaholidays.co.uk

ČSA
V Celnici 5. **Map** 4 D3. **Tel** 23 90 07 007. w csa.cz

Czech Centre London
116 Long Acre, London WC2E 9PA. **Tel** 020 7836 3669. w london.czech centres.cz

Czech Tourist Authority – Czech Tourism
Vinohradská 46, Praha 2.
Tel 221 580 611.
w czechtourism.com

Hotels.com
Tel 239 014 224 (CZ);
Tel 0800 028 3906 (UK);
Tel 020 3024 8216 (UK).
w uk.hotels.com

Osprey City Holidays
5 Thistle Street, Edinburgh EH2 1DF.
Tel 0131 243 8098.
w ospreyholidays.com

Tour & Explore
62 George Street, Croydon, Surrey CR0 1PD.
Tel 020 8234 1532.
w tourandexplore.co.uk

Travelsphere
Tel 01858 898 723 (UK).
w travelsphere.co.uk

US Agencies

Czech Centre New York
321 E 73rd Street, New York, NY 10021.
Tel 646 422 3399.
w new-york.
czechcentres.cz

Embassy of the Czech Republic
3900 Spring of Freedom Street NW, Washington, DC. **Tel** 202 274 9100.
w mzv.cz/washington

Private Rooms and Self-Catering Apartments

IN UK

Regent Holidays
6th Floor, Colston Tower, Colston Street, Bristol BS1 4XE. **Tel** 020 3553 0275.
w regent-holidays.co.uk

IN PRAGUE

American Express Business Travel Centre
Na Příkopě 19. **Map** 3 C4.
Tel 222 800 100.
w americanexpress.cz

Apartmentplan.cz
U Demartinky 3, Praha 5.
Tel 606 688 970.
w apartmentplan.cz

Autoturist
Na Strži 1837/9, Praha 4.
Tel 261 104 401.

AVE
Pod Barvířkou 6/747, Praha 5.
w avehotels.cz

Čedok
Na Příkopě 18. **Map** 4 D4.
Tel 224 197 632.
w cedok.com

Estec
Vaníčkova 5, Prague 6.
Tel 233 107 511.
w hoteldiscount.cz

hotel.cz
Sokolovská 194, Praha 9.
Tel 222 539 539.
w hotel.cz

Prague City Apartments
Karolíny Světlé 4.
Map 3 A5.
Tel 800 800 722 (CZ);
0808 120 2320 (UK);
1 877 744 1222 (US).
w prague-city-apartments.cz

Prague City Tourism/ Prague Information Service
Staroměstské náměstí 1.
Map 3 B3.
Tel 221 714 714.
Rytířská 12.
Map 3 C4.
Václavské náměstí 42 (kiosk).
Map 4 D5.
Václav Havel Airport, Terminals 1 & 2.
w prague.eu

Travel Agency of Czech Railways
Perlová 3. **Map** 3 C5.
Tel 972 243 053.
w cdtravel.cz

Hostels

Hostel Jednota
Opletalova 38. **Map** 4 D5.
Tel 224 230 037.
w alfatourist.cz

Traveller's Hostel
Dlouhá 33. **Map** 3 C3.
Tel 777 738 608.
w travellers.cz

Camping

Aritma Džbán
Nad Lávkou 5, Praha 6.
Tel 725 956 457.
w campdzban.eu

Camp Dana Troja
Trojská 129, Troja.
Tel 283 850 482.
w campdana.cz

Intercamp Hostel Kotva
U ledáren 1557/1, Braník, Praha 4.
Tel 244 461 712.
w kotvacamp.cz

Prague Accommodation Service
Nad Bertramkou 11, Praha 5. **Tel** 602 309 435.
w stopin-prague.com

Prague-Hotel
w prague-hotel.ws

Prague-Stay.com
Na Perštýně 2. **Map** 3 B5.
Tel 222 311 084.
w prague-stay.com

Praha.st
Trojská 14, Praha 8.
Tel 277 001 710.
w praha.st

Where to Stay

Apartments

Little Quarter

Appia Hotel Residence Ⓚ Ⓚ
Šporkova 3/322, Praha 1
Tel *257 215 819*   Map 2 D3
Ⓦ appiaresidencesprague.cz
This historic hotel has elegantly
decorated rooms and apartments
for up to four people.

Hunger Wall Residence Ⓚ Ⓚ
Plaská 615/8, Praha 5
Tel *257 404 040*   Map 2 E5
Ⓦ prague-rentals.com
Well-furnished apartments are
housed in an early 20th-century
building. Service is exemplary.

Nicholas Hotel Residence Ⓚ Ⓚ
Malostranské nám. 5, Praha 1
Tel *731 452 791*   Map 2 E3
Ⓦ thenicholashotel.com
Set in an 18th-century palace, this
hotel has gorgeous rooms with
kitchenettes. The staff are helpful.

New Town

Elysee Apartments Ⓚ Ⓚ
Václavské náměstí 43, Praha 1
Tel *221 455 111*   Map 4 D5
Ⓦ hotelelyseeprague.cz
These compact, well-equipped
apartments are in the heart of
the city, with on-site parking.

Further Afield

Prague Classic Rental Ⓚ
Sázavská 6, Praha 2
Tel *222 516 466*
Ⓦ praguecr.com
For true Prague living, stay in one
of these eight buildings with a
range of apartments.

Charming exterior of Hotel Hoffmeister,
near Prague Castle

Boutique/Design

Old Town

Barcelo Ⓚ Ⓚ
Celetná 29, Praha 1
Tel *800 222 515*   Map 4 D3
Ⓦ barcelo.com
Housed in a restored 17th-century
building, the modern, comfortable, air-conditioned rooms here
also have free Wi-Fi.

Prague Castle and Hradčany

Domus Henrici Ⓚ Ⓚ
Loretánská 11, Praha 1
Tel *220 511 369*   Map 1 C3
Ⓦ domus-henrici.cz
This good-value, quiet historic
hotel offers rooms equipped with
modern amenities.

Hotel Hoffmeister Ⓚ Ⓚ
Pod Bruskou 7, Praha 1
Tel *251 017 111*   Map 2 F2
Ⓦ hoffmeister.cz
The imposing Hoffmeister
has airy rooms, lovely outdoor
spaces and an excellent spa.

Little Quarter

Domus Balthasar Ⓚ Ⓚ
Mostecká 5, Praha 1
Tel *220 199 499*   Map 2 E3
Ⓦ domus-balthasar.cz
Bright, cosy rooms combine
stylish design with traditional
touches at the Domus Balthasar.

New Town

987 Prague Hotel Ⓚ Ⓚ
Senovážné náměstí 15, Praha 1
Tel *255 737 200*   Map 4 E4
Ⓦ 987praguehotel.com
This great-value hotel near the
main station and Wenceslas
Square offers well-decorated
rooms and suites.

**Falkensteiner Hotel
Maria Prag** Ⓚ Ⓚ
Opletalova 21, Praha 1
Tel *222 211 229*   Map 4 E5
Ⓦ falkensteiner.com
A mix of Neo-Classical style and
innovatively decorated rooms.
There is also a wellness spa.

Hotel Pav Ⓚ Ⓚ
Křemencova 13, Praha 1
Tel *221 502 111*   Map 5 B1
Ⓦ hotel-pav.cz
This reliable hotel offers elegantly
furnished rooms, good service
and free Wi-Fi access.

Hotel Sovereign Ⓚ Ⓚ
Politických vězňů 16, Praha 1
Tel *221 111 000*   Map 4 D5
Ⓦ sovereignhotel.cz
Rooms are simple and clean
at this relaxing hotel. There is
an on-site sauna, steam bath
and gym.

Majestic Plaza Ⓚ Ⓚ
Štěpánská 33, Praha 1
Tel *221 486 100*   Map 5 C1
Ⓦ hotel-majestic.cz
Both Art Deco and Biedermeier-
style rooms feature at this popular
hotel. There are great views from
the seventh floor.

Metropol Ⓚ Ⓚ
Národní třída 33, Praha 1
Tel *246 022 100*   Map 3 B5
Ⓦ metropolhotel.cz
The rooms at this sleek hotel
with glass-walled design are
comfortable but small. Some
offer views of Prague Castle.

Noir Ⓚ Ⓚ
Legerova 35, Praha 2
Tel *224 104 111*   Map 6 D3
Ⓦ hotelnoir.cz
Contemporary black-and-white
designer rooms are offered at this
pet-friendly hotel. There is also a
cosy garden café.

Further Afield

Red and Blue Design Hotel Ⓚ
Holečkova 13, Praha 5
Tel *220 990 100*
Ⓦ redandbluehotels.com
Good-sized designer rooms with
bathrooms decorated in shades
of either red or blue. Offers
complimentary breakfast.

Ametyst Ⓚ Ⓚ
Jana Masaryka 11, Praha 2
Tel *222 921 921*
Ⓦ hotelametyst.com
This townhouse-style hotel has
comfortable rooms featuring
wall art that is up for sale.

Angelo Ⓚ Ⓚ
Radlická 1g, Praha 5
Tel *234 801 111*
Ⓦ angelohotel.com
A colourful design concept
dominates the rooms, which
offer additional work space.

Art Hotel Praha Ⓚ Ⓚ
Nad Královskou oborou 53, Praha 7
Tel *233 101 331*
W arthotel.cz
Rooms feature contemporary art.
The lobby area is as impressive
as the private garden.

Budget

Old Town

Prague Square Hostel Ⓚ
Melantrichova 10, Praha 1
Tel *224 240 859* **Map** 3 B4
W praguesquarehostel.com
This hostel is clean, offers free
breakfast and has attentive staff.
It's also in an excellent location.

U Červené Židle Ⓚ
Liliová 4, Praha 1
Tel *296 180 018* **Map** 3 B4
W redchairhotel.com
Rooms are modern and roomy,
with charming touches. The lobby
is beautiful, and staff great.

Černý Slon Ⓚ Ⓚ
Týnská 1, Praha 1
Tel *222 321 521* **Map** 3 C3
W hotelcernyslon.cz
This luxurious historic hotel has
welcoming staff and individually
designed rooms with great views.

Modrá Růže Ⓚ Ⓚ
Rytířská 403/16, Praha 1
Tel *224 404 100* **Map** 3 C4
W hotelmodraruze.cz
Here there are 52 basic rooms,
plus spacious suites in the tower
and two disabled-friendly rooms.

U Medvídků Ⓚ Ⓚ
Na Perštýně 7, Praha 1
Tel *224 211 916* **Map** 3 B5
W umedvidku.cz
Connected to a historic brewery,
this hotel has charming rooms
with Gothic rafters and lovely
Renaissance painted ceilings.

Jewish Quarter

Florentina Boat Ⓚ
Dvořákovo nábřeží, Praha 1
Tel *739 002 550* **Map** 3 A2
W florentinaboat.cz
This floating boat hotel with
well-appointed cabins is moored
between Čechův most and
Mánesův most. The sun deck
offers great views of Prague Castle.

Hostel Franz Kafka Ⓚ
Kaprova 14/13, Praha 1
Tel *776 790 049* **Map** 3 B3
W hostelfranzkafka.com
This good-value hostel provides
single rooms, doubles and dormi-
tories with shared bathrooms.

Upscale penthouse with contemporary decor at the Mosaic House

Travellers' Hostel Ⓚ
Dlouhá 33, Praha 1
Tel *224 826 662* **Map** 3 C2
W travellers.cz
This popular hostel and pension
is located close to several pubs
and clubs. It's a great place to
meet other travellers.

Little Quarter

Hotel Kampa Ⓚ
Všehrdova 16, Praha 1
Tel *257 404 444* **Map** 2 E5
W sivekhotels.com
Hidden away near the serene
Kampa Park, this hotel has rooms
featuring historical touches.

Little Town Hotel Ⓚ
Malostranské náměstí 11, Praha 1
Tel *242 406 965* **Map** 2 E3
W littletownhotel.cz
This stark but modern hotel in a
medieval palace is a great budget
option for the Little Quarter.

Pension Dientzenhofer Ⓚ
Nosticova 2, Praha 1
Tel *257 311 319* **Map** 2 E4
W dientzenhofer.cz
At this famous pension, the large
rooms are shabby chic. The garden
offers river views.

Dům u Velké Boty Ⓚ Ⓚ
Vlašská 30/333, Praha 1
Tel *257 532 088* **Map** 2 D3
W dumuvelkeboty.cz
Homey charm, period furnishings
and friendly owners make for a
personalized stay.

New Town

Hotel Museum Ⓚ
Mezibranská 15, Praha 1
Tel *296 325 186* **Map** 6 D1
W hotelmuseum.cz
The large rooms here are simply
but tastefully furnished. The
delicious breakfast is a bonus.

Jerome House Ⓚ
V Jirchářích 13, Praha 1
Tel *730 896 595* **Map** 5 B1
W jeromehousehotel.cz
The Jerome House is a little stark
but convenient. It is good value
for the location, with basic but
comfortable rooms.

DK Choice

Mosaic House Ⓚ Ⓚ
Odborů 4, Praha 2
Tel *221 595 350* **Map** 5 B1
W mosaichouse.com
This environmentally conscious
hotel offers trendy rooms
ranging from dorms to four-star.
Some rooms have terraces that
give splendid views of the city.
A bustling bar and restaurant
with friendly and attentive staff
make this a welcoming place
for travellers of all ages.

Further Afield

Anna Ⓚ
Budečská 17, Praha 2
Tel *222 513 111*
W hotelanna.cz
The rooms have Art Nouveau
interiors at this excellent
value hotel, with a beautiful
breakfast room.

Dahlia Inn Ⓚ
Lípová 1444/20, Praha 2
Tel *222 517 518*
W dahliainn.com
This small hotel has charming
and comfortable rooms, as well
as friendly staff.

Vitkov Ⓚ
Koněvova 114
Tel *242 453 003* **Map** Off map
W hotel-vitkov.cz
This modern, basic hotel at a
busy crossroads in the Žižkov
district offers great value.

For more information on types of hotels *see page 187*

Hotels with Character

Old Town

Hotel Aurus ⓀⓀ
Karlova 3, Praha 1
Tel *222 220 262*   Map 3 A4
🆆 aurushotel.cz
The rooms at this small, old-world, family hotel are distinctive with antique furnishings.

DK Choice

Hotel Josef ⓀⓀ
Rybná 20, Praha 1
Tel *221 700 111*   Map 3 C3
🆆 hoteljosef.com
This all-white and glass designer hotel with bright touches and great service has an interesting layout. Two buildings are connected by a courtyard and offer unique design elements. The lobby is a showpiece in itself. Enrol for a morning sight-seeing jog through the city.

U Zlatého Stromu ⓀⓀ
Karlova 6, Praha 1
Tel *222 220 441*   Map 3 A4
🆆 uzlatehostromu.com
The 18th-century decor is impressive, and uniquely designed rooms have modern amenities.

Unitas ⓀⓀ
Bartolomějská 9, Praha 1
Tel *224 230 533*   Map 3 B5
🆆 unitas.cz
Located in a quiet lane, this former convent has enormous rooms and splendid bathrooms.

Jewish Quarter

Hotel Haštal Ⓚ
Haštalská 1077/16, Praha 1
Tel *222 314 335*   Map 3 C2
🆆 hotelhastalprague.com
This Art Nouveau-style hotel is the oldest family-run establishment in the centre of the city.

Maximilian ⓀⓀ
Haštalská 14, Praha 1
Tel *225 303 111*   Map 3 C2
🆆 maximilianhotel.com
This designer hotel is decorated with muted colours and Art Deco touches. Try the superb breakfast.

Prague Castle and Hradčany

Hotel Monastery ⓀⓀ
Strahovské nádvoří 13, Praha 1
Tel *233 090 200*   Map 1 B4
🆆 hotelmonastery.cz
Located in the peaceful garden of Strahov Monastery (*see pp120–21*),

Spacious and cosy room, U Zlaté Studně

this romantic hotel with cosy, modern rooms offers unforget-table views of the city.

Lindner Hotel Prague Castle ⓀⓀ
Strahovská 128, Praha 1
Tel *226 080 000*   Map 1 B4
🆆 lindner.de
Located behind Prague Castle, this beautifully reconstructed former stable is a must-visit.

Little Quarter

Charles Hotel ⓀⓀ
Josefská 1, Praha 1
Tel *211 151 300*   Map 2 E3
🆆 hotel-charles.cz
Just off Charles Bridge, this hotel, housed in a historic building, has charming, Baroque-style rooms with all modern amenities.

Sax ⓀⓀ
Jánský vršek 328/3, Praha 1
Tel *257 531 268*   Map 2 D3
🆆 hotelsax.cz
Decked out in 50s, 60s, and 70s decor, this colourful hotel makes for a memorable stay. The rooms are simple yet cosy.

Augustine Hotel ⓀⓀⓀ
Letenská 12/33, Praha 1
Tel *266 112 233*   Map 2 F3
🆆 theaugustine.com
This former monastery features Cubist-style rooms and a cellar brewery. The restaurant is housed in a glass-covered courtyard.

DK Choice

U Zlaté Studně ⓀⓀⓀ
U zlaté studně 166/4, Praha 1
Tel *257 011 213*   Map 2 E2
🆆 goldenwell.cz
Situated beneath Prague Castle, in the maze of the Little Quarter streets, the "Golden Well" offers lovely, elegantly furnished rooms with splendid views of the city. The hotel also houses one of the city's top restaurants.

New Town

DK Choice

Fusion ⓀⓀ
Panská 9, Praha 1
Tel *226 222 800*   Map 4 D4
🆆 fusionhotels.com
The stripped down, industrial chic-style rooms here feature contemporary decor. A six-person bed is just one of its unique features. There is a bar and a restaurant, and staff are committed to ensuring that guests have a good time.

Hotel Yasmin ⓀⓀ
Politických vězňů 12, Praha 1
Tel *234 100 100*   Map 4 D5
🆆 hotel-yasmin.cz
Located close to Wenceslas Square, the Yasmin offers comfortable rooms with fresh, contemporary decor.

DK Choice

Icon ⓀⓀ
V Jámě 6, Praha 1
Tel *221 634 100*   Map 5 C1
🆆 iconhotel.eu
The facilities at this hip hotel with efficient staff and wonderful rooms include a spa, a fashionable lounge and a tapas bar-restaurant serving Spanish cuisine. In-room iPod connections and all-day breakfast are just a few of the bonuses.

Further Afield

Clarion Congress Hotel Prague ⓀⓀ
Freyova 33, Praha 9
Tel *211 131 139*
🆆 clarioncongresshotel prague.com
This large, contemporary Congress hotel features a wellness centre, plus a number of bars and restaurants renowned for their excellent cuisine.

Moods ⓚⓚ
Klimentská 28, Praha 1
Tel *420 222 330 100*
Ⓦ hotelmoods.com
This family-friendly hotel offers its guests, among other things, an all-day breakfast. A stay here is an enjoyable experience.

Riverside Praha ⓚⓚ
Janáčkovo nábřeží 15, Praha 5
Tel *225 994 611*
Ⓦ mamaison.com
A historic boutique hotel with a fairytale exterior, the Riverside Praha boasts an exquisite location on the banks of the Vltava.

Luxury
Old Town
Grand Hotel Praha ⓚⓚ
Staroměstské náměstí 22, Praha 1
Tel *221 632 556* **Map** 3 C3
Ⓦ grandhotelpraha.cz
Located opposite the Astronomical Clock, this Baroque palace has rooms decorated with murals and antique furnishings.

Ventana ⓚⓚ
Celetná 7, Praha 1
Tel *221 776 600* **Map** 3 C3
Ⓦ ventana-hotel.net
Experience Art Nouveau luxury in enormous rooms and suites with amazing Old Town views.

Hotel Paříž ⓚⓚⓚ
U Obecního domu 1, Praha 1
Tel *222 195 195* **Map** 4 D2
Ⓦ hotel-paris.cz
Beautiful rooms and decor make for a luxurious stay at arguably Prague's best-known hotel.

Pachtuv Palace ⓚⓚⓚ
Karolíny Světlé 34, Praha 1
Tel *234 705 111* **Map** 3 A4
Ⓦ pachtuvpalace.com
Frescoes, chapel ceilings and architectural gems dominate the interiors of this palace.

Jewish Quarter
President ⓚⓚ
Nám. Curieových 100, Praha 1
Tel *234 614 100* **Map** 3 B2
Ⓦ hotelpresident.cz
Fabulously furnished rooms, a renowned restaurant and business facilities are found here.

Four Seasons ⓚⓚⓚ
Veleslavínova 2a/1098, Praha 1
Tel *221 427 000* **Map** 3 A3
Ⓦ fourseasons.com/prague
Superbly located on the banks of the Vltava river, this hotel offers classic Four Seasons luxury.

Intercontinental ⓚⓚⓚ
Pařížská 30, Praha 1
Tel *296 631 111* **Map** 3 B2
Ⓦ icprague.com
Comfortable rooms and a variety of dining options are available at the Intercontinental.

Prague Castle and Hradčany
Savoy ⓚⓚ
Keplerova 6, Praha 1
Tel *224 302 430* **Map** 1 B3
Ⓦ hotelsavoyprague.com
Slightly dated, but lovely nonetheless, this place offers a complimentary minibar.

Little Quarter
Alchymist ⓚⓚⓚ
Tržiště 19, Praha 1
Tel *420 257 286 011* **Map** 2 D3
Ⓦ alchymisthotel.com
The royally-furnished rooms here are distinct from one another. The facilities include a great spa.

Aria ⓚⓚⓚ
Tržiště 9, Praha 1
Tel *420 225 334 111* **Map** 2 E3
Ⓦ ariahotel.net
The thematic rooms here are dedicated to musical styles or famous composers. Guests have private access to the Vrtba Garden.

New Town
Hotel Beseda ⓚⓚ
Vladislavova 20, Praha 1
Tel *222 500 222* **Map** 3 C5
Ⓦ hotelbesedaprague.cz
Just a few steps from Wenceslas Square, traditional luxury is offered here. It caters to business travellers and families with kids.

Sheraton Prague Charles Square Hotel ⓚⓚ
Žitná 8, Praha 2
Tel *225 999 999* **Map** 5 C1
Ⓦ sheratonprague.com
Come here for a hip lobby, sleek rooms with modern amenities and sophisticated dining venues.

Boscolo Prague ⓚⓚⓚ
Senovážné náměstí 13, Praha 1-
Tel *224 593 111* **Map** 4 E4
Ⓦ prague.boscolohotels.com
Close to the main train station, this hotel boasts Italian opulence and an impressive spa.

DK Choice
Radisson Blu Alcron ⓚⓚⓚ
Štěpánská 40, Praha 1
Tel *800 900 811* **Map** 6 D1
Ⓦ radissonblu.com/hotel-prague
This historic Art Deco hotel features rooms and suites with high ceilings and period furnishings combined with excellent amenities and good service. The in-house Michelin-starred Alcron restaurant is highly recommended.

Further Afield
NH Praha ⓚ
Mozartova 1, Praha 5
Tel *257 153 111*
Ⓦ nhprague.com
The rooms here are spacious. Take a cable car to the on-site restaurant with beautiful views.

Andel's Hotel ⓚⓚⓚ
Stroupežnického 21, Praha 5
Tel *296 889 688*
Ⓦ andelshotel.com
The well-equipped rooms here feature contemporary designs, and the breakfast buffet is great.

The Mark Luxury Hotel Prague ⓚⓚⓚ
Hybernská 12, Praha 1
Tel *226 226 111*
Ⓦ grandmark.cz
Housed in a former Baroque palace, this hotel has a gorgeous courtyard garden.

Le Palais ⓚⓚⓚ
U Zvonařky 1, Praha 2
Tel *234 634 111*
Ⓦ lepalaishotel.eu
This *belle époque* hotel has brightly coloured rooms, attentive staff and a great wellness centre.

Homey yet elegant interiors of The Mark Luxury Hotel Prague

For more information on types of hotels *see page 187*

WHERE TO EAT AND DRINK

Restaurants in Prague, just like the tourist economy, have improved in recent years. For decades, state-licensed eating and drinking establishments had little incentive to experiment or progress. But attitudes have changed. New restaurants are opening constantly, many of them foreign-owned, offering the discerning diner an ever-increasing choice. The restaurants described in this section reflect the change,

though many only serve a limited range of standard Western dishes in addition to the staple Czech meals. *Recommended Restaurants* summarizes the key features of the restaurants and cafés listed in this guide, which are organized by area. Information on pubs, beer halls and bars appears on pages 206–207. Compared to Western European prices, eating out in Prague is still cheap.

Tips on Eating Out

Because of the huge influx of tourists, eating out has changed in character. The lunch hour can be any time from 11am to 3pm, and for most Czechs, the normal time for the evening meal is around 7pm. However, many of the restaurants stay open late and it is possible to get a meal at anytime from 10am until 11pm. Kitchens close 30 minutes to one hour earlier than stated closing times.

During spring and summer, the large numbers of visitors tend to put a strain on many of Prague's more popular restaurants. To be certain of a table, especially in the very well-known restaurants, it is advisable to book in advance.

The city centre is full of restaurants, and there are several off the normal tourist track. Prices also tend to be lower the further you go from the centre.

Places to Eat

The importance of a stylish yet comfortable setting, and food

which is inspired rather than just prepared, is slowly beginning to trickle down to Prague's better and more innovative restaurants. The places which follow this maxim are generally the best.

One of the simplest places to eat is the sausage stand, a utilitarian establishment that is very common in Central Europe. The sausages can either be eaten standing at the counter or taken away cold. For a late-night meal, your best bet is often a *gyros* (kebab) or pizza served from a street stand.

For greater comfort, head for a café *(kavárna)*. Cafés range from loud, busy main street locations to quieter bookstore establishments. All have fully stocked bars and many serve a variety of food from simple pastries and sandwiches to full-blown meals. Opening hours differ widely, but many open early in the morning and are good for a quick, if not quite a Western-style, breakfast.

Brunch buffets, complete with champagne and jazz, are

Outside dining in a charming garden courtyard

available at a number of the city's fine-dining establishments. Brunch costs no more than Kč600, so it is a great option for those who want to experience high quality food without breaking the bank.

A restaurant is called a *restaurace*; a *vinárna* specializes in wine and may have small snacks to match the drinks.

Plain Czech food is normally available at the local beer hall *(pivnice)* or pub *(hospoda)*, though the emphasis at this type of place is normally on drinking rather than eating.

Reading the Menu

Never judge a restaurant by the standard of its menu translations – mistakes are common in every class of restaurant. Many menus still list the weight of meat served. Typically, you'll need to order main meal accompaniments like potatoes, rice or dumplings separately, unless the menu specifically includes it. The same applies to salads and other side dishes *(see pp194–5 for The Flavours of Prague)*.

A boat restaurant in the Old Town, at the bank of the Vltava

Tourists eating at a restaurant in the Old Town Square

Extra Costs

In some restaurants or bars, the waiter may bring nuts to your table. Yes, they are for you to eat, but at a price equal to, or higher than, an appetizer. You will not insult anybody by telling the waiter to take them away. The same applies to appetizers brought round by the waiter.

You may notice extra charges you don't recognize when you check your bill. But they may well be legitimate, as cover charges (usually Kč10–25) might include such items as milk, ketchup, bread and butter might be charged for. Finally, a 21 per cent tax is normally included in the menu.

Etiquette

You don't have to wait to be seated in snack bars and smaller eateries. It is also quite normal

Fine dining amid stained-glass Art Deco splendour

for others to join your table if there is any room. No restaurant has an official dress code, but people tend to dress up when dining in upmarket restaurants.

Payment and Tipping

The average price for a full meal in the centre of Prague ranges from about Kč250 to Kč1,100 per person and more, depending on the type of establishment. In some restaurants the waiter may write your order on a piece of paper and then leave it on your table for the person who comes around when you are ready to pay. Tipping in the Western sense is rare; most Czechs round the bill up to the nearest 10 or 100 crowns. Most restaurants accept major credit cards, but ask before the meal to make sure. Cafés, pubs and bakeries often accept only cash.

Vegetarians

The situation for vegetarians in Prague is improving as awareness increases. Fresh vegetables are available throughout the year, and numerous restaurants offer vegetarian and vegan options. Nevertheless, even when a dish is described as meatless, it's always worth double-checking. Vegetarians should particularly beware of menu sections called *bez masa* as, whilst the literal translation of this word is "without meat", its actual meaning is that meat is not the main ingredient in the dishes listed.

Disabled Travellers

Many restaurants still do not cater specifically for the disabled. The staff will almost always try and help, but Prague's ubiquitous stairs and basements will defeat all but the most determined.

Reservations

There is generally no need to reserve a table at lunchtime or on weekday evenings in Prague. If you are planning to eat dinner on a Friday or Saturday evening, however, particularly in Prague's better known restaurants, it is advisable to book in advance. Reservations can be made in person, by telephone or occasionally online. Alternatively, online booking companies will make a free reservation for you. Your booking is confirmed by email and you pay as usual at the restaurant.

Recommended Restaurants

Prague offers an astonishing array of cuisines, from French and Asian to traditional and modern Czech fare *(see Flavours of Prague pp194–5)*. Traditional Czech involves dishes with lots of meat, potatoes or dumplings, while modern Czech is where enterprising chefs are taking the old recipes and making them fresher and lighter.

Our restaurants are divided into six geographical areas: Old Town, Jewish Quarter, Prague Castle and Hradčany, Little Quarter, New Town and Further Afield. We've selected the best from across the city, and encourage you to move out of the centre and explore some other neighbourhoods for more variety and cheaper prices. The specially recommended restaurants, marked as "DK Choice", have been chosen because they offer a special experience – either for the superb cuisine, for enjoying a traditional Czech dining night out, for the excellent value, or a combination of these.

The Flavours of Prague

While few visitors come to Prague for the food, there is far more to contemporary Czech cuisine than the Central European norm of meat, potatoes and dumplings. Czech food remains based on seasonally available ingredients, while a simple, no-fuss approach allows natural flavours to dominate most dishes. The staples of Czech cooking are pork, beef, game and carp, which tend to be served grilled or roasted, accompanied by a light sauce and vegetables. They are also used in sour soups, known as *polévky*. It is unlikely that you will leave Prague without tasting *knedlíky* (dumplings), either savoury or sweet.

Blueberries

Atmospheric U Pinkasů cellar bar and restaurant *(see p203)*

Meat

The Czech favourite is pork *(vepřové)*. It appears in countless dishes, including soups, goulash and sausages, or can be served on its own, either grilled or (more commonly) roasted and served with sliced dumplings and sweet-sour cabbage *(Vepřo-knedlozelo)*. It also appears in other forms, notably as Prague ham *(Pražska šunka)*, a succulent,

lightly smoked meat usually eaten with bread at breakfast or with horseradish as a starter at suppertime.

Veal, occasionally served in the form of breadcrumbed, fried Wiener schnitzel *(smažený řízek)*, is popular.

Beef in the region has never been up to international standards, and needs to be prepared well to be edible.

The Prague favourite is *Svíčková*, sliced, roast sirloin, served in a cream sauce with dumplings and sliced lemon. If cooked well, it can be tender and delicious. Beef is also used in goulash and stews. Most of the beef served in top restaurants is likely to be imported. Czech lamb *(jehněčí)* is not the best in the world, either, though for a short period from mid-March to mid-May, there is

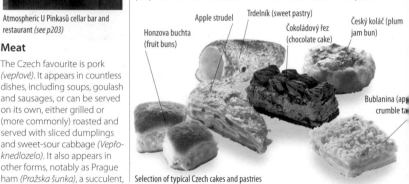

Apple strudel — Trdelník (sweet pastry)

Honzova buchta (fruit buns)

Čokoládový řez (chocolate cake)

Český koláč (plum jam bun)

Bublanina (ap[p] crumble ta[rt]

Selection of typical Czech cakes and pastries

Local Dishes and Specialities

Knedlíky (dumplings), either savoury *(špekové)* in soups or sweet *(ovocné)* with fruits and berries, are perhaps Bohemia's best-known delicacy. Once a mere side dish, they have now become a central feature of Czech cuisine, as Postmodern chefs rediscover their charms and experiment with new and different ways of cooking and serving them. Other specialities of the region include *Drštková polévka*, a remarkably good tripe soup, which – although an acquired taste – has also seen something of a revival in recent years as better restaurants add it to their menus. Duck and pheasant remain popular in Prague and, with the city surrounded by fine hunting grounds, such game is always of top quality. Pork, though, is the city's (and the nation's) most popular food, served roasted on the bone, with red cabbage.

Stuffed eggs

Polévka s játrovými knedlíčky
Soup with liver dumplings is a common dish in the Czech Republic.

Venison and other game meats feature on many menus around the city

Czechs are unwilling to pay the higher prices these goods demand. As a result, the hardy cabbage remains the country's top vegetable, used in numerous different ways, such as raw as a salad, or boiled as an accompaniment to roast meats. The Czech version of *sauerkraut, kyselé zelí,* is ubiquitous. Mushrooms, too, are well liked, and find their way in to many sauces, especially those served with game.

good lamb available in Prague's markets, where it is usually sold whole, complete with the head which is used to make soup.

Game

There is a wide variety of game to be found in the forests around Prague. Depending on the season (the best time is autumn), you will find duck, pheasant, goose, boar, venison, rabbit and hare on many menus. Duck is probably the most popular game dish, usually roasted with fruits, berries or sometimes with chestnuts, and served with red cabbage. Small pheasants, roasted whole with juniper and blueberries or cranberries, are also popular, while venison is often served grilled with mushrooms. Rabbit and hare are usually presented in spicy, goulash-style sauces.

Vegetables

Fresh vegetables are becoming more popular as an accompaniment to meals. Note, however, that Czechs tend to boil their vegetables into oblivion. While more and more imported, out-of-season produce is finding its way into supermarkets, many

Fresh vegetables on a Prague market stall

Best Local Snacks

Sausages Street stalls and snack bars all over the city sell traditional sausages (*klobásy*), pickled sausages (*utopence*), frankfurters (*párky*) or bratwurst, served in a soft roll with mustard.

Chlebíčky Open sandwiches on sliced baguette are found in any delicatessen or snack bar in Prague. Toppings are usually ham, salami or cheese, always accompanied by a gherkin (*nakládaná okurka*).

Pivní sýr Beer cheese is soaked in ale until it becomes soft. It is served spread on bread and eaten with pickles or onions.

Nakládaný hermelín This whole round cheese is pickled in oil with onions and paprika. A firm favourite in pubs.

Palačinky Pancakes are filled with ice cream and/or fruits and jam, and are topped with lashings of sugar.

Pečený kapr s kyselou omáčkou Carp with sour cream and lemon is popular, especially at Christmas.

Vepřové s křenem Pork is served roasted, on the bone, with red cabbage and either sauerkraut or horseradish.

Ovocné knedlíky Sweet dumplings are filled with fruits or berries, usually blueberries or plums.

What to Drink in Prague

Czech beers are famous around the world, but nowhere are they drunk with such appreciation as in Prague. The Czechs take their beer *(pivo)* seriously and are very proud of it. Pilsner and its various relations originate in Bohemia. It is generally agreed that the best Pilsners are produced in Bohemia – and all the top producers are not far from Prague. Beers can be bought in bottles and, best of all, on draught. Canned beer is made mostly for export, and no connoisseur would ever drink it. The Czech Republic also produces small quantities of wine, both red and white, mainly in Southern Moravia. Little of it is bottled for export. Mineral water can be found in most restaurants; Mattoni and Dobrá voda (meaning good water) are the two most widely available brands.

Gambrinus, legendary King of Beer, and trademark of a popular brand of Pilsner

Pilsner and Budweiser

The best-known Czech beer is Pilsner Urquell. Clear and golden, with a strong flavour of hops, Pilsner is made by the lager method: bottom-fermented and slowly matured at low temperatures. The word "Pilsner" (now a generic term for similar lagers brewed all over the world) is derived from Plzeň (in German, Pilsen), a town 80 km (50 miles) southwest of Prague, where this type of beer was first made in 1842. The brewery that developed the beer still makes it under the name Plzeňský prazdroj (original source), better known abroad as Pilsner Urquell. A slightly sweeter beer, Budweiser Budvar is brewed 150 km (100 miles) south of Prague in the town of České Budějovice (in German, Budweis). The American Budweiser's first brewer adopted the name after a visit to Bohemia in the 19th century.

Traditional copper brew-kettles in Plzeň

Budweiser logo

Pilsner Urquell logo

Types of Czech Beer

Originally, Czech beers were divided into draft, lager and special beers, according to the concentration of malt they contained (known as original gravity). However, in 1997, a new system was introduced that is more in line with EU practices. Czech beer now falls into one of four main groups according to colour – light *(světlé)*, semi-dark *(polotmavé)*, dark *(tmavé)* and cut *(řezané)*. Within these groups are a further 11 sub-groups categorized by measures of alcohol, sugar, wheat and yeast content, as well as the method of final adjustment of the beer. Confusingly, pubs still use the old system of categorization by original gravity.

Kozel beer label

Beer and Beer Halls

Staropramen

Gambrinus

Velkopopovický kozel

Budweiser Budvar

Plzeňský prazdroj (Pilsner Urquell)

The real place to enjoy Czech beer is a pub or beer hall (*pivnice*). Each pub is usually supplied by a single brewery (*pivovar*), so only one brand of beer is available, but several different types of beer are on offer. The major brands include Pilsner Urquell and Gambrinus from Plzeň, Staropramen from Prague, and Velkopopovický Kozel from Velké Popovice, south of Prague. The usual drink is draught light beer (*světlé*), but a number of beer halls, including U Fleků (*see p155*) and Chalice Restaurant (*see p154*) also serve special, strong dark lagers (ask for *tmavé*).

A half litre of beer (equivalent to just under a pint) is called a *velké* (large), and a third of a litre (larger than a half pint) is called a *malé* (small). The waiters bring beers and snacks to your table and mark everything you eat and drink on a tab. You should be aware that in some pubs there is a tacit assumption that all the customers want to go on drinking until closing time, so don't be surprised if more beers arrive without you having ordered them. If you don't want them, just say no. The bill is only totted up when you are ready to leave.

People enjoying a drink in Café Lávka, near the Charles Bridge

Wines

Czech wine producers have not yet emulated the success of other East European wine-makers. The main wine-growing region is in Moravia, where most of the best wine is produced for local consumption. Some wine is also made in Bohemia, around Mělník, just north of Prague. The whites are made mostly from Riesling, Müller-Thurgau or Veltliner grapes (*polosuché* is demi-sec and *suché* is sec). Rulandské (Pinot) is an acceptable dry white. The reds are slightly better, the main choices being Frankovka and Vavřinecké. In the autumn, a semi-fermented young, sweet white or red wine called *burčák* is sold and drunk across the capital.

Rulandské, white and red

Czech Spirits and Liqueurs

In every restaurant and pub, you'll find Becherovka, a bitter-sweet, amber herbal drink served both as an aperitif and a liqueur. It can also be diluted with tonic (called Beton). Other local drinks include Borovička, a juniper-flavoured spirit, and plum brandy or Slivovice. The latter is clear, strong and an acquired taste. Imported spirits and cocktails are more expensive.

Becherovka

Where to Eat and Drink

Old Town

Las Adelitas
Mexican Map 3 B4 Ⓚ
Malé náměstí 13, Praha 1
Tel *222 233 247*
Go around the corner from the
Astronomical Clock to savour
authentic Mexican food at
this neighbourhood eatery.
Try the freshly prepared *burritos,
enchiladas* and *quesadillas*. Also
check out the interesting array
of Mexican beers and tequilas.

Atmoška
Czech-International Map 3 A4 Ⓚ
Smetanovo nábřeží 14, Praha 1
Tel *222 222 114*
Fantastic views of Prague Castle
and Charles Bridge are the main
draws at Atmoška. It boasts a
young, cool clientele and lots of
vegetarian options. Welcoming
atmosphere and friendly staff.

Country Life
Vegetarian Map 3 B4 Ⓚ
Melantrichova 15, Praha 1
Tel *224 213 366* **Closed** *Sat*
Best bargain lunch in town.
The self-serve buffet has freshly
made hot and cold vegetarian
dishes; pay by weight. Also try
the excellent sandwiches, salads,
soups and desserts.

Golden Tikka
Indian Map 3 A5 Ⓚ
Konviktská 9, Praha 1
Tel *222 211 462*
Diners can enjoy a range of
traditional vegetarian and meat-
based dishes at this non-smoking
restaurant. There is also a lunch
menu served Monday to Friday,
and a takeaway option.

Grand Café Orient
International Map 3 C3 Ⓚ
Celetná 34, Praha 1
Tel *224 224 240*
Located in the House of the Black
Madonna *(see p67)*, the world's
only Cubist café offers a beautiful
buffet-bar and elegant lighting,
all designed by Josef Gočár in
keeping with the Cubist ethos.

Kabul
Afghan Map 3 A5 Ⓚ
Krocínova 316/5, Praha 1
Tel *224 282 509*
An eclectic menu, welcoming
staff and a local feel – Kabul
offers reasonable, but hearty
Afghan dishes and pizza.
Expect crowds at lunchtime.

DK Choice

Lehká Hlava
Vegetarian Map 3 A4 Ⓚ
Boršov 2/280, Praha 1
Tel *222 220 665*
The best vegetarian restaurant
in Prague has a creative take on
international cuisine and trippy,
cool interiors. The extensive
menu ranges from Asian to
Mexican to Lebanese. The Thai
red curry with tofu is a treat,
and the *quesadilla* will force
you to skip dessert. There are
many vegan offerings as well.

Maitrea
Vegetarian Map 3 C3 Ⓚ
Týnská ulička 6/1064, Praha 1
Tel *221 711 631*
This beautiful restaurant offers
a well-designed menu that
includes Asian and Mexican
dishes. Great lunch specials
are also available.

Price Guide
Prices are based on a three-course meal
per person, with a half-bottle of house
wine, including tax and service.

Ⓚ	under Kč500
ⓀⓀ	Kč500–800
ⓀⓀⓀ	over Kč800

Raw Deli
Vegan Map 3 B5 Ⓚ
Národní třída 25, Praha 1
Tel *722 060 007*
This casual eatery uses raw
ingredients in dishes such as
Asian noodles, salads, vegan
burgers and sushi, plus a range
of cold-pressed juices and
home-made chocolates.

U Provaznice
Czech Map 3 C4 Ⓚ
Provaznická 3, Praha 1
Tel *224 232 528*
Locals and visitors come to this
cheerful pub in an excellent
location for its reasonably priced
menu. Be prepared to find it
packed at lunchtimes.

Divinis
Italian Map 3 C3 ⓀⓀ
Týnská 21, Praha 1
Tel *222 325 440*
This stylish Italian restaurant
serves superbly prepared dishes
that are created using high-
quality ingredients shipped
in from Italy.

Klub Architektů
International Map 3 B4 ⓀⓀ
Betlémské náměstí 5A, Praha 1
Tel *224 248 878*
Despite the name, you are
unlikely to encounter many
architects or artists at this funky
cellar restaurant, but you will
find delicious international main
courses and a long wine list.

Pepe Lopez
Mexican Map 3 C4 ⓀⓀ
Na Příkopě 25, Praha 1
Tel *776 300 003*
Importing ingredients directly
from Mexico, this vibrant restau-
rant is as authentic as they come.
After dinner, stay on for the
extensive range of tequila or a
cocktail, and enjoy a salsa class.

Restaurace U Tří Zlatých Lvů
Czech Map 3 B5 ⓀⓀ
Uhelný trh 1, Praha 1
Tel *224 284 118*
The Restaurant at The Three
Golden Lions provides contem-
porary Czech cuisine, such as
roast pork ribs served in a spicy

Welcoming interiors of Lehká Hlava, Prague's finest vegetarian restaurant

The warm, opulent dining room at Francouzská Restaurace

marinade with garlic bread and two sauces. Wash it all down with Pilsner or Kozel Dark beer.

Staroměstská
Czech **Map** 3 C3
Staroměstské náměstí 19, Praha 1
Tel *224 213 015*
Classic Czech dishes are served at this long-established traditional inn. In the warmer months, it is possible to dine alfresco, while enjoying wonderful views of the Old Town Square.

Století
International **Map** 3 A5
Karolíny Světlé 21/320, Praha 1
Tel *222 220 008*
Prompt service and delicious food is offered at this often missed, though centrally located, restaurant. The Czech dishes on the menu are creatively named and prepared.

U Tří růží
Czech **Map** 3 B4
Husova 10/232, Praha 1
Tel *601 588 281*
This brew house makes its own beer and serves classic Czech dishes. Six fresh beers are always on tap.

Ambiente Brasileiro
Brazilian **Map** 3 B3
U Radnice 8, Praha 1
Tel *224 234 474*
Choose from a variety of dishes at this all-you-can-eat buffet. Traditional Brazilian *churrasco* is paraded around the restaurant on skewers.

Bellevue
International **Map** 3 A4
Smetanovo nábřeží 18, Praha 1
Tel *222 221 443*
Views of Charles Bridge and the castle are welcome complimentary extras at this otherwise pricey, upmarket restaurant. Make sure you book in advance.

Francouzská Restaurace
French **Map** 4 D3
Náměstí republiky 5, Praha 1
Tel *222 002 784*
Delicious dishes almost overshadowed by the Art Nouveau interiors. They also serve Czech and international cuisine. Strong wine list.

Kogo
Italian **Map** 3 C4
Havelská 499/27, Praha 1
Tel *224 214 543*
A good location makes this eatery an ideal spot for lunch or dinner. Savour solid Italian cuisine in spacious and lovely surroundings.

Mlýnec
Czech **Map** 3 A4
Novotného lávka 9, Praha 1
Tel *277 000 777*
Mlýnec serves a nice range of meals made with locally sourced meat and fish. Sunday roast lunch.

Platina
Czech **Map** 3 A5
Karolíny Světlé 29, Praha 1
Tel *239 009 244*
Relish modern Czech cuisine with an inventive touch at this eatery. The seasonally changing menu focuses on using local ingredients. Summer barbecue on the terrace.

Red Pif
International **Map** 3 A5
Betlémská 9, Praha 1
Tel *222 232 086* **Closed** *Sun*
This industrial-chic restaurant and wine shop offers a small but delicious menu and a great wine list. Beautifully designed interiors.

Le Terroir
French-International **Map** 3 B4
Vejvodova 1, Praha 1
Tel *602 889 118* **Closed** *Sun & Mon*
One of Prague's top gastronomic experiences, and the best place for wine lovers. The food is equally good and well prepared.

V Zátiší
International **Map** 3 B4
Liliová 1, Praha 1
Tel *222 221 155*
For a memorable dining experience with excellent food and service, reserve a table at V Zátiší. Expert staff add to the pleasure.

VinodiVino
Italian **Map** 3 C3
Štupartská 769/18, Praha 1
Tel *222 311 791*
This restaurant and wine bar features specialities from southern Italy. The small menu is well-designed, with signature offerings.

Zdenek's Oyster Bar
Seafood **Map** 3 C3
Malá Štupartská 636/5, Praha 1
Tel *725 946 250*
Serious seafood restaurant with an intriguing oyster bar. Try the generous platters of oysters and clams. Don't miss the lobster roll, the most authentic example in Prague.

Jewish Quarter

Apetit
Czech **Map** 3 C2
Dlouhá 736/23, Praha 1
Tel *222 329 853*
This subterranean eatery serves a wide variety of fish and seafood, traditional Czech specialities and steaks. Also on offer is a selection of Moravian wines.

Bakeshop
International **Map** 3 C2
Kozí 1, Praha 1
Tel *222 316 823*
Locals and visitors alike come to this elegant venue for delicious coffee and sweet and savoury baked treats like pastries, muffins and quiches, plus salads and soups. There is also an attractive outdoor seating area.

View of the impressive wine cellar at French restaurant Le Terroir

For more information on types of restaurants *see page 193*

DK Choice

Lokál Ⓚ
Czech   **Map** 3 C2
Dlouhá 33, Praha 1
Tel *222 316 265*
Fun, old-style Czech pub with
well-done Czech classics and
lots of fresh Pilsner Urquell beer.
Modern lighting, long tables
and wooden chairs create a cosy
ambience. Service is excellent
and the food is tasty.

My Raw Café Ⓚ
Vegetarian   **Map** 4 D2
Dlouhá 39, Praha 1
Tel *603 889 016*
My Raw Café processes all food
at a maximum temperature of
42° C to retain healthy enzymes
and vitamins.

Prague Beer Museum Ⓚ
Czech   **Map** 4 D2
Dlouhá 46, Praha 1
Tel *732 330 912*
Enjoy delicious fare while refreshing
your knowledge of beer at this
spot set in 13th-century cellars.

Aldente Trattoria Vineria ⓀⓀ
Italian   **Map** 3 C2
Vězeňská 4, Praha 1
Tel *222 313 185*
Try the seasonal dishes at this
casual *trattoria* with a good
range of Italian wines. Specials
change weekly.

Fish and Chips ⓀⓀ
British   **Map** 3 C2
Dlouhá 21, Praha 1
Tel *606 881 414*
Traditional British fish and chips
is the star of the menu here, but
there are also soups, sandwiches,
salads and grilled fish or meat.

Krčma ⓀⓀ
Czech   **Map** 3 B3
Kostečná ulice 4, Praha 1
Tel *226 219 386*
This classical tavern in a cellar
setting near the posh Pařížská

The airy, blond-wood setting at the
informal Mistral Café

Understated elegance at the highly praised La Degustation

Street offers traditional cuisine
and live music. Good list of draft
beers and wines.

Mistral Café ⓀⓀ
International   **Map** 3 B3
Valentinská 56/11, Praha 1
Tel *222 317 737*
A casual place near the Old Town,
Mistral offers good food in a
bright, minimalist setting.

V Kolkovně ⓀⓀ
Czech   **Map** 3 C3
V Kolkovně 8, Praha 1
Tel *224 819 701*
Visit this popular brewery restau-
rant for the excellent fresh beer,
speedy service and heaping
plates of Czech delicacies.

La Belle Epoque ⓀⓀⓀ
American   **Map** 3 A3
Křižovnická 8, Praha 1
Tel *222 321 926*
Tex-Mex specialities, with an
emphasis on steak, served in a
rustic setting. Argentinian beef
and New Zealand lamb feature
prominently on the menu.

La Casa Argentina ⓀⓀⓀ
Argentinian   **Map** 3 C2
Dlouhá 35/730, Praha 1
Tel *222 311 512*
The swinging seats at the bar are
just one feature of the jungle-like
interiors at this eatery, which is
usually packed with guests.

DK Choice

La Degustation ⓀⓀⓀ
Czech-International **Map** 3 C2
Haštalská 18, Praha 1
Tel *222 311 234*
For the ultimate Czech
dining experience step into
La Degustation. Six or 11
courses of fresh, flavourful
food are paired with wines.
Chefs prepare each tiny dish
with considerable care for
ingredients and design, and
are supported by pleasant and
knowledgeable waiting staff.

Dinitz ⓀⓀⓀ
Jewish   **Map** 3 B2
Bílkova 12, Praha 1
Tel *222 244 000*
Located behind the Spanish
Synagogue, Dinitz offers some of
the best kosher food in Prague. The
menu ranges from steak and pasta
to Middle Eastern specialities.

La Finestra in Cucina ⓀⓀⓀ
Italian   **Map** 3 B3
Platnéřská 90/13, Praha 1
Tel *222 325 325*
La Finestra in Cucina's small
menu offers Italian favourites
cooked to perfection. Beautiful
surroundings and delicious food.
Great service and wine list.

DK Choice

Grosseto Marina ⓀⓀⓀ
Italian   **Map** 3 A3
Alšovo nábřeží, Praha 1
Tel *605 454 020*
Enjoy superb service, beautiful
river views over Prague Castle
and excellent Italian food – on
a boat. The top deck is a great
place to have a drink, with or
without descending below
deck for a lovely dinner of
pasta, fish, meat, or even
pizza. An early evening visit is
the best time to watch the sun
set and the city lights glow.

King Solomon ⓀⓀⓀ
Jewish   **Map** 3 B3
Široká 8, Praha 1
Tel *224 818 752*
Traditional Kosher Jewish cooking
with a Czech touch. Veal, deer
and lamb are sourced locally.
Bread is made on site and offered
alongside hummus and tahini.

La Veranda ⓀⓀⓀ
Italian-French **Map** 3 B2
Elišky Krásnohorské 10/2, Praha 1
Tel *224 814 733*   **Closed** *Sun*
Bright and homey interiors greet
guests at La Veranda. Chefs use
a variety of organic and locally
sourced products in their dishes.

Prague Castle and Hradčany

Kavárna Nový Svět
International   Map 1 B2
Nový Svět 2, Praha 1
Tel *242 430 700*   **Closed** *Wed*
Tucked away in picturesque Nový Svět, this small café is the perfect place in which to warm up with a soup, a snack or just a good cup of coffee.

Malý Buddha
Asian   Map 1 B3
Úvoz 46, Praha 1
Tel *220 513 894*
Located near Prague Castle, Malý Buddha, or Little Buddha, serves a range of Vietnamese dishes, as well as potent teas and exotic juices.

Peklo
Czech   Map 1 B4
Strahovské nadvoří 1, Praha 1
Tel *220 516 652*
Peklo offers classic Czech dining in a 12th-century location beneath Strahov Monastery *(see pp120–21)*. The house speciality, "stuffed devil's hoof", is worth trying.

Host
Czech-International   Map 1 C3
Loretánská 15, Praha 1
Tel *728 695 793*
Good, fair-priced food in a major tourist hub. Classic Czech food is well done at this eatery. Modern interiors with great views.

Villa Richter
International   Map 2 F2
Staré zámecké schody 6/251, Praha 1
Tel *702 205 108*
This venue is essentially two restaurants in one. Piano Nobile serves Central European dishes with a modern touch; Terra offers well-priced Czech fare.

Little Quarter

Bohemia Bagel
American   Map 2 E4
Lázeňská 19, Praha 1
Tel *257 218 192*
This popular eatery offers wholesome burgers, bagels and sandwiches. Reservations are recommended at breakfast.

U Knoflíčků
Czech   Map 2 E5
U Lanové Dráhy 1, Praha 1
This simple Czech café offers cakes and sandwiches at pocket-friendly, out-of-Prague prices.

U Kocoura
Czech   Map 2 E3
Nerudova 205/2, Praha 1
Stern service is offset by excellent food at this eatery, including the traditional *vepřo-knedlo-zelo* (roasted pork with bread dumplings and cabbage).

U Malého Glena
International   Map 2 E4
Karmelitská 23, Praha 1
Tel *257 531 717*
Well-executed burgers, ribs, Tex-Mex and a small selection of Czech dishes at this casual eatery. Tiny jazz club in the cellar.

Bar Bar
International   Map 2 E5
Všehrdova 17, Praha 1
Tel *257 312 246*
Fun, casual neighbourhood place with an intriguing interior. Large selection of dishes on the menu and a good choice of wines.

DK Choice

Café Lounge
International   Map 2 E5
Plaská 615/8, Praha 1
Tel *257 404 020*
Beautiful interiors with a secret courtyard, delicious fresh soup, great coffee and a creative evening menu make this a go-to place from morning till night. There's a special coffee and wine each week, and the pastry chefs are extremely talented at making imaginative desserts. Welcoming staff, too.

Kočár z Vídně
Austrian   Map 2 F4
Saská 520/3, Praha 1
Tel *777 043 793*
For authentic Austrian food in Prague, stop by this eatery. Try the well-done *wiener schnitzel* (veal coated in breadcrumbs). Extensive Austrian wine list.

Konírna
Czech   Map 2 E4
Maltézské náměstí 10, Praha 1
Tel *257 534 121*
Traditional Czech cooking with a modern twist. Konírna's menu has old recipes not found in many restaurants.

Luka Lu
Balkan   Map 2 E4
Újezd 33, Praha 1
Tel *257 212 388*
Unique interiors, friendly service and well-prepared fish, pasta and barbeque specialities. There is streetside and outdoor seating in the courtyard.

Malostranská beseda
Czech-International   Map 2 E3
Malostranské náměstí 21, Praha 1
Tel *257 409 112*
Traditional Czech food and beer served in an elegant building in the heart of the Little Quarter. A buzzing place for lunch.

Nebozízek
International   Map 2 D5
Petřínské sady 411, Praha 1
Tel *257 315 329*
One of the city's best park restaurants, offering indoor and outdoor dining with a view. Standard fare at decent prices.

Café de Paris
French   Map 2 E4
Maltézské náměstí 4, Praha 1
Tel *603 160 718*
Considered one of the best brasseries in Prague with an excellent menu featuring their speciality "Entrecôte Café de Paris" – a steak served with a special sauce made from a secret recipe.

Vibrant and cheerful dining room at Luka Lu

For more information on types of restaurants *see page 193*

Outstanding city view from the rooftop terrace, Terasa U Zlaté Studně

Café Savoy Ⓚ Ⓚ Ⓚ
Czech-French **Map** 2 F5
Vítězná 5, Praha 5
Tel *257 311 562*
This charming and bustling restaurant features impressive interiors with a Neo-Renaissance ceiling dating back to 1893. Offers lovely coffee, light lunches and gourmet meals.

Coda Ⓚ Ⓚ Ⓚ
International **Map** 2 E3
Tržiště 9, Praha 1
Tel *225 334 761*
Elegant, musically themed interiors and a rich menu featuring unique flavours and a special Czech section. The rooftop terrace is ideal for an afternoon drink.

Restaurace Tbilisi Ⓚ Ⓚ Ⓚ
Georgian **Map** 2 E3
Tomášská 14/21, Praha 1
Tel *257 313 130*
A stylish, modern restaurant with expressive interiors designed in black and white, Tbilisi offers a variety of Georgian dishes cooked over charcoal, as well as fine Georgian wines.

Spices Ⓚ Ⓚ Ⓚ
Asian **Map** 2 E4
Nebovidská 459/1, Praha 1
Tel *233 088 888*
Spices is the go-to place for an inventive selection of delicious pan-Asian dishes and mouth-watering cocktails. The modern decor combines with Renaissance-style vaulted ceiling.

Terasa U Zlaté Studně Ⓚ Ⓚ Ⓚ
International **Map** 2 E2
U Zlaté studně 4, Praha 1
Tel *257 533 322*
Also known as "At the Golden Well", this neighbourhood restaurant offers a beautiful

interior and stunning views. The menu is perfectly prepared and served. In the summer, dine on the rooftop terrace.

U Malířů Ⓚ Ⓚ Ⓚ
Czech-International **Map** 2 E4
Maltézské náměstí 11, Praha 1
Tel *257 530 000*
Gorgeous historic interiors and an interesting menu featuring modern Czech cuisine are what attracts diners to this place. With friendly and helpful staff, it is an excellent venue for a quiet dinner.

New Town

Café Louvre Ⓚ
Czech-International **Map** 3 B5
Národní třída 22, Praha 1
Tel *224 930 949*
A Czech institution, Café Louvre offers a good variety and quality of food, including an excellent selection of cakes, pastries and coffees. Play a game of pool in the on-site billiards room.

Café Slavia Ⓚ
Czech-International **Map** 3 A5
Smetanovo nábřeži 2, Praha 1
Tel *224 218 493*
Traditional Prague café with a full menu, lovely Art Deco interiors and pretty windows. The wonderful cake selection makes for a lovely afternoon break. There is often live music in the evenings.

Dynamo Ⓚ
International **Map** 5 A1
Pštrossova 29, Praha 1
Tel *224 932 020*
Dynamo is a design gem with a good range of excellent vegetarian options, plus a handful of Czech dishes and an Italian pasta selection.

Klub Cestovatelů Ⓚ
Lebanese **Map** 5 A1
Masarykovo nábřeží 22, Praha 1
Tel *734 322 729*
Tasty food, good service and relaxing interiors – this is an enjoyable riverside spot for lunch or dinner.

Miss Saigon Ⓚ
Vietnamese-Japanese **Map** 5 B1
Myslíkova 26, Praha 2
Tel *222 560 328*
Great sushi and pho (noodle soup) along with a wide range of other specialities – all well-prepared and served in a relaxed dining space.

Svatováclavská Cukrárna Ⓚ
Czech **Map** 5 B2
Václavská pasáž, Karlovo náměstí 6, Praha 1
Tel *224 916 774*
For a taste of things outside Prague, head to this simple 1930s café for a glass of cheap Turkish coffee and a wedge of strudel.

Fama Ⓚ Ⓚ
Czech **Map** 3 C5
Vladislavova 18, Praha 1
Tel *224 949 305* **Closed** *Sun*
Creative, well-presented dishes on a diverse menu served in a modern dining room. Lots of Pilsner Urquell to accompany the food.

Home Kitchen Ⓚ Ⓚ
International **Map** 5 C1
Jungmannova 8, Praha 1
Tel *734 714 227* **Closed** *Sun*
Casual, homey place that's great for a quick lunch. The seasonally changing menu features daily soups, salads and sandwiches.

Lemon Leaf Ⓚ Ⓚ
Thai-International **Map** 5 B1
Myslíkova 14, Praha 2
Tel *224 919 056*
A wide array of Thai, Burmese and continental dishes are pre-pared using fresh ingredients. The restaurant also offers a good range of wines and draught beers.

DK Choice

Nota Bene Ⓚ Ⓚ
Czech **Map** 6 D2
Mikovcova 4, Praha 2
Tel *721 299 131* **Closed** *Sun*
A fascinating, rotating beer list and locally sourced Czech specialities make Nota Bene one of the hottest places around. There is also a beer hall in the basement that only serves beer and snacks. The inviting interior has exposed brick decor. Book in advance.

Novoměstský Pivovar
Czech-International   ⓚⓚ   **Map** 5 C1
Vodičkova 20, Praha 1
Tel *222 232 448*
Classic Czech dishes served in a working brewery. Novoměstský Pivovar is a great place to expand your knowledge of beer.

Solidní Jistota
International   ⓚⓚ   **Map** 5 A1
Pštrossova 21, Praha 1
Tel *602 387 598*   **Closed** *Mon & Tue*
Hearty fare including burgers, steak and chicken wings are served at this casual place, which also has an on-site night club. Prices are good and the food is satisfying. Open till late.

U Pinkasů
Czech   ⓚⓚ   **Map** 3 C5
Jungmannovo nám. 15/16, Praha 1
Tel *221 111 152*
Beloved beer hall with typical interiors, food and beer. U Pinkasů could be considered a tourist trap, but it still attracts the locals.

Ultramarin
Thai-International   ⓚⓚ   **Map** 3 B5
Ostrovní 32, Praha 1
Tel *224 932 249*
Stylish restaurant with a good selection of dishes including grilled meats. There's an on-site night club, which serves cocktails.

Universal
French-International   ⓚⓚ   **Map** 5 B1
V Jirchářích 6, Praha 1
Tel *224 934 416*
Casual yet chic French bistro with a classic menu and interiors that match the relaxed vibe.

Alcron
International   ⓚⓚⓚ   **Map** 6 D1
Štěpánská 40, Praha 1
Tel *222 820 410*   **Closed** *Sun*
This intimate, Michelin-starred restaurant has a small, fascinating menu with some of the most creative dishes in Prague.

Bresto
French-Italian   ⓚⓚⓚ   **Map** 3 C1
Štěpánská 31, Praha 1
Tel *222 212 810*
You'll find creative cooking and a great wine list, making it perfect for a full meal or a snack break.

Čestr
Czech   ⓚⓚⓚ   **Map** 6 E1
Legerova 75/57, Praha 1
Tel *222 727 851*
The speciality here is locally sourced beef (more than 20 cuts) cooked many ways. The wine list is extensive.

Cicala Trattoria
Italian   ⓚⓚⓚ   **Map** 6 D1
Žitná 43, Praha 1
Tel *222 210 375*   **Closed** *Sun*
This *trattoria* offers a taste of Italy in its brick-lined cellar space and modern ground floor restaurant. *Bucatini all'amatriciana* (pasta with a tomato and pancetta sauce) is one of the house specialities.

Como
Mediterranean   ⓚⓚⓚ   **Map** 4 D5
Václavské náměstí 818/45, Praha 1
Tel *222 247 240*
A good dining option on Wenceslas Square is hard to find, but this place offers tasty dishes, served by friendly staff. Try the beautifully cooked leg of lamb.

El Emir
Lebanese   ⓚⓚⓚ   **Map** 3 C4
Václavské náměstí 1, Praha 1
Tel *224 281 099*
Extensive, flavourful menu featuring fresh fish and lots of mezze. Oriental-style decor and a pleasant atmosphere.

Ginger & Fred
French   ⓚⓚⓚ   **Map** 5 A2
Jiráskovo náměstí 6, Praha 2
Tel *221 984 160*
Located atop the famed Dancing House. Modern French food is served in gorgeous interiors.

Visitors enjoying drinks at U Pinkasů, Prague's popular beer hall

Miyabi
Japanese   ⓚⓚⓚ   **Map** 5 C1
Navrátilova 10, Praha 1
Tel *296 233 102*   **Closed** *Sun*
Miyabi is one of the oldest Japanese restaurants in town and offers delicious and expert cooking. Excellent sushi and stylish interiors.

Renommé
Czech-French   ⓚⓚⓚ   **Map** 5 A1
Na struze 1, Praha 1
Tel *224 934 109*
Located just around the corner from the National Theatre, this small and elegant family-run restaurant serves seasonal meals with an emphasis on foie gras and fish.

Suterén
Czech-Central
European   ⓚⓚⓚ   **Map** 5 A1
Masarykovo nábřeží 26, Praha 1
Tel *224 933 657*   **Closed** *Sun*
Housed in an Art Nouveau building, this place specializes in game and poultry dishes, but it also has a good selection of seafood options.

DK Choice

U Emy Destinnové   ⓚⓚⓚ
International   **Map** 5 C2
Kateřinská 7, Praha 2
Tel *224 918 425*   **Closed** *Sun*
Well-cooked, creative food is served here, along with excellent wine, which is matched by the service. U Emy Destinnové does Black Angus beef and seafood expertly well. Tableside cooking and a tank from which to choose your own lobster and crab add to the entertainment value.

Cream-coloured walls with an array of unusual objects, Universal

For more information on types of restaurants *see page 193*

Wooden floors, neutral colours and paper screens at Japanese restaurant Hanil

Žofín Garden ⓀⓀⓀ
International **Map** 5 A1
Slovanský Ostrov, Praha 1
Tel *774 774 774*
Lovely garden restaurant located on one of the Vltava river's islands. Excellent family spot with enjoyable food.

Zvonice ⓀⓀⓀ
Czech-International **Map** 4 D4
Jindřišská věž, Praha 1
Tel *224 220 009*
A wide variety of dishes are served here. The specialities are boar and venison. Located in an old Gothic belfry, this restaurant is hard to beat for atmosphere.

Further Afield

Dhaba Beas Ⓚ
Vegetarian
Bělehradská 90, Praha 2
Tel *725 940 016*
Spartan, cheap and popular self-service curry house. Recipes – all of them vegetarian – are culled from the traditional cuisine of northern India.

Hanil Ⓚ
Japanese
Slavíkova 24, Praha 3
Tel *420 222 715 867*
Excellent sushi and friendly service make Hanil a place to seek out. The house speciality is the popular Korean dish, *bulgogi*.

Kofein Ⓚ
Czech-International
Nitranská 9, Praha 3
Tel *273 132 145*
Czech-inspired tapas and a range of internationally leaning mains; their daily specials are always recommended. Cosy dining area.

Pho Vietnam Tuan & Lan Ⓚ
Vietnamese
Slavíkova 1657/1, Praha 2
Tel *224 221 665* **Closed** *Sun*
For authentic Vietnamese cuisine stop by this eatery, which is constantly overflowing with folks crazy for its quality dishes and great prices. Try the spring rolls.

Radost FX Ⓚ
Vegetarian **Map** 6 E2
Bělehradská 120, Praha 2
Tel *603 193 711*
Sunday brunch is especially busy at this popular spot, and during peak lunch and dinner hours, it can also be hard to find a seat.

La Boca ⓀⓀ
International
Truhlářská 10, Praha 1
Tel *222 312 073*
Cosy restaurant in a busy neighbourhood. The menu includes tapas, fresh pasta, and savoury desserts. There is also a children's menu.

Hybernia ⓀⓀ
Czech-International
Hybernská 7/1033, Praha 1
Tel *224 226 004*
Traditional Czech cuisine with a modern twist is served here. The Hybernia is very popular throughout the day. There is a large bar area and outdoor terrace seating.

Mailsi ⓀⓀ
Pakistani
Lipanská 1, Praha 3
Tel *222 717 783*
A one-of-a-kind restaurant in Prague, Mailsi's simple interior belies the authentic and flavourful food coming out of the kitchen.

Mash Hana ⓀⓀ
Japanese
Badeního 3, Praha 6
Tel *224 324 034* **Closed** *Sun & Mon*
Excellent Japanese food in a warm, welcoming ambience. The chef is the first person guests see on entering this bright restaurant.

Mozaika Burger & Co ⓀⓀ
Czech/International
Nitranská 13, Praha 3
Tel *224 253 011* **Closed** *Sun*
Home-made burgers with meat sourced from local suppliers, plus house-baked buns and breads and natural wines, all served in a trendy setting.

Občanská Plovárna ⓀⓀ
Thai
U Plovárny 8, Praha 1
Tel *257 531 451*
Set on the banks of the Vltava, this restaurant has a modern interior and excellent Thai food, especially the spicy curries.

Olympos ⓀⓀ
Greek
Kubelíkova 9, Praha 3
Tel *222 722 239*
A large variety of well-prepared Greek dishes are served at this eatery. Don't miss the special Greek cheeses. The relaxed atmosphere makes it easy to while away an afternoon or evening here.

Osteria Da Clara ⓀⓀ
Italian
Mexická 7, Praha 10
Tel *271 726 548* **Closed** *Sun*
Out of the way, but worth the trip. Serves excellent, simply prepared dishes and has a good wine list.

Key to prices *see page 198*

Pastička ⓚⓚ
Czech
Blanická 25, Praha 2
Tel *222 253 228*
Designed in the style of Irish pubs,
Pastička is a perfect blend of old-
fashioned beer hall and modern
gastro-pub. Choose from an
impressive selection of beers and
wines as well as good, filling food.

The Pind ⓚⓚ
Indian
Korunní 1151/67, Praha 3
Tel *222 516 085*
Customers head to The Pind for
excellent Indian food with a spicy
kick. The dining area is lovely, and
the staff are welcoming.

DK Choice

La Terrassa ⓚⓚ
Spanish
*Janáčkovo nábřeží - Dětský
ostrov, Praha 5*
Tel *725 161 616*
Enjoy tapas and other freshly
made Spanish specialities on
a beautifully renovated boat
on the Vltava. The staff are
perfectly attentive and knowledgeable about the wine list.
The food and service are so
good that guests will want
to come again, even if they
have to sit below deck.
Highly recommended for
summer dining.

Villa Voyta ⓚⓚ
International
K Novému Dvoru 124/54, Praha 4
Tel *241 049 401*
Set in an Art Nouveau building
of the same name, this charming
restaurant uses fresh, locally
produced ingredients in its
dishes. Friendly ambience.

Sumptuous dining room in one of Prague's most stylish restaurants, SaSaZu

Aromi ⓚⓚⓚ
Italian
Náměstí Míru 6, Praha 2
Tel *222 713 222*
The Italian chef here creates a
small but tasty menu of classic
favourites. Daily specials based
on fresh seasonal ingredients.

Aureole ⓚⓚⓚ
Asian-fusion
Hvězdova 1716/2b, Praha 4
Tel *222 755 380*
This is the highest restaurant in
Prague and it has a stunning
interior. The menu is heavily
inspired by the Orient and
includes sushi and curry.

Café Imperial ⓚⓚⓚ
Czech-International
Na Poříčí 15, Praha 1
Tel *246 011 440*
Creative cooking is what distin-
guishes this eatery, which also
offers a Czech menu selection,
breakfast and daily lunch specials.

Oliva ⓚⓚⓚ
Mediterranean
Plavecká 404/4, Praha 2
Tel *222 520 288*
Lovely, family-run restaurant
with a focus on fresh, creative
cooking. Dishes are carefully
sourced and expertly prepared
and served.

DK Choice

Sansho ⓚⓚⓚ
International
Petrská 25, Praha 1
Tel *222 317 425*   **Closed** *Sun
& Mon*
With no set menu, Sansho
prepares everything daily,
based on what they source
from local farmers. The dining
room is family-style, and the
casual approach includes an
open kitchen and friendly
staff. Chefs place a premium
on the quality of their meat
cuts, but there's always
something on the menu
for vegetarians.

DK Choice

SaSaZu ⓚⓚⓚ
Asian
*Bubenské nábřeží 306,
Praha 7*
Tel *284 097 455*
This pleasant restaurant,
awarded a Michelin Bib
Gourmand, offers excellent
food from Indonesia, Thailand
and Vietnam. The opportunity
to experiment with a variety of
flavours does not happen often,
but guests will be rewarded
throughout with innovative
dishes. Don't rush – this is a
meal to savour.

Art Nouveau ceramic wall tiling and mosaic ceiling, Café Imperial

For more information on types of restaurants *see page 193*

Pubs, Beer Halls and Bars

Prague has somewhere to suit practically everyone's taste, from sophisticated cocktail bars to traditional Czech cellar pubs. One particular breed of pub, the themed Irish, English or sports bar, caters mainly to the large number of young English men who travel to Prague on stag weekends. The real charm of drinking in Prague is that it's possible to stroll around the Old Town and find places to meet and drink with Czechs and expatriates alike. If you sit at an empty table, don't be surprised if others join you. In some traditional Czech pubs, a waiter will automatically bring more beer as soon as you appear close to finishing, unless you indicate otherwise. It pays to expect the unexpected in Prague – in some supposedly upmarket places, the waiters' attitude can be surly and unhelpful, while in the humblest pub, you may find service to be efficient and courteous.

Traditional Pubs and Beer Halls

Traditionally, Czech pubs either serve food or are large beer halls dedicated to the mass consumption of beer. The words *hostinec* and *hospoda* used to indicate a pub with food, whereas a *pivnice* served only beer, but over time the distinctions have faded.

Recommended for the brave, **The Golden Tiger** (U Zlatého Tygra) is a loud Czech literati pub, wall-to-wall with mostly male regulars. (This is where the Czech president, Vaclav Havel took Bill Clinton to show him local beer culture.) **U Fleků** has brewed its unique beer, Flekovské, since 1499. For authenticity, and Budvar, try **U Medvídků** which is not far away from the National Theatre *(see pp156–7)* and the Old Town Square. **U Vejvodů** is a former traditional Czech pub which has embraced tourism, with large tables and waiters who understand English. You lose something in authenticity but the beer is good, the food decent and there's usually a place to sit. The traditional *hospoda* scarcely comes more so than **U Pinkasů**, hidden behind Wenceslas Square in a quaint courtyard.

Cocktail Bars

Prague now has almost more cocktail bars than you could shake a swizzle stick at, but there are some that stand out. On Pařížská, Prague's Fifth Avenue, you'll find **Bugsy's**. This bar has even printed their own cocktail bible, though towards the end of the week, it does become somewhat overtaken by burly men in long coats. Among the least expensive bars in Prague are **Bar Konvice** (Kettle) and nearby **Propaganda**. For drinks with a view, head to the highest bar in town, **Oblaca** in Žižkov TV Tower. In **Beer Factory**, you can tap your own beer, sample cocktails or just listen or dance to music.

Irish Pubs and Theme Bars

Prague now has theme bars in all shapes and sizes, with still the most common being the ubiquitous Irish pub. **Caffreys** is one of Prague's most popular – and pricier – Irish bars, located off the Old Town Square. **Rocky O'Reilly's** is the biggest Irish pub in town, and a rowdy place, packed to the rafters if there is a big football match on the television. **Jáma** is a lively pub with great bar food that serves Prague's best burger, among other attributes. Just a stone's throw away from Charles Bridge is possibly the only Irish-Cuban hybrid pub anywhere, the noisy and fun **O'Che's**.

La Casa Blu is an atmospheric South American bar where the Chilean, Peruvian, Mexican and Czech staff create a carnival-type atmosphere.

Bohemian Hangouts

Not only in the geographical heart of Bohemia, these bars also represent the unconventional side of Prague city-life. **Al Capone's** is one of the most famous, not to say notorious, drinking dens in the Old Town, host to a parade of visitors and locals. **Chapeau Rouge** is a rowdy college joint that is a guaranteed all-nighter, with a street-level bar that's loads of fun and a downstairs club that's hopping most of the night. Over the Vltava in the Castle district, you'll find **U Malého Glena**, which translates roughly to "at Little Glen's", and is one of the longest surviving expatriate bars in the city. Not far away is **Jo's Bar & Garáž**, which has also stood the test of time as an expat hangout. It's a small, cavernous pub, Mexican eatery and disco, and becomes quickly packed.

Sports Bars

Sports bars have taken off in Prague, with places like **Lion & Ball** or **The PUB**, with its deck of TV screens. Another popular sports bar further from the city centre is **Club Velbloud** in Žižkov.

Café Society

The city is embedded in café society, ranging from old-fashioned smoky joints to cafés within bookstores, boutiques and billiard halls. Some are restaurants, others focus on drinking, but all serve alcohol. Located inside the Cubist House of the Black Madonna *(see p67)* is **Grand Café Orient**. Other places to see and be seen are **Ebel** in the Old Town and **Slavia**, by the river opposite the National Theatre. For a perfect meeting place, try the **Grand Café Praha** opposite the Old Town Square's Astronomical Clock, or the light-filled **EMA Espresso Bar**.

DIRECTORY

Traditional Pubs and Beer Halls

The Beer House
Pivovarský Dům
Lípová 15.
Map 5 C2.
Tel 296 216 666.
[w] pivovarskydum.com

The Black Bull
U Černého Vola
Loretánské nám 1.
Map 1 B3.
Tel 606 628 929.

The Golden Tiger
U Zlatého Tygra
Husova 17. **Map** 3 B4.
Tel 222 221 111.
[w] uzlatehotygra.cz

Kolkovna-Olympia
Vítězná 7. **Map** 2 E5.
Tel 251 511 080.
[w] kolkovna.cz

Monastery Brewery Strahov
Strahovské nádvoří 301/10.
Map 1 B4.
Tel 233 353 155.
[w] klasterni-pivovar.cz

The Shot Out Eye
U Vystřeleného Oka
U Božích bojovníků 3.
Tel 222 540 465.
[w] uvoka.cz

U Fleků
Křemencova 11.
Map 5 B1.
Tel 224 934 019.
[w] ufleku.cz

U Kalicha
Na Bojišti 12–14.
Map 6 D3.
Tel 224 912 557.
[w] ukalicha.cz

U Medvídků
Na Perštýně 7.
Map 3 B5.
Tel 224 211 916.
[w] umedvidku.cz

U Pinkasů
Jungmannovo náměstí 15/16. **Map** 3 C5.
Tel 221 111 152.
[w] upinkasu.cz

U Vejvodů
Jilská 4. **Map** 3 B4.
Tel 224 219 999.
[w] restauraceu vejvodu.cz

Cocktail Bars

Aloha
Dušní 11. **Map** 3 B2.
Tel 602 251 392.
[w] alohapraha.cz

Bar Konvice
Bartolomějská 11.
Map 3 B5.
Tel 224 240 588.

Beer Factory
Václavské náměstí 58.
Map 6 D1.
Tel 234 101 117.
[w] beer-factory.cz

Bugsy's
Pařížská 10. **Map** 3 B2.
Tel 840 284 797.
[w] bugsysbar.com

Hemingway Bar
Karolíny Světlé 26.
Map 3 A5.
Tel 773 974 764.
[w] hemingwaybar.cz

Oblaca
Žižkov TV Tower,
Mahlerovy sady 1.
Tel 210 320 086.
[w] towerpark.cz

Propaganda
Pštrossova 29. **Map** 5 A1.
Tel 224 932 285.
[w] propagandabar.cz

Irish Pubs and Theme Bars

Black Angels
Staroměstské nám. 29.
Map 3 B3.
Tel 224 213 807.
[w] blackangelsbar.cz

Caffreys
Staroměstské nám. 10.
Map 3 B3.
Tel 224 828 031.
[w] caffreys.cz

La Casa Blu
Kozí 15. **Map** 3 C2.
Tel 224 818 270.
[w] lacasablu.cz

Dubliner
Týn 1 – Ungelt. **Map** 3 C3.
Tel 224 895 404.
[w] aulddubliner.cz

George & Dragon
Staroměstské nám. 11.
Map 3 B3.
[w] georgeanddragon prague.com

Jáma (The Hollow)
V jámě 7. **Map** 5 C1.
Tel 222 967 081.
[w] jamapub.cz

James Joyce
U Obecního dvora 4.
Map 4 D3.
Tel 224 818 851.

J.J. Murphy's
Tržiště 4. **Map** 2 E3.
Tel 257 535 575.
[w] bestirishbarprague. com

Merlin
Bělehradská 68A.
Map 6 E2.
Tel 222 522 054.
[w] merlin-pub.cz

O'Che's
Liliová 14. **Map** 3 C3.
Tel 222 221 178.
[w] oches.com

Rocky O'Reilly's
Štěpánská 32. **Map** 3 A5.
Tel 222 231 060.
[w] rockyoreillys.cz

Bohemian Hangouts

Al Capone's
Bartolomějská 3.
Map 3 B5.
Tel 224 241 040.
[w] alcapones.cz

Chapeau Rouge
Jakubská 2. **Map** 3 C3.
Tel 222 316 328.
[w] chapeaurouge.cz

Duende
Karolíny Světlé 30.
Map 3 A4.
Tel 774 486 077.
[w] barduende.cz

Jo's Bar & Garáž
Malostranské nám 7.
Map 2 E3.
Tel 257 531 422.
[w] josbar.cz

U Malého Glena
Karmelitská 23.
Map 2 E4.
Tel 257 531 717.
[w] malyglen.cz

Sports Bars

Club Velbloud
Hraniční 3, Praha 3.
Map 6 D1.
Tel 739 936 696.

Lion & Ball
Týnská ulička 3.
Map 3 C3.
Tel 777 000 780.
[w] sportbar.cz

The PUB
Veleslavínova 3.
Map 3 A3. **Tel** 222 312 296. [w] thepub.cz

Café Society

Café Imperial
Na Poříčí 15.
Map 4 D3.
Tel 246 011 440.
[w] cafeimperial.cz

Café Lounge
Plaská 8. **Map** 2 E5.
Tel 257 404 020.
[w] cafe-lounge.cz

Ebel Coffee
Řetězová 9.
Map 3 B4.
Tel 224 895 788.
[w] ebelcoffee.cz

EMA Espresso Bar
Na Florenci 3.
Map 4 E3.
Tel 730 156 933.
[w] emaespressobar.cz

Grand Café Orient
Dům U Černé Matky Boží
Ovocný trh 19.
Map 3 C3.
Tel 224 224 240.
[w] grandcafeorient.cz

Grand Café Praha
Staroměstské nám. 22.
Map 3 B3.
Tel 221 632 522.
[w] grandcafe.cz

Kávovarna
Palác Lucerna,
Štěpánská 61.
Map 4 D5.
Tel 224 224 537.

Slavia
Národní třída 1.
Map 3 A5.
Tel 224 218 493.
[w] cafeslavia.cz

Nightlife

Nightlife in Prague is as lively as in other European cities. A constant stream of visitors and a spirited local crowd has seen to that. Cheap drink, cutting-edge performers, liberal gambling and prostitution laws all help pull in the crowds. Prague is also now firmly established as a tour-stop for major American and UK pop and rock acts, with venues such as the Tipsport and O2 arenas playing host to big names at least once a month.

On a more local level, Prague's club scene is a proven testing ground for up-and-coming bands, and its dance/music events, which are heavily influenced by nearby Berlin, are renowned for being experimental. Prague's gay and lesbian scene is buzzing, and the local population is among the most tolerant in mainland Europe.

Discos and Nightclubs

The biggest club in the city is the **Lucerna Music Bar**, which offers a varied programme – either live local bands or a DJ playing classic hits – in an unusual basement ballroom in the beautiful, but run down, Lucerna building. It fills up quickly however, so make sure you get there early.

Karlovy Lázně is another large club, which sometimes has live bands. **Zlatý Strom** offers techno/ house together with 1970s, 1980s and 1990s dance tunes until 5am in a spectacular medieval cellar setting.

The trendier clubs, more likely to be playing cutting-edge music, include **Nebe** and **Radost FX**, where the city's most affluent are attracted by a constant diet of house music and plush decor, together with **Fatal Music Club** and **SaSaZu**. The **Double Trouble** is popular with visiting stag parties, which means it can get quite rowdy. For enthusiasts looking for genuinely experimental and original hardcore house and techno music, the best place to go is **Roxy**, where sets are often accompanied by art-house video projections. Roxy regularly hosts live rock bands, including a number of big-name bands. The **Crossclub** offers a wide variety of music ranging from dubstep to hardcore.

Rock and Pop Clubs

Lovers of live rock music are well served in Prague. One school of thought feels that the anarchic influence of Prague's pioneering 1980s rock bands helped – however inadvertently – bring down the Communist regime. There are today a large number of popular rock venues – generally small clubs and cafés – which host a variety of different groups. The indigenous scene continues to thrive – Prague's own rock bands play both their own compositions as well as cover versions of more famous numbers, many singing in English. Higher-profile, more internationally renowned Western bands play in Prague regularly, usually at the **Tipsport Arena** or **O2 Arena**.

The **Rock Café** and the **Vagon**, both very popular venues, offer regular concerts followed by discos. Other venues include the **Futurum Music Bar**, open till the early hours. **Palác Akropolis** in Žižkov is great for visiting foreign bands. The Lucerna Music Bar and Roxy also host regular bands.

Jazz

The roots of jazz in Prague can be traced not only to the American tradition but also to the pre-war heyday of Prague's famous jazz players, such as Jaroslav Ježek. Even during the Communist period, Prague was an internationally renowned centre of jazz, never failing to attract the biggest names. Dizzy Gillespie, Stan Getz, Duke Ellington and Buddy Rich all played in Prague during the 1960s and 1970s.

Today, Prague's many jazz clubs play all forms, from Dixieland to swing. One of the leading and most popular jazz venues in the city is the **Jazz Club Reduta**, which has daily jazz concerts at around 9pm. When former US President Bill Clinton asked his Czech counterpart Vaclav Havel if he could play some jazz during a state visit to Prague in January 1994, the Czech president took him to the Jazz Club Reduta. The **Jazz Boat** is a great way to see the sights from the river and relax to local jazz. At the **AghaRTA J azz Centrum**, you can hear a high standard of playing. **U Malého Glena** has regular live blues, jazz and funk, as does **Jazz Republic**, with performances every night from 9pm. For serious enthusiasts, the International Jazz Festival (various venues) and the Bohemia Jazzfest in Old Town Square, both held every few years, attract talent from all over the world. **Blues Sklep** is a relative newcomer to Prague's jazz scene and offers an inventive schedule, showcasing acts from jazz, blues and other genres.

Gay and Lesbian Venues

With even mainstream clubs such as Radost FX holding regular gay nights, it is no wonder that Prague is considered one of Europe's hottest gay destinations. The scene is liberal and diverse. Clubs are split into various categories, with **Termix** being a loud and lively disco, and always packed. **Drake's Club** is a less in-your-face venue, and popular with visitors, while the city's most famous gay venue, **Friends**, is a cocktail bar. Friends has a steady following among expat and local men who are less interested in cruising than in just having a drink with like-minded folks. **Temple**, a gay centre, features a bar, disco, sex shop and hotel on the same premises.

The website www.prague.gayguide.net is a valuable resource for all things gay in Prague, including gay-friendly hotels, guesthouses and groups and associations.

Adult Prague

Prague has seen itself become the sex tourism capital of Europe since 1989, partly thanks to ubiquitous cheap beer and the mistaken assumption that prostitution is legal in the country. The law is, in fact, deliberately opaque. While locals may seem fairly tolerant towards the sex industry and associated night-life, and some clubs and venues hosting prostitution have a veneer of respectability, visitors are well advised to steer clear.

DIRECTORY

Discos and Nightclubs

Club Hany Bany
Tel 736 611 777.
W clubhanybany.cz

Coyotes Prague
Malé náměstí 2.
Map 3 B4.
Tel 224 216 000.
W coyotesprague.cz

Crossclub
Plynární 1096/23.
Tel 736 535 010.
W crossclub.cz

Double Trouble
Melantrichova 17.
Map 3 B4.
Tel /34 767 938.
W doubletrouble.cz

Fatal Music Club
Rokycanova 29, Praha 3.
Tel 222 783 463.
W fatalclub.cz

Karlovy Lázně
Novotného lávka,
Smetanovo nábřeží 198.
Map 3 A4.
Tel 222 220 502.
W karlovylazne.cz

Lucerna Music Bar
Vodičkova 36.
Map 3 C5.
Tel 224 217 108.
W musicbar.cz

Misch Masch
Veletržní 61, Praha 7.
W mischmasch.cz

Nebe
V Celnici 4. **Map** 4 D3.
Tel 774 370 033.
Also at: Václavské Náměstí 56. **Map** 6 D1.
Tel 608 129 535.
Křemencova 10.
Map 5 B1.
Tel 608 370 038.
W nebepraha.cz

Občanská Plovárna
U Plovárny 8.
Map 3 A2.
Tel 257 531 451.
W obcanskaplovarna.cz

Radost FX
Bělehradská 120.
Map 6 E2.
Tel 224 254 776.
W radostfx.cz

Roxy
Dlouhá 33.
Map 3 C3.
W roxy.cz

SaSaZu
Bubenské nábřeží 306,
Praha 7.
Tel 284 097 444.
W sasazu.com

Újezd
Újezd 18. **Map** 2 E5.
Tel 251 510 873.
W klubujezd.cz

Zlatý Strom
Karlova 6.
Map 3 A4.
Tel 222 220 441.
W zlatystrom.cz

Rock and Pop Clubs

Futurum Music Bar
Zborovská 7, Praha 5.
Map 2 F5.
Tel 257 328 571.
W futurum.musicbar.cz

Klub Lávka
Novotného lávka 1.
Map 3 A4.
Tel 774 991 119.
W lavka.cz

O2 Arena
See p221.

Palác Akropolis
Kubelíkova 27.
Tel 296 330 911.
W palacakropolis.cz

Rock Café
Národní 20.
Map 3 B5.
Tel 224 933 947.
W rockcafe.cz

Tipsport Arena
See p221.

Vagon
Národní třída 25.
Map 3 B5.
Tel 733 737 301.
W vagon.cz

Jazz Clubs

AghaRTA Jazz Centrum
Železná 16.
Map 3 C4.
Tel 222 211 275.
W agharta.cz

Blues Sklep
Liliová 10.
Map 3 B4.
Tel 608 848 074.
W bluessklep.cz

Jazz Boat
Boat: Gate No. 2, under Čechův Bridge,
Dvořákovo nábřeží.
Map 3 B2.
Tel 731 183 180.
W jazzboat.cz

Jazz Club Reduta
Národní třída 20.
Map 3 B5.
Tel 224 933 487.
W redutajazzclub.cz

Jazz Club U Staré Paní
Michalská 9.
Map 3 B4.
Tel 605 285 211.
W jazzstarapani.cz

Jazz Republic
28. října 3.
Map 3 C5.
Tel 224 282 235.
W jazzrepublic.cz

U Malého Glena
Karmelitská 23.
Map 2 E4.
Tel 257 531 717.
W malyglen.cz

Gay and Lesbian Venues

Alcatraz
Bořivojova 773/58,
Praha 3.
Tel 222 711 458.

Drake's Club
Zborovská 50, Praha 5.
Map 2 F5.
Tel 257 326 828.
W drakes.cz

Escape
V jámě 8. **Map** 5 C1.
Tel 777 153 876.
W escapeclub.xxx

Friends
Bartolomějská 11.
Map 3 B5.
Tel 226 211 920.
W friendsprague.cz

Heaven
Gorazdova 11.
Map 5 A3.
Tel 224 921 282.
W heaven.cz

Klub 21
Římská 21, Praha 2.
Map 6 E1.
Tel 222 364 720.
W klub21.cz

Temple
Seifertova 3, Praha 3.
Map 4 F4.
Tel 722 212 952.
W clubtemple.cz

Termix
Třebízského 4a.
Tel 222 710 462.
W club-termix.cz

SHOPPING IN PRAGUE

With its wide, pedestrianized streets, classy shopping malls, souvenir shops and antiques *bazars*, Prague is established as one of Europe's leading shopping destinations. Almost all of the major US and Western European retailers have established outlets in the city. The quality of goods manufactured in the Czech Republic – from glass and china to hand-woven carpets and wooden toys – is always of a high standard. Most of Prague's best shopping areas are in the centre of the city, and you can spend a whole day just diving in and out of small speciality shops and large department stores. For a different shopping experience, the few traditional markets in the city offer everything from vegetables and fresh fruit to imported Russian caviar, toys, clothes, furniture, Czech crafts and electrical parts. Large malls are dispersed further out on the outskirts of Prague but are easily accessible by car or metro.

Opening Hours

Most of Prague's shops open from 10am to 6pm Monday to Friday and from 9am to 1pm on Saturdays, although supermarkets are open for much longer, from 7am until 9 or 10pm.

Food stores open earlier too, most of them at 7am – reflecting the early working day of many locals – and close at around 9pm. Some Vietnamese convenience stores are open 24 hours (you can find one at Národní and two close to I.P. Pavlova metro station). Department stores and the big shopping centres and malls are open daily between 8am and 9pm, with their supermarkets starting an hour earlier and closing an hour later. All are open on Sundays, except on holidays. Some Tesco supermarkets (Skalka, Novodvorská Plaza and Nový Smíchov) open at 6 or 7am and close at midnight, while three others (at Avion Shopping Park, OC Letňany and NC Eden) are open round the clock.

In the centre, around Old Town Square and Celetná and Karlova streets, many shops rely almost entirely on tourists for their trade, so have adapted their opening hours accordingly. They are usually open daily from 10am until late evening. Some close at 11pm. All the shops are at their most crowded on Saturdays, and for stress-free shopping, it's often better to wander around them during the week. Prague's market in

An antiques shop on Bridge Street, in Prague's Little Quarter

Havelská is open daily, while River Town market is open Monday to Saturday. Opening times for both are from 7am until the evening.

How to Pay

Most staple goods, such as food, are cheaper than comparable items in Western Europe and the US, as long as they do not need to be imported. However, with more and more multinationals, such as Boss and Pierre Cardin, moving into the city, prices are slowly starting to rise.

The total price of goods should always include Value Added Tax (this is 20 per cent of the total price, depending on what is being sold). Cash payments can usually only be made in Czech crowns *(koruna)*, though some shops now take euros. The exchange rate in supermarkets such as Tesco, Billa and Albert can sometimes be even better than in the exchange offices. Smaller shops appreciate it if you pay the exact amount and at times may refuse to accept banknotes of Kč1,000 and above. All major credit and charge cards are widely accepted *(see p230)*.

If you are a non-EU resident, you can get the VAT back on purchases exceeding Kč2,000. To be able to do this, you must be sure, when you make a purchase, to ask at the cash till for a tax-free cheque. When you go back to the airport for your return flight, make your way to the special desk at departures for reclaiming your VAT costs. Be prepared to show your items, receipts and cheques. Once that is done, the staff will refund the VAT.

Sales and Bargains

Following the examples of the Western stores, sales are becoming more popular. As a result, it is now quite normal for clothes to be sold off cheaper at the end of each season. There is also an increasing number of post-Christmas sales in the shops found around Old Town Square, Wenceslas Square, Na Příkopě and 28. října.

If you want vegetables, fruit, meat or other perishable produce, buy them at the beginning of the day, when the best quality goods are still on sale. There is no point in waiting till the end of the day in the hope of getting bargains, as is the case in Western shops that reduce prices to get rid of perishable items.

Where to Shop

Most of Prague's best shops are conveniently located in the city centre, especially in and around Wenceslas Square, though the souvenir shops lining Nerudova on the way up to the castle are also well worth your time. Many of these shopping areas have been pedestrianized, making for leisurely window-shopping, although they can get rather crowded. There are a number of department stores which sell an eclectic range of Czech and Western items, with more opening all the time. The well-known department store **Kotva** (The Anchor), lies in the centre of the city. It was built in 1975

and its four storeys offer a wide range of Western goods, particularly fashion and electronics, with the bonus of an underground car park. But compared to Western department stores, Kotva has a smaller selection of goods than you may be accustomed to, and is now struggling to compete with the newer and more glamorous **Palladium** shopping mall across the square. Prices for some of the more luxurious items on sale, such as perfumes, can often be equivalent to the Western ones.

Another popular store is **Tesco**. This has a good selection of Czech and Western products in a bland 1970s building on Národní třída. The city's oldest department store is **Bílá Labut'** (The White Swan) in Na Poříčí. It was opened shortly before the occupation of Czechoslovakia in 1939 and was the first building in Prague to have an escalator. It has since fallen on hard times but is still worth a browse for the building alone.

Debenhams, another famous name from Western Europe, has opened an enormous store on Wenceslas Square, and its home furnishings department on the third floor is very popular with locals.

The outskirts of Prague are now home to massive shopping parks, with large hypermarkets. Tesco has several branches, including

DIRECTORY

Department Stores

Bílá Labut'
Na Poříčí 23.
Map 4 E3.
Tel 22 23 20 227.

Debenhams
Václavské náměstí. 21.
Map 4 D5.
Tel 22 10 15 047.

Kotva
Revoluční 1.
Map 4 D3.
Tel 22 48 01 111.

Palladium
Náměstí Republiky 1.
Map 4 D3.
Tel 22 57 70 250.
W **palladiumpraha.cz**

Tesco
Národní třída 63/26.
Map 3 B5.
Tel 22 28 15 111.

in Nový Smíchov, in OC Letňany and at Zličín, next to the equally enormous IKEA.

Markets and Malls

Prague city centre is not blessed with a great market for most of the year, though the Christmas Gift Market in Old Town Square is worth visiting. The city's major central market, **Havelská tržnice** (see p215), sells mainly fresh produce and cheap souvenirs. Another large market is **Pražská tržnice** (take the metro to Vltavská). The best of Prague's flea markets is **Buštěhrad Collector's Market** (see p215), a glorified car-boot sale close to Lidice. Various markets – farmer's, Christmas and Easter – are organized in front of Arkády Pankrác building (see p215).

Western-style shopping malls are common in Prague. Na Příkopě – between Náměstí Republiky and Václavské náměstí – is home to five: **Palladium**, **Slovanský dům**, **Myslbek**, **Černá růže** and **Koruna Palace** (see p215). Further out, but close to metro stations, are **Arkády Pankrác**, **Nový Smíchov** and **Atrium Flora** (see p215). There are also other malls on the outskirts of Prague, all with huge car parks.

A second-hand bookshop in Prague

What to Buy in Prague

There is a huge selection of goods available in Prague's shops. Prague's more traditional products, such as Bohemian crystal, china, wooden toys and antiques, make great souvenirs, and there are still some real bargains to be picked up around the city, though you will need to shop around. Increasingly popular are the more unusual, though less authentic, historic goods which are sold by many of Prague's street shops. These include Soviet army medals, Red Army uniforms and Russian dolls. Lovely Czech gems are also worth investigating, particularly garnets.

You should watch out for an increasing number of fakes which are now appearing in the market.

Prague also has several *bazar* shops which stock a range of items at cheaper prices. Items are often unusual and good bargains can be found. **Bazar Nekázanka** is a small, popular shop full of second-hand goods. For furniture bargains, **Antik Bazar** is well worth a visit.

Glass and China

Bohemian glass and china have always been ranked among the finest in the world. From huge, decorative vases to delicate glass figurines, the vast selection of glass and china items for sale is daunting. Crystal, glass and china can be quite different depending on where they are made. Lead crystal ranges in lead content from 14 to 24 per cent, for example. Always make sure you are fully aware of what you are buying.

Some of the best glass and china in Bohemia is produced at the Moser glassworks in Karlovy Vary and sold at **Moser**.

The deep blood-red Bohemian garnet, the Czechs' de facto national stone, is highly popular and can be purchased as jewellery in many of the stores which also sell glass, including **Crystal Direct**, **Czech Crystal** and **Erpet Bohemia Crystal**. Another great store to visit is **Artěl**, which sells mouth-blown glassware designed by Karen Feldman.

However, prices for certain goods, especially classically designed vases, decanters and bowls are starting to reflect the increasing popularity of Bohemian crystal. The days when such goods could be purchased in Prague for half the Western European price are over. Yet, value for money remains high, and you can still pick up bargains if you shop around carefully. Remember that many of the modern pieces are just as lovely and much cheaper.

Bohemian porcelain, while not as celebrated as Bohemian

crystal, also makes an excellent gift or souvenir. **Český Porcelán**, the country's most famous factory, is in Dubí, close to the town of Teplice, an hour's drive towards the German border from Prague, and its factory shop offers wonderful bargains. Český Porcelán also has a shop in Prague. Other names worth looking out for include Royal Dux Bohemia, Haas & Czjzek, A. Ruckl & Sons and Toner.

Because of the fragile nature of the goods, many shops will pack anything you buy there. But if you go for a more expensive piece, it is worth looking into insurance before you leave Prague.

Antique Shops

Given its history as a major city in the Habsburg empire, Prague is a great place to hunt for antiques. Hidden treasures seemingly lurk around every corner, and prices are still generally lower than in the West. Most of the city's shopping districts have a large number of antique shops: Old Town is full of them, as is the Royal Route from the castle. Look out for Bohemian furniture, glass and porcelain, as well as military and Soviet memorabilia.

Antique shops that are well worth exploring include **Dorotheum**, **Starožitnosti pod Kinskou** and **Pražské Starožitnosti**. **Military Antiques** is a haven for all army fanatics. For goods over Kč1,000, check with the shop whether you will need a licence to export them.

You should watch out for an increasing number of fakes which are now appearing in the market.

Traditional Crafts

The traditional manufacture of high-quality, hand-crafted goods still survives in modern-day Prague. The variety of the merchandise available in the shops – hand-woven carpets, wooden toys, table mats, beautifully painted Easter eggs, baskets, figurines in folk costumes and ceramics – are all based on Czech and Moravian folk crafts and then enriched with modern elements. You can buy traditional craft items from many market stalls as well as a fair number of shops.

Making items from clay is an ancient craft in the Czech Republic. **Česká Keramika** has a long tradition of manufacturing ceramics.

A jewellery shop known for using only the best Czech garnets mounted in stylish, contemporary settings is **Studio Šperk**. You should also look out for a chain of shops called **Manufaktura** (Handmade), which sells goods made only in the Czech Republic and has a huge choice of hand-carved decorative items, as well as original cosmetics.

A number of street vendors around Old Town Square also sell handmade items including jewellery and puppets. Czech wooden items are of the highest quality (*see* Speciality Shops, *pp214–15*).

Books

There are numerous bookshops in Prague, reflecting the city's rich literary heritage. Many of them sell English-language books. **Neo Luxor – Palác knih** offers a great selection of books on its three floors. There are several branches scattered around the city.

Maps and guides to Prague in English can be bought at **Knihkupectví Academia**. Other specialist bookshops include **Knihkupectví Fišer** and **Kanzelsberger**, with locations around the city. **Franz Kafka Bookshop** sells editions of the author's works in a variety of languages. Prague also has second-hand bookshops. **Antikvariát Dlážděná** is one of the best and has a vast selection. **Antikvariát Ztichlá Klika** deals in antiquarian books as well as 20th-century avant-garde works.

The legendary **Globe** café and bookstore has been a good place to find second-hand English books and enjoy the city's best cappuccino since 1993. The Globe is known for hosting regular literary events and art exhibitions, as does the newer **Shakespeare & Sons**, which also holds film nights and poetry readings. Another well-stocked English bookshop is **Oxford Bookshop**, which is also linked to a huge e-book store (Mega Books CZ).

If you are after Czech books or CDs, try **Levné knihy** (Cheap Books) or **Knihkupectví Daniel**, both located close to the massive Tesco store on Národní třída.

DIRECTORY

Glass and China

Artěl
Celetná 29 (entrance at Rybná 1). **Map** 3 C3.
Tel 224 815 085.

U lužického semináře 7.
Map 2 F3.
Tel 251 554 008.
W **artelshop.com**

Český Porcelán
Perlová 1. **Map** 3 B4.
Tel 224 210 955.
W **cesky.porcelan.cz**

Crystal Direct
Karlova 24.
Map 3 A4.
Tel 222 220 126.
W **crystaldirect.cz**

Czech Crystal
Karlova 44.
Map 3 A4.
Tel 222 327 987.
W **czechcrystal.com**

Erpet Bohemia Crystal
Staroměstské náměstí 27.
Map 3 C3.
Tel 224 229 755.
W **erpetcrystal.cz**

Moser
Na příkopě 12.
Map 3 C4.
Tel 224 211 293.

Also at: Staroměstské náměstí 15. **Map** 3 C3.
Tel 221 890 891.
W **moser-glass.com**

Antique Shops

Antik Bazar
Jana Želivského 2, Žižkov.
Tel 603 480 904.
W **antik-bazar.cz**

Bazar Nekázanka
Nekázanka 17.
Map 4 D4.
Tel 224 210 550.
W **nekazanka.cz**

Dorotheum
Ovocný trh 2. **Map** 3 C4.
Tel 224 222 001.
W **dorotheum.cz**

Military Antiques
Hybernská 40.
Map 4 F4.
Tel 222 222 657.

Pražské Starožitnosti
Zdeněk Uhlíř
Mikulandská 8.
Map 3 B5.
Tel 224 930 572.

Starožitnosti pod Kinskou
Náměstí Kinských 7,
Praha 5 – Smíchov.
Tel 257 311 245.
W **antique-shop.cz**

Gifts and Souvenirs

Česká Keramika
Bělohorská 248/65,
Praha 6 – Břevnov.
Tel 730 132 885.

Manufaktura
Also at: Karlova 26.
Map 3 A4.

Melantrichova 17.
Map 3 B4.

Celetná 12. **Map** 3 C3.

Mostecká 17. **Map** 2 E3.

Zlatá ulička u Daliborky 7 & 21 Prague Castle.
Map 2 E2.
Tel 230 234 376.
W **manufaktura.cz**
(several branches)

Studio Šperk
Dlouhá 19.
Map 3 C3.
Tel 224 815 161.
W **drahonovsky.cz**

Books

Antikvariát Dlážděná
Dlážděná 7. **Map** 4 E4.
Tel 222 243 911.
W **adplus.cz**

Antikvariát Ztichlá Klika
Betlémská 10–14.
Map 3 A5.
Tel 222 221 150.
W **ztichlaklika.cz**

Franz Kafka Bookshop
Staroměstské náměstí 12.
Map 3 B3.
Tel 222 321 454.

Globe
Pštrossova 6.
Map 5 A1.
Tel 224 934 203.
W **globebookstore.cz**

Kanzelsberger
Václavské náměstí 42.
Map 4 D5.
Tel 224 217 335.
W **dumknihy.cz**

Knihkupectví Academia
Václavské náměstí 34.
Map 4 D5.
Tel 221 403 840.
W **academia.cz**

Knihkupectví Daniel
Levné knihy
Národní třída 38.
Map 3 C5.
Tel 224 946 668.

Knihkupectví Fišer
Fišer Knihkupectví
Kaprova 10.
Map 3 B3.
Tel 222 320 733.

Levné knihy
Spálená 43/104.
Map 3 B5.
Tel 224 930 766.

Neo Luxor – Palác knih
Václavské náměstí 41.
Map 4 D5.
Tel 296 110 336.
(two of several branches)

Oxford Bookshop
Opletalova 5/7.
Map 4 E5.
Tel 224 220 521.
W **oxfordbookshop.cz**

Shakespeare & Sons
U Lužického semináře 10.
Map 2 F3.
Tel 25 75 31 894.
W **shakes.cz**

Markets, Malls and Speciality Shops

Take your pick – super-modern mall or traditional market. Prague has them both, although do remember that Prague's main market is at some distance from the city centre at Holešovice. Malls have sprung up everywhere in the city, and Prague has made a name for itself as a leading place to find all sorts of odd bits and pieces in any number of speciality stores. From Fabergé eggs to Jewish *yarmulkas*, you'll find it in Prague.

Markets

Prague's markets offer a vast range of goods, although most are aimed at locals, offering fruit and vegetables, cheap clothing and electronics. The largest market in the city, **River Town** (Holešovická tržnice), was converted from a former slaughter-house. The market now sells fresh fruit and vegetables, and all kinds of poultry, as well as fish, textiles, flowers, electronics, antiques, toys and furniture. These are all sold in several large halls and in outdoor stalls. The market is generally open from Monday to Saturday, 7am to 8pm.

In Havelská, right in the centre of the city, is **Havelská tržnice**, which mainly sells fruit, vegetables and cheap souvenirs. It is open daily, 7am–7pm.

You will also enjoy foraging through the junk, antiques, furniture and military memorabilia (none of which comes with a promise of a refund or guarantee) at the out-of-town **Buštěhrad Collectors Market**, allegedly the third-largest market of its kind in Europe. You can get there by public transport, taking a bus from Dejvická or Zličín metro stations. The market is only open on the second and fourth Friday and Saturday of the month, from 6am to noon. Another flea market worth visiting, Bleší trhy Praha, is at Kolbenova metro station, and is open 6am–1:30pm at weekends.

Old Town Square plays host to an excellent and very popular Christmas Market from the end of November through the New Year's holiday. Besides the stalls selling gifts and toys, there are others selling hot wine and sausages, and there is also a small children's play area. The Square also hosts the city's Christmas tree and a number of open-air winter concerts.

Malls

There is an increasing number of Western-style shopping malls in Prague, which are more popular and often much better than the old department stores, offering better value and a greater range of high-quality goods. In the very centre of town on Náměstí Republiky (on metro B), **Palladium** has hundreds of shops and restaurants on five levels. Just down the street, on Na příkopě, the upmarket **Myslbek**, **Černá růže** and **Koruna Palace** (metro A and B) are home to a great number of chic boutiques and jewellery stores. In addition, at **Slovanský dům**, there is a multiplex cinema as well as a fabulous Kogo restaurant.

You can also take the metro to visit three-storey galleries **Arkády Pankrác** (metro C) and **Atrium Flora** (metro B). **Nový Smíchov** at Anděl (metro B) is home to a two-storey Tesco, as well as multiplex Cinestar Cinemas *(see p219)* nearby. Other shopping destinations include **Quadrio**, at Spálená, and **Florentinum**, next to Masaryk train station.

Very popular is the huge **Centrum Chodov** (metro C), with 200 shops. **Galerie Harfa**, close to the O2 Arena, has an ice-skating rink on the roof, which is free for public use (Českomoravská, metro B). At the furthest outskirts of the city, at both ends of metro line B, there are many hypermarkets and malls, including **Metropole Zličín**, which also has a multiplex cinema. The largest mall in the country, **OC Letňany** (metro line C and shuttle bus) is close to the D8 motorway. **Šestka** can be useful for last-minute shopping, as it is situated just next to the airport and served by bus Number 119 between Dejvická and Václav Havel Airport.

Street Stalls

Street stalls and wandering vendors are not officially allowed to operate in most areas of Prague, though a number of vendors are permitted to sell souvenirs around Charles Bridge. Street stalls are allowed near the entrance to the Old Jewish Cemetery in the Jewish Quarter, and they also line the Old Castle Steps from Malostranská metro station up to the castle's eastern gate.

As most of these sellers are well vetted, the goods on sale tend to be reasonably good quality, though you are unlikely to find any real bargains, and much of what is on sale can be bought cheaper in souvenir stores.

Speciality Shops

Bohemia and Moravia have long been known for their fine wooden toys. You will find a number of shops selling them throughout the city, especially in Old Town, but beware of cheap imports. You can be sure of the genuine article at **Hračky Traditional Toys** near the castle, Beruška in New Town and **Sparky's House of Toys**, just off Na příkopě, a treasure trove for children of all ages. Older children might also like **Games & Puzzles** on Wenceslas Square, which specializes in all sorts of mind teasers, including handmade wooden labyrinths.

If you are looking for something a little quirky, but very Czech, try **Botanicus** near Old Town Square, which sells all-natural and all-Czech health and beauty products, from soap to massage oil. Another popular store is **Qubus**, which sells anything and everything, as long as it is the height of modern design.

Most of the weird and wonderful things on sale were designed by young Czechs. There are a number of other unique and interesting stores in Prague. The **Spanish Synagogue Gift Shop** sells torah pointers, *yarmulkas*, watches and other Jewish gifts. **Le Patio** on Národní is a shop specializing in original illuminations and candelabra, as well as top-quality restored furniture imported from India, and tables and chairs made by some outstanding Czech blacksmiths. Another favourite

for design fans is **de.fakto**, an upmarket version of IKEA, in the centre of the city. **Art Deco Galerie** is an upmarket junk shop with gorgeous period-pieces, glass, accessories, home furnishings and second-hand clothing. The prize for most bizarre shop in Prague must go to **Original Stoves by Trakal**, a store specializing in the restoration of historic stoves.

Food and Delicatessens

Prague's supermarkets are well stocked with the basic foodstuffs. **Delicacies-lahůdky** is a

small shop with meat and fish counters. **Paul** sells breads, fancy cakes and eclairs, plus some local delicacies. For freshly baked bread, visit the bakers around Wenceslas Square and Karmelitská Street. **Paneria** shops sell a good selection of patisseries and sandwiches.

For the best selection of local and international delicacies, however, try **Bakeshop** on Kozí just off Old Town Square. You'll find breads and baked goods, as well as brownies, cookies and sandwiches. It's great for a snack, an informal lunch or to pick up supplies for a picnic.

DIRECTORY

Markets and Malls

Arkády Pankrác
Na Pankráci 86, Pankrác.
Tel 225 111 100.
[W] arkady-pankrac.cz

Atrium Flora
Vinohradská 151, Žižkov.
Map 6 F1.
Tel 255 741 712.
[W] atrium-flora.cz

Buštěhrad Collectors Market
Bleší trhy, Buštěhrad.
Tel 608 967 157.
[W] bustehradantik.cz

Centrum Chodov
Roztylská 19, Chodov.
Tel 272 173 677.
[W] centrumchodov.cz

Černá růže
Na příkopě 12.
Map 3 C4.
Tel 221 014 111.
[W] cernaruze.cz

Florentinum
Na Florenci 15, Praha 1.
[W] florentinum.cz

Galerie Harfa
Českomoravská 2420/15a, Praha 9.
Tel 266 055 600.
[W] galerieharfa.cz

Havelská tržnice
Havelský trh. **Map** 3 C3.

Koruna Palace
Václavské náměstí 1.
Map 3 C5.
Tel 224 219 526.
[W] koruna-palace.cz

Metropole Zličín
Řevnická 1, Zličín.
Tel 226 081 540.
[W] metropole.cz

Myslbek
Na příkopě 19–21 & Ovocný trh 8.
Map 3 C4.
[W] ngmyslbek.cz

Nový Smíchov
Plzeňská 8.
Tel 251 101 061.
[W] novysmichov.eu

OC Letňany
Veselská 663, Praha 9.
Tel 221 742 400.
[W] oc-letnany.cz

Palladium
Náměstí Republiky 1.
Map 4 D3.
Tel 225 770 250.
[W] palladiumpraha.cz

Quadrio
Spálená 2121/22.
Map 3 B5.
Tel 224 054 023. [W] quadrio.cz

River Town
(Holešovická tržnice)
Bubenské nábřeží 13, Praha 7.

Slovanský dům
Na příkopě 22.
Map 3 C4.
[W] slovanskydum.com

Šestka
Fajtlova 1090/1, Praha 6.
Tel 225 023 100.
[W] oc-sestka.cz

Speciality Shops

Art Deco Galerie
Michalská 21. **Map** 3 B4.
Tel 224 223 076.
[W] artdecogalerie-mili.com

Botanicus
Týn 3. **Map** 3 C3.
Tel 234 767 446.
[W] botanicus.cz

de.fakto
Michalská 7, Vejvodova 3.
Map 3 B4.
Tel 224 233 815.
[W] defakto.cz

Games & Puzzles
Václavské náměstí 38.
Map 6 D1. **Tel** 224 946 506. [W] hras.cz

Hračky Traditional Toys
Loretánské náměstí 3.
Map 1 B3.
Tel 603 515 745.

Original Stoves by Trakal (Stará Kamna)
Karmelitská 21. **Map** 2 E4.
Tel 257 534 203.
[W] starakamna.cz

Le Patio
Jungmannova 30.
Map 3 C5.
Tel 224 934 402.
Also at: Dušni 8. **Map** 3 C3.
Tel 222 310 310.
[W] lepatio.cz

Qubus
Rámová 3. **Map** 3 C2.
Tel 295 568 123.
[W] qubus.cz

Spanish Synagogue Gift Shop
Věžeňská 1.
Map 3 B2.

Sparky's House of Toys
Havířská 2.
Map 3 C4.
Tel 224 239 309.
(one of several branches)
[W] sparkys.cz

Foods and Delicatessens

Bakeshop
Kozí 1.
Map 3 C2.
Tel 222 316 823.
[W] bakeshop.cz

Delicacies-lahůdky
Zlatý Kříž
Jungmannovo náměstí 19.
Map 3 C5.
Tel 222 519 451.

Paneria
Kaprova 3.
Map 3 B3.
Tel 702 127 704.
[W] paneria.cz
Also at: Radlická 3185, Anděl, Praha 5.
Tel 702 127 714.
Seifertova 39, Žižkov.
Tel 702 127 717.
(several branches)

Paul
Václavské náměstí 46.
Map 4 D5.
Tel 739 542 257.

ENTERTAINMENT IN PRAGUE

Prague offers a wide variety of entertainment for its visitors, with something for every taste and interest. Whether you prefer opera to jazz or mini-golf to a football match, there is plenty to choose from. Movie buffs can choose from many of the latest Hollywood blockbusters, a lot of them in English with subtitles. For the adventurous, mime and fringe theatre are both thriving. Prague has a superb musical tradition, which includes symphony orchestras, opera, musicals, jazz and folk music. Concerts are performed throughout the year, in venues which range from Baroque palaces to public parks and gardens. Even if you don't speak Czech, you can still enjoy the city's cultural offerings. Some plays can be seen in English, and for many types of entertainment, music, dance and sport, a knowledge of the language isn't necessary at all.

Practical Information

The best place to look for information about what's on and where in Prague is in the English-language newspaper *The Prague Post (see p233)*. This provides details of the best entertainment and cultural events which will be of interest to an English-speaking audience. Those events that are in English or have translation facilities are marked. Other sources of information are the leaflets and City Guides given out at the ticket agencies in the city, such as **Ticketpro** or **Ticketportal**. In addition, there are two online bulletin boards in English, www.expats.cz and http://prague.tv, aimed at expats and visitors. You can also buy a booklet called *Přehled*, printed in English and available from any PIS office. For a comprehensive rundown of events, buy *Culture in Prague*, a detailed monthly publication listing information

A performance of *Cosí Fan Tutte* at the Mozart Festival

on a variety of local exhibitions, concerts and theatre.

Booking Tickets

Tickets can be bought in advance from the box office at most venues. You can also book tickets in advance by writing to, or ringing, the venue. Remember that many of the city's box offices may not have any English speakers available. Tickets for the opera or for any of the performances at the **National Theatre** can also be booked online. The more popular events tend to become heavily booked up in advance by tour groups – particularly during the summer – and by season-ticket holders. However, standby tickets are usually available about an hour before the show. If this isn't practical and you want to be sure of a ticket on a particular day, it is better to buy them at a booking agency. The drawback to using agencies, however, is that commission on these tickets can be high, sometimes doubling the

Puppet Theatre

Puppetry has a long tradition in Prague and is still strongly represented. The most famous puppet show in the city is held at the **Spejbl and Hurvínek Theatre** *(see p219)*. The show revolves around Daddy Spejbl and his reprobate son Hurvínek. Other puppet theatres include the **National Marionette Theatre** *(see p219)*, known for its entertaining puppet rendition of Mozart's *Don Giovanni*. The **Theatre in Dlouhá Street** *(see p219)* and the **Puppet Empire** *(see p219)* also put on puppet shows occasionally. Check listings *(see pp224–5)*.

Theatre puppets

original price. Your hotel receptionist may also be able to get you tickets.

Ticket Prices

Ticket prices are generally cheap compared to Western prices, except for certain popular performances, most notably during the Prague Spring International Music Festival *(see p52)*. Prices range from around Kč100 for a small fringe production to up to Kč3,000 for a performance by an internationally famous orchestra. Paying by credit card is usually only acceptable at ticket agencies.

The Neo-Classical Estates Theatre (Stavovské divadlo; *see p218*)

Elegant interior of the Rudolfinum auditorium *(see p221)*

Ticket Touts

There have been cases of counterfeit tickets being sold, especially for the larger rock concerts. To be safe, always buy your tickets at reputable agencies or at the venue itself.

Late-night Transport

Prague's metro *(see pp242–3)* stops running shortly after midnight, while the normal bus and tram service also ends around midnight. Then the city's extensive night bus and tram service takes over. Timetables are displayed at each stop. Night trams and buses are regular and efficient and it is likely that there will be a tram or bus stop near your

hotel. Taxis provide the most certain form of late-night transportation, but beware of unscrupulous drivers trying to overcharge you *(see p240)*. It is often a good idea to try to walk a little way from the theatre before you hail a cab; the fare will probably be a lot cheaper. Ask at your hotel before you go out to find out what the best transport options are.

Music Festivals

The most famous music festival of all is the Prague Spring International Music Festival, held between May and June *(see p52)*. Hundreds of international musicians come to Prague to take part in the celebrations. Other music festivals include Mozart's Prague *(see p52)*, held in May, and Strings of Autumn *(see p54)* that takes place later in the year.

Spectators at a football match at Generali Arena *(see p221)*

DIRECTORY

Booking Agents

Bohemia Ticket
Na Příkopě 16.
Map 4 D4.
Tel 224 215 031.
W bohemiaticket.cz

DC Service
Maiselova 4.
Map 3 B3.
Tel 224 816 346.
W visitprague.cz

National Theatre tickets
Tel 224 901 448.
W narodni-divadlo.cz

**Prague City Tourism/
Prague Information Service**
Staroměstské náměstí 1.
Map 3 B3.
Tel 221 714 714.
W prague.eu

Ticket Art
Politických vězňů 9.
Map 4 D5.
Tel 222 897 552.
W ticket-art.cz

Ticket Portal
Politických vězňů 15.
Map 4 D5.
Tel 224 091 438.
W ticketportal.cz

Ticket Stream
Koubkova 8. **Map** 6 E3.
Tel 224 263 049.
W ticketstream.cz

Ticketpro
Václavské náměstí 38.
Map 3 C5.
W ticketpro.cz

The Performing Arts and Films

Prague has always been known for its artistic heritage. Theatre has played an important role in the city's cultural development, and in recent decades the range of entertainment has expanded considerably. Even during the Communist period, Prague remained a centre of experimental theatre, not least with the emergence of Black Light Theatre in the 1960s. Today, this tradition continues, with new theatre groups emerging all the time, ever more experimental. In general, the theatre season runs from September to June. During the summer, open-air performances are given in Prague's gardens and parks. For those who prefer to dance till dawn, relax to the sound of jazz or take in a movie – you will find plenty to entertain you in this city.

English-language Performances

Many theatres in Prague have started to stage a number of English-language productions, especially in the summer months. Even if the play is not performed in English, some venues use supertitles to provide a translation. For details, check the listings *(see Listings and Tickets pp224–5)*.

Major Theatres

Prague's first permanent theatre was built in 1738, but the city's theatrical tradition dates from the Baroque and Renaissance periods.

The **National Theatre** *(see pp156–7)* is Prague's main venue for opera, ballet and plays. The neighbouring New Stage is another important venue. It is also the main stage for the multimedia **Laterna Magika** company, which is one of Prague's best-known theatre groups as well as being at the forefront of European improvisational theatre.

Other major theatres in the city include the **Comedy Theatre** and the "stone theatres." These gained importance during the 19th century and include the **Vinohrady Theatre** and the **Estates Theatre** *(see p67)* – one of the most respected in Prague. The Prague Municipal Theatre is an acting company whose plays appear in turn at the **ABC Theatre** and the **Rokoko Studio of Drama**. The **Kolowrat Theatre** is based in the Kolowrat Palace.

Fringe Theatres

These originated during the 1960s and won renown for their fight against the status quo. The groups are still very innovative and largely experimental. They perform in small theatres, and many of Prague's best actors and actresses have developed their skills while working for some of these companies.

Fringe theatres include the **Dramatic Club**, well known for its supporting ensemble; the **Ypsilon Studio**, with one of the finest acting companies in the city; **Theatre Na Fidlovačce**, which stages a mix of musicals and straight drama; the large **Theatre Below Palmovka**, renowned for its mix of classical and modern plays; and the **Theatre in Celetná**. One of Prague's most spectacular theatrical and music venues is **Křižík's Fountain**, at the Exhibition Ground, where classical concerts are held and full orchestras perform to stunning lightshows. The **Semafor Theatre** is the home of the tremendously popular comedian, Jiří Suchý.

Pantomime, Mime and Black Light Theatre

Some of the most popular theatre entertainment in Prague is pantomime, mime and Black Light Theatre. In the latter, the use of UV lighting and fluorescent objects, and costumes, against a darkened stage creates a stunning visual spectacle. None of the three genres requires any understanding of Czech and all are strongly represented.

Jiří Srnec's Black Light Theatre is one of the major venues for Black Light Theatre performance. **Ta Fantastika** is another. These and others are listed in the directory.

Dance

In Prague, opera and ballet companies traditionally share the National Theatre, where the Czech Republic's best permanent ballet company is based. The **Prague State Opera** also has a resident ballet ensemble that is keen to usurp the reputation of the National Theatre company as the city's best. The tickets for the ballet at both major venues are even lower than for opera performances. You can also watch ballet performances at the Estates Theatre. **Ponec** is an experimental performance dance space dedicated to modern dance, and hosts the annual Tanec Praha international festival of contemporary dance and movement theatre in June.

Cinemas

Although Prague doesn't show all the latest Hollywood blockbusters, more than 80 per cent of the films shown are recent US productions, most of them in English with Czech subtitles. Multiplex cinemas are now big business. The largest of these multiplexes – the **Cinema Cities**, which can be found in Flóra, Zličin, Háje, Anděl, Letňany, Hostivař, and one in the centre in **Slovanský Dům** – boast eight to ten screens. **Světozor** is great for catching Czech films with English subtitles. **Bio Oko** is an art house cinema with a great café and an ambitious repertoire of contemporary Czech films as well as classics. **Lucerna** is a lovely cinema to visit, with a beautiful interior. Other cinema options are listed in the directory.

DIRECTORY

Theatres

ABC Theatre
Divadlo Abc
Vodičkova 28.
Map 3 C5.
Tel 222 996 115.
W **mestskadivadla prazska.cz**

Black Light Theatre of Prague
Divadlo V Rytířské
Rytířská 31.
Map 3 C4.
Tel 224 186 114.
W **blacktheatre.cz**

Broadway
Na příkopě 31.
Map 3 C4.
Tel 225 113 311.

Comedy Theatre
Divadlo Komedie
Jungmannova 1.
Map 5 B1.
Tel 224 216 015.

Dramatic Club
Činoherní Klub
Ve Smečkách 26.
Map 6 D1.
Tel 211 151 877.
W **cinoherniklub.cz**

Estates Theatre
Stavovské Divadlo
Železná 11.
Map 3 C4.
Tel 224 901 448.
W **narodni-divadlo.cz**

Jiří Srnec's Black Theatre
Černé Divadlo Jiřího Srnce
Palác Savarin,
Na příkopě 10. **Map** 3 C4.
Tel 774 574 475.
W **srnectheatre.com**

Kolowrat Theatre
Divadlo Kolowrat
Ovocný trh 6.
Map 3 C3.
Tel 224 901 448.
W **narodni-divadlo.cz**

Křižík's Fountain
Křižíkova Fontána
Výstaviště, Praha 7.
Tel 723 665 694.
W **krizikovafontana.cz**

Laterna Magika
Národní třída 4.
Map 3 A5.
Tel 224 901 448.
W **laterna.cz**

National Marionette Theatre
Národní Divadlo Marionet
Žatecká 1. **Map** 3 B3.
Tel 224 819 322.
W **mozart.cz**

National Theatre
Národní Divadlo
Národní třída 2.
Map 3 A5.
Tel 224 901 448.
W **narodni-divadlo.cz**

Puppet Empire
Říše Loutek
Žatecká 1.
Map 3 B3.
Tel 222 324 565.
W **riseloutek.cz**

Reduta Theatre
Divadlo Reduta
Národní třída 20.
Map 3 B5.
Tel 224 933 487.
W **redutajazzclub.cz**

Rokoko Studio of Drama
Divadlo Rokoko
Václavské náměstí 38.
Map 4 D5.
Tel 222 996 185.
W **mestskadivadla prazska.cz**

Semafor Theatre
Divadlo Semafor
Dejvická 27, Praha 6.
Tel 233 901 384.
W **semafor.cz**

Spejbl and Hurvínek Theatre
Divadlo Spejbla A Hurvínka
Dejvická 38, Praha 6.
Tel 224 316 784.
W **spejbl-hurvinek.cz**

Ta Fantastika
Karlova 8.
Map 3 A4.
Tel 222 221 366.
W **tafantastika.cz**

Theatre Below Palmovka
Divadlo Pod Palmovkou
Zenklova 34, Praha 8.
Tel 283 011 127.
W **divadlopod palmovkou.cz**

Theatre in Celetná
Divadlo v Celetné
Celetná 17. **Map** 3 C3.
Tel 222 326 843.
W **divadlovceletne.cz**

Theatre in Dlouhá Street
Divadlo v Dlouhé
Dlouhá 39. **Map** 3 C3.
Tel 221 778 629.
W **divadlovdlouhe.cz**

Theatre Na Fidlovačce
Divadlo Na Fidlovačce
Křesomyslova 625.
Map 6 E5.
Tel 241 404 040.
W **fidlovacka.cz**

Vinohrady Theatre
Divadlo Na Vinohradech
Náměstí Míru 7. **Map** 6 F2.
Tel 224 257 601.

WOW
Na příkopě 31. **Map** 3 C4.
Tel 225 113 194.
W **wow-show.com**

Ypsilon Studio
Studio Ypsilon
Spálená 16. **Map** 3 B5.
Tel 224 947 119.

Dance

Ponec
Husitská 24a/899, Praha 3.
Tel 222 721 531.
W **divadloponec.cz**

Prague State Opera
Státní Opera Praha
Wilsonova 4.
Map 6 E1.
Tel 224 901 448.
W **narodni-divadlo.cz**

Cinemas

Bio Oko
Františka Křížka 15,
Praha 7.
Tel 233 382 606.
W **biooko.net**

Cinema City Flóra
Vinohradská 151,
Praha 3 – Žižkov.
Tel 255 742 021.
W **cinemacity.cz**

Cinema City Galaxie
Arkalycká 3/951,
Praha 4 – Háje.
Tel 255 742 021.
W **cinemacity.cz**

Cinema City Nový Smíchov
Plzeňská 8, Praha 5.
Tel 255 742 021.
W **cinemacity.cz**

Cinema City Slovanský Dům
Na příkopě 22.
Map 3 C4.
Tel 255 742 021.
W **cinemacity.cz**

Cinema City Zličín
Řevnická 1, Praha 5.
Tel 255 742 021.
W **cinemacity.cz**

Cinestar Anděl
Radlická 1e, Praha 5.
Tel 800 288 288.
W **cinestar.cz**

Cinestar Černý Most
Chlumecká 6, Praha 9.
Tel 800 288 288.
W **cinestar.cz**

Evald
Národní třída 28.
Map 3 B5.
Tel 221 105 225.
W **evald.cz**

Kino Aero
Biskupcova 31, Praha 3.
Tel 608 330 088.
W **kinoaero.cz**

Kino Atlas
Sokolovská 371/1,
Praha 8.
Tel 222 312 737.
W **kinoatlas.cz**

Lucerna
Vodičkova 36.
Map 3 C5.
Tel 224 216 972.
W **lucerna.cz**

Mat
Karlovo náměstí 19.
Map 5 B2.
Tel 224 915 765.

Světozor
Vodičkova 41.
Map 3 C5.
Tel 224 946 824.
W **kinosvetozor.cz**

Music and Sports

Prague may not match the vibrancy of Vienna or Budapest, but it certainly can hold its own among Europe's leading cultural destinations. During the holiday season, concerts of classical and Baroque music are held in churches and palaces around the city. Another great attraction for music lovers are Prague's music festivals *(see pp52–4)*.

Sports fans are well served too, with top-class ice hockey and Champions League football.

Opera

Since Richard Wagner's *The Mastersingers of Nurnburg* officially opened Prague's State Opera House on 5 January 1888, Prague has been a centre of operatic excellence. Today, two highly competitive world-class opera companies give opera top billing on Prague's cultural calendar. And while the low Soviet-era prices of yore are now long gone, top-price seats range from Kč1,000 to 1,200, which makes opera in Prague more accessible than most cities in Europe.

The two major companies, the National and the State, both perform exclusively in their own theatres – the National Opera Company in the **National Theatre** *(see pp156–7)*; the State Opera Company at the **Prague State Opera**. The latter presents a predominantly classical Italian repertoire, always in the orginal language, and performances are always popular. Tickets should be bought in advance. The National Opera Company has a more experimental repertoire, and most of its operas are performed in Czech.

To view a Czech opera, by Czech composers such as Smetana or Dvořák, the National Theatre is your best opportunity. A branch of the National Theatre, the **Estates Theatre** *(see p219)*, performs mainly classical, Italian operas in the original language.

Classical Music

The Czech Philharmonic Orchestra (CPO) has been based at the magnificent **Rudolfinum** *(see p86)* since giving its first concert there in January 1896, when it was conducted by no less a personality than Antonín Dvořák, whose name the Rudolfinum's grand hall now carries. Finding immediate success with the public in Prague and abroad (the Philharmonic travelled to London on tour as early as 1902), the orchestra is today recognized by music lovers as one of the finest in the world.

The post of chief conductor of the CPO is one of the most revered appointments in classical music; currently the post is filled by Jiří Bělohlávek. Almost all contemporary Czech music, including the celebrated 2000 work *Requiem* by Milan Slavický, premiered at the Rudolfinum. The programme is varied, however, and the works of Czech composers share the limelight with those of their foreign counterparts.

Besides the Rudolfinum, the main concert venue for classical music is the Smetana Hall, found in the **Municipal House** *(see p66)*. Other permanent concert halls include the **Atrium in Žižkov**, a converted chapel, the **Clementinum** and the imposing **Congress Centre Prague**. With 20 halls and 50 rooms, as well as exhibition space covering 13,000 sq m (140,000 sq ft), the Congress Centre can host all kinds of events, with up to 9,300 participants and visitors.

Music in Churches and Palaces

Concerts performed in the numerous churches and palaces around Prague are extremely popular. Many of these buildings are normally closed to the public, so this is the only chance to see them from inside. Major churches include the **Basilica of St James** *(see p67)*; the **Church of St Giles** *(see p77)*; the **Church of St Nicholas** *(see pp128–9)* in the Little Quarter; the **Church of St Nicholas** *(see p72)* in the Old Town; the **Church of St Francis** in Knights of the Cross Square *(see p81)*; **St Vitus's Cathedral** *(see pp102–105)* and **St George's Basilica** *(see p100)*. Other important venues are the **Lobkowicz Palace** *(see p101)* and the **Sternberg Palace** *(see pp112–13)*. It's worth checking the listings magazines *(pp224–5)* for the specific dates and timings of concerts.

World Music

A small number of clubs and bars in Prague offer ethnic music. The **Palác Akropolis** hosts diverse performances daily in an atmospheric, converted 1920s-theatre building. The Akropolis has hosted the likes of Ani Difranco, Apollo 440 and Transglobal Underground. Concerts of all kinds of music are held at the **National House of Vinohrady** on a variety of occasions. Some of the better jazz clubs *(see pp208–209)* also feature world musicians and bands on a regular basis. Another place worth checking out is **La Bodequita del Medio**, a Cuban restaurant that features Cuban performers some weekend evenings.

Sports

Czechs are crazy about most sports, and given their habit of winning international competitions in any number of events on a regular basis, it is not surprising. The biggest spectator sports are ice hockey and football, in that order of importance.

The main Czech ice hockey league is the best in Europe after the Russian league (KHL), and both US NHL and KHL rosters are filled with Czech players. Prague has two teams in the top division, Sparta and Slavia. Sparta plays its home games at the **Tipsport Arena**, where tickets cost from Kč80 onwards. Slavia play at the **O2 Arena**, built for the 2004 Ice Hockey World Championship, held in, but surprisingly not won by, the Czech Republic. Tickets here cost Kč100 and up. There are three games a week throughout the season, from September to May, so you should be able to catch a game.

Czech football has long been admired throughout the world, and the national team has played better than expected on several occasions. The domestic league is less admired, as many of the country's top stars play in richer leagues elsewhere in Europe. The country's leading team, Sparta Prague, however, is a perennial

qualifier for the European Champions League, which guarantees a procession of big-name opponents. Tickets for Champions League games (played September to December, depending on Sparta's progress) sell out quickly. Home matches of the Czech Republic are also played at **Generali Arena**, commonly known as Letná.

If you want to get active, you may have to travel a little further out of town, as sports facilities are not extensive in central Prague. Squash, however, is very popular, and there are a number of courts in the city centre, including **ASB** on Wenceslas Square. Mini-golf is on offer at

the **Minigolf SK Tempo Praha**. The **Czech Lawn Tennis Club** on Štvanice Island also offers 14 clay courts and six indoor courts that can be rented by the general public all day at the weekends and until 3pm on weekdays.

Aquapalace Praha is the largest water park in Central Europe, with many pools, a health centre and the large Sauna World, which has a wide range of Finnish saunas and a Roman spa. During the summer, various sports can be performed at **Beachklub Pankrác** or at **Žluté lazně**, which is located on the banks of Vltava river. **Fun Island** is a sports and relaxation centre at Císařská louka (Imperial Meadow) island.

DIRECTORY

Music Venues

Academy of Music
Hudební Fakulta Amu
Malostranské náměstí 13.
Map 2 E3.
Tel 234 244 136.
Ⓦ hamu.cz

Atrium in Žižkov
Atrium Na Žižkově
Čajkovského 12, Praha 3.
Tel 222 721 838.
Ⓦ atriumzizkov.cz

Basilica of St James
Bazilika Sv. Jakuba
Malá Štupartská.
Map 3 C3.

Church of St Francis
Kostel Sv. Františka
Křižovnické náměstí.
Map 3 A4.

Church of St Giles
Kostel Sv. Jiljí
Husova 8. **Map** 3 B4.

**Church of St Nicholas
(Little Quarter)**
Kostel Sv. Mikuláše
Malostranské náměstí.
Map 2 E3.

**Church of St Nicholas
(Old Town)**
Kostel Sv. Mikuláše
Staroměstské náměstí.
Map 3 B3.

**Church of Sts Simon
and Jude**
Kostel Sv. Šimona A Judy
Dušní ulice. **Map** 3 B2.
Ⓦ fok.cz

Clementinum
Zrcadlová Síň Klementina
Mariánské náměstí 5.
Map 3 B3.
Ⓦ klementinum.com

**Congress Centre
Prague**
Kongresové Centrum Praha
5. května 65, Praha 4.
Tel 261 171 111.
Ⓦ kcp.cz

Lobkowicz Palace
Lobkovický Palác
Jiřská 3/1, Pražský hrad.
Map 2 E2.
Tel 233 312 925.
Ⓦ lobkowicz.cz

**Music Theatre
in Karlín**
Hudební Divadlo Karlín
Křižíkova 10. **Map** 4 F3.
Tel 221 868 666.
Ⓦ hdk.cz

Prague State Opera
Státní Opera Praha
Wilsonova 4. **Map** 6 E1.
Tel 224 901 448.
Ⓦ narodni-divadlo.cz

**Rudolfinum – Dvořák
Hall**
Rudolfinum – Dvořákova Síň
Alšovo nábřeží 12.
Map 3 A3.
Tel 227 059 227.
Ⓦ ceskafilharmonie.cz

St George's Basilica
Bazilika Sv. Jiří
Jiřské náměstí,
Pražský hrad.
Map 2 E2.

St Vitus's Cathedral
Katedrála svatého Víta
Pražský hrad.
Map 2 D2.

Sternberg Palace
Šternberský Palác
Hradčanské náměstí 15.
Map 1 C3.
Tel 233 090 570.

World Music

**La Bodeguita
del Medio**
Kaprova 5.
Map 3 B3.
Tel 224 813 922.
Ⓦ bodeguita.cz

**National House
Vinohrady**
Národní dům
Náměstí Míru 9. **Map** 6 F2.
Tel 221 596 111.
Ⓦ nardum.cz

Palác Akropolis
Kubelíkova 27.
Tel 296 330 911.
Ⓦ palacakropolis.cz

Sporting Venues

Aquapalace Praha
Commercial Zone
Průhonice.
Tel 271 104 111.
Ⓦ aquapalace.cz

ASB Squash
Václavské náměstí 13–15.
Map 3 C5.
Tel 224 232 752.

**Beachklub Praha –
Pankrác**
Horáčkova, Praha 4.
Tel 724 337 967.
Ⓦ beachklub.cz

**Czech Lawn Tennis
Club**
Štvanice 38, Praha 7.
Tel 222 316 317.
Ⓦ cltk.cz

Fun Island
Císařská louka, Praha 5.
Tel 702 161 802.

Generali Arena
Milady Horákové 98,
Praha 7.
Tel 296 111 400.
Ⓦ sparta.cz

**Minigolf SK
Tempo Praha**
Zálesí 1074/5, Praha 4.
Tel 608 730 620.

O2 Arena
Českomoravská 17,
Praha 9.
Tel 266 771 000.
Ⓦ o2arena.cz

Tipsport Arena
Za Elektrárnou 419,
Praha 7.
Tel 266 727 443.
Ⓦ tipsportarena-
praha.cz

Žluté lázně
Podolské nábřeží 3/1184,
Praha 4 – Podolí.
Tel 777 409 009.
Ⓦ zlutelazne.cz

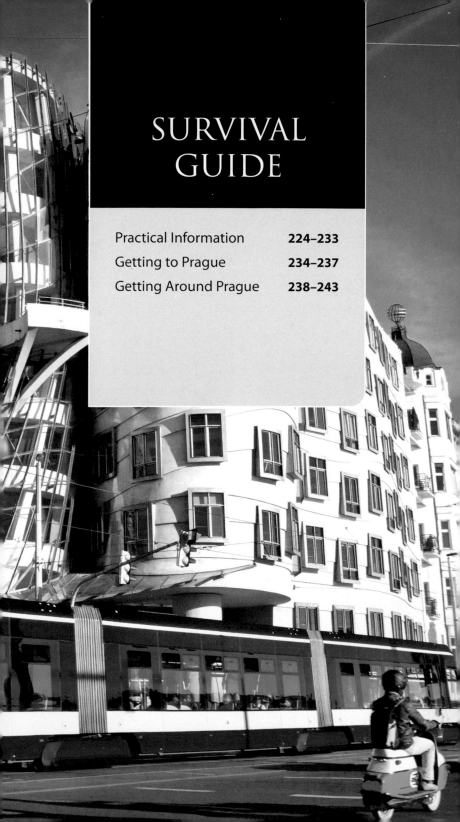

SURVIVAL
GUIDE

PRACTICAL INFORMATION

Since the fall of the Iron Curtain in the late 1980s, the Czech Republic has not only joined the European Union, but has also held its presidency. In that time, Prague has transformed into a true European capital city, and today all facilities – hotels, banks, restaurants and information centres – are of a high standard. Even so, a little forward planning remains worthwhile. Researching a sight to check when it is open and how best to get there can save a lot of time and inconvenience. Prague's transport system is straightforward, and most of the city's sights are located within walking distance of one another. In general, prices are not as low as they once were, making hunting out bargains in the less touristy parts of the city a worthwhile exercise. Prague is a safe city for tourists, but pick-pocketing is rife, as are scams involving taxis, restaurants in the city centre and money changers.

When to Go

One of the best times to visit Prague is during the summer when the weather is warm, although the city can be rather crowded then. Other busy times of the year for the Czech capital are Easter and the run-up to Christmas *(see pp52–5)*. The main sights, such as the Old Town Square, are always packed during these periods, but the crowds give Prague a carnival atmosphere. It is worth bearing in mind that some sights are closed between October and April.

Be sure to bring a raincoat in the summer, warm clothes in winter when temperatues regularly drop below freezing, and sturdy shoes all year round. Climate and rainfall charts can be found on *pages 53–5*.

Visas and Passports

A valid passport or, where applicable, an ID card is needed when entering the Czech Republic from any country outside the Schengen Zone.

British nationals must have a valid passport, but visas are not required. Visitors from the United States, Canada, Australia and New Zealand need a valid passport with a minimum of 90 days remaining on it, and they can stay for up to three months without a visa. As visa requirements do change, visitors are advised to contact the Czech embassy or consulate, or check details with their travel agent before travelling. If you need a visa, you can obtain one from your nearest Czech embassy or consulate.

Customs Information

For non-EU visitors, customs allowances per person are 2 litres (3.6 pints) of wine, as well as 1 litre (1.8 pints) of spirits and 200 cigarettes. The maximum value of currency that can be brought into or taken out of the country is €10,000. Sums in excess of this must be declared to the customs authority. To export authentic antiques, you need to obtain a special licence *(see Shopping p212)*.

VAT (value added tax) can be claimed back on items totalling Kč1,000 or more that are taken out of the country within 30 days of the date of purchase.

A branch of the Prague Information Service in Staroměstské náměstí

Travel Safety Advice

Visitors can get up-to-date travel safety information from the Foreign and Commonwealth Office in the UK, the State Department in the US and the Department of Foreign Affairs and Trade in Australia.

Tourist Information

There are a number of tourist information offices and specialized agencies in Prague that provide advice on anything from accommodation and travel to restaurants and guided tours.

The **Prague City Tourism** is the city's best source of tourist information. It has three offices in the city centre and one at the airport, and provides visitors with advice, maps and listings *(see pp216–17)* in English, German, Russian, French, Czech, Spanish, Italian, Japanese and Chinese. If you want similar information on the rest of the country, visit the **Czech Republic Information Centre** or **Čedok**, the country's largest tour operator.

Language

Czechs are now as likely to speak Italian, Spanish and French as English and German, so navigating the city has become much easier. However, be aware that the level of customer service does vary.

Listings and Tickets

There are hundreds of galleries, museums, clubs and theatres scattered throughout the city,

Entry tickets for some of
Prague's major tourist sights

and to find out what's on, it is best to consult a listings paper. Online, listings can be found on the Prague Information Service (PIS) website and at www. expats.cz and www.prague.tv. The comprehensive Czech-language listings book *Přehled* is best explained by a PIS worker.

The price of admission to museums varies widely, from Kč40 to around Kč300. Most churches are free, with a collection box for donations at the door. Tickets for enter-tainment events can be bought from booking agencies or at the venue itself *(see pp216–17)*. Some hotels can also book tickets for you; alternatively, try a large travel agent in the city centre.

Opening Hours

This guide lists the opening hours for individual museums, galleries and churches. Most of the city's major sights can be visited throughout the year, but many of Prague's gardens

and the castles outside the city are open only from 1 April to 31 October. Visiting hours are normally from 9am to 5pm daily, but during the summer months, opening times are extended to 6pm. Note that final admission times can often be as much as an hour earlier. Gardens stay open until 8pm in July and August. Most museums and several castles are closed on Monday. The National Museum is closed on the first Tuesday of the month, and the Jewish Museum is closed on Saturday. Museum Night in June is an opportunity to visit collections for free between 7pm and 1am. A free transport service between the museums is also in operation.

Opening hours of Prague's shops vary widely. Many businesses are open between 7am and 6pm Monday to Friday, and 8am to noon on Saturday. Department stores generally stay open until between 7 and 9pm on Saturday and Sunday. Prague does not have a standard day for late-night shopping, although many of the more expensive tourist shops stay open until around 10pm on most nights.

Banks are open from 8am to 5pm Monday to Friday. Restaurants, cafés and bars all have varied opening hours *(see pp192–3)*. Most bars open from 10am and, with no licensing laws, often stay open until everyone leaves.

A person taking photographs of one of Prague's many picturesque sights

Children riding the miniature train at Prague Zoo

Travellers with Special Needs

Facilities for the disabled are slowly increasing in Prague. The prevalence of narrow streets and uneven paving, especially in the centre, do contribute to problems, but ramps are being added to allow easier access into buildings. Hotels are introducing facilities for travellers with special needs, and transport options have also improved, with low access on Prague's trams and lifts installed in many metro stations. Visit the Prague Public Transport Company website at www.dpp.cz to plan your journey using wheelchair-accessible metro stations, trams and buses, and three special bus lines for wheelchair-users. Timetables at tram stops indicate which services are wheelchair-accessible.

The PIS (see p225) distributes a superb booklet, *Accessibility Atlas for People with Impaired Mobility.* Published by the **Prague Organization for Wheelchair Users**, it contains all the information you need to make the most out of your stay in Prague. The PIS also provides maps and guides in Braille in various languages.

Between the PIS office and the Old Town Square's Astronomical Clock is a 24-hour wheelchair-accessible toilet. Press the buzzer by the wheelchair logo for access.

Travelling with Children

Czechs are tremendously family-oriented and love well-behaved children. When travelling on public transport, it is not unusual for strangers to offer to help – for example by vacating seats for parents with young children. If you have a pram, indicate this clearly to tram drivers, and they will allow extra time for you to get on board. Children are welcome in bars and restaurants, but remember that the Czech Republic has not introduced a smoking ban yet. However, there are a number of non-smoking restaurants with designated kids' areas for hassle-free dining experiences for parents. **Bohemia Bagel** is another restaurant with a dedicated kids' area. Baby-changing facilities are free in any branch of McDonald's, **Mothercare** and Marks & Spencer, while public toilets often cost Kč5–10. Breast-feeding in public is not very common but perfectly acceptable. Staying in an apartment may be a better option than a hotel if you have children.

Modern playgrounds abound in Prague – try the ones at Letná (Map 3 A1) and Riegrovy Sady (Map 6 F1). The zoo (see p162) and the adjacent **Botanical Garden** make an excellent day out, as do the bobsleigh track at **Bobsled Prague**, **The Museum of Miniatures**, **Choco Story Museum**, the **Public Transport Museum** and, in the summer, **Aquapalace Praha** (see p221) or **Podolí Pool**. For more ideas, visit www.kidsinprague.com.

Senior Travellers

Many international hotels, car-hire firms and airlines offer discounts for seniors with proof of pensioner status. *Důchodce/ Důchodkyně* means "pensioner" in Czech, so keep an eye out for this word at ticket offices, although museums, concert halls and sights may offer a discount only to Czech pensioners. The public transport system allows discounts only to Czech seniors. However, public transport in Prague is among the cheapest in Europe.

Student Travellers

If you are entitled to an International Student Identity Card (ISIC), it is worth getting one before travelling to Prague. Admission charges to most of Prague's major attractions, such as museums, galleries, castles and other historic buildings, are up to

International Student Identity Card

50 per cent cheaper on production of a valid ISIC card (for example, admission to Prague Castle is half the price of the full entrance fee). Students can also get cheaper coach and train travel. If you are looking for somewhere low-cost to stay, many youth hostels in the centre of the city offer student discounts (see Where to Stay, pp186–7). Some restaurants, such as **Pizzeria Einstein**, offer discounts as well.

Time

Prague is on Central European time, which is Greenwich Mean Time (GMT) plus 1 hour. Summer time runs effectively from the end of March up until the end of October – this is GMT plus 2 hours. New York is 6 hours behind Prague, and Los Angeles is 9 hours behind. Sydney is 9 hours ahead (10 in summer), while Moscow and Johannesburg are 2 and 1 hours ahead respectively.

Electricity

The electricity supply in Prague is 230V AC, and two-pin plugs are used. For British or US plugs, an adaptor is needed. Adaptors can be purchased in any large electrical shop such as Dat Art or Electro World in malls (*see p215*).

Conversion Chart

Imperial to Metric
1 inch = 2.54 centimetres
1 foot = 30 centimetres
1 mile = 1.6 kilometres
1 ounce = 28 grams
1 pound = 454 grams
1 pint = 0.6 litre
1 gallon = 4.6 litres

Metric to Imperial
1 millimetre = 0.04 inch
1 centimetre = 0.4 inch
1 metre = 3 feet 3 inches
1 kilometre = 0.6 mile
1 gram = 0.04 ounce
1 kilogram = 2.2 pounds
1 litre = 1.8 pints

Responsible Tourism

Czechs are great nature-lovers and, therefore, fairly green. Large municipal recycling bins are prevalent across the city, encouraging the recycling of books, clothes, furniture and other items. Organic food and clothing are becoming popular. **Country Life** operates an organic farm and bakery to supply its own and others' shops and restaurants, while **Suvi** is Prague's first organic fashion store, with clothes designed and made in Central Bohemia by local people. **Manufaktura** sells handmade wooden ornaments, toys and utensils, recycled paper and more. In supermarkets, try to buy Czech products to support the local economy. Look out for Kubík juices, Kofola (the Czech-Slovak alternative to Coca-Cola), Mattoni, Dobrá voda and Korunní still and sparkling water, and Orion and Opavia biscuits and sweets. Seasonal markets are also good for local produce.

Look out for the EU Ecolabel flower logo on various products and services. **Adria Hotel** and **Hotel Adalbert** have earned this endorsement by conserving water and energy, and recycling and decreasing waste.

Ecotourism is another aspect of the Czech Republic's commitment to environmental sustainability. **Greenways**, a local NGO, publishes maps and guides for cycling to and around the country, while the **European Centre for Eco Agro Tourism** offers a Green *Holiday Guidebook* to the Czech Republic in various languages.

EU Ecolabel logo

Religious Services

The city offers houses of prayer for most religions.

DIRECTORY

Personal Security and Health

Compared to many Western cities, Prague is relatively safe. Even if you do not need emergency help from the police, you should feel free to approach them at any time for advice of any kind – they are generally helpful to the tourist population. If you should need emergency medical care during your stay in Prague, it will be given free. An increasing number of English-speaking services are available, including health centres, pharmacies and dentists (see opposite).

A Prague police station sign

The Police and Security Services

In Prague, you will come across several kinds of policemen and -women and members of various security services. Report any problems to a uniformed state police officer at a police station. The main stations are marked on the Street Finder maps (see pp244–55). The state police carry guns and can arrest a suspect. They patrol the streets on foot or drive grey, blue and yellow patrol cars. The municipal police, the other main security force, is divided into different sections. Special mobile police stations are set up during tourist high season in locations such as the Old Town Square. They are staffed by multilingual officers

Municipal police badge

State police badge

to enable tourists to report crimes and seek on-the-spot advice. The **Tourist Police Station** is where you should go to report any losses and thefts. The office is manned 24 hours a day, seven days a week. For lost property, it is worth trying the **Ztráty a nálezy** (lost-and-found office) on Karolíny Světlé. The traffic police regulate parking, including clamping and issuing fines (see p241), speeding and drink-driving. It is illegal to drive with any alcohol in your bloodstream, and if you are caught, the penalties are severe. If you have a serious traffic accident, you must immediately ring the state police. It is against the law to move anything before the police get there.

You will also see private security guards that tend to guard banks and be used as security at football matches. They are armed with truncheons.

What to be Aware of

Prague is a safe and unthreatening city to walk around. Violence and robberies are rare in the city centre. Crimes against tourists are usually limited to petty pilfering from cars and hotels, and the only really prevalent issue – pickpockets. Using your common sense should help you to avoid trouble. Always remember to keep your bag in sight and avoid carrying your passport, wallet and valuables in your back pocket or in an open bag. It is best to leave them in your hotel safe. Thieves tend to operate in busy areas such as crowded trams, metro cars and popular sights. Be careful when watching the hourly movements of the Old Town Square's Astronomical Clock, for instance. Pickpockets are skilled and use very clever diversionary tactics. Be aware and keep everything safe and close. It is very unlikely that anything stolen will ever be recovered. Never leave anything of value in your car and try to park in an underground car park.

It is always advisable to take out adequate insurance before you arrive in Prague since it is difficult to arrange once there. Report any thefts to the state or municipal police for future insurance claims.

Prague is generally safe for women travelling on their own. However, one place that is advisable to avoid at night if you are a woman alone

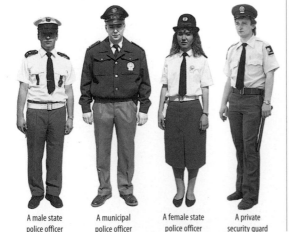

A male state police officer

A municipal police officer

A female state police officer

A private security guard

is Wenceslas Square, because local men might assume that you are one of the city's prostitutes.

Prague has some less-than-reputable bars and cafés that stay open into the early hours. Bars with the words "non-stop" and "herna" are synonymous with shady characters gambling on slot machines. See the bars and cafés listings on *pp206–207* for recommended venues to visit. Be aware that the more touristy restaurants and many taxi drivers have a tendency to overcharge. It is best to take a taxi from a Fair Place taxi rank *(see p240)*. Keep all of your receipts.

Before you travel, take photocopies of all essential documents, including your passport. Place your passport in your hotel safe and carry the photocopy with you when you are out and about. You are expected to have your passport with you only when driving.

In an Emergency

Your hotel should be able to put you in touch with a local doctor if necessary, but if you need immediate help, Prague's emergency services are available 24 hours a day. Non-Czech speakers should call 112; an English-speaking operator will translate via a three-way

Prague traffic police car

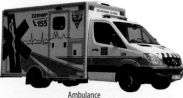

Ambulance

conversation to the service you need. Hospitals with casualty units are marked on the Street Finder maps *(see pp244–55)*.

Health Care and Pharmacies

All EU nationals are entitled to free health care in the Czech Republic. To claim medical treatment, visitors must have a European Health Insurance Card (EHIC card), which should be presented to the physician along with a valid form of identification. Not all treatments are covered by the card, so additional medical insurance is definitely advisable.

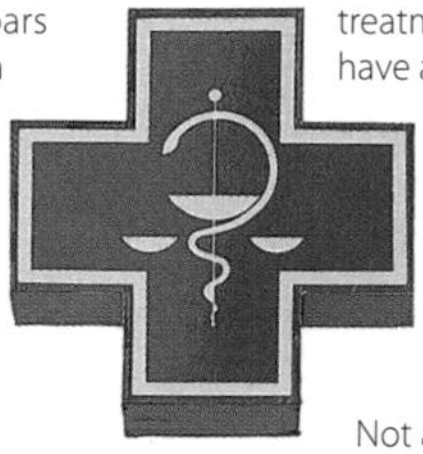

Medical tourism is increasingly popular; **Health Centre Prague** offers cheaper procedures than in the rest of Europe.

There are also 24-hour pharmacies *(lékárna)* with staff who are qualified to give advice and administer simple remedies. If you want an English-speaking doctor, visit the **Diplomatic Health Centre** for foreigners at Na Homolce. Alternatively, try the privately run **Canadian Medical Center** or, for dental care, **Elite Dental Prague**. You will need to take a passport and a means of payment with you.

Those with respiratory problems should be aware that between October and March, sulphur dioxide levels in Prague occasionally exceed the World Health Organization's accepted levels. With increasing car ownership in the city and a lack of funding for alternative fuels, this situation seems unlikely to improve, so if you think you may be affected by fumes, be sure to take any medication you might need with you on your trip.

DIRECTORY

Emergency Numbers

Emergency Operator
Tel 112 (in English).

Ambulance
Tel 155.

Police
Tel 158 (state)/156 (municipal).

Fire
Tel 150.

Police

Tourist Police Station
Jungmannovo náměstí 9.
Map 3 C5.

Lost Property Bureau

**Lost and Found
(Ztráty a nálezy)**
Karoliny Světlé 5.
Map 3 A5.
Tel 224 235 085.
Open 4am–4pm Mon–Fri (to 5:30pm Mon & Wed; to 2pm Fri).

Medical Centres

Canadian Medical Center
Veleslavínská 1.
Tel 724 300 301 (24 hours)
Open 8am–6pm Mon–Fri (to 8pm Tue & Thu), 9am–2pm Sat.
W cmcpraha.cz

**Diplomatic Health Centre
(Nemocnice Na Homolce)**
Roentgenova 2.
Tel 257 271 111.
Open 24 hours a day.
W homolka.cz

Elite Dental Prague
Vodičkova 5. **Map** 3 C3.
Tel 222 510 888.
Open 8am–8pm Mon–Thu, 8am–4pm Fri.
W elitedental.cz

Health Centre Prague
Vodičkova 28, 3rd entrance, 2nd floor.
Map 3 C5.
Tel 603 433 833 (24 hrs).
Open 8am–5pm Mon–Fri.
W doctor-prague.cz

24-Hour Pharmacies

Lékárna Palackého
Palackého 5. **Map** 3 C5.
Tel 224 946 982.

Lékárna u Sv. Ludmily
Belgická 37. **Map** 6 F3.
Tel 222 513 396.

Banking and Local Currency

With its increasingly international profile, Prague is becoming more expensive, although residential sections of the city remain cheaper than the tourist centre. Banks now have international desks staffed by multilingual cashiers, and ATMs dot the city streets. Credit cards are widely accepted, although in smaller outlets, it is wise to ask first, while traveller's cheques can be changed only in banks. It is worth bearing in mind that bureaux de change usually take some commission regardless of their "zero" claims.

Banks and Bureaux de Change

The large, modern banks generally found in the city centre all open between 9am and 5pm or 6pm Monday to Friday. Hundreds of bureaux de change are found in tiny shops throughout the city. However, despite sometimes offering better exchange rates than the banks, their commission charges (often hidden in the small print) are huge, often as high as 12 per cent. Compare this to the 1–5 per cent charged by banks, along with a minimum commission of Kč20–50. The only advantage of these exchange offices is their convenience. Many are open late every day, some offer a 24-hour service and queues are rare.

Most of the larger hotels will also change foreign currency for you, but again commission rates may be very high. If you have some Czech currency left over from your stay, you can reconvert your money. All banks will reconvert your extra crowns for a small commission. Finally, never change your money on the black market. As well as being illegal, the rate is not any

higher than banks or exchanges, and it is guaranteed you will be given notes that are not legal tender.

A better way to access your money than changing cash is to withdraw crowns using your debit card. Check with your bank to find out how much it will charge you for the use of this service.

A zero-commission bureau de change shopfront in Prague

ATMs

There are ATMs *(bankomats)* all over the centre of Prague, and using them is the easiest method to get your Czech currency. Many ATMs are located inside banks (in the entrance), but they are accessible even if the branch is closed. They accept most major credit and debit cards, and information is available in English, German, French and Czech. ATMs in the Czech Republic issue crowns only (no euros or dollars). The vast majority dispense Kč200 or Kč500 notes, occasionally Kč1,000 and Kč2,000 notes.

Façade of the Česká Spořitelna bank

Credit Cards

Paying by credit card is becoming more popular in Prague – not only in hotels and restaurants, but also in supermarkets and shops. Even if an outlet displays a credit card sign, do not assume they will accept all types of card as payment. In a restaurant, it is better to ask before ordering your meal to avoid difficulties later. The cards most often accepted are American Express, VISA and MasterCard. Most banks will allow cash advances (up to your limit) on your card.

DIRECTORY

Banks

Česká Národní Banka
Na příkopě 28. **Map** 3 C4.
Tel 224 411 111. **W** cnb.cz

Česká Spořitelna
Rytířská 29. **Map** 3 C4.
Tel 800 207 207. **W** csas.cz

Československá Obchodní Banka
Na příkopě 18. **Map** 3 C4.
Tel 800 300 300.

Komerční Banka
Václavské náměstí 42.
Map 4 D5. **Tel** 955 545 111.
W kb.cz

Moneta
Hybernská 20. **Map** 4 D3.
Tel 211 490 611.
W moneta.cz

UniCredit Bank
Náměstí Republiky 3a. **Map** 4 D3.
Tel 955 959 835.
W unicreditbank.cz

Bureaux de Change

Eurochange
Opletalova 30. **Map** 4 E5.
Tel 224 243 614.

Exchange
Náměstí Franze Kafky 2.
Map 3 B3.
Tel 800 225 588.

Inter Change
Rytířská 26. **Map** 3 C4.
Tel 224 221 757.
One of several branches.
W interchange.cz

Currency

The currency in Prague and the Czech Republic is the Czech crown (*koruna*), which is abbreviated as Kč (the international abbreviation is CZK). *Hellers* (of which there are 100 to the crown) have been phased out.

The Czech crown is the best and usually the only possible currency to use when making payments in cash. Some hotels and shops accept payment in euros, but the exchange rate may not always be favourable. Tesco accepts euros and gives change in Czech crowns at the going bank rate, as does Marks & Spencer, where they accept pounds sterling as well.

Banknotes

Czech banknotes are available in the denominations Kč100, Kč200, Kč500, Kč1,000, Kč2,000 and Kč5,000.

Kč5,000 note

Kč2,000 note

Kč1,000 note

Kč500 note

Kč200 note

Kč100 note

1 crown (Kč1)

2 crowns (Kč2)

Coins

Coins come in the following denominations: Kč1, Kč2, Kč5, Kč10, Kč20 and Kč50. All the coins have the Czech emblem, a lion rampant, on one side.

5 crowns (Kč5)

10 crowns (Kč10)

20 crowns (Kč20)

50 crowns (Kč50)

Communications and Media

The main Czech telephone service is called Telefónica O2 Czech Republic. O2 provides a comprehensive digital network of phones across the country and, along with Vodafone and T-Mobile, constitutes the Czech mobile market. Wi-Fi zones and Internet cafés can be found all over Prague; the latter are often in courtyards or on the first floor of buildings. Česká Pošta remains an efficient postal service within the Czech Republic and overseas.

O2 phone boxes in Prague

Public Telephones

Despite the growing use of mobile phones, there are still many public phones in the Czech Republic; indeed, there are more phone boxes here than in most European countries.

O2 public phones accept cash (euros and Czech crowns), credit cards and phonecards. Depending on which phone you find, you can send a text message and an email as well as make a call. In hotels, you can usually get a direct line, but commission charges on the calls are often exorbitant. Remember also that international calls can be extremely expensive, no matter what time of day you phone. The cheapest way to call abroad is via an international call office.

You can buy phonecards (telefonní karta) from tobacconists (tabáks) and newsstands, and from post offices, supermarkets and petrol stations. Two popular cards are Karta X, a pre-paid calling card that permits you to make national and international calls from any phone; and Trick, a multifunctional card that can be used to pay for telephone calls and Internet services.

On all phones in the country, the dialling tone is a short note followed by a long one; the ringing tone consists of long regular notes, and the engaged signal has short and rapid notes. All Czech phone numbers have nine digits, and Prague numbers start with a 2.

Mobile Phones

Czech mobile phones operate on a GSM band of 900/1800 MHz, the same standard in use throughout Europe, but different from that used in the United States. US cell phones will work provided they are tri-band phones and that the service provider allows for international roaming. To avoid high roaming fees, you can obtain local pay-as-you-go SIM cards, which give you a temporary telephone number and allow you to make calls and send text messages on the local network.

Pay-as-you-go cards are very well priced. You pay for credit but the SIM card is free. The three main mobile-phone operators are Telefónica O2 (www.cz.o2.com), Vodafone (www.vodafone.cz) and T-Mobile (www.t-mobile.cz). Czech mobile numbers start with a 6 or 7.

Internet Access

Most hotels offer guests some form of in-room internet access, through either a wireless or a LAN connection. Wireless connections may not be reliable, depending on how far your room is from the router. If Internet access is important to you, it's best to mention this at the hotel reception when checking in and request a room with a strong wireless signal. Most hotels will usually also have a public computer terminal for guests to surf the Internet or, failing that, they will allow guests to quickly check their emails on the hotel computer. The receptionist should know the location of the nearest café with Wi-Fi access.

Traditional internet cafés across Prague are being replaced by cafés with a

Reaching the Right Number

• Czech directory enquiries and operator	1180
• International directory enquiries and to make a collect call	1181
• International call followed by the country code	00
• In case of emergencies (Police)	158
• Emergency operator (English)	112

Wi-Fi connection. The few internet cafés that remain offer reasonable rates, around Kč1–2 per minute. Just because the word "café" is part of the name, do not assume they will serve coffee – or that the coffee will be drinkable if they do. As for those establishments offering free wireless access, connections are usually pretty fast. If there's a password, the staff will tell you what it is.

Post office sign

Postal Services

There are a number of post offices in Prague (see Street Finder Maps on pp244–55). The best and largest one is the **Main Post Office** in Jindřišská, just off Wenceslas Square. It has a huge variety of services, including a large phone room where you can make international calls. This service operates from 7am to 11pm. The Main Post Office offers easy-access information in English, and swift and efficient service. Take a ticket when you enter the building, then wait until the electronic display indicates which booth you should go to. If you want to buy some of the Czech Republic's attractive stamps, go to window 29 (no ticket required).

The Main Post Office on Jindřišská is open from 2am to midnight. Most other post offices offer more regular business hours, from 8am to 6pm or 7pm Monday to Friday, and from 8am until noon on Saturday.

There is no first- or second-class mail in the Czech Republic, but the majority of letters usually arrive at their destination within a few days. If you want to send something valuable through the post, use the registered mail service, which is reliable.

Postcards and letters can be posted in the many orange post boxes scattered around Prague. Both take around five working days to arrive in the UK and about a week to get to the US. Stamps can be bought from post offices, newsagents or tabáks – they will also be able to tell you what stamps you need. All parcels and registered letters need to be handed in at a post office, rather than placed in post boxes.

For emergency parcels and packages that need to arrive quickly, you can use an international courier service, such as **DHL** or **FedEx**, rather than the post office.

Post restante letters are delivered to the Main Post Office in Jindřišská Street. Go to window 1 or 2 (open 7am to 8pm Monday to Friday and 7am to noon Saturday) with your passport or other official identification.

Newspapers

Prague has several newspapers but none in English. For news in English, go to www.ctk.eu for translated articles. Other online resources on Prague are www.expats.cz, www.prague.tv and www.praguemonitor.com.

Most of the newsstands located around Wenceslas Square and other popular tourist spots sell the main quality European newspapers such as The Times, The Guardian, El País and Die Zeit, as well as US papers such as the International Herald Tribune.

TV and Radio

Czech television dubs everything, so local TV is not much use to non-Czech speakers. However, most hotels have freeview news channels, and the larger chains have packages that include film channels.

You can listen to the BBC World Service on 101.1FM; it is also possible to listen to the BBC online, by logging on to www.bbc.co.uk. One of the most popular local stations is Radio 1 (91.9MHz), which has an English-language show, High Fidelity (8–11pm Fri). Another weekly English-language show, The Friday Ripple (5–7pm Fri), is on Radio Wave (www.wave.cz).

Copy of The Prague Post

DIRECTORY

Internet Cafés and Call Shops

Internet Café InterLogic
Budějovická 1123/13,
Praha 4.
Tel 241 734 617.

Relax Café Bar
Dlážděná 4.
Map 4 E4.
Tel 224 211 521.
 relaxcafebar.cz

Postal Services

DHL
Václavské náměstí 47.
Map 4 D5.
Tel 840 103 000/220 300 111.
w dhl.cz

FedEx
Tel 800 133 339.
w fedex.com/cz

Main Post Office
Jindřišská 14.
Map 4 D5.
Tel 221 131 445/604 221 504.
w ceskaposta.cz

Tobacconist's, where you can also buy stamps and phonecards

GETTING TO PRAGUE

Prague is located right at the heart of Europe and enjoys good transport connections with the rest of the continent. There are direct flights every day from most of Europe's major cities and, via Delta Airlines and ČSA, from selected cities in the USA. There are no direct flights from Australia, however. International coach transport is efficient and inexpensive, but journey times can be off-putting. Prague is well served by international railways, but as this is a popular means of getting to Prague trains tend to get booked up early, especially in the summer. The main train station (Hlavní nádraží) is close to Wenceslas Square and the city centre and, except for the airport, other major points of arrival are also fairly central.

Travelling by Air

Prague has good flight connections to most major European cities. More than 40 international airlines fly to Prague's Václav Havel Airport (Letiště Václava Havla). If you are travelling from the United States, **Delta Airlines** operates a limited number of non-stop flights from Atlanta and New York. There are no Australian or New Zealand carriers flying direct to Prague, although you can fly **British Airways** with a stop in London. Other major airlines include **KLM**, **Air France**, **Lufthansa**, **Emirates** and **Czech Airlines** (**ČSA**). It takes about 1 hour and 50 minutes to fly from London to Prague, and about 9 hours from the east coast of North America.

Tickets and Fares

Prague has become increasingly popular with budget carriers, both as a hub and a destination. Both **easyJet** and **Jet2.com** fly regularly between Prague and several cities in the UK; **Ryanair** also flies direct to Brno, Czechia's second city. **Smart Wings**, **Wizz Air** and **German Wings** are popular budget carriers that connect Prague to destinations in the rest of Europe. Booking online or by phone as early as possible will get you the best prices from these budget airlines, and taking only cabin luggage keeps the price down too.

APEX (advanced purchase) tickets can be a cheap option, but they have stringent conditions attached to them. These include having to book your ticket at least a month in advance and severe penalties if you cancel your flight.

If you ring well in advance, airlines will quote you the standard fare, but the price may be lowered nearer the time if seats remain unsold – this is rarely the case in the summer months, however, as Prague is such a popular destination. You may get a better deal in winter (except over the Christmas and New Year period when prices

Czech Airlines plane coming in to land

rise again). Students and regular business travellers may be able to get discounts at any time of year. Children under two who do not occupy a separate seat usually pay 10 per cent of the adult fare. If you do get a cheap deal, ensure that you will get a refund if your travel agent goes out of business.

Prague Airport

Prague's only international airport is at Ruzyně, 15 km (9 miles) northwest of the city centre. The airport is modern, clean, efficient and functional. It offers all that you would expect from an international airport: ATMs and 24-hour exchange facilities; car rental offices; a duty-free shop; a post office and a left-luggage office.

The airport was thoroughly modernized at the start of the millennium, including the addition of a new terminal. Terminal 1 is used for intercontinental flights, including those to the UK, North America, the Middle East, Africa and Asia. All domestic flights and flights to destinations within the EU and other Schengen countries are served by

Departures board in Terminal 2 at Prague Airport

Terminal 2. The two terminals are connected and are only a short walk apart. There is also a business-class lounge and catering facility, as well as a shopping centre within the Marriott Courtyard Hotel, which is located just across the airport forecourt.

Terminal 3, also known as the South Terminal, is further away and used only for general aviation and private planes.

CEDAZ bus operating between the airport and the city

Transport from the Airport to the City

Getting to and from Prague airport is easy, relatively fast and economical, unless you fall victim to one of Prague's infamous taxi scams (see p240). Allow at least 60 minutes to reach the airport by road from the city centre at rush hour, though on a good day, it could take as little as 30 minutes. Travelling by a combination of the metro and standard bus takes about 45 minutes depending on connections.

The airport is linked to the city centre by a regular minibus service run by **CEDAZ**. For the return trip to the airport, there is a bus stop at V Celnici street, a short distance from Náměstí Republiky. Buses leave every 30 minutes from 7:30am to 7pm, and tickets cost Kč150 per person.

A regular public bus service runs to the airport from Dejvická

metro (bus 119) and from Zličín metro (bus 100). Between midnight and 5am, the 510 night bus will take you into the city every half hour for the standard Kč32 public transport ticket. The Airport Express bus stops at Dejvická, Masarykovo nádraží, Náměstí Republiky and Hlavní nádraží; it runs every half-hour between 5:45am and 9:15pm and costs Kč60.

For a service on demand to and from the airport, both **AAA Radiotaxi** and **FIX Airport Cars** are reliable options and offer a 47 per cent discount on a return trip. They can take you to addresses outside the city, and they can even be used to tour the rest of the Czech Republic.

Alternatively, there are always taxis waiting in front of the terminal. Taxis provided by AAA and FIX Airport Cars offer a fixed price. The prices are comparable for most of the other companies, but it should not cost more than Kč600 to get to the city centre.

DIRECTORY

Airport Information

Václav Havel Airport
Tel 220 111 888. **W** prg.aero

Main Airlines

Air France
W airfrance.com

British Airways
W ba.com

Czech Airlines (ČSA)
V Celnici 5. **Map** 4 D3.
Tel 239 007 007. **W** csa.cz

Delta Airlines
W delta.com

EasyJet
W easyjet.com

Emirates
W emirates.com

German Wings
W germanwings.com

Jet2.com
W jet2.com

KLM
W klm.com

Lufthansa
Tel 234 008 234.
W lufthansa.com

Ryanair
W ryanair.com

Smart Wings
W smartwings.com

Wizz Air
W wizzair.com

Airport Bus

CEDAZ
Tel 220 116 758. **W** cedaz.cz

Taxi Transfers

AAA Radiotaxi
Tel 14 014/222 333 222/
729 331 133. **W** aaataxi.cz

FIX Airport Cars
Tel 722 555 525.
W airportcars.cz

The airport forecourt, from which buses and taxis can be taken into town

The Art Nouveau façade of Hlavní nádraží, the main train station in Prague

Travelling by Train

Rail travel is an enjoyable and environmentally friendly way to travel to and from Prague. Prague is connected by rail to all the major capitals of Europe. International trains have dining cars and couchettes, but tickets are often more expensive than budget air fares so it is always worth comparing the price of both options. Buy well in advance to ensure a seat and get the best possible deal.

The railways in the Czech Republic are run by České Dráhy (ČD). There are several types of train run by ČD. These include the *rychlík* (express) trains; the *osobní* (passenger) trains, which form a local service and stop at all stations; the EX, or national express, for longer distances; the SC (Supercity), which is the fastest and most comfortable train service between Prague, Františkovy Lázně and Ostrava; and the EC (Eurocity), or international express.

Alternatively, Regiojet and Leo Express make for a cheaper and more comfortable option to Pardubice, Olomouc and Ostrava, with extensions to the Slovak cities of Žilina, Poprad (Tatry) and Košice.

Tickets can be bought in advance. If you want to buy a ticket just before your train leaves, be warned that queues at ticket booths can be long, especially on Fridays and Sundays. First-class carriages exist on most trains and guarantee you a seat. In the timetable, an "R" in a box by a train number means you must have a seat reserved on that train. An "R" without a box means a reservation is recommended. If you are caught in the wrong carriage, you have to pay an on-the-spot fine.

Train Stations

The biggest and busiest railway station in Prague is Hlavní nádraží, which is only a 5-minute walk from Wenceslas Square. After a thorough renovation, the Art Nouveau station now features a gleaming interior with shops, restaurants, a pub and even a jeweller's. As well as shops, the lower ground floor has an inexpensive left-luggage facility and the central ticket office (open 3:30am–00:30am). In this ticket hall, there is also **ČD Travel**, where all international rail tickets, including those for Eurostar, are sold by multilingual station staff. Many international trains also stop at Nádraží Holešovice.

Prague's oldest train terminal, Masarykovo nádraží, serves mainly Prague's suburbs and a few other domestic routes. Similarly, many domestic routes are served from Smíchov.

Travelling by Coach

Coach connections from Prague to many of the major European cities have improved immeasurably, and tickets tend to sell out quickly. Some Czech towns – such as Karlovy Vary, Hradec Králové, Český Krumlov and Terezín – are much easier to reach by coach than train.

The city's main bus terminal is Florenc, on the northeastern edge of the New Town. There is also a smaller station at Anděl called Na Knížecí. The Florenc terminal stays open from 4am until midnight and offers food outlets, information kiosks, inexpensive left-luggage facilities and tickets sales from such companies as **Eurolines** and **Student Agency** to name just two. During the summer months, there are hundreds of coach trips to all the major coastal resorts in southern Europe. These get booked up quickly by Czechs, so buy your ticket well in advance and be sure to reserve a seat.

A uniformed railway employee

Travelling by Car

To drive a car in the Czech Republic, you must be at least 18 years of age. Most foreign driving licences, including Canadian, US and EU ones, are recognized. New Zealand and Australian drivers, however, should get an International Driving Licence before leaving home.

If you bring your own car to Prague, by law you must carry the following with you at all times: a valid driver's licence; vehicle

A Eurolines long-haul coach

Prague's Major Rail and Coach Stations

The major points of arrival by train and coach are all fairly central and easily accessible by metro – the nearest metro to each terminal is shown in the boxes along with more detailed travel information.

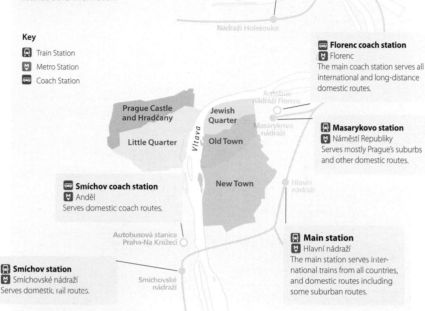

🚊 Holešovice station
Ⓜ Nádraží Holešovice
This is the main Prague railway station for select international destinations, including Berlin, Vienna and Budapest.

Key

🚊 Train Station
Ⓜ Metro Station
🚌 Coach Station

Nádraží Holešovice

🚌 Florenc coach station
Ⓜ Florenc
The main coach station serves all international and long-distance domestic routes.

Autobus. nádraží Florenc

Prague Castle and Hradčany

Jewish Quarter

Vltava

Masarykovo nádraží

Little Quarter

Old Town

🚊 Masarykovo station
Ⓜ Náměstí Republiky
Serves mostly Prague's suburbs and other domestic routes.

🚌 Smíchov coach station
Ⓜ Anděl
Serves domestic coach routes.

New Town

Hlavní nádraží

Autobusová stanice Praha-Na Knížecí

🚊 Main station
Ⓜ Hlavní nádraží
The main station serves inter-national trains from all countries, and domestic routes including some suburban routes.

🚊 Smíchov station
Ⓜ Smíchovské nádraží
Serves domestic rail routes.

Smíchovské nádraží

Typical road sign showing the directions to target destinations

registration card; a hire certificate or, if you are borrowing the car, a letter signed by the owner and authorized by a recognized body, such as the AA or RAC, giving you permission to drive it; and a third-party insurance document (or home insurance, for EU citizens).

If you drive on the motorway, you will also need to display a special highway sticker available at the border, petrol stations and post offices. Other items you have to carry at all times are a set of replacement bulbs, red warning triangles, a first-aid kit and a safety vest. You also have to display a national identification sticker. Headlights must be used at all times, even during daylight hours. It is compulsory to wear seat belts if fitted, and children under 12 years of age are not allowed in the front seat. When you are driving, it is strictly forbidden to have any alcohol in your blood or to use a mobile phone.

There are good motorway connections to all the major cities in the Czech Republic, including Plzeň and Brno, and many more are under construction.

The speed limit on motorways is 130 km/h (81 mph); on dual and single carriageways, 90 km/h (56 mph); and in urban areas, 50 km/h (31 mph). The traffic police patrolling the roads are very vigilant, and any infringements are dealt with harshly. There are also occasional road blocks to catch drunken drivers. Visit www.motorway.cz for more details on driving on Czech motorways.

DIRECTORY

Train Travel

ČD Travel
Plaha Hlavní nádraží, Wilsonova 80. **Map** 4 E5. **Tel** 840 112 113/ 972 243 051. 🌐 **cd.cz**

Coach Travel

Eurolines
Florenc Coach Station. **Map** 4 F3. **Tel** 731 222 111. 🌐 **elines.cz**

Student Agency
Florenc Coach Station. **Map** 4 F3. **Tel** 841 101 101.
🌐 **studentagency.cz**

Car Travel

Budget
Prague Airport, main station. **Map** 4 E5. **Tel** 235 325 713.
🌐 **budget.cz**

Car Breakdown/Service/ Accidents
Tel 1230 (ÚAMK)/1240 (Autoklub Bohemia Assistance).

GETTING AROUND PRAGUE

The centre of Prague is conveniently small, and most of the sights can be reached comfortably on foot. However, to cross the city quickly, or to visit a more remote sight, the public transport is efficient, clean and cheap. It is based on trams, buses and the underground (metro) system, all of which are run by the Prague Public Transport Company (Dopravní podnik hlavního města Prahy). Throughout this guide, the best method of transport is given for each sight. The metro and trams serve the city centre, while buses are used to reach the suburbs. The entire system is simple to use – only one ticket is needed for all three forms of transport. Bus, tram and metro routes are found on city maps, available at most city centre *tabáks*, bookshops and newsagents; or refer to the map on the inside back cover of this guide.

Green Travel

Prague has a fantastic public transport system. Buses serve the outer suburbs, thereby decreasing congestion on central streets, where trams, cars, bikes, pedestrians and even horses jostle for space. Comprehensive and 24-hour public transport means that driving a car is unnecessary.

Prague is also wonderfully compact, so walking between sights is not just possible but preferable. Cycling is another good way of getting around. Renting a bike is easy *(see p241)*.

The last Thursday of each month sees the Auto*Mat Critical Mass bike ride, which sets off from Jiřího z Poděbrad square at 6pm.

The Transport System

The best way of getting around central Prague by public transport is by tram or metro. Prague's rush hours are between 6am and 8am and 3pm and 5pm, Monday to Friday. However, more trains, trams and buses run at these times, so crowding is not usually a problem. Some bus routes to the suburbs only run during peak hours.

Tickets

Prague's transport network relies on the honour system. Be aware that periodic checks are carried out by plain-clothes ticket inspectors who levy a large on-the-spot fine if you don't have a valid ticket. Transfer tickets cover the entire system and allow 30 or 90 minutes of travel after validation. Buy the ticket before you travel and validate it in the machines provided, or you will be travelling illegally.

Tickets are available for Kč24 (for 30 minutes of travel including transfers) or Kč32 (for 90 minutes), and can be used on all forms of public transport, including the funicular railway that runs from Újezd up Petřín Hill; the boat service (lines P1–6); and the railway network (lines R and S). For shorter journeys around the city centre, the 30-minute transfer ticket will usually suffice.

Longer-term tickets are often more convenient and a good idea if you are planning on seeing many tourist sights

24-hour ticket   30-minute ticket

around the city. They offer unlimited rides for a number of days – a one-day ticket costs Kč110 and a three-day ticket is Kč310.

Children aged between 6 and 15 pay reduced prices – they pay half the fare on Kč24, Kč32 and Kč110 tickets.

Tickets may be purchased from the automatic machines at the entrance of all metro stations, at some tram or bus stops, and at *tabáks* (tobacconists), newsagents and some shops. For more information on transport routes, maps and tickets, visit the Prague Transport Information website or one of the information offices listed below.

DIRECTORY

Prague Public Transport Information Centres
Muzeum metro station, main station. **Open** 7am–9pm daily.
Václav Havel Airport, Terminals 1 & 2. **Open** 7am–9pm daily.
Holešovice train station, Anděl. **Open** 7am–9pm Mon–Fri, 9:30am–5pm Sat.

Prague Transport Information
Tel 296 191 817. **w** dpp.cz

A visitor to Prague cycling around the city on a hired bike

A busy tram on the streets of Prague

Travelling by Tram

Trams are Prague's oldest method of public transport. Horse-drawn trams appeared on the streets in 1879, but by 1891, the first electric tram was in operation. The metro may be faster in terms of travelling distances, but when you factor in descending to and ascending from stations, the tram system is actually the most efficient, not to mention pleasant, way of getting around the city. Some lines operate only in the rush hour, and there are several night trams, all of which pass by Lazarská in the New Town.

The tram system is run by the **Prague Public Transport Company**. Tram tickets are also valid for travel on the metro and buses. You have to buy your ticket before you board a tram. Once you have entered, you will see a small, yellow punching machine on two or three metal poles just inside the doors. Insert your ticket, and it will be validated automatically. If you do not punch your ticket, it is not valid, and if you are caught by a ticket inspector, you will have to pay an on-the-spot fine. Make sure you buy the correct ticket for your desired journey as you will also be fined for an incorrect ticket. Each tram stop has a timetable – the stop underlined is where you are standing. The stops below that line indicate where that tram is heading.

Trams run every 4 to 20 minutes. Doors either open and close automatically or by pushing a button. The current stop and the next stop are announced in Czech. The metro closes shortly after midnight. A small number of night trams run every 30 minutes. These trams (numbers 51–59) are marked by white numbers on a dark background at the stop.

Tram Signs

These are found at every tram stop and tell you which trams stop there, and in what direction each tram is going.

Tram logo

Numbers indicate which trams stop here

The direction each tram is heading in

Name of the tram stop

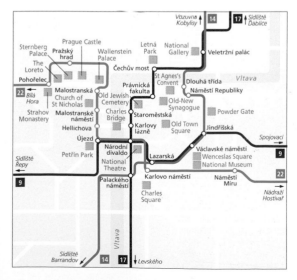

Useful Tram Routes

These three tram routes are the most useful for getting around the centre of Prague. They pass many of the major sights on both sides of the Vltava, so they are also a cheap, pleasant way of sightseeing. Routes may be diverted in summer during roadworks.

Key

■ Major sight

— Tram route

O Tram stop (selected stops only)

A typical, modern public bus on the streets of Prague

Travelling by Bus

Most visitors to Prague are likely to use a bus only to travel to and from the airport *(see p235)*, or if they visit the zoo. By law, buses are not allowed in the city centre because the streets are too narrow. Instead, they are used to transport people from the suburbs to tram and metro stops outside the centre.

Unless you have enough small change, you must purchase a ticket before you board a bus. Tickets are available from the vending machines at the entrance of metro stations, *tabáks* (tobacconists) and all the usual agents *(see p238)*.

You must validate your ticket in the punching machine on the bus. When buying a ticket, choose either a Kč24 transfer ticket allowing 30 minutes of travel, or a Kč32 ticket, which is valid for 90 minutes. You have to push a button to open the doors on most buses, though some open automatically. There is a high-pitched warning signal when doors are about to close. You are expected to give up your seat for the elderly, the disabled and people with small children.

Bus timetables are located at every stop. They have the numbers of all the buses that stop there and the timetable for each route. The frequency of buses varies considerably. In the rush hour, there may be 12 to 15 buses an hour; at other times, as few as three.

There are more than 25 buses that run during the night, serving the outer areas not covered by the tram and metro system. These buses are numbered in the 500s and 600s.

Travelling by Taxi

Taxis in Prague are a useful but frustrating form of transport. All taxis are privately owned, and there are many unscrupulous drivers who are out to charge as much as they can get away with. Never take a taxi from outside a hotel or tourist sight, as these are most likely to be operated by drivers who fall into this category; the only taxis safe to hail on the street are Fair Place taxis (www.prague-taxi. co.uk/taxi-fair-place.htm). Drivers in the Fair Place scheme guarantee a fair price, a safe ride, a professional approach and high standards. There are around 50 Fair Place taxi ranks across Prague.

Official taxis have a roof lamp and the company name, registration number and basic price list must be displayed on both front doors. Prices currently are Kč40 boarding fee, Kč28/km travel and Kč6/ minute waiting. After the journey, the driver is obliged to print an official receipt. To get an idea of taxi prices in Prague, look at one of the Fair Place price leaflets, available for free in hotels and train stations.

If you think you have been scammed by a taxi driver, take their name and number so you can report them to the police *(see pp228–9)*. The best way not to be taken advantage of is to use a Fair Place taxi or have your hotel or restaurant call another reputable firm.

Unless your Czech pronunciation is good, always have your destination written down in Czech.

PĚŠÍ ZÓNA

Pedestrian zone

Pedestrian crossing

Street or square name and Prague district

VÁCLAVSKÉ NÁM.
NOVÉ MĚSTO-PRAHA.1

Street number   City registration number

Walking

Walking around Prague is the most enjoyable way to see the city. Some pedestrian crossings are controlled by traffic lights, but be sure to cross only when the green man is showing, and even then, check the road carefully before you do so. It is now illegal for drivers to ignore pedestrian crossings, but for years they were allowed to do so, and old habits die hard. Be especially careful at crossings that do not have traffic lights.

Bear in mind that trams do have priority at pedestrian crossings, which can be confusing. They also travel at high speeds, occasionally coming upon you with little warning. Considering the uneven cobbled streets, the steep hills and the mass of tram lines, flat, comfortable shoes for walking are strongly recommended.

Yellow AAA taxis at a Fair Place taxi rank

Cycling

One of the greenest and best ways of getting around Prague is by bike. First-timers will benefit from taking a tour first to get the lay of the land since bike lanes are rare. Renting a bike is easy, and most rental places, such as **Praha Bike**, also arrange good tours. Bike paths line both sides of the Vltava, and there is a series of biking/hiking trails linking Prague to Vienna (www.pragueviennagreenways.org).

A boat tour on the Vltava run by Prague Venice Boats

Driving

Most visitors are better off not driving around the centre of Prague. The city's complex web of one-way streets, the pedestrianized areas around the historic core of the city and a severe shortage of parking spaces make driving very difficult. Prague's public transport system is a much more efficient way of travelling around the city.

If you do decide to drive, be aware that on-the-spot fines for traffic violations are common. You must drive on the right, and the law states that both driver and front- and back-seat passengers should wear seat belts. The speed limit in the city is 50 km/h (31 mph) unless a sign indicates otherwise.

Parking spaces in the centre are scarce, and the penalties for illegal parking are harsh. Meter parking from 8am to 6pm costs Kč30–40 per hour. Orange zones allow parking for 2 hours and green zones for 6; blue zones are reserved for residents. To use the meter, insert coins for the amount of time you need and display your receipt prominently on the dashboard.

Unfortunately, car theft is rife, and expensive Western cars are a favourite target. Try to park in an official – preferably underground – car park (see the Street Finder maps pp244–55).

MIMO ZÁSOBOVÁNÍ
One-way traffic and No stopping except for deliveries

Better yet, park at one of the guarded car parks (look for the "P+R" symbol) at the edge of the city and use public transport to get in.

If you are towed, call the police (Tel 156) to locate your car. The maximum fine is Kč1,300 (Kč850 if you stop them in the process), plus Kč150 parking fee, and Kč200 for each subsequent day. If you get clamped, a sticker lists the number to call to have the clamp removed.

Sightseeing Tours

Many firms offer trips around Prague's major sights, as well as outings to castles such as Karlštejn and Konopiště (see p169). Tours usually start from Náměstí Republiky (Republic Square) and from the upper part of Wenceslas Square. These trips can be expensive, but prices vary, so check what's on offer before you make a booking. The Jewish Museum (see p87) organizes trips around the Jewish Quarter. For those on a tight budget, the PIS (see p225) offers some of the cheapest tours in town. Tours can also be booked through Čedok (see p225).

A trip on tram 91, run by the Museum of Municipal Mass Transport, is one of the cheapest and best city-centre tours. It starts off at the Exhibition Ground (see pp178–9) and travels around the Old Town, the New Town and the Jewish Quarter. This service runs from Easter to the middle of November every weekend and public holiday. Tickets can be bought on board. Tram 22 will take you from the city up to the castle.

Sightseeing tours in horse-drawn carriages are run from the Old Town Square. Walking and bike tours give a level of detail to Prague unseen from speedier modes of transport, while boat tours (see pp56–9) allow for fantastic views of major sights.

DIRECTORY

Sightseeing Tour Operators

Martin Tour Praha
Main Office: Štěpánská 61.
Map 5 C1. **Tel** 777 318 198.
Ⓦ martintour.cz

Prague Walking Tours
Dlouhá 37. **Map** 4 D2.
Tel 608 200 912.
Ⓦ praguer.com

Praha Bike
Dlouhá 24. **Map** 3 C3.
Tel 732 388 880.
Ⓦ prahabike.cz

Precious Legacy
Kaprova 13. **Map** 3 B3.
Tel 222 321 954.
Ⓦ legacytours.net

Premiant City Tour
Na Příkopě 23. **Map** 4 D4.
Tel 606 600 123 (24 hours).
Ⓦ premiant.cz

Private Prague Guide
Blanická 25.
Map 6 F2. **Tel** 773 103 102.
Ⓦ private-prague-guide.com

Travelling by Metro

The underground railway, known as the metro, is the quickest (for longer journeys) and most comfortable form of transport in Prague. It is managed by the Prague Public Transport Company, and its construction began in 1967. It has three lines, A, B and C. The straightforward layout and clear signs make finding your way around the system very easy. Trains run between 5am and midnight.

The metro sign for
the underground railway

Finding Your Way Around the Metro

Metro entrances are not always easy to spot. Look for a sign displaying the letter "M" within an upside-down triangle. The colour of the sign (green, yellow or red) indicates which line the station is on. The street entrance will normally lead you down a flight of steps.

Once you have purchased your ticket and passed through the unmanned ticket barriers – you must validate your ticket here – continue down the escalators to the trains. At the bottom of each escalator is a long central corridor with a platform on either side for trains travelling in either direction. Signs suspended from the ceiling indicate the direction in which the trains are travelling. The edges of the platforms are marked with a white, broken line that should not be crossed until the train stops. You may have to push a button to open the train doors, which play a recorded warning message when they are about to close. During the journey, the name of the next station is announced in Czech.

Line A (green) is the most useful for tourists, because it covers all the main areas of the city centre – Prague Castle, the Little Quarter, the Old Town and the New Town – as well as the main shopping area around Wenceslas Square.

Displayed above some seats are disabled signs. These chairs should be given up for the elderly, the disabled and those with small children.

The spacious interior of Nádraží Veleslavín metro station

Automatic Ticket Machines

You can buy transport tickets at designated ticket sellers (see p238) or at the yellow automatic ticket machines in the metro station. The ticket machines, and tickets themselves, may vary in design and colour, but they are still applicable to all forms of transport. The machines offer a choice of tickets at varying prices – for adults and children – as well as a choice of languages (either Czech or English).

1 Check which price band is the right one to meet your requirements, then press the appropriately labelled button. Once validated, a transfer ticket is valid for 30 or 90 minutes (Kč24 or Kč32 respectively).

2 If you want more than one ticket – whether of the same price band or another – press the relevant buttons; the total amount owed will be displayed on screen.

3 If you are sure of your choice of ticket, insert coins into this slot. Most machines give change.

4 Collect your ticket, plus any change that may be due to you, from the large slot at the base of the machine.

Making a Journey by Metro

1 To decide which line to take, find your destination and its nearest metro station on the Street Finder *(see pp244–55)*, then plot your route on a metro map. The Prague metro is fairly straightforward to use; Line A is green, line B is yellow and line C is red. Metro maps can be obtained free of charge at most metro stations. A metro map has also been included at the end of this book.

The central corridor with platforms either side and signs indicating the direction of trains

2 Two types of standard metro transfer tickets are available *(right)*. Choose between a 24Kč ticket for 30 minutes or a 32Kč ticket for 90 minutes. You can also buy tickets for unlimited travel within a 24-hour period or for periods of 1 or 3 days *(far right)*.

4 This sign, hanging from the ceiling, is visible when you come down the escalator. It shows the direction of the trains on each platform. This one says that the train's final station *(Stanice)* on the left is Háje, so from the metro map you know the train is travelling south.

3 Before going down the escalators, you must stamp your ticket in one of these machines. If the ticket has not been stamped, it is not valid, and you will have to pay a fine if caught. A ticket must only ever be stamped once.

"Stanice" means station

"Směr" means direction

Name of station

5 This sign along the central platform indicates the station on line C where you are (red circle) and those stations where you can transfer to the other lines (A and B). For stations to the left of the red circle, follow the arrow to the left, and vice-versa for stations to the right.

The red circle indicates which station you are in

6 Once you are at your stop, follow the exit signs *(Výstup)* leading out of the metro system. Some metro stations have numerous exits. Local street maps at the exit should help you decide which is best for you.

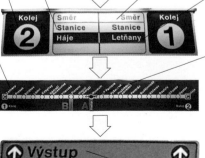

STREET FINDER

The map references given for all the sights, hotels, restaurants, bars, shops and entertainment venues described in this book refer to the maps in this section only. A complete index of street names and all the places of interest marked, can be found on the following pages. The key map (right) shows the area of Prague covered by the *Street Finder*. This map includes sightseeing areas, as well as districts for hotels, restaurants, pubs and entertainment venues. In keeping with Czech maps, none of the street names in the index or on the Street Finder have the Czech word for street, *ulice*, included (though you may see it on the city's street signs). For instance, Celetná ulice appears as Celetná in both the index and the Street Finder. The numbers preceding some street names are dates. In our index, we ignore the numbers, so that 17. listopadu (17 November), is listed under "L".

Key

	Major sight
	Place of interest
	Other building
Ⓜ	Metro station
⊟	Train station
🚌	Coach station
⊞	Tram stop
🚟	Funicular railway
⊜	River boat boarding point
𝒊	Tourist information office
➕	Hospital with casualty unit
🏛	Police station
✝	Church
✡	Synagogue
═	Railway line
—	City wall
—	Pedestrian street

Scale of Map Pages

0 metres   200

0 yards   200

1:8,400

Aerial view of the Baroque Church of St Nicholas in the Old Town Square

The imposing twin towers of the Church of
St Peter and St Paul on top of Vyšehrad rock

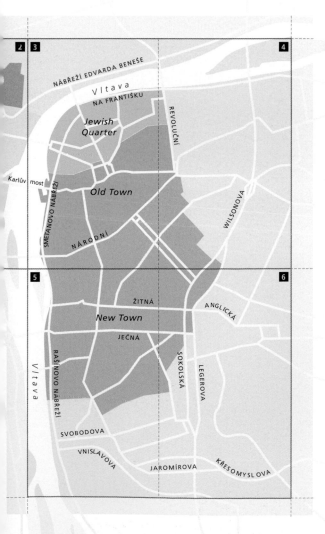

0 metres   500
0 yards   500

Street Finder Index

The order of the names in the index is affected by the *háček*, the accent like an inverted circumflex (*háček* means "little hook"). In the Czech alphabet, **č**, **ř**, **š** and **ž** are treated as separate letters. Street names beginning with **ř**, for example, are listed after those beginning with **r** without an accent.

Churches, buildings, museums and monuments are marked on the Street Finder maps with their English and Czech names. In the index, both forms are listed. However, English names for streets and squares, such as Wenceslas Square, do not appear on the maps. Where they are listed in the index, the Czech name is given in brackets in the form that appears on the map.

Useful Words

dům	house
hrad	castle
kostel	church
klášter	convent, monastery
most	bridge
nábřeží	embankment
nádraží	station
náměstí	square
sady	park
schody	steps
třída	avenue
ulice	street
ulička	lane
zahrada	garden

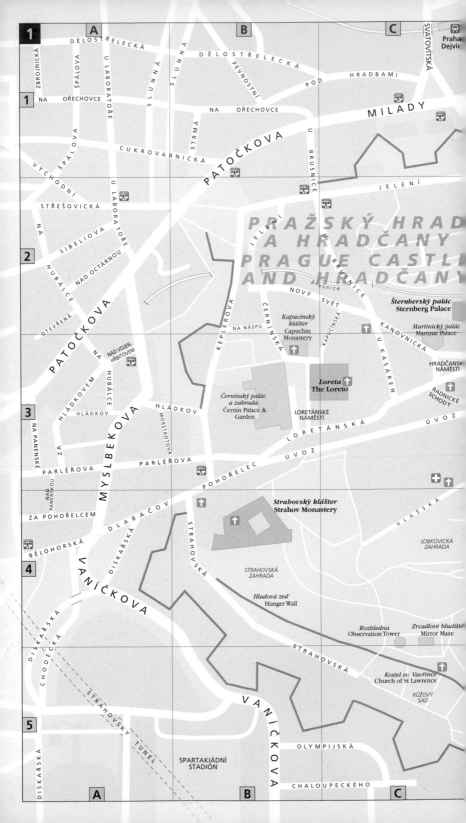

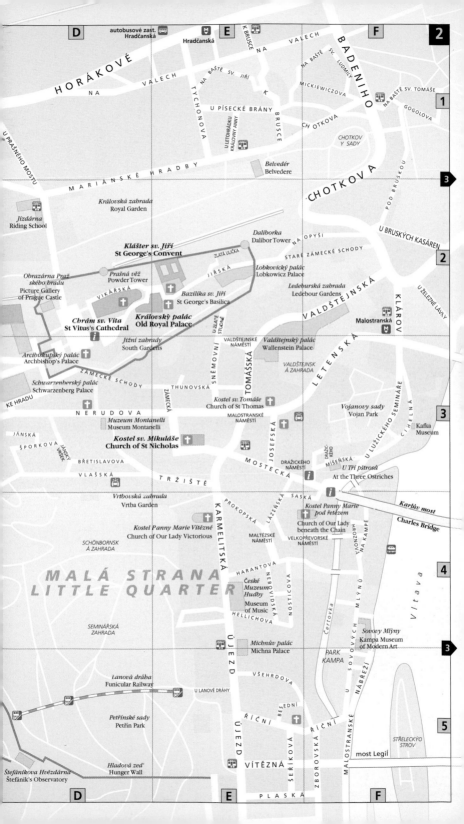

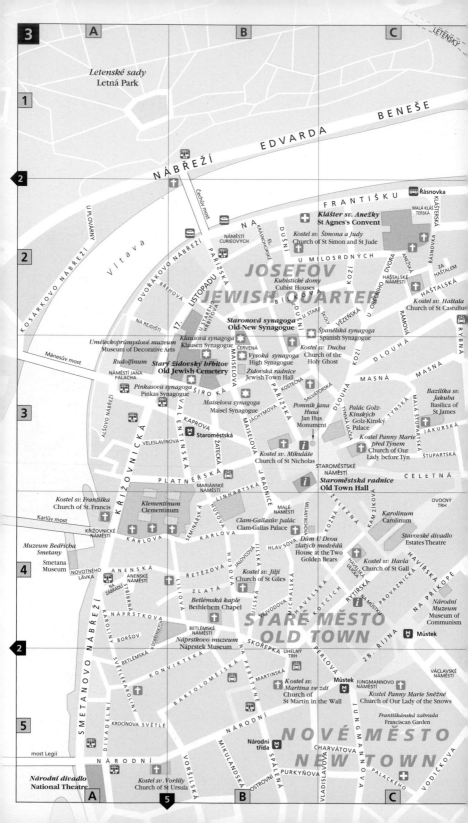

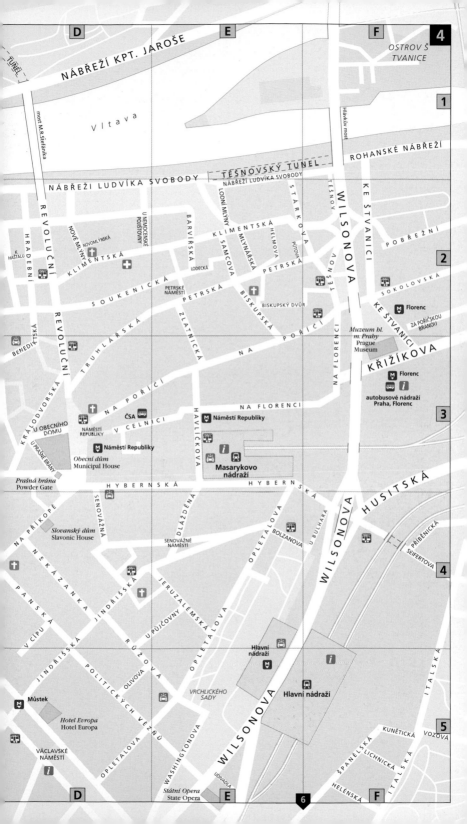

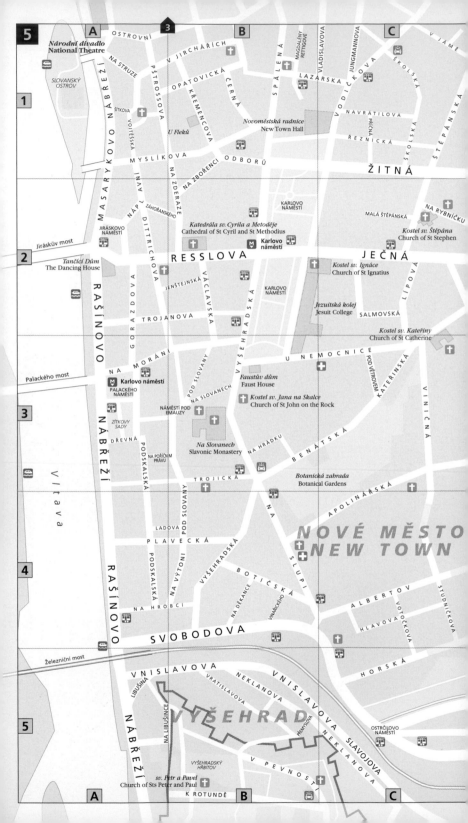

General Index

Acknowledgments

Dorling Kindersley wishes to thank the following people who contributed to the preparation of this book.

Main Contributor

Vladimír Soukup was born in Prague in 1949. He worked for the daily newpaper, *Evening Prague*, for 20 years, eventually becoming Deputy Chief Editor. He has written a wide range of popular guides to Prague.

Additional Contributors

Ben Sullivan, Lynn Reich, Wendy Wrangham.

Design and Editorial

Managing Editor Carolyn Ryder
Managing Art Editor Steve Knowlden
Senior Editor Georgina Matthews
Senior Art Editor Vanessa Courtier
Editorial Director David Lamb
Art Director Anne-Marie Bulat
Production Controller Hilary Stephens
Picture Research Susie Peachey, Ellen Root
Designer Nicola Erdpresser, Sangita Patel
Consultant Helena Svojsikova
Maps Caroline Bowie, Simon Farbrother, James Mills-Hicks, David Pugh (DK Cartography)
Revisions Team
Tanveer Abbas Zaidi, Namrata Adhwaryu, Tora Agarwala, Emma Anacootee, Jasneet Arora, Shruti Bahl, Mark Baker, Claire Baranowski, Kate Berens, Marta Bescos, Hilary Bird, Louise Cleghorn, Michelle Crane, Russell Davies, Marc Di Duca, Stephanie Driver, Emer FitzGerald, Rebecca Flynn, Fay Franklin, Anna Freiberger, Camilla Gersh, Alistair Gunn, Lydia Halliday, Elaine Harries, Charlie Hawkings, Kaberi Hazarika, Christine Heilman, Claire Jones, Jan Kaplan, Bharti Karakoti, Juliet Kenny, Sumita Khatwani, Dr Tomáš Kleisner, Rahul Kumar, Rakesh Kumar Pal, Maite Lantaron, Jude Ledger, Colette Levitt, Darren Longley, Susannah Marriott, Wilf Matos, Alison McGill, Jacy Meyer, Sonal Modha, Casper Morris, Vikki Nousiainen, Catherine Palmi, Helen Partington, Jay Pesta, Marianne Petrou, Filip Polonský, Arun Pottirayil, Private-Prague-Guide.com, Khushboo Priya, Robert Purnell, Rada Radojicic, Sands Publishing Solutions, Avijit Sengupta, Azeem Siddiqui,
Rituraj Singh, Beverly Smart, Tracy Smith, Scott Stickland, Marian Sucha, Will Tizzard, Priyanka Thakur, Daphne Trotter, Conrad Van Dyk, Vinita Venugopal, Ajay Verma, Deepika Verma, Christopher Vinz, Sophie Wright, Debra Wolter.

Additional Photography

Mark Baker; DK Studio/Steve Gorton; Jiri Dolezal; Nigel Hudson; Jiri Kopriva; Ian O'Leary; Otto Palan; Filip Polonský; Frantisek Preucil; Rough Guides/Jon Cunningham, /Eddie Gerald, /Natascha Sturny; M Soskova; Clive Streeter; Alan Williams; Peter Wilson; Wendy Wrangham.

Picture Credits

a = above; b = below/bottom; c = centre; f = far; l = left; r = right; t = top.

Works of art on the pages detailed have been reproduced with the permission of the following copyright holders: Aristide Maillol *Pomona* 1910 © ADAG, Paris, and DACS, London, 2011: 166bc; Gustav Makarius Tauc (An der Aulenkaut 31, Wiesbaden, Germany) under commission of the Minorite Order in Rome: 37br.

The Publishers are grateful to the following individuals, companies and picture libraries for permission to reproduce their photographs:

123RF.com: Viacheslav Baranov 147tl.

Alamy Images: Anna Stowe Travel 10bl; Radim Beznoska 193tl; Petr Bonek 23cra, 40tr; Paul Brown 230c; Frank Chmura 234bl; © CTK/ Rene Fluger 27crb; CHL / Widmann 199br; CTK 54c, 142; CZ Prague/Dennis Chang 232cla, 238bl; Eye Ubiquitous 71tc; Chris Fredriksson 81br, 147br, 195c; Kevin George 203tr; isifa Image Service s.r.o 119cra; INTERFOTO 64cl; Sterba Martin, Horazny Josef 35crb; B. O'Kane 13c; J. Pie 192bl; PjrTravel 5cr; Profimedia International S.R.O/Michaela Dusíková 84tr, 179bl, 226tl; Josef Sedmak 108–9; **Archiv für Kunst und Geschichte, Berlin:** 19b, 20tr, 20bc(d), 20br(d), 21tl(d), 21tc(d), 21tr(d), 21bc(d), 22bl, 25crb(d), 31ca(d), 34bl, 36cla(d), 37clb, 37bl(d), 45tl, 52br(d), 107crb, 116tr, Erich Lessing 30cl(d),

33bl(d), 90tr, 91br; **Archív Hlavniho Mesta. Prahy (Clam- GallasůvPalác)**: 25clb, 26bl, 29br, 30br, 32bc, 35cb, 35bc, 74br, 136br, 137br(d), 138crb; **Augustine Hotel**: 185bc.

Bildarchiv Preussischer Kulturbesitz: 21bl(d), 31br, 36br, 70tr(d), 106bl(d); **Bridgeman Art Library, London**: Prado, Madrid 31tl; Rosegarten Museum, Constance 28cla. **Budweiser Budvar**: 196cr, 197tr.

Cedaz, Ltd: 235tr; **Česká Tisková Kancelár**: 21br, 37cra; **Comstock**: George Gerster 12cla; Jean-Loup **Charmet**: 35bl, 64cl; **Zdenek Chrappek**: 52cl; **Corbis**: Christophe Boisvieux 82, 158; **Czech National Bank**: 231.

La Degustation: 200tr; **Dopravní podnik hl. m. Prahy**: 238cr, 242tr, 243cr; **Dreamstime.com**: Abxyz 99tc; Anky10 99cr; Artur Bogacki 35cr, 172; Pavel Dospiva 16br; 130br; Editor77 8-9; Frbird 62; Rostislav Glinsky 242cl; Jekurantodistaja 13br; Josefkubes 161br; Pavel Kavalenkau 229clb; Kitsen 195tl, Liberty 12bc; Miroslav Liska 148br; Peter Lovás 39cr; Lukyslukys 146br; Marbenzu 171b; Mihaiciolan 145ca; Milonk 170bl; Milan Palicka 169tr; Quixoticsnd 222-223; Richair 234cr; Rudi1976 4cr; Krzysztof Slusarczyk 40bl; Lee Snider 39cb; Petr Svec 110b; Pawel Szczepanski 2–3; Vitaly Titov & Maria Sidelnikova 12tr; Richard Van Der Woude 101tr, 106cl; Zkk600 60-1.

EU Ecolabel Help Desk: 227cra; **Courtesy of Eurolines UK**: 236br; **Mary Evans Picture Library**: 138br, 223.

Fotolia: © Tanya 64br; **Francouzska Restaurace**: 199tl.

Getty Images: DEA / A. DAGLI ORTI 33br; Heritage Images 35tl; Hulton Archive 20bl; Universal Images Group 36c; Roger Viollet 36bl; **Golden Well Hotel, Prague**: 202tl; **Grafoprint Neubert**: 33cb, 40clb, 118cl.

Hanil: 204t; **Hidden Places Residences & Boutique Hotels**: 186bl; **Hutchison Library**: Libuše Taylor 53br, 54c, 176bc.

The Image Bank: Andrea Pistolesi 16b;

iStockphoto.com: Dark_Eni 122; Narvikk 235bl. **Kancelář Prezidenta Republiky**: 22–3, 23tc, 23bl, 23br, 24cla; **Oldrich Karasek**: 11tr, 58cb, 64cla, 103bl; 103br, 134tr, 135bl; 176tr, 197crb, 217tr, 233tl; **Karlštejn**: 27tl; Vladimír Hyhlík: 26–7; The Mark Luxury Hotel Prague: 191br; **Karel Kestner**: 37bc; **Klementinum**: 25tl; Dalibor Kusák: 168–9 all, 170–1 all.

Lindner Hotel Prague Castle: 184cl; **The Lobkowicz Collections**: 99br; **Luka Lu Restaurant, Prague**: 201br.

Ivan Malý: 216cr. **Lehká Hlava, Prague**: 198bl; **Mistral Café**: 200bl; **Mosaic House, Prague**: 189tr; **Xoaher Musavvir**: 154tl. **Muzeum Hlavního Města Prahy**: 34–5; **Muzeum hl. M. Prahy/Müllerova vila**: 163bl; **Muzeum Montanelli**: The secret of Pavla Aubrechtova, The Kabinet of Vladimir Gebauer photo by Oto Palan 124cla; **Muzeum Poštovní Známky**: 149cl.

Národní Galerie v Praze: 26br; Grafická sbírka 29bl, 33tl, 69bl, 71cb, 102tr, 104br, 121tl, 125cb, 129br, 138bc, 157br, 175bl, 180hl; Klášter sv. Anežky 41tr, 85tl, 94–5 all, 133bl; Klášter sv. Jiří 18, 39cl,, Šternberský palác 40cl, 112–3 all, 114–5 all, Veletržni Palac 164–5 all; Zbraslav Monastry 42bl; **Národní Muzeum v Praze**: Vlasta Dvořáková 22crb, 28–9, 28bl, 28bc, 28br, 29t, 29cl, 29cr, 29crb, 31bl, 75bl, 77br, Jarmila Kutová 22cl, 22clb, 24bl, Dagmar Landová 30bl, Muzeum Antonína Dvořáka 41b, Muzeum Bedřicha Smetany 34cl, Prokop Paul 77b, Tyršovo Muzeum; 149bl; **Národní Technické Muzeum**: Gabriel Urbánek 43tr.

Obrazárna Pražského Hradu: 100bl; **Österreichische Nationalbibliothek, Wien**: 27cb, 28cb.

Photographers Direct: Chris Barton 10cra; Eddie Gerald 11bc; **Photolibrary**: Robert Harding Travel/Yadid Levy 194c. Pivovarské **Muzeum**: 196tr; **Pivovary Staropramen**: 197ftl; **Prague Information Service**: www.prague-info. cz 133cra; **Bohumír Prokůpek**: 27bl, 32clb, 120cl, 121cr, 121bl.

Reciprocity Images: www.photographersdirect. com/Jason Langley 240br; Rex Features Ltd: Alfred 37tr; Riverside Praha: 184br; Robert Harding Picture Library: Michael Jenner 128cl; Christopher Rennie105tr; Peter Scholey 32cl, 129cla; ROPID: 239cl, 239cr, 240tl, 243cr.

SABMiller: 196cl, 196crb, 196br, 197tl, 197tc, 197ftr; SaSaZu, Prague: 205tc; STA Travel Group: 226c; Státní Ústredni Archiv: 25br; Státní Ústav Památkové Péče: 25c; Státní Židovské Muzeum: 41cr, 87tc, 87clb, 92tl; Lubomír Stiburek, www. czfoto.cz: 57bc, 163tr, 243tc, 249bca, 250cr; Marian Sucha: 57tl, 127tr, 174tr, 197bl; SuperStock: age fotostock/Christian Beier 38; Hemis.fr 182-3; imagebroker.net 96; Svatovítský Poklad, Pražský Hrad: 23tr, 26clb, 42tr.

Uměleckoprůmyslové Muzeum v Praze: 41tl, 149c, 149clb, 149cb, Gabriel Urbánek 30clb, 43bl; Universal Restaurant, Prague: 203bl; Univerzita Karlova: 27ca; U Pinkasu Restaurant: 194cla.U Zlaté Studně: 190tr.

Zoo Praha: 162tr; ZZS HMP: 229bl.

Front endpaper:
Alamy: CTK Rbr
Corbis: Christophe Boisvieux Rtr ;
Dreamstime.com: Frbird Rcr;
iStockphoto.com: Dark_Eni Lbc
SuperStock: imagebroker.net Lcl.

Map cover:
4Corners: Maurizio Rellini / SIME.

Cover Picture Credits

Front main and spine top:
4Corners: Maurizio Rellini / SIME.
Back:
Dreamstime.com: Noppasin Wongchum

All other images © Dorling Kindersley.
For further information,
see: www.dkimages.com

Phrase Book

In Emergency

Help!	Pomoc!	po-*mots*
Stop!	Zastavte!	za-*stav-te*
Call a	Zavolejte	za-*vo-ley-te*
doctor!	doktora!	dok-*to-ra!*
Call an	Zavolejte	za-*vo-ley-te*
ambulance!	sanitku!	sa-*nit-ku!*
Call the	Zavolejte	za-*vo-ley-te*
police!	policii!	poli-*tsi-yi!*
Call the fire	Zavolejte	za-*vol-ey-te*
brigade!	hasiče	ha-*si-che*
Where is the	Kde je	gde *ye*
telephone?	telefón?	tele-*fohn?*
the nearest	nejbližší	ney-*blish-ee*
hospital?	nemocnice?	ne-*mots-nyitse?*

Communication Essentials

Yes/No	Ano/Ne	ano/*ne*
Please	Prosím	pro-*seem*
Thank you	Děkuji vám	dye-*ku-ji* vahm
Excuse me	Prosím vás	pro-*seem* vahs
Hello	Dobrý den	do-*bree* den
Goodbye	Na shledanou	na s-*hle-da-no*
Good evening	Dobrý večer	dob-*ree* vech-*er*
morning	ráno	rah-*no*
afternoon	odpoledne	od-*po-led-ne*
evening	večer	ve-*cher*
yesterday	včera	vche-*ra*
today	dnes	dnes
tomorrow	zítra	zeet-*ra*
here	tady	ta-*di*
there	tam	tam
What?	Co?	tso?
When?	Kdy?	gdi?
Why?	Proč?	proch?
Where?	Kde?	gde?

Useful Phrases

How are you?	Jak se máte?	yak-*se* mah-*te?*
Very well,	Velmi dobře	vel-*mi* dob-*rzhe*
thank you.	děkuji.	dye *kuyi*
Pleased to meet you.	Těší mě.	tyesh-*ee* mye
See you soon.	Uvidíme se	u-*vi-dyee-me-se-*
	brzy.	br-*zi*
That's fine.	To je v	to *ye* vpo-
	pořádku.	*rzhahdku*
Where is/are…?	Kde je/jsou …?	gde *ye/yso* …?
How long does	Jak dlouho to trvá	yak *dlo* ho to tr-*va*
it take to get to´?	se dostat do..?	se do-*stat do…?*
How do I get to…?	Jak se dostanu k..?	yak se do-*sta-nu k* …?
Do you speak	Mluvíte	mlu-*vee-te*
English?	anglicky?	an-*glits-ki?*
I don't understand.	Nerozumím.	ne-*ro-zu-meem*
Could you speak	Mohl(a)* byste	mohl- (*a*) bis-*te*
more slowly?	mluvit trochu	mlu-*vit* tro-*khu*
	pomaley?	po-*maley?*
Pardon?	Prosím?	pro-*seem?*
I'm lost.	Ztratil(a)*	stra-*tyil (a)*
	jsem se.	y*sem se.*

Useful Words

big	velký	vel-*kee*
small	malý	mal-*ee*
hot	horký	hor-*kee*
cold	studený	stu-*den-ee*
good	dobrý	dob-*ree*
bad	špatný	shpat-*nee*
well	dobře	dob-*rzhe*
open	otevřeno	ot-*ev-rzhe-no*
closed	zavřeno	zav-*rzhe-no*
left	do leva	do *le-va*
right	do prava	do *pra-va*
straight on	rovně	rov-*nye*
near	blízko	blee-*sko*
far	daleko	da-*le-ko*
up	nahoru	na-*ho-ru*
down	dolů	do-*loo*
early	brzy	br-*zi*
late	pozdě	poz-*dye*
entrance	vchod	vkhod
exit	východ	vee-*khod*
toilets	toalety	toa-*leti*
free, unoccupied	volný	vol-*nee*
free, no charge	zdarma	zdar-*ma*

Making a Telephone Call

I'd like to place a	Chtěl(a)* bych	khtyel(*a*) bikh
call.	volat.	vo-*lat*
I'd like to make a	Chtěl(a)* bych	khtyel(*a*) bikh
reverse-charge call.	volat na účet	volat na oo-*chet*
	volaného.	volan-*eh-ho*
I'll try again later.	Zkusím to	skus-*eem* to
	později.	poz-*dyey*
Can I leave	Mohu nechat	mo-*hu ne-khat*
a message?	zprávu?	sprah-*vu?*
Hold on.	Počkejte.	poch-*key-te*
Could you speak	Mohl(a)* byste	mo-*hl (a) bis-te*
up a little, please?	mluvit hlasitěji?	mluvit *hla-si-tyey?*
local call	místní hovor	meest-*nyee hov-or*

Sightseeing

art gallery	galerie	ga-*ler-riye*
bus stop	autobusová	au-*to-bus-o-vah*
	zastávka	za-*stah-vka*
church	kostel	kos-*tel*
garden	zahrada	za *hra-da*
library	knihovna	knyi-*hov-na*
museum	muzeum	muz-*e-um*
tourist	turistické	tooristi-*tske*
information	informace	in-*for-ma-tse*
train station	nádraží	nah-*dra-zhee*
closed for the	státní	staht-*nyee*
public holiday	svátek	svah-*tek*

Shopping

How much does	Co to stojí?	tso to sto-*yee?*
this cost?		
I would like …	Chtěl(a)* bych ….	khtyel(*a*) bikh…
Do you have …?	Máte …?	maa-*te …?*
I'm just looking.	Jenom se dívám.	ye-*nom se*
		dyee-*vahm*
Do you take	Berete kreditní	be-*re-te* kred-*it*
credit cards?	karty?	nyee **karti**?
What time do	V kolik	v ko-*lik*
you open/	otevíráte/	o-*te-vee-rah-te/*
close?	zavíráte?	za vee rah-*te?*
this one	tento	ten-*to*
that one	tamten	tam-*ten*
expensive	drahý	dra-*hee*
cheap	levný	lev-*nee*
size	velikost	vel-*ik-ost*
white	bílý	bee-*lee*
black	černý	cher-*nee*
red	červený	cher-*ven-ee*
yellow	žlutý	zhlu-*tee*
green	zelený	zel-*en-ee*
blue	modrý	mod-*ree*
brown	hnědý	hnyed-*ee*

Types of Shop

antique shop	starožitnictví	sta-*ro zhit--*
		nyits-tvee
bank	banka	bank *a*
bakery	pekárna	pe-*kahr-na*
bookstore	knihkupectví	knih-*kupets-tvee*
butcher	řeznictví	rzhez-*nyits-tvee*
camera shop	obchod	op-*khot*
	s fotoaparáty	sfoto-*aparahti*
chemist		
(prescriptions etc)	lékárna	leh-*kah-rna*
chemist	drogerie	drog-*erye*
(cosmetics,		
toiletries etc)		
delicatessen	lahůdky	la-*hoo-dki*
department store	obchodní dům	op-*khod-nyee doom*
grocery	potraviny	pot-*ra-vini*
glass	sklo	sklo
hairdresser		
(ladies)	kadeřnictví	ka-*derzh-nyits-tvee*
(mens)	holič	ho-*lich*
market	trh	trkh
newsstand	novinový	no-*vi-novee*
	stánek	stah-*nek*
post office	pošta	posh-*ta*
supermarket	samoobsluha	sa-*mo-ob-slu-ha*
tobacconist	tabák	ta-*bahk*
travel	cestovní	tses-*tov-nyi*
agency	kancelář	kantse-*laarzh*

* alternatives for a female speaker are shown in brackets

Staying in a Hotel

Do you have a vacant room?	Máte volný pokoj?	mah-te vol-nee po-koy?
double room	dvoulůžkový pokoj	dvo-loozh-kovee po-koy
with double bed	s dvojitou postelí	sdvoy-to pos-telee
twin room	pokoj s dvěma postelemi	po-koy sdvye-ma pos-tel-emi
room with a bath	pokoj s koupelnou	po-koy s ko-pel-no
porter	vrátný	vraht-nee
hall porter	nosič	nos-ich
key	klíč	kleech
I have a reservation.	Mám reservaci.	mahm rez-ervatsi

Eating Out

Have you got a table for …?	Máte stůl pro …?	mah-te stool pro …?
I'd like to reserve a table.	Chtěl(a)* bych rezervovat stůl.	khtyel(a) bikh rez-er-vov-at stool
breakfast	snídaně	snyee-danye
lunch	oběd	ob-yed
dinner	večeře	vech e-rzhe
The bill, please.	Prosím, účet.	pro-seem oo-chet
I am a vegetarian.	Jsem vegetarián(ka)*.	ysem veghe-tariahn(ka)
waitress!	slečno!	slech-no
waiter!	pane vrchní!	pane vrkh-nyee!
fixed price menu	standardní menu	stan-dard-nyee men-u
dish of the day	nabídka dne	nab-eed-ka dne
starter	předkrm	przhed-krm
main course	hlavní jídlo	hlav-nyee yeed-lo
vegetables	zelenina	zel-en-yin-a
dessert	zákusek	zah-kusek
cover charge	poplatek	pop-la-tek
wine list	nápojový lístek	nah-po-yo-vee lee-stek
rare (steak)	krvavý	kr-va-vee
medium	středně udělaný	strzhed-nye ud-yel-an-ee
well done	dobře udělaný	dobrzhe-ud-yel-an-ee
glass	sklenice	sklen-yitse
bottle	láhev	lah-hev
knife	nůž	noozh
fork	vidlička	vid-lich-ka
spoon	lžíce	lzhee-tse

Menu Decoder

biftek	bif-tek	steak
bílé víno	bee-leh vee-no	white wine
bramborové knedlíky	bram-bo-ro-veh kne-dleeki	potato dumplings
brambory	bram-bo-rí	potatoes
chléb	khlehb	bread
cibule	tsi-bu-le	onion
citrónový džus	tsi-tron-o-vee dzhuus	lemon juice
cukr	tsukr	sugar
čaj	chay	tea
čerstvé ovoce	cher-stveh-o-vo-ce	fresh fruit
červené víno	cher-ven-eh vee-no	red wine
česnek	ches-nek	garlic
dort	dort	cake
fazole	fa-zo-le	beans
grilované	gril-ov-a-neh	grilled
houby	ho-bi	mushrooms
houska	hous-ka	roll
houskové knedlíky	ho-sko-veh kne-dleeki	bread dumplings
hovězí	hov-ye-zee	beef
hranolky	hran-ol-ki	chips
husa	hu-sa	goose
jablko	ya-bl-ko	apple
jahody	ya-ho-di	strawberries
jehněčí	ye-hnye-chee	lamb
kachna	kakh-na	duck
kapr	ka-pr	carp
káva	kah-va	coffee
krevety	krev-et-i	prawns
kuře	ku-rzhe	chicken
kyselé zelí	kis-el-eh zel-ee	sauerkraut
maso	ma-so	meat
máslo	mah-slo	butter
minerálka perlivá/ neperlivá	min-er-ahl-ka purl-i-vah/ ne-purl-i-vah	mineral water fizzy/ still
mléko	mleh-ko	milk

mořská jídla	morzh-skah-yeed-la	seafood
ocet	ots-et	vinegar
okurka	o-ku-rka	cucumber
olej	oley	oil
párek	paa-rek	sausage/frankfurter
pečené	petsh-en-eh	baked
pečené	pech-en-eh	roast
pepř	peprzh	pepper
polévka	pol-eh-vka	soup
pomeranč	po-me-ranch	orange
pomerančový džus	po-me-ran-ch-- o-vee dzhuus	orange juice
pivo	pi-vo	beer
rajské	rayskeh	tomato
ryba	rib-a	fish
rýže	ree-zhe	rice
salát	sal-at	salad
sůl	sool	salt
sýr	seer	cheese
šunka	shun-ka	ham
vařená /uzená	varzh-enah u-zenah	cooked smoked
telecí	te-le-tsee	veal
tuna	tu-na	tuna
vajíčko	va-yee-chko	egg
vařené	varzh-en-eh	boiled
vepřové	vep-rzho-veh	pork
voda	vo-da	water
vývar	vee-var	broth
zelí	zel-ee	cabbage
zelenina	zel-enyina	vegetables
zmrzlina	zmrz-lin-a	ice cream

Numbers

1	jedna	yed-na
2	dvě	dvye
3	tři	trzhi
4	čtyři	chti-rzhi
5	pět	pyet
6	šest	shest
7	sedm	sedm
8	osm	osm
9	devět	dev-yet
10	deset	des-et
11	jedenáct	ye-de-nahtst
12	dvanáct	dva-nahtst
13	třináct	trzhi-nahtst
14	čtrnáct	chtr-nahtst
15	patnáct	pat-nahtst
16	šestnáct	shest-nahtst
17	sedmnáct	sedm-nahtst
18	osmnáct	osm-nahtst
19	devatenáct	de-va-te-nahtst
20	dvacet	dva-tset
21	dvacet jedna	dva-tset yed-na
22	dvacet dva	dva-tset dva
23	dvacet tři	dva-tset-trzhi
24	dvacet čtyři	dva-tset chti-rzhi
25	dvacet pět	dva-tset pyet
30	třicet	trzhi-tset
40	čtyřicet	chti-rzhi-tset
50	padesát	pa-de-saht
60	šedesát	she-de-saht
70	sedmdesát	sedm-de-saht
80	osmdesát	osm-de-saht
90	devadesát	de-va-de-saht
100	sto	sto
1,000	tisíc	tyi-seets
2,000	dva tisíce	dva tyi-see-tse
5,000	pět tisíc	pyet tyi-seets
1,000,000	milión	mi-li-ohn

Time

one minute	jedna minuta	yed-na min-uta
one hour	jedna hodina	yed-na hod-yin-a
half an hour	půl hodiny	pool hod-yin-i
day	den	den
week	týden	tee-den
Monday	Pondělí	pon-dye-lee
Tuesday	Úterý	oo-ter-ee
Wednesday	Středa	strzhe-da
Thursday	Čtvrtek	chtvr-tek
Friday	Pátek	pah-tek
Saturday	Sobota	so-bo-ta
Sunday	Neděle	ned-yel-e

alternatives for a female speaker are shown in brackets